The Sikh View on Happiness

Also available from Bloomsbury:

Beyond Religion in India and Pakistan, Virinder S. Kalra and Navtej K. Purewal
Prem Rawat and Counterculture, Ron Geaves
Sikhism: A Guide for the Perplexed, Arvind-Pal Singh Mandair

The Sikh View on Happiness

Guru Arjan's Sukhmani

Kamala Elizabeth Nayar and Jaswinder Singh Sandhu

BLOOMSBURY ACADEMIC
LONDON • NEW YORK • OXFORD • NEW DELHI • SYDNEY

BLOOMSBURY ACADEMIC
Bloomsbury Publishing Plc
50 Bedford Square, London, WC1B 3DP, UK
1385 Broadway, New York, NY 10018, USA
29 Earlsfort Terrace, Dublin 2, Ireland

BLOOMSBURY, BLOOMSBURY ACADEMIC and the Diana logo are trademarks of Bloomsbury Publishing Plc

First published in Great Britain 2020
This paperback edition published in 2021

Copyright © Kamala Elizabeth Nayar and Jaswinder Singh Sandhu, 2020

Kamala Elizabeth Nayar and Jaswinder Singh Sandhu have asserted their right under the Copyright, Designs and Patents Act, 1988, to be identified as Authors of this work.

For legal purposes the Acknowledgements on p. ix constitute an extension of this copyright page.

All rights reserved. No part of this publication may be reproduced or transmitted in any form or by any means, electronic or mechanical, including photocopying, recording, or any information storage or retrieval system, without prior permission in writing from the publishers.

Bloomsbury Publishing Plc does not have any control over, or responsibility for, any third-party websites referred to or in this book. All internet addresses given in this book were correct at the time of going to press. The author and publisher regret any inconvenience caused if addresses have changed or sites have ceased to exist, but can accept no responsibility for any such changes.

A catalogue record for this book is available from the British Library.

A catalog record for this book is available from the Library of Congress.

ISBN: HB: 978-1-3501-3987-9
PB: 978-1-3502-6693-3
ePDF: 978-1-3501-3988-6
eBook: 978-1-3501-3989-3

Typeset by Integra Software Services Pvt. Ltd.

To find out more about our authors and books visit www.bloomsbury.com and sign up for our newsletters.

Contents

List of illustrations	vi
Preface	vii
Acknowledgements	ix
Note on translation	xi
1 The pursuit of happiness in Indic religions	1
2 Guru Arjan's life, work and martyrdom	21
3 The ritual function of the *Sukhmani*	47
4 The *Sukhmani*: Teachings and practice	67
5 A path towards meaningful living	101
6 Understanding Guru Arjan's *Sukhmani*: Summary and conclusions	123
The *Sukhmani: The Pearl of Happiness* (An English Translation)	133
Summary of the four watches of the day (*Astapadis* 1–12)	192
Summary of the four watches of the night (*Astapadis* 13–24)	193
Glossary of Punjabi terms	194
Notes	199
References	237
Index	248

Illustrations

Figures

1.1	The sources of suffering	12
4.1	The six forms of happiness	94
4.2	The Sikh formula of happiness	97
5.1	The multi-layered person	103
5.2	The distress cycle	108

Tables

2.1	Earlier sources on Guru Arjan's meetings with Sri Chand: From mid-1800s to early 1900s	33
2.2	Later sources on Guru Arjan's meetings with Sri Chand: From mid-1900s to the present	37

Preface

Indic perspectives on the pursuit of happiness (*sukh*) are grounded in spirituality. Since religions originating in the Indian subcontinent share the common belief that the primary source of suffering is bondage to the cycle of birth, death and rebirth (*sansar*), they focus on liberation from *sansar* as the ultimate goal. These religious traditions are, however, set apart by their explanations about the nature of bondage, specific causes of affliction (*kalesh*) and its cures. While the more ancient traditions (like the Upanishads, Patanjali's Yoga and Theravada Buddhism) require mental and physical discipline within the context of world renunciation, the later devotional traditions (like Mahayana Buddhism and Bhakti sects) emphasize the accessibility of intrinsic religious practice for the common or lay people. Similarly, Sikhism – the youngest world religion born out of Indian soil – embraces a spiritual path accessible to those living in the world as householders.

The *Sukhmani* (The Pearl of Happiness) is the most celebrated text composed by Guru Arjan (1563–1606 CE), the fifth of a succession of ten human Gurus, who together established the Sikh religion (*Sikhi*). Guru Arjan's *Sukhmani* addresses the existential problem of suffering (*dukh*) and sheds light on how to overcome the human condition of suffering. However, since the attainment of happiness is not merely the result of removing or overcoming *dukh*, the *Sukhmani* also provides valuable insights into human nature, the cultivation of well-being, and the pursuit of happiness for householders navigating the trials and turbulence that come with mundane existence. More specifically, the *Sukhmani* underscores *Nam* – the expression of the One essence in all existence – as both the panacea for human suffering and the ultimate means to liberation from *sansar* even as the text highlights 'detached engagement' as a critical constituent of wellness. Overall, the *Sukhmani* illustrates the Sikh existential, psychological and spiritual perspective on well-being and happiness. And, as one of the more popular Sikh texts, the recitation of the *Sukhmani* is also central to Sikh practice.

Along with an original English translation of the *Sukhmani*, the present work provides an analysis of the devotional text. First, the book provides a broader context of joy (*sukh*) and suffering (*dukh*) in Indic religions for a sharper understanding of the *Sukhmani* message regarding the pursuit of happiness.

Second, it examines the historical, social and religious context of the *Sukhmani* in order to come to a more accurate understanding and interpretation of the text. Third, it analyses the main spiritual teachings expounded in the *Sukhmani*. Fourth, the study demonstrates the practical application of Sikh teachings in the contemporary context. In doing so, it underscores the existential, psychological and spiritual insights into the human problem of suffering and explores the *Sukhmani*'s therapeutic value in helping adherents improve their wellness. The underlining of the Sikh view on well-being and happiness can add to the contributions made by other Indic traditions, such as Patanjali's Yoga and Theravada Buddhism, especially since these earlier religious and philosophical systems were meant for the renunciate.

More broadly, the analysis here seeks to contribute a greater understanding of the development of Sikh thought. While much has been written on Guru Nanak and his teachings as the foundation of this spiritual tradition, the evolution of Sikh beliefs has been less explored. More important, given the sparseness of available literature on Sikh spiritual teachings in contrast to the substantial amount of work on Sikh history, this work should also prove useful to scholars and students studying Sikh religion and history in particular or South Asian religions in general. In addition, the textual analysis and translation of the *Sukhmani* should be of interest to the many diasporan Sikhs who find learning about their scripture a challenge, given the language barrier and limited analytical resources available on Sikh spirituality. Last, although this work specifically focuses on the Sikh tradition, it is also relevant for those professionally or personally interested in Eastern spirituality and happiness or wellness studies.

Acknowledgements

I was first introduced to *Sikhi* in 1974 when I moved to my paternal grandmother's house in Rajouri Garden in west Delhi. The neighbourhood primarily consisted of post-1947 refugees, both Hindu and Sikh. Even though my grandmother was a devout Hindu, the name Jaswant Kaur was engraved in stone beside the entrance gate of the family home. She was named Durga Devi at her birthplace in Saro Chak, situated in the Gujrat district of the Punjab in present-day Pakistan. She was, however, given the Sikh name Jaswant Kaur upon marrying my grandfather Jamna Das, who was a Hindu from the village of Kunjah. The name Jaswant Kaur was chosen for her at the wedding ceremony when the presiding scripture was randomly opened and *j* was the first letter of the page. This was evidently a practice among some Hindus, who gave Sikh names as a safeguard.

More significant was my relationship with the Talwar family. My grandmother's neighbour and good friend, the late Tej Kaur (wife of the late Harcharan Singh), was a mother of seven children – Kanwaljeet Kaur, Iqbal Singh, Harbhajan Singh, 'Biri' (Jasbir Kaur), the late 'Jeeti' (Surjeet Kaur), 'Rumy' (Jatinder Kaur) and 'Bunty' (Inderpal Singh). I have fond childhood memories of playing, going to *Shukravaar* bazaar, watching Ram-*lila* from the rooftop, celebrating the marriages of Biri-*didi* and Jeeti-*didi*, etc. The air was filled with enthusiasm. After all, Rajouri Garden was a neighbourhood largely made up of partition survivors. The thought of this place of refuge becoming the site of the 1984 anti-Sikh massacre would have been unimaginable. For me, Guru Arjan's *Sukhmani* is fitting here as the text inspirits hope amid the despair.

The *gurdwara* is the place where Sikhs gather to inspirit themselves with *Nam* resounding in the devotional singing of hymns (*kirtan*). My most cherished memories are those in which I accompanied Biri-*didi* and her family to listen to *kirtan* at the local *gurdwara* in Nehru market. It was in their company that I began to appreciate *kirtan*. Even now, when I hear the sacred words (*shabad*) 'Chant *Nam*, O my friend and companion' (*Nam japo, mere sajan saina*), they come to mind. In a sense, they were my initial congregation (*sadh sangat*).

In the research and writing of this study, I have benefited from the help of many. First and foremost, I would like to acknowledge my co-author, Jaswinder Singh Sandhu, who collaborated on the translations and aided me with his expertise in counselling psychology and Sikh spirituality. I am also thankful to the students enrolled over the years in the courses on the Sikh religion that I teach at Kwantlen Polytechnic University. The class discussions have been an encouragement to me in terms of undertaking and conceptualizing the project. I would also like to express my sincere appreciation to Bob Fuhr and Greg Jenion for their collegiality and kind support in my research pursuits since I first arrived at Kwantlen in 2002. I am also grateful to the two blind peer reviewers for their positive feedback and suggestions for refining the manuscript. I am as well appreciative to both Amrita Kaur and Yadvinder Singh of Auckland, New Zealand, for performing the opening *salok* of the *Sukhmani* to the Gauri *rag*, during their Vancouver *kirtan* tour in July 2017.

My co-author, Jaswinder Singh Sandhu, would like to thank Naina Khera-McRackan for reaching out and encouraging us to undertake another *gurbani* translation project. Thanks are also owed to the British Columbia Foundation for the Study of Sikhism, especially Gurhimat Singh Gill for his assistance in the translation process and his sharing of resources otherwise difficult to obtain. Bloomsbury Academic editors Camilla Erskine and Lucy Carroll provided excellent support.

I would like to express my gratitude to my father, Baldev Raj Nayar, for both his guidance over the years and assistance in editing the present manuscript. I am likewise grateful to my husband, who has been an on-going source of motivation and support. Also, I am thankful to our two daughters – Shardha Kaur and Sangeeta Kaur – for their encouragement for the project; and, of course, to Kingston (aka *kaddu*), the family's Tibetan spaniel who, to our amusement, enjoys listening to *kirtan* in *rag*. Last, I would like to acknowledge Harkirat Singh Brar, who in 2017 – at the mere age of twenty-four years – tragically drowned in Harrison Lake (British Columbia). With a whole life ahead, Harkirat Singh had a profound understanding of the joys and sorrows that this life brings. His knowledge of, and love for, *gurbani* was truly inspirational.

Although indebted to many, we alone bear the responsibility for the work, in the final analysis.

Kamala Elizabeth Nayar

Note on translation

The original translation offered here of the *Sukhmani* into the English language – along with the additional verses by Guru Arjan, the preceding Sikh Gurus and Bhai Gurdas used in the analysis – has been done from a medieval form of Punjabi. The non-technical language of this genre of hymns from the *Guru Granth Sahib* can be problematic. In order to avoid awkward constructions, we have in some places provided a loose translation, not always following the literal pattern of Punjabi grammar. Since the *Sukhmani* is highly and creatively structured, we have kept its original organization in twenty-four parts (*astapadi*) with each part comprising eight verses (*pauri*).

We have been particularly attentive to the specific phraseology and imagery of the Sikh tradition. Previous translations of the *Guru Granth Sahib* in its entirety or in parts have, for the most part, been based on colonial or Christian templates that have at times changed the connotative meaning of Sikh teachings.[1] More recently, the translations available online have fluctuated between using Christian (e.g. translating *Ek Oankar* ['the One creator-creation'] as 'Lord') and New Age (e.g. translating *Ek Oankar* as 'cosmic energies' or 'cosmic frequencies') terminology.

Employing the *Sikhi* perspective, we have in the process of translating adhered to the basic premise that the verses ultimately point to the Sikh spiritual goal of connecting with *Ek Oankar* as it manifests in all of creation. We have therefore retained all the epithets (defined in the glossary), in order to provide a full picture of how *Ek Oankar* is described in the *Guru Granth Sahib* and to shed light on how Guru Arjan has employed the epithets to illustrate the qualities of *Ek Oankar*.[2] In doing so, our translations provide a fuller appreciation of Guru Arjan's artistry in portraying Ultimate Reality.

While the aim of these translations has been to capture the meaning of Sikh teachings in the modern English idiom, we have also retained certain key concepts in their original form in order to most accurately reflect Sikh thought. These key concepts are explained in both the analysis and the glossary. The translations, moreover, maintain the gender neutrality of the sacred verses, since the inner dimension of a person is genderless. Going beyond gender, the verses at the same time embody both the masculine and feminine qualities of Ultimate Reality, as depicted by the Sikh Gurus.

We use the abbreviation *GGS* and provide the standardized page number for citations of the translated verses taken from the *Guru Granth Sahib*. However, when we cite verses taken from the *Sukhmani*, we provide the *astapadi* number, followed by the verse number. Finally, while throughout the entire book we employ the original Punjabi terms, in Chapter 1 we also identify our use of Skt (Sanskrit) and Pali terms.

1

The pursuit of happiness in Indic religions

The *Sukhmani* (The Pearl of Happiness) is the most celebrated text composed by Guru Arjan (1563–1606 CE), the fifth of a succession of ten human Gurus,[1] who together established the Sikh religion or *Sikhi* (experiential or lived path of learning).[2] Consistent with the writings of the first four Sikh Gurus who had preceded Guru Arjan, the *Sukhmani* teaches the central importance of *Nam* – the expression of the One essence in all existence. In doing so, the devotional text underscores *Nam* as both the panacea to overcome human suffering (*dukh*) and the ultimate means to liberation from the cycle of birth, death and rebirth (*sansar*). Questions surrounding the source of, and the cure for, suffering are prominent themes in the major religions originating in the Indian subcontinent, including Hinduism, Buddhism, Jainism and Sikhism.

Broadly, Indic religions focus on the means to liberation from *sansar*, because the state of human bondage to the continual cycle of rebirth is regarded as the primary source of suffering. Even though Indic religious traditions share this worldview, they are set apart by their explanations about the specific causes of, and the remedies for, suffering or affliction (*kalesh*; Skt. *klesha*). From the standpoint of the development of Indic religions, the more ancient traditions tend to focus on mental and physical discipline within the context of world renunciation, as the sole means to liberation.[3] In contrast, the later devotional traditions are more oriented towards the accessibility of intrinsic religious practice for the common or lay people.[4]

As taught by Guru Nanak (1469–1539 CE), the founder of *Sikhi*, existential suffering can be eliminated by renouncing the ego while continuing to live in society.[5] Although *Sikhi* is often described as a 'householder religion',[6] Guru Nanak's spiritual approach actually rejects the traditional path of the householder, even as it explicitly establishes the Sikh position as against that of world renunciation in the pursuit of liberation.[7] Guru Nanak's case about ego-renunciation and social involvement is most prominently explained in the *Siddh Goshth* (Discourse to the Siddhs). Guru Nanak holds the position that while the individual ego (*ahankar*) is caught in the web of the world's illusions (*maya*),[8] *Nam* is the panacea that provides liberation from such influence and entanglement.[9]

Building on Guru Nanak's perspective about ego-renunciation in the larger context of social involvement,[10] Guru Arjan significantly provides valuable and practical teachings on the cure for affliction (*kalesh*). In fact, the first *astapadi* (part of a hymn comprising eight verses) of the *Sukhmani* text explains how mindful remembrance of *Nam* results in the removal of *kalesh*:

> Remember mindfully, mindfully, and attain happiness,
> > tension and *kalesh* vanish from the body.
> Be mindful of the One who cares for the universe,
> > and whose *Nam* is chanted by countless people, in a myriad of ways.
> … Those yearning for a vision of Your Oneness,
> > Nanak, I can be saved in their company. (*Sukhmani* 1.1)

Indeed, the *Sukhmani* addresses the existential problem of suffering (*dukh*), and sheds light on how to overcome the human condition of suffering for those navigating the trials and turbulence that come with mundane existence. However, since the attainment of happiness is not merely the result of removing or overcoming *dukh*, Guru Arjan's *Sukhmani* also provides valuable insights into human nature, the cultivation of wellness and the pursuit of happiness for people living as householders in the world. More specifically, the text underscores *Nam* as the panacea for human suffering even as it highlights 'detached engagement' as a critical constituent of well-being. In sum, the *Sukhmani* illustrates Guru Arjan's existential, psychological and spiritual perspective on wellness and happiness.

Before commencing the analysis of the *Sukhmani* in terms of its insights on well-being and happiness, it is important to first explore how various Indic religious and philosophical traditions understand the nature of suffering (*dukh*) and happiness (*sukh*).

Suffering and happiness in Indic religions

The axial age in the Indian subcontinent is marked by the birth of three major Indic religious streams – the Upanishadic, Jaina and Buddhist traditions.[11] Indo-Aryan migration towards the Gangetic plains in North India, and the subsequent development of towns in the region (c. 900–600 BCE),[12] gave rise to different religious systems, like Buddhism and Jainism, that opposed Brahminic hegemony. Dissenting traditions emerged because the urban people were not receptive to the monopoly of the Brahmin 'priestly' class (Skt. *varna*) over existing religious knowledge and ritual practices.[13] In reaction to Vedic ritualism and the perceived futility of the materialistic goal-orientation of Vedic fire and animal sacrifice (Skt. *yajna*) – including the pursuit of boons in this life and in heaven (Skt. *svarga*) – the Upanishadic, Theravada Buddhist and Jaina traditions emphasized metaphysical enquiry. In doing so, these traditions took on the new distinct worldview of the cycle of birth, death and rebirth (Skt. *samsara*).[14] Bondage to *samsara* is the result of good or bad action (Skt. *karma*). Actions, which are accumulated in the past and present life, shape the circumstances for rebirth. Since the major source of suffering is bondage to *samsara*, the ultimate goal is liberation from this continual cycle of suffering. Accordingly, experiential wisdom is necessary to break the bonds of *karma* and ultimately *samsara*.

While maintaining the Brahminic view of society (i.e. the *varna* system), the Upanishadic challenge (c. 900–500 BCE) to Vedic ritualism (even though there are also mythic and ritual passages in the Upanishads) views sacrifice and its materialistic goals as both an inferior and an ineffective means to the new goal of liberation. Rather, the Upanishadic tradition espouses *jnana* – the metaphysical understanding of the true nature of Reality – as the ultimate goal of liberation. *Jnana* is attained through physical and mental discipline within the context of world renunciation. Renouncing the material world is regarded as the prerequisite for the pursuit of liberation and involves a life of celibacy, asceticism, rigorous Vedic study and meditation.

World renunciation came to be regarded as the necessary act for those pursuing liberation because it provided the necessary 'greenhouse-like' environment conducive for renunciates to break free from all desires and attachment. Not only is desire a source of suffering, but it is also an obstacle to acquiring experiential wisdom necessary for liberation. Desire connotes the state of attachment, including attachment to the notion of a better rebirth. Desire for joyful or pleasurable experiences, even of a spiritual nature, gives rise to attachment whereby the sense of 'I' (i.e. ego) misidentifies itself as the true self (Skt. *atman*). More specifically, allowing the illusory nature of the world (*maya*) to simultaneously stimulate and subdue the mind results in a state of entanglement with *maya*, which creates a 'smoke screen' between the sense of 'I' and the true self. Conversely, detachment from desire and the sense of 'I' results in the awareness of one's true nature:

> Now, this is the aspect of his that is beyond what appears to be good, freed from what is bad, and without fear.
> It is like this. As a man embraced by a woman he loves is oblivious to everything within or without, so this person embraced by the self (*atman*) consisting of knowledge is oblivious to everything within or without.
> Clearly, this is the aspect of his, where all desires are fulfilled, where the self is the only desire, and which is free from desires and far from sorrow.[15]

Awareness eradicates the smoke screen of illusions and, in turn, cures affliction and suffering.

Renunciation and the removal of the *kleshas*

Klesha (Punjabi *kalesh*) is a key concept in Indic religious traditions, especially in the Yoga philosophical school. While there have prevailed different Vedic, Buddhist, Jaina and Tantric practices for controlling bodily and mental processes – even as some practices may have emerged from non-Aryan sources[16] – there are many references to yogic discipline in the Upanishads.[17] Yogic practice is primarily described as the controlling of the senses to attain discriminating wisdom.[18] While yogic practice preceded Patanjali's *Yoga Sutras* (*c.* 100 BCE), the text is regarded as the formalization of classical yoga in the Indian subcontinent, which then came to be considered as one of the six Hindu orthodox philosophical schools.[19]

The Samkhya School is regarded as the theoretical foundation of the Yoga School's practical orientation towards spiritual attainment.[20] Samkhya metaphysics is based on a dualistic realism. There are two eternal realities: (1) the self or pure consciousness (Skt. *purusha*) and (2) matter (Skt. *prakriti*). These two eternal realities are under the influence of the three constituents or attributes (Skt. *gunas*) that are considered to make up the material world.[21] Bondage occurs when *purusha* forgets its true nature and its actual relationship with *prakriti*. That is, *purusha* as pure consciousness misidentifies itself as *prakriti*, including the physical body, the senses and the ego. This results in *purusha* losing awareness of its true nature as pure consciousness.[22]

The classical tradition of yoga, which is often referred to as the 'royal way' of discipline (Skt. *raja-yoga*), focuses on controlling the intellectual faculties.[23] In the *Yoga Sutras*, Patanjali delineates a practical system of mental and physical exercises to both overcome the senses and ego and attain discriminating knowledge about the true nature of *purusha* or pure consciousness. Therefore, within the context of an ascetic lifestyle, the discipline and goal entail both gaining control over the mind and dismantling all corrupting forces:

> The active performance of yoga involves ascetic practice, study of sacred lore, and dedication to the Lord of Yoga.
> Its purpose is to cultivate pure contemplation and attenuate the forces of corruption.
> The forces of corruption are ignorance, egoism, passion, hatred, and the will to live.
> Ignorance is the field where the other forces of corruption develop, whether dormant, attenuated, intermittent, or active.
> Ignorance is misperceiving permanence in transience, purity in impurity, pleasure in suffering, an essential self where there is no self.
> Egoism is ascribing a unified self to the organs and powers of perception, such as the eye and the power to see.
> Passion follows from attachment to pleasure.
> Hatred follows from attachment to suffering.
> The will to live is instinctive and overwhelming, even for a learned sage.[24]

Patanjali identifies five specific poisons or causes of affliction (Skt. *klesha*): (1) ignorance (Skt. *avidya*), (2) egoism (Skt. *asmita*), (3) passion (Skt. *raga*), (4) hatred (Skt. *dvesha*) and (5) the will to live (Skt. *abhinivesha*). The first *klesha* is *avidya* or spiritual 'ignorance',[25] which is the basis of all affliction, and results from not truly knowing or lacking an awareness of the true self. Ultimately, suffering (Skt. *duhkha*) arises when the individual self misidentifies itself as separate from the outside world, especially since personal impressions, desires, misconceptions, conflict and changes in the outside world bring about discomfort.[26] The second *klesha* is *asmita* or 'egoism', which is rooted in the sense of I-am-ness.[27] Egoism relies on the other three *kleshas* for a false sense of permanence.

The third *klesha* is *raga* or 'passion and attraction' to the enjoyable qualities of the body and mind.[28] Attraction most often involves the realm of sensual-pleasure. For instance, sight, taste, smell, sound or touch can stimulate sensual-pleasure. However, whatever the object of attraction may be, the experience of joy or happiness is short-lived because it is impermanent in nature. Therefore, all objects, experiences, situations or persons are accompanied with pain since any form of attachment can generate grief, loss or anxiety. The fourth *klesha* is *dvesha* or 'hatred and aversion'. It is the opposite of attraction.[29] Aversion – like attraction – involves the realm of sensual-pleasure. However, in the case of aversion, objects, experiences, situations or people are avoided and hated because they bring discomfort.

Lastly, the fifth *klesha* is *abhinivesha* or 'the will to live'.[30] Clinging to life is viewed as the most difficult affliction to overcome, because the fear of death is imprinted as a *karmic* formation on the psyche. Since the five *kleshas* are the sources of suffering, healing entails the removal of these five afflictions or 'corrupt forces'. The removal of the various *kleshas* is achievable primarily through meditation,[31] an intrinsic spiritual practice that cultivates a state of detachment from the ego. Detachment breaks the snares of *maya*, *kleshas* and worldly pressures and, in turn, gives rise to joy and happiness.

Along with the Upanishads and the subsequent development of the Yoga-Samkhya philosophical schools,[32] the axial age marks the birth of Buddhism.[33] According to tradition, the founder of Buddhism, Gautama Buddha (*c.* 624–544 BCE), renounced his royal family life and took on ascetic practices after seeing the 'three' miseries (an old person, a sick person and a corpse) and an ascetic in the hope of finding a solution to suffering. During his own spiritual quest, however, the Buddha became disenchanted with yogic meditation because he found the resulting trances to be transient in nature. Likewise, he also found that the various extreme forms of ascetic practices, like self-denial, to be exhausting and thus ineffective. Subsequently, the Buddha began to practise and teach the Middle Way of renunciation. That is, the practice of asceticism with an orientation towards sustaining the body, rather than depriving it. Upon attaining enlightenment, the Buddha gained insight into the Four Noble Truths about suffering.

As described in the *Dhammapada*,[34] the Buddha's Four Noble Truths espouse that (1) life is suffering (Pali *dukka*); (2) the source of suffering is desire (Skt. *trishna*; Pali *tanha*), including the craving for existence; (3) suffering can be extinguished (Skt. *nirvana*; Pali *nibbana*); and (4) the cessation of suffering is achievable through the Eightfold Path.[35] More specifically, the *Dhammapada* explains how perception – accompanied by the rise of mental states, including attachment, hate and desire – is the source of suffering:

> Preceded by perception are mental states,
> For them is perception supreme,
> From perception have they sprung.
> If, with perception polluted,
> One speaks or acts,
> Thence suffering follows
> As a wheel the draught ox's foot.[36]

While 'polluted' perception is regarded as the source of suffering, 'pure' perception is achievable with the practice of mindful thought and action:

> Preceded by perception are mental states,
> For them is perception supreme,
> From perception have they sprung.
> If, with tranquil perception, one speaks or acts,
> Thence ease follows
> As a shadow that never departs.[37]

Realization or insight into the *dhamma*, especially the Four Noble Truths, is viewed as the remedy for all suffering and the means to happiness.[38] The Buddha's Four Noble Truths have been foundational and paradigmatic for later Buddhist doctrinal and sectarian developments.[39]

According to the second noble truth, desire is the primary source of suffering and it gives rise to bodily and mental defilements or afflictions (Pali *kilesa*). There are three basic or root defilements – delusion, greed and hate. These three root defilements are personified as the three daughters of Mara or the King of Death, the antithesis of *dhamma*. According to Buddhist hagiographical literature, Mara unsuccessfully sent his three daughters to tempt and divert the Buddha from his path towards enlightenment. The three afflictions are also represented in the form of animals – the pig (delusion), the rooster (lust or greed) and the snake (hate) – at the centre of the wheel of life on the 'maps' of *samsara*.

The three main *kilesas* are the hindrances that cause all beings to generate *karma* and suffer in the cycle of rebirth. Moreover, these three chief *kilesas* are the source of all other *kilesas* or unwholesome qualities in the form of various bodily and mental defilements.[40] The *Pali Canon* refers to additional *kilesas*, and regards them as hindrances to wisdom.[41] For instance, within a discourse framework, the *Sutta Pitika* (Basket of Discourse) of the *Pali Canon* mentions them:

> On returning from his almsround, after his meal he sits down, folding his legs crosswise, setting his body erect, and establishing mindfulness before him. Abandoning covetousness for the world, he abides with a mind free from covetousness; he purifies his mind from covetousness. Abandoning ill will and hatred, he abides with a mind free from ill will, compassionate for the welfare of all living beings; he purifies his mind from ill will and hatred. Abandoning sloth and torpor, he abides free from sloth and torpor, percipient of light, mindful and fully aware; he purifies his mind from sloth and torpor. Abandoning restlessness and remorse, he abides unagitated with a mind inwardly peaceful; he purifies his mind from restlessness and remorse. Abandoning doubt, he abides having gone

beyond doubt, unperplexed about wholesome states; he purifies his mind from doubt. (18)

Having thus abandoned these five hindrances, imperfections of the mind that weaken wisdom, quite secluded from sensual pleasures, secluded from unwholesome states, he enters upon and abides in the first *jhana* (concentration state) which is accompanied by applied and sustained thought, with rapture and pleasure born of seclusion. (19)[42]

In the process of leading an ascetic lifestyle, one eliminates the five hindrances, including: (1) covetousness, (2) ill will-hate, (3) sloth-torpor, (4) restlessness-remorse and (5) doubt.

Furthermore, the *Abhidhamma Pitika* (Basket of Virtue) of the *Pali Canon* provides a list of ten defilements (*dasa kilesavatthuni*): (1) greed (*lobha*), (2) hate (*dosa*), (3) delusion (*moha*), (4) conceit (*mana*), (5) wrong views (*micchaditthi*), (6) doubt (*vicikiccha*), (7) torpor (*thinam*), (8) restlessness (*uddhaccam*), (9) shamelessness (*ahirikam*) and (10) recklessness (*anottappam*).[43] There are also other lists of *kilesas* in post-*Pali Canon* literature, including the treatise on Theravada Buddhist doctrine called the *Visudhimagga* (Path of Purification), which was written in Pali by Buddhaghosa (c. early 400 CE).[44] For example the *Visudhimagga* regards greed, hate and delusion as the three defilements,[45] which are also at the root of all other *kilesas* (including pride, jealousy and doubt).[46]

The goal of Buddhist practice is to gain control over all desires and to perfect one's actions. In doing so, one becomes aware of impermanence, including the experience of insubstantiality of the personal self (Pali *anatta*). *Arhants* (Skt. 'noble ones'; Buddha-like) are the enlightened ones, who will have no rebirth as they no longer crave anything, including the benefits of meditation. Significantly, according to the Buddha, only those free from defilements deserve being a monk:

One not free of defilements,
Who will don a yellow robe,
That one, devoid of control and truth,
Is not worthy of a yellow robe.

But one who, well placed in virtues,
Would be with defilements ejected,
Endowed with control and truth,
That one is worthy of a yellow robe.[47]

Liberation is referred to as *nibbana* 'to cool by blowing', which connotes the extinguishing of fire and, more specifically, blowing out the *kilesas* that bind one to the cycle of rebirth. Therefore, *nibbana* is the return to an unagitated state.

Indic metaphysical enquiry that emerged during the axial age – which has as its single-minded goal of enlightenment and personal contentment – regards the renunciation of mundane pursuits as the prerequisite for conquering both desire and affliction. Indeed, the highest value is placed upon world renunciation. However, society at the same time requires people to live in the world, especially to procreate. Moreover, while renunciates provide religious teachings to the laity or householders, they are dependent on the offerings made by householders.[48] In effect, the Hindu tradition made a serious attempt to reconcile the earlier Vedic path of religious and social action and the opposing austere Upanishadic path of renunciation.

The householder and desire

The Classical Hindu tradition resolves the tension between the ideal of renunciation and the necessity of people having to live in the world, by establishing the goals of sacrifice and renunciation as part of a schema of four different life stages (Skt. *ashrama*).[49] According to the *varna-ashrama-dharma* schema,[50] there are four aims of life: (1) the fulfilment of social and religious duty (Skt. *dharma*), (2) the acquisition of prosperity and power (Skt. *artha*), (3) the experience of sensual-pleasures (Skt. *kama*) and (4) the attainment of liberation (Skt. *moksha*). While there are four human goals, the first three (*dharma*, *artha* and *kama*) are meant to be fulfilled during the householder stage of life (Skt. *grihastha-ashrama*). That is, householders are obliged to fulfil certain social or religious obligations, and to follow prescriptions to be prosperous and have progeny.[51]

During the last stage of life (Skt. *samnyasa-ashrama*), one is however required to renounce the material world in order to pursue the ultimate goal of *moksha*, which is open only to the privileged males belonging to the three upper-Hindu classes that are regarded as twice-born (Skt. *dvija*).[52] While those of non-*dvija* status (i.e. men belonging to the *shudra* class and women) cannot aspire to achieve *moksha* in their present life, the householder goals suffice for them during their entire life even as they can hope for a better rebirth. For instance, those with non-*dvija* status can perform renunciate-like practices, such as fasting and observances for one's husband (Skt. *pati-vrata*), in order to attain merit in this life so that they may be reborn with *dvija* status in the next life and eventually aspire to attain liberation. The pursuit of liberation requires world renunciation, including the householder goal of *kama* (desire, wish or lust).

Kama refers to the desire for that which brings pleasure to the senses. Although sexual desire or lust dominates religious discourse, *kama* may be with or without reference to sex.[53] While a householder is meant to both enjoy sex and procreate, there is a warning about the potential dangers of lust. That is, *kama* is potentially addictive and always runs the risk of becoming a vice.[54] Unlike gambling, drinking alcohol and hunting, sexual activity is the only potential vice necessary for existence;[55] that is, it involves the human instinct for both creation and self-preservation.

Just as Hindu religious pursuit includes abstaining from sensual-pleasure, the *Bhagavad Gita* (c. 100 BCE–100 CE) also teaches that householders can attain the spiritual ideal of renunciation by sacrificing the ego.[56] Although Krishna discusses three paths,[57] his teaching about the renunciation of the fruits of one's actions (Skt. *nis-kama-karma-yoga*) is of central importance. The *Bhagavad Gita* teaches that one has to fulfil one's inherent social and religious duty for the sake of attaining *moksha* at the personal level and for the maintenance of the social order at the community level. Accordingly, householders can – when detached from the fruits of their actions – acquire spiritual benefit. Of course, this path of action (Skt. *karma-marga*) is within the context of one's social class and stage-in-life (Skt. *varna-ashrama-dharma*).

In relation to the perspective that desire is the main cause of suffering, there emerge two significant questions: Can one truly alleviate suffering or overcome desire while living in the world? And, more specifically, how can social engagement help in getting rid of affliction?

Sikhi, suffering and social responsibility

Guru Nanak (1469–1539 CE), the revered founder and the first of a line of ten Sikh Gurus, laid the foundations of *Sikhi*. As aforementioned, Guru Nanak's *Siddh Goshth* teaches that the ego can be renounced while living as a householder (*grahasti*). Similar to the teachings of the *Bhagavad Gita*, the basic requirement is to renounce the fruits of one's actions (Skt. *nis-kama-karma-yoga*). The fundamental difference here, however, is that for Guru Nanak this path of action is not to be pursued according to either *varna-ashrama-dharma* or the principle of *dvija*.[58] Although one is required to fulfil family and social duties in the context of ego-renunciation, social involvement goes beyond striving for traditional householder goals. Indeed, Guru Nanak's vision for social involvement is fundamentally about improving the state of humanity (*sarbat da bhalla*),⁵⁹ and reflects his understanding of, and concern about, the sources of human suffering.

Based on his devotional compositions, one can delineate Guru Nanak's spiritual perspective on *dukh* (suffering, sorrow, pain or grief). Continuous with other Indic religions, human bondage to *sansar* is the major source of suffering. Indeed, pain is inevitable since humans are caught in the cycle of suffering. Besides this understanding of human bondage, Guru Nanak differentiates four causes of suffering:

> First is the suffering (*dukh*) of hunger,
>   and the other is of separation;
> Then is the suffering (*dukh*) of oppression and death.
> Another is the suffering (*dukh*) of ailments
>   rushing through the body;
> O naïve doctor, don't apply the medicine! (1)
> O naïve doctor, don't apply the medicine!
> As pain (*dard*) occurs, the body continues to suffer.
> Such medicine has no effect, brother. (1) [Pause]
>
> Forgetting the Beloved, and indulging in pleasures;
> Then disease spreads throughout the body.
> The ignorant mind receives punishment;
> O naïve doctor, don't apply the medicine! (2)
>
> Sandalwood is of value when it has fragrance;
> The body is of value when it has the breath.
> When breathing ceases, the body withers away;
> After that, nothing is consumed. (3)
>
> The body is golden, and one's being is pure;
> When a single particle contains the untainted *Nam*.
> All suffering (*dukh*) and disease are eradicated;
> Nanak: Saved by the True *Nam*. (4)⁶⁰

According to Guru Nanak, people endure pain when they experience: (1) separation, primarily from *Nam*, resulting in anxiety and fear; (2) physical deprivation, such as hunger and thirst; (3) bodily ailments, like disease and infection; and (4) oppression and death.

Guru Nanak's belief that suffering arises from oppression and tyranny is evident in his 'Babar-bani' – the verses about the first Mughal Emperor Zahiruddin Muhammad Babur (1526–30 CE) and his annexation of North

India.⁶¹ Guru Nanak explicitly expresses the idea that these external forces need to be acknowledged and addressed.⁶² Notwithstanding that notion, Guru Nanak considers the brutality of oppression to be only secondary to the pain of separation:⁶³

> If my body were to suffer,
>   if sin and curse were to eclipse,
>   if blood drinking kings held power over my head,
>   even so, You will be praised and yearning will never cease.⁶⁴

Indeed, Guru Nanak views separation from *Nam* as a much more severe type of pain to endure – even harsher than social and political oppression – because 'spiritual suffering' is the fundamental form of suffering that affects both mind and body.

Along with the four types of suffering, Guru Nanak also teaches that when humans are self-centred (i.e. separated from *Nam*) or guided by their egos (*manmukh*), they are caught in a continual cycle of *dukh-sukh-dukh*: 'From suffering (*dukh*) sprouts happiness (*sukh*), from pleasure (*sukh*) comes suffering (*dukh*).'⁶⁵ Caught in this vicious cycle of suffering, humans seek pleasure as an 'escape' to alleviate their pain. Seeking pleasure, however, results in more suffering because the experience of pleasure is not permanent. Moreover, in the effort to escape pain, individuals run the risk of becoming unwell, addicted and/

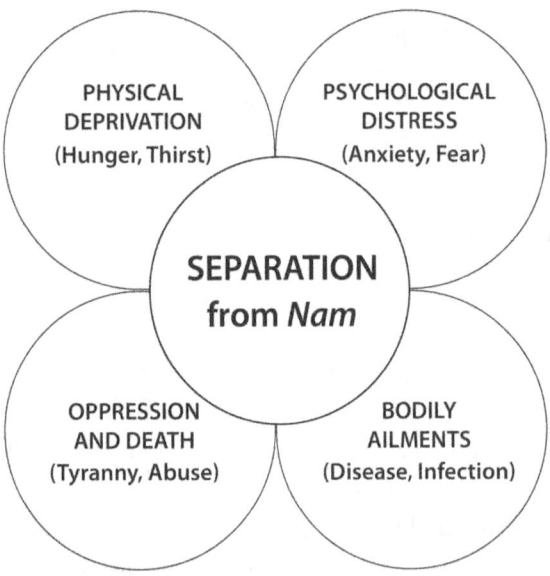

Figure 1.1 The sources of suffering.

or falling in the grip of the five evils.[66] As the experience of separation intensifies, the pain worsens. In effect, individuals become caught in the continual cycle of suffering-pleasure-suffering (*dukh-sukh-dukh*) and eventually drown in the ocean of existence (*sansar*).

On the other hand, the experience of *dukh* can also lead to a profound awareness of one's separation from *Nam*. While the source of suffering (*dukh*) is pleasure (*sukh*), suffering (*dukh*) is also regarded as the cure for ego-centredness: 'Suffering (*dukh*) is the cure, pleasure (*sukh*) is the disease, no awareness [of the One] in pleasure (*sukh*).'[67] Indeed, the experience of *dukh* can serve as a catalyst for change. That is, with the heightened awareness of the impermanence of life, one can more deeply connect with *Nam*.

It is important to note here that the word *sukh* has various interpretations. In order to accurately interpret the word *sukh*, the entire verse has to be taken into serious consideration. For instance, when *sukh* refers to the immediate gratification of desire for pleasure or comfort, it is viewed as a disease or source of suffering:

> The ignorant indulges in pleasures, it's all suffering (*dukh*);
> From pleasures (*sukh*) arise disease, thus resulting in sin;
> Gratification creates grief, separation and death.[68]

On the other hand, *sukh* can also mean happiness in the context of joyful acceptance of the various aspects of human existence:

> Those who serve obtain honor;
> Nanak: Praise the Treasure of virtues.
> Sing and listen with love in the heart,
>   shed suffering (*dukh*) and bring happiness (*sukh*) home.[69]

While the former usage of the term *sukh* (i.e. pleasure or comfort) is immediate in time, the latter connotation of the subsequent employment of the term (i.e. happiness) is joy and peace that are integrated into one's being. Indeed, the pursuit of happiness is not merely the result of removing or overcoming *dukh* in order to attain happiness, but it also involves the cultivation of wellness. And, according to Guru Nanak, one ultimately has to transcend duality or a dualistic mode of thinking:

> This coming and going
>   ends through the *shabad*.
> The One watches and blesses.

> One suffers from the disease of duality,
> and *Nam*, the cure, is forgotten.
> The one who has been inspired to understand
> is liberated through the *shabad*.
> Nanak: The Emancipator saves those
> who have distanced themselves
> from ego and duality.[70]

The concept of transcending duality also relates to the duality of *dukh* and *sukh*. That is, the goal is to accept the existential reality of both *dukh* and *sukh*:

> Nanak: It is absurd to be spared from suffering (*dukh*) and to ask for comfort (*sukh*);
> Suffering and comfort are the two garments given to a person at the door;
> When words are not effective, it is better to be silent.[71]

In actuality, life entails both *dukh* and *sukh*. For those who resist this fact, there is likely to be more suffering, but they can become aware of the non-duality of *dukh-sukh* with the support of *Nam*: 'Pleasure and suffering are alike, when one has the support of *Nam*.'[72] And, those who see *sukh* and *dukh* alike, they are unaffected by either: 'Recognize pleasure (*sukh*) and suffering (*dukh*) as alike; *shabad* is the way of happiness' and 'The experience of pleasure and suffering is given by You (*Guru*), the *gurmukh* is unaffected'.[73] In effect, the *gurmukh* (one who follows the will of *Guru* or the Gurus' teachings) transcends the dualistic nature of *dukh* and *sukh*, and attains happiness and peace.

Along with the general Indic philosophical understanding that the source of *dukh* is the result of actions (*karam*) done in a past or current life, Guru Nanak also teaches that both *dukh* and *sukh* are under the control and part of the will of *Ek Oankar* (the One creator-creation): 'According to the cosmic order (*hukam*) there are the exalted and the lowly. As a result of *hukam*, suffering (*dukh*) and happiness (*sukh*) are experienced.'[74] But, while *dukh* and *sukh* are viewed as under the control of *Ek Oankar*, importantly one should not ignore psychological distress, self-deprivation, neglect of physical ailments or surrender to abuse. Guru Nanak teaches that suffering is a result of both inner forces (ego-centredness) and external forces (social injustice and political oppression).[75] For the inner forces, one should follow the path of inner awareness and concentration on *Nam*, whereas for the external forces, one should perform selfless service (*seva*) for the betterment of humanity, including helping those in need or fighting against injustice and oppression.

Guru Nanak views social involvement as an integral component of spiritual development. While Classical and Bhakti Hindu philosophers contended that everyone is equal at the spiritual level, they accepted, unlike Guru Nanak, the Brahminic social order at the societal level. Guru Nanak, on the other hand, challenged the *varna* system and its associated discriminatory notion of purity and pollution. Instead of *varna-ashrama-dharma*, Guru Nanak's teachings about *dharam* (Skt. *dharma*) integrate his concerns of both the internal and external sources of suffering. The fulfilment of Sikh *dharam* involves the remembrance of *Nam* (*simran*) to break down ego-centredness and alleviate the pangs of spiritual separation as well as the practice of selfless service (*seva*) to help attenuate or combat the external sources of human suffering. In doing so, Sikh *dharam* strives for both the attainment of contentment and the cultivation of compassion.[76] Hence, the goal is to find a balance between the internal quest for contentment and the external concern for social justice and harmony.

The constituents of Sikh *dharam* or how a Sikh should live are also reflected in the triadic prescription of *Nam-dan-ishnan*: *Nam* (Name) refers to the remembrance of *Ek Oankar*, *dan* (charity) denotes the social value of *seva* and *ishnan* (purification) entails personal mental and physical cleanliness.

> The *gurmukh* is blessed with *Nam*, *dan* and *ishnan*.
> The *gurmukh* experiences effortless contemplation.
> The *gurmukh* attains honor in the court.
> The *gurmukh* merges with the supreme Being, the destroyer of fear.
> The *gurmukh* performs good deeds and inspires others to do the same.
> Nanak: The *gurmukh* unifies with the One.[77]

These three principles provide a holistic approach to individual spiritual attainment and community development.[78] While *ishnan* involves cleansing the mind and body through remembrance, the unifying experience with *Nam* fosters the spirit of *seva*:

> The essence of *Nam* is in all.
> Without *Nam*,
>   one is afflicted with suffering and death.
> When essence merges with the Essence,
>   the mind is fulfilled.
> Duality disappears, enters the home of oneness.
> The breath blows thunderously in the tenth door.
> Nanak: The Unmoveable is attained effortlessly.[79]

Guru Nanak's message of *Nam-dan-ishnan* can be regarded as the 'blueprint' for the three core principles of how a Sikh should live that were prescribed in the 1950 *Sikh Reht Maryada* (Sikh Code of Conduct and Conventions): (1) chanting *Nam* (*Nam japo*), (2) honest livelihood (*kirat karo*) and (3) sharing a tenth of one's earnings for the betterment of humanity (*vand ke chhako*).[80] More recently, the *Sikh Reht Maryada* has prescribed:

> A Sikh's personal life should comprehend:
>
> 1. Meditation on *Nam* and the scriptures (*nam bani da abhiasa*)
> 2. Leading life according to the Gurus' teachings (*gurmati di rahini*)
> 3. Altruistic voluntary service (*seva*)[81]

As taught by Guru Nanak, a Sikh should strive to attain the truth and – more significantly – apply that truth in one's daily life.[82]

Modern scholarship previously demonstrated how *Sikhi* has been – through a 'Sant synthesis' – influenced by Hindu (Vaishnava) Bhakti, the *hath-yoga* of the Nath tradition and the mysticism of Sufism.[83] Indeed, the *nirgun bhagats* (poet-saints who praise the formless one) in northern India, from the fifteenth to the seventeenth century, generally tended to teach a more 'radical' devotional path to liberation in which the realization of God is to be attained through devotional meditation on the *Nam*. They explicitly rejected all institutional forms of religion, including the notion of revelation (as in the Vedas or Qur'an), places of worship (*mandir, masjid*), temple rituals, yogic practices, pilgrimage places, religious texts and the need for clergy. While similarities among the *nirgun bhagats* did exist, they were not members of a single group or movement. As argued by Mann, earlier scholars (like McLeod) perhaps overlooked the differences among the *nirgun bhagats* because they focused on the various non-Sikh *bhagats* (like Kabir, Namdev and Ravidas) included in the *Guru Granth Sahib*. While the verses of the *nirgun bhagats* that are included in the Sikh scripture would reflect the similarities shared between them and Guru Nanak, an analysis of these verses alone has overshadowed some substantial differences.[84]

No doubt, Guru Nanak is commonly revered as a *sant* or a *nirgun bhagat* based on his many devotional compositions and his call for the devotion of *Nam*, the expression of the formless one. However, several scholars have more recently highlighted some substantial departures of *Sikhi* from *nirgun* Bhakti, including the positive value placed on manual labour and selfless service (*seva*) for the welfare of humanity, as well as Guru Nanak's establishment of the Guru-seat (*gur-gaddi*) at Kartarpur and appointment of a successor for his followers.[85]

These differences account for the continuation and development of the distinct community referred to as the Sikh Panth.

Moreover, Guru Nanak spoke out against many contemporaneous religious, socio-economic and political beliefs and practices in North India that he believed to be either unhealthy or unjust. Indeed, he had 'a strong sense of vision that compelled him to proclaim his message for the ultimate benefit of his audience and to promote socially responsible living'.[86] Well known for his critique of the caste system and the hypocrisy associated with it, Guru Nanak put high value on manual labour and selfless service (*seva*).[87] His socio-political orientation can also be viewed as reflecting his spiritual and existential understanding of suffering. This was also addressed and supported by key institutions of the Sikh Panth, such as the *sangat* (congregation), the *pangat* or *Guru ka langar* (community meal), the *dharamsal* (religious sanctuary, original Sikh place of worship) and the *shabad-Guru* (Guru's words) as the central authority in community life.[88] These key institutions established by Guru Nanak in fact address the internal and external sources of suffering, such as ego-centredness, mental distress, physical deprivation and social alienation.

Building on Guru Nanak's spiritual approach to alleviating suffering (*dukh*), Guru Arjan composed the *Sukhmani* (The Pearl of Happiness), a lengthy text that not only addresses the existential problem of suffering but also provides valuable insights into the human pursuit of well-being and happiness for all members of society. A careful reading of the *Sukhmani* provides us a profound understanding of the Sikh approach to happiness in the course of navigating through the trials and turbulence of the material world. Besides, the lucidity of the work has allowed it to evolve into a central and popular Sikh text. As part of Guru Arjan's accomplishments in both organizing the Sikhs and forging a communal identity, the *Sukhmani* provides a blueprint for putting Sikh spiritual values into practice, at both the individual and collective levels.

Intellectual context and approach of the study

Sikhi has, for the most part, been studied in a vacuum even as it is often overshadowed in the West by the popularity of Patanjali's Yoga and Buddhism. While much attention has been given to the latter two, *Sikhi* has been overlooked in terms of its insights into human nature and spiritual understanding of both well-being and happiness. In part, the explanation for this situation lies internally in the nature of Sikh Studies; that is, *Sikhi* is a relatively new and emerging field within the larger discipline of religion. Moreover, enquiry into the Sikh tradition has been polarized from the mid-nineteenth up to the late twentieth century.[89] This polarization emerged in the context of British colonial rule and the Singh Sabha movement: the orientalists or early European scholars were interested in understanding Sikh religion (Trumpp, Macauliffe) and history (Cunningham),[90] while Sikh scholars (Sahib Singh, Teja Singh) had as their objective the crystallization of a distinct Sikh identity.[91]

This Orientalist-Sikh relation can be viewed as the template for the dynamic interaction between the 'traditional historians' and the 'critical historians' of the twentieth century. On the one hand, the 'traditional historians' (Trilochan Singh, Daljeet Singh) have had as their aim the defence of the Sikh faith and assertion of a Sikh identity.[92] On the other hand, the 'critical historians' (McLeod, Harjot Singh Oberoi, Pashaura Singh) have had as their primary objective the determination of historical fact with respect to the development of Sikh tradition, including concern about the authenticity of texts and their authorship, and historical accuracy in the interpretation of texts.[93] Subsequently, the 'traditional historians' came to perceive the 'critical historians' as attacking Sikh faith and identity, while the 'critical historians' viewed the 'traditional historians' as being insensitive to the canons of scholarly research and the quest for historical facts.[94]

More recently, with the rise of post-colonial, post-modernist and feminist challenges to the earlier structural-functional paradigms of the 'homogenous Other', there has emerged much theoretical discussion around the issues of fluidity in the development of Sikhism (rather than taking a linear approach to its development), interpreting the tradition (using *Sikhi* instead of Sikhism frames), heterogeneity (i.e. various sectarian renditions) of the tradition and the complexity of identity (as opposed to a single essential Sikh identity). All of this has, in turn, made for greater importance and value being accorded to both the impact of the Singh Sabha movement and the colonial context on historical reconstructions of the Sikh tradition, and the role of agency in the study of *Sikhi* and Sikh communities.[95]

The present study certainly recognizes the importance of the relevant issues surrounding historical authenticity and accuracy, and they form a significant aspect of it. Related to the field of Indology, this work includes an enquiry into the historical accuracy and consistency of the corpus of Sikh literature, including the hagiographies (*sakhis*) about Guru Arjan.[96] Yet, 'improbable' events described in the hagiographies may well have some religious significance beyond the domain of history. Therefore, the study also takes into serious consideration that which does not strictly emerge as historical fact. Consequently, while this analysis examines historical accuracy and consistency, it does so without losing sight of that which is important to the Sikh tradition. And, while historical context is undoubtedly important in looking at religious development, a mere historical reconstruction may well fall far short in understanding matters relating to religious beliefs and practices. This work therefore not only aims to take into consideration the historical context of the *Sukhmani*, but also seeks to explore the metaphorical meanings contained in the *Sukhmani* and the religious significance of the events in the hagiographies about Guru Arjan. In doing so, the study also draws on oral knowledge, mainly communicated by Sikh religious preachers (*gianis*).

In addition, instead of solely employing Western philosophical categories and theories to deconstruct the tradition or of using modern psychological concepts to frame the spiritual teachings, we hope to shed light on how *Sikhi* addresses the existential problem of suffering and the pursuit of happiness from within the tradition itself as well as from within the larger framework of Indic religions. This approach is vital, since Indic perspectives on happiness are grounded in spirituality, while modern understandings of happiness pertain to the mental and emotional dimensions of the human condition.[97] Indeed, according to modern psychology, including positive psychology, happiness involves meaningful engagement, an optimistic outlook and pleasant emotions, along with the understanding that life comes with its ups and downs.[98] On the other hand, Indic traditions distinguish two main sources of happiness: (1) extrinsic, the fulfilling of desires and avoidance of displeasure or suffering, and ultimately (2) intrinsic, the spiritual experience of oneness as a result of transcending the ego.[99]

The research for this study consists of four main components: (1) an analysis of the primary sources of the Sikh tradition, including the *Sukhmani* and other verses composed by the Sikh Gurus as well as other religious literature; (2) an analysis of the primary sources of Hinduism and Buddhism, including religious texts on *dharma*; (3) an examination of the secondary sources of the Indic religious and philosophical traditions in general, and of the Sikh tradition more specifically; and (4) an analysis of the *Sukhmani* from the perspective of the text's existential and psychological insights into the human problem of suffering and the pursuit of happiness. While handling these tasks, elements of wellness and happiness studies are also incorporated into the study. In the light of the foregoing discussion, this study seeks to provide tentative answers to questions pertaining to suffering, healing, well-being and happiness in the Sikh tradition.

Aims of the study

In general, the present study contextualizes Guru Arjan's *Sukhmani* within the broader framework of Indic religions as well as within the Sikh tradition. More specifically, the study underlines the *Sukhmani* as a significant contribution to the Sikh spiritual tradition. The chief aims of this work are: (1) to provide an understanding of the *Sukhmani* within the larger framework of the pursuit of happiness in the light of the concepts of *dukh* and *sukh* in Indic religions; (2) to delineate the historical, social and religious context of the *Sukhmani*; (3) to underscore the location of the *Sukhmani* in the development of *Sikhi*; (4) to offer an analysis of Guru Arjan's key spiritual teachings contained in the *Sukhmani*; (5) to highlight key Sikh psychological concepts and illustrate the application of *gurmat* values (or values taught by the Sikh Gurus); and, last, (6) to provide an original English translation of the *Sukhmani*.

An analysis of the *Sukhmani* involves an exploration of four useful textual dimensions: (1) the historical life-situation of the author of the text (Chapter 2); (2) the intended purpose, audience and function of the text (Chapter 3); (3) the spiritual perspective of the text (Chapter 4); and (4) the implications of the text for the cultivation of well-being and the attainment of happiness (Chapter 5). As indicated, before commencing the analysis on the *Sukhmani* and its teachings on the pursuit of happiness, it is necessary to first provide the composition's socio-historical context, specifically pertaining to Guru Arjan's life, works and martyrdom, the topic of the next chapter.

2

Guru Arjan's life, work and martyrdom

Guru Arjan (1563–1606), the fifth Sikh Guru, is highly revered by Sikhs for having built the Harmandar Sahib (also known as the Golden Temple)[1] in Amritsar and for having compiled the initial Sikh canon titled the *Adi Granth*. While Guru Arjan's initiatives consolidated the organizational and doctrinal aspects of the Sikh community (the Panth), they were also part of the larger aim to unify the expanding community amid the changing religious, social and political environment in the Punjab. Although Arjan's guruship (1581–1606) began and, for the most part, continued under Mughal Emperor Akbar's rule (1556–1605) and the latter's policy of religious pluralism, it came to a tragic end with Mughal Emperor Jahangir's reign (1605–27) and his evident religious intolerance towards the Sikh Panth.[2]

Building on the tradition developed by the Sikh Gurus who had preceded him, Guru Arjan consolidated the Sikh Panth. Indeed, his life, work and martyrdom 'perfectly represent all that Guru Nanak had founded and anticipated'.[3] The striking feature about Guru Arjan's *Sukhmani* is not only that the text builds on the spiritual teachings of Guru Nanak (including concepts like *Nam-dan-ishnan*),[4] but also that its message echoes through Guru Arjan's actions, most profoundly at the time of his execution. Guru Arjan's devotional compositions should, therefore, be viewed and understood in the light of both his life and his martyrdom, especially since 'tradition complements scripture'[5] here. That is, tradition provides a more complete interpretation of Guru Arjan's teachings.

Traditional narratives about Guru Arjan provide a larger context for his scriptural texts as they shed light on his character and existential situation. It is for this reason that Guru Arjan's *Sukhmani* should be read with an understanding of his life story, including his balanced approach to living in the world, his dedicated effort in consolidating the Sikh Panth, his hostile relations with his eldest brother Prithi Chand and the events surrounding his martyrdom, all of which can be drawn from scriptural and more contemporary Sikh literature.

While ambiguity and historical inconsistency may exist, especially in the retelling of his martyrdom, the hagiographies or traditional narratives – at the very least – provide a context for his teachings.[6]

Hagiographies are 'multifaceted narratives' that provide a historical texture.[7] While historical context is important in looking at religious developments, a mere historical reconstruction may fail in highlighting the significance of religious phenomena.[8] Since the narratives are very much cherished and celebrated in the Sikh tradition, they can reveal the reverence in which Guru Arjan has been held by Sikh followers. Moreover, depending on their religious worldview, narratives also shed light on sectarian differences. Indeed, academic enquiry also needs to shed light on religious phenomena that matter and make sense to the tradition.

There are three main traditional sources from which an account of Guru Arjan's life can be drawn: (1) *Guru Granth Sahib*, (2) Bhai Gurdas's *Varan* and (3) *Gur Pratap Suraj* (1843). The first source, *Guru Granth Sahib*, the primary Sikh scripture, includes texts like the *Sukhmani* authored by Guru Arjan as well as verses by several court bards (*bhatts*) in praise of Guru Arjan (*GGS*, 1406–09).[9] The second source, Bhai Gurdas's *Varan*, is an interpretive commentary on the *Guru Granth Sahib*, which Guru Arjan designated as the 'key' to understanding *shabad-Guru* (Guru's words).[10] The third source, *Gur Pratap Suraj* (Manifestation of the Sun, also known as *Suraj Prakash*), is Bhai Santokh Singh's magnum opus on the lives of nine Sikh Gurus (Guru Angad to Guru Gobind Singh) and Banda Singh Bahadur.[11]

It is important to note here that, while the *Gur Pratap Suraj* is regarded as a monumental source of history about the Sikh Gurus, scholars trained in historiography view its hagiographical character as problematic.[12] Moreover, the *Gur Pratap Suraj*'s author – Bhai Santokh Singh (1787–1843) – represents the Nirmala sect,[13] an order of celibate Sikh-Sanskrit scholars. Although the Nirmala Sikhs have played an important role in the preservation of Sikh history,[14] they are regarded as Sanatan Sikhs because they hold a worldview that combines *sanatan* or ancient Hindu beliefs and *Sikhi*. Sikhs at large accept comparative religious studies and inter-religious discourse (*vichar*);[15] however, various Sikhs' voice dissent over the Nirmala tendency to illustrate *Sikhi* through a Hindu-Vedantic worldview.[16] Despite these two shortcomings, the *Gur Pratap Suraj* serves as an important source for religious discourse or sermons (*katha*) in the *gurdwara*, and contains the most narratives about Guru Arjan.

This chapter provides a general overview of Guru Arjan's life, work and martyrdom, based on Sikh scriptural sources (*Guru Granth Sahib* and Bhai Gurdas's *Varan*), later Sikh literature (such as the *Gur Pratap Suraj*) and contemporary scholarship. In doing so, it reveals the religious, social and political circumstances during which Guru Arjan composed the *Sukhmani*. Furthermore, the chapter critically examines the narratives about how Sri Chand assisted Guru Arjan in composing the *Sukhmani*. In the light of Guru Arjan's life and work, the chapter illustrates the particular sectarian orientation of this narrative and its various renditions.

Before examining the life and martyrdom of Guru Arjan, it is necessary, however, to first analyse the distinctive roles and contributions of the Sikh Gurus who came before him. Such an examination provides the essential background on the early development of *Sikhi* even as it contextualizes Guru Arjan's role within the Sikh Panth.

The Panth inherited by Guru Arjan

As in the case of the other Sikh Gurus, Guru Arjan had a distinctive role in the development of the Sikh tradition. His organizational and doctrinal initiatives certainly strengthened the expanding Sikh Panth. Despite Guru Arjan's unique contributions in historical time (*kal*), it is the Sikh belief that all ten Gurus were of the same essence. As Bhatt Mathura explains:

> Recognize Guru Nanak as embodying the light of *Har*.
> From there came [Guru] Angad, his essence merged with the essence.
> With [Guru] Angad's mercy, [Guru] Amar [Das] became *Satgur*.
> [Guru] Amar Das bestowed Guru Ram [Das] the canopy of immortality.
> Touched by a vision of Guru Ram Das, speech became ambrosial, thus speaks Mathura.
> With the eyes, see the image of Guru Arjan as the proven leader.[17]

According to *Sikhi*, there is one Guru, often referred to as Nanak, along with the ten complete or self-realized humans regarded as the embodiments of the timeless (*akal*) light. Bhai Gurdas explains Guru Arjan's spiritual stature thus:

> *Niranjan* is beyond description, beyond birth, timeless and infinite.
> The great light of *Paramesar* is beyond that of the sun and moon.
> The light shines continuously, and is praised by all worldly life.
> The world salutes the primal Being, the supporter. ...
> Guru Arjan is [one with] the true Creator.[18]

> The light in his father, grandfather and forefathers is within Guru Arjan.
> The throne was attained through the trade of *shabad* awareness.[19]

Therefore, Guru Arjan was as much a successor of Guru Nanak as was Guru Angad (the second Sikh Guru).[20] *Guru* connotes Ultimate Reality (i.e. *Ek Oankar*) or the embodiment of that reality, such as the ten human Gurus who uttered the sacred word (*shabad-Guru*). While Guru Nanak's works served as the spiritual foundation and inspiration for the later Sikh Gurus, he also established Guru as the central authority of the Panth.

One of Guru Nanak's initiatives that distinguishes him from many other contemporary religious mystics (*sants*) is that, before he passed on, Guru Nanak, significantly, appointed a successor to take his place as the central authority of the Panth. Importantly, Guru Nanak chose neither of his own two sons, Sri Chand and Lakhmi Das. Rather, in 1539 Guru Nanak appointed Bhai Lehna, whom he regarded as an ideal devotee of the *Guru*, as his successor.[21] In order to prevent the possibility of his own sons claiming entitlement to lead and to inherit property, Guru Nanak advised Bhai Lehna to establish his Guru-seat (*gur-gaddi*) at Khadur.[22] Guru Nanak gave Bhai Lehna the name Angad 'limb of the body', reflecting his deep connection with the Panth.[23]

As the successor, Guru Angad (1504–52) continued Guru Nanak's relatively small following. Despite its small size, Guru Angad had the challenging task not only of continuing and expanding the Panth after the passing of Guru Nanak, but also to do so in the face of Sri Chand's opposition to him for having succeeded the *gur-gaddi*.[24] Guru Angad strengthened both the *sangat* (congregation) and the *pangat* (communal meal) institutions, by opening more religious centres. In addition to composing some hymns, Guru Angad also 'adopted and modified' the *lande-mahajini* script (used in northern India by *khatris* for accounting), which he used in making copies of Guru Nanak's compositions for distribution.[25] The script came to be called *gurmukhi* (from the Guru's mouth), which was later used in writing the *Adi Granth*, and subsequently by Sikhs in general for writing in Punjabi. Besides his religious and literary initiatives, Guru Angad also gave importance to physical activity, like wrestling, which can be viewed as an antecedent to the later tradition of martial (*gatka*) training within the Panth.

In 1552, Guru Angad appointed Amar Das Bhalla (1479–1574) as his successor, based on the latter's devotion and commitment to the Sikh Panth. While Amar Das Bhalla was born into a Vaishnava family and lived in Basarke (a village on the outskirts of what later became known as Amritsar), at the age of sixty he embraced *Sikhi* upon meeting Guru Angad and hearing the Sikh Gurus' messages. Guru Angad's sons, Dasu and Datu, however, contested their father's decision; in fact, Dasu installed himself as 'guru' at Khadur.[26] Subsequently,

Guru Amar Das built a well at Goindval, where he established his *gur-gaddi*,[27] and built Goindval Sahib as a *tirath* (pilgrimage place). Later, Emperor Akbar visited this holy place and received *langar* (community dining).[28]

While he continued the Panth's established institutions, Guru Amar Das made a more explicit break with Hindu traditions. For instance, he replaced the singing of Hindu hymns with the recitation of Sikh texts at birth, marriage and death ceremonies. Guru Amar Das also spoke out against caste, child marriage, *sati* and the rule forbidding widow remarriage. He denounced as well the Islamic practice of veiling.[29] In order to meet the needs of the growing Sikh Panth, Guru Amar Das also established the *manji* system of twenty-two seats through which people were appointed to spread *Sikhi*.[30] He designated both women and men to collect offerings and conduct worship at the various religious centres.

Guru Amar Das, further, gathered and compiled a four-volume collection of hymns referred to as the *Goindval Pothis*. They were compiled in an effort to preserve an authentic collection of sacred texts and to prevent 'unripe utterances' (*kachi bani*) or even fake works from entering the Sikh Panth.[31] The *Goindval Pothis* are written in Gurmukhi script and organized according to classical Indian musical measure (*rag*; Skt. *raga*). They include the devotional works of Guru Amar Das, the two preceding gurus (Guru Nanak and Guru Angad) and several *bhagats* (like Kabir, Ravidas and Namdev) to broaden the Panth's base. Guru Amar Das composed many texts, with his most celebrated composition being *Anand* (Bliss).[32] In *Anand*, Guru Amar Das describes the bliss a devotee experiences when immersed in *Har* (an epithet for *Ek Oankar*):

> O my mind, may you always remain with *Har*.
> My mind, remain with *Har*, suffering shall disappear.
> You will be accepted, and all endeavours completed.
> *Swami* is the all-powerful Master, why be forgetful?
> Nanak says: O my mind, always remain with *Har*.[33]

In 1574, Guru Amar Das appointed his son-in-law Jetha Sodhi (1534–81) as his successor.[34] Since Punjabi society is patrilineal, it was revolutionary for Guru Amar Das to grant his son-in-law the Guru-seat (*gur-gaddi*) instead of either of his two sons, Mohan and Mohari.[35] Upon his appointment, Jetha was named Guru Ram Das. While Guru Amar Das requested Guru Ram Das to build a new centre for the Panth in view of the expanding community, the initiative also circumvented the potential conflict over the legal claim that either of his two sons could make on the centre at Goindval.[36] In 1577, Guru Ram Das began building a large pool meant for ritual bathing on land that had been gifted to his wife by Emperor Akbar at the centre of an ancient town.[37] Subsequently, it became known as Ramdaspur (also known as Guru da Chak or Chak Ram Das).[38] Having a large business class to draw upon for financial support, Guru Ram Das sent agents (*masand*) to collect donations for the construction of sacred pools and free kitchens.[39]

Guru Ram Das made great efforts in spreading the Sikh teachings and promoting *langar*. While he continued the traditions laid down by the previous Sikh Gurus, Guru Ram Das is most celebrated for his musical genius. Not only did he compose many devotional texts, but as a highly skilled musician Guru Ram Das also introduced eleven new *rags* to the tradition. While he did not compile any *pothis* including his own work, Guru Ram Das encouraged a professional class of scribes to preserve and distribute *gurbani* because of his concern about maintaining the authenticity of the Gurus' hymns.[40]

Guru Ram Das was father to three sons – Prithi Chand, Mahan Dev and Arjan. Despite the fact that Arjan was the youngest, he was chosen as the successor in 1581 based on his suitability for guruship.[41] Although the Panth's tradition of succession was solely based on spiritual merit, the appointment of Guru Arjan was justified on both the original principle of such merit and the new practice of keeping succession within the Sodhi clan. This additional practice can be interpreted as a form of favouritism (i.e. keeping the *gur-gaddi* title within the family). On the other hand, Guru Arjan's appointment broke with primogeniture – the rule that inheritance and leadership are to be passed down to the eldest son – since Guru Arjan was the youngest son.

This break with custom in fact resulted in a lot of tension between Guru Arjan and Prithi Chand; the latter as the eldest son felt entitled to acquire the Guru-seat (*gur-gaddi*).[42] For instance, Prithi Chand objected when Mohari (Guru Amar Das's son) invested Guru Arjan with the turban, a Khatri custom indicating succession.[43] Perhaps many sacred verses, justifying Guru Arjan's succession, were composed in reaction to this opposition.[44] Bhai Gurdas makes the case:

> With the merit of past deeds, possessions return to the rightful home.
> Seated as the head of the Sodhi clan, Ram Das was declared as *Satgur*.
> In perfect harmony, he enlightened Amritsar.
> A game played by the Beloved, where the Ganges returns to the ocean.
> Receive what is deserved, without effort nothing is held in the hands.
> Arjan, the son, arrived in the home, and was declared Guru by the world.
> The Guruship remained with the Sodhi clan, unbearable for others [to do].
> That which belongs in the home stays in the home.[45]

Indeed, this justification of Arjan's appointment to the Guru-seat was imperative, given Prithi Chand's antagonism towards the radical break from primogeniture, which then became a source of internal factionalism within the Sikh Panth.

The life of Guru Arjan

Not only was Arjan the first Sikh Guru to have been born in a Sikh family, but also both his father and maternal grandfather were Sikh Gurus. Therefore, narratives about Guru Arjan in the *Gur Pratap Suraj* are also found in the sections on Guru Amar Das (his maternal grandfather) and Guru Ram Das (his father). Since Guru Arjan (1563–1606) was born at Goindval – the centre of the Sikh Panth under Guru Amar Das – he was introduced to *Sikhi* and the activities of the Panth from a very young age. During his childhood, Arjan was in the care of Guru Amar Das, who is described as having been very fond of Arjan.[46]

As a child, Arjan learnt *gurmukhi* from Bhai Buddha and Sanskrit from a couple of *pandits* (Kes and Gopal), even as he participated in oral recitation of *gurbani* with Bhai Gurdas and Bhai Savan Mal.[47] In addition, Arjan was also trained in the *rags*; he later used all thirty *rags* that his father used.[48] In 1574, at around the age of eleven, Arjan moved with his family to Ramdaspur, the new centre of the Panth. In 1579, at the age of sixteen, Arjan married Ganga Devi, just two years prior to taking over the Guru-seat.[49] Sixteen years passed before they were able to have their only child; in 1595, they had a son named Hargobind.

Following the passing of Guru Ram Das in 1581, Arjan succeeded to the Guru-seat. As part of his mission, Guru Arjan further developed the institutional aspects of the Sikh Panth, which, in turn, unified and strengthened it. Guru Arjan continued the projects that his father had started, such as building sacred pools (*sarovar*) at Ramdaspur, Ramsar (pool of Ram) and Santokhsar (pool of contentment). Upon finishing the pool at Ramdaspur, Guru Arjan had the Harmandar Sahib (temple of *Har*) built uniquely in the middle of the sacred pool with a walkway leading up to it. The temple's simplicity and modest size are immediately striking. What is more, entry into the temple evokes humility because one has to descend below ground level to the base of the temple structure in order to meet with *Guru*.

Upon the completion of the Harmandar Sahib (*c.* 1601), Ramdaspur became the Sikh holy city of Amritsar (pool of nectar). Guru Arjan also began building other towns like Tarn Taran in the Majha region and Kartarpur in the Jalandhar region of the Punjab. Bhai Gurdas describes Guru Arjan's effort in the expansion of the Panth:

> Spreading the message in the four directions, countless *sangats* arrived.
> The *langar* operates with *shabad-Guru*, created by the perfect One.
> Under a spotless canopy, the *gurmukh* attains the supreme state of *Braham*.[50]

Guru Arjan instituted the practice of Sikh families sharing their earnings (later established as *dasvand*) to the Guru's charity box (*Guru ki golak*) to support the expanding Sikh Panth.[51] Also, as a means to finance the construction of the sacred pools, temples and new towns, he reorganized the *masand* system (initially set up by his father Guru Ram Das). The *masand* network flourished throughout the Punjab and beyond, thus strengthening the Panth's economic base.[52]

Besides his efforts at advancing the institutional aspects of the Sikh Panth, Guru Arjan had to contend with Prithi Chand's antagonism. As aforementioned, a conflict had emerged between Guru Arjan and his elder brother Prithi Chand over the fact that the latter did not inherit the Guru-seat. Traditional scholars tend to hold the perspective that this tension emerged after Arjan was appointed as the successor; however, 'alienation' may have begun even prior to this event as a result of the preferential treatment Prithi Chand felt his parents gave to Arjan.[53] For example, Arjan triumphed over Prithi Chand when their parents were seemingly testing their character; when the parents requested them to attend a wedding in Lahore, Prithi Chand refused to go while Arjan obeyed their command.[54]

Once Guru Arjan succeeded to the Guru-seat, Prithi Chand went against him. This opposition gave rise to internal factionalism within the Sikh Panth. Bhai Gurdas describes Prithi Chand as 'the rascal (*mina*), with his hidden agenda, spread madness'.[55] Prithi Chand both sought assistance from a local state official (Sulhi Khan) to plot against Guru Arjan and prepared his own son Manohar Das, better known as Miharvan, for guruship.[56] There are many hagiographies that echo this tension over succession, even over the future successor of Guru Arjan. For instance, there are narratives about how (1) Prithi Chand and his wife Karmo were pleased, when Guru Arjan and his wife were unable to conceive a child, in the hope that their own son Miharvan could become the sixth guru; (2) Prithi Chand and Karmo were upset upon the birth of Guru Arjan's son Hargobind; (3) Prithi Chand's desire for Miharvan to succeed guruship was rekindled when Hargobind was struck with smallpox; (4) Prithi Chand made a couple of attempts to have Hargobind killed (by poison and by a cobra);

and (5) the Minas composed and distributed *kachi bani* as *gurbani* to Sikhs in Amritsar.⁵⁷ From the perspective of the Sikh Gurus, Prithi Chand was the founder of the 'Mina' group, whereas the followers of Prithi Chand referred to their tradition as *Miharvan sampraday*. The Mina sect was the only major sect established during the period of the Sikh Gurus;⁵⁸ however, there had also been other progeny of the previous Sikh Gurus who competed for the Guru-seat.

Any sectarian rivalry or emergence of a splinter group presents the risk of corrupting, diluting or influencing the Panth by: (1) establishing competing *deras* or settlements in various locations, (2) creating their own scriptures while using hymns of the Sikh Gurus and (3) creating *sakhis* that suggest a 'legitimate' connection with any of the Sikh Gurus.⁵⁹ Complaints against Guru Arjan were made to the Mughal authorities many times, and there are many references to the detractors (*nindaks*) in Guru Arjan's works.⁶⁰ Bhai Gurdas and Bhai Buddha made attempts to attenuate the tensions within the Panth, but to no avail.⁶¹ Prithi Chand's opposition thus made it necessary for Guru Arjan to hold his ground by protecting both his position as Guru of the Panth and his authority to appoint his successor. Notwithstanding this posture, there are also references that underscore how Guru Arjan still remained kind to Prithi Chand.⁶²

Guru Arjan's Panthic initiatives to help those in need, especially following the famine caused by drought (1595),⁶³ seemingly impressed Emperor Akbar.⁶⁴ Consistent with his own policy of religious pluralism and his own development of the syncretistic 'religion of God' (*Din-i-Ilahi*),⁶⁵ the emperor wanted to observe the Sikh Panth in person. Akbar and his entourage visited Goindval on 4 November 1598, during which they met Guru Arjan.⁶⁶ Several weeks later, Emperor Akbar reduced the province's land revenue tax.⁶⁷ Around this time, Guru Arjan also began to compile the sacred writings of the Sikh Gurus into a unified canon.

The *Adi Granth*

Along with asserting the correct line of Sikh Gurus (*gur-gaddi*) and increasing the number of holy places (*tirath*), Guru Arjan also created the *Adi Granth* – the initial version of the Sikh canon. The *Adi Granth* as the authoritative Sikh holy book was a critical Panthic development because it provided a standardized structure to Sikh doctrine.⁶⁸ Guru Arjan's motive for creating and installing the *Adi Granth* is often attributed to his desire to preserve the authenticity of the Gurus' words (*gurbani*) within the Sikh Panth. Since Prithi Chand of the

Mina sect had begun compiling an anthology of Sikh writings in which he was including his own works, Guru Arjan had to address the issue of the circulation of inauthentic texts (*kachi bani*).[69]

Indeed, Guru Arjan compiled an authentic canon of Sikh devotional compositions in order to safeguard the Panth. In fact, following Guru Arjan's martyrdom, Prithi Chand proclaimed himself as the sixth guru and then his son Miharvan proclaimed himself as the seventh guru on the ground that they were the 'real' Sikhs who had remained true to Guru Nanak's tradition, as against Guru Hargobind whom they critiqued as having joined in activities of the Mughal state, including warfare and hunting.[70] Regardless, the Sikh Panth's position has remained that the Mina sect goes against the teachings of the *Guru Granth Sahib* (the highest authority), as further discussed in 'Sectarian Narratives about the *Sukhmani*' below.

While internal factionalism has been regarded as a primary motive in compiling the *Adi Granth*, Emperor Akbar's visit to Goindval is described as the inspiration behind Guru Arjan doing so. Following Guru Arjan's meeting with Emperor Akbar and his entourage, the former is said to have begun compiling a text sealed with an authoritative status, as a 'holy' book for the Sikh Panth,[71] just as there existed the eternal or unauthored Vedas within the Hindu tradition and the *Pali Canon* in Theravada Buddhism.[72] Guru Arjan hired textual specialists and scribes to create a canon as a distinct alternative to the Vedas and the Qur'an.

When Guru Arjan succeeded to the Guru-seat in 1581, he is said to have received a large body of sacred hymns, including Guru Ram Das's works and the *Goindval Pothis* (collection of hymns Guru Amar Das had put together).[73] There is, besides, a narrative about Guru Arjan having to persuade his maternal uncle, Mohan, into giving him the hymns of the first three Gurus and having to send disciples around in search of any other copies that may have been made.[74] According to tradition, the *Goindval Pothis* passed through a single line of transmission from one Sikh Guru to the succeeding one and then incorporated into the *Adi Granth* by Guru Arjan. More recently, however, historians have underscored the complexity in the compilation of the *Adi Granth* since there are at least two extant *Goindval Pothis* (and, at least, two more that have not been located or were destroyed) and that Guru Arjan used other sources as well when compiling the *Adi Granth*.[75]

Guru Arjan compiled the *Adi Granth* based on several principles, which have been delineated from his editorial decisions: (1) doctrinal consistency, (2) the ideal of a balanced life, (3) a spirit of optimism, (4) the ideal of inclusiveness and (5) the concern for a distinct Sikh identity.[76] While the *Adi Granth* provides a cohesive collection of the Sikh Gurus' teachings, Guru Arjan also incorporated selected works of fifteen *bhagats* (like Kabir, Ravidas and Sheikh Farid) associated with the Hindu and Muslim traditions. Such incorporation was, however, not at the cost of any distinct Sikh beliefs. Rather, the works of the *bhagats* concur with the teachings of the Sikh Gurus. And, Guru Arjan's inclusion of the *bhagats* is consistent with Guru Nanak's principle of transcending the religious divide of Hindus and Muslims (as well as of caste divisions), all of which was permissible in the socio-political context of Emperor Akbar's policy of religious tolerance. By creating a canon, Guru Arjan established a standardized doctrine for the Sikh Panth.[77]

Sectarian narratives about the *Sukhmani*: 'Guru Arjan meets Sri Chand'

According to tradition, Guru Arjan composed the *Sukhmani* on the banks of Ramsar sarovar (Amritsar), where he found both shade and peace from the town developing around Harmandar Sahib.[78] Based on the fact that the composition is included in the *Adi Granth* and that it is a 'work of great maturity', McLeod claims that the *Sukhmani* was written just prior to 1604.[79] While the precise dates for the text are not known, it is generally accepted that the *Sukhmani* was composed around 1600, about the time that Guru Arjan was also compiling the *Adi Granth*, especially since the *Sukhmani* is included in an early draft of the scripture called the Guru Nanak Dev University Manuscript no. 1245 (1599 CE).[80] Significantly, the *Sukhmani* describes the illusions of the material world, which fit in with the historical context of (1) the sectarian competition, especially from Prithi Chand, then existing within the Sikh Panth and (2) the growing hostility from within the Mughal Empire towards the Sikh Panth, since an orthodox faction that opposed Mughal Emperor Akbar and his policies was now in ascendance.

Contemporary Sikh preachers speak of how Guru Nanak's elder son, Sri Chand, met Guru Arjan when he was writing the *Sukhmani*. After having written the sixteenth *astapadi*, Guru Arjan requested Sri Chand to participate in the composition of the *Sukhmani*. Sri Chand responded by giving Guru Arjan the introductory *salok* of the *Japji*: '*adi sachu jugadi sachu hai bhi sachu Nanak hosi bhi sachu*' (i.e. GGS, 1). This *salok* was thereupon inserted by Guru Arjan at the beginning of the seventeenth *astapadi* (i.e. GGS, 285).[81] While Bhai Santokh Singh's *Gur Pratap Suraj* (1843) makes no mention of Sri Chand meeting Guru Arjan (or of the former assisting the Guru in composing the *Sukhmani*), it does contain a narrative (*sri chand ji ne bheta mangee*) about Sri Chand sending his disciple Kamalia to collect a yearly stipend from Guru Arjan.[82]

It is interesting to note that Macauliffe, who relies heavily on the *Gur Pratap Suraj*, tends not to reiterate narratives that are seemingly controversial.[83] Significantly, while he also does not refer to the narrative about Sri Chand giving the modified *salok* of *Japji* to Guru Arjan, Macauliffe does briefly mention that Guru Arjan met and conversed with Sri Chand at Barath, when the former was travelling throughout the Punjab to propagate *Sikhi*, as well for himself to stay away from Prithi Chand.[84] The interaction between Guru Arjan and Sri Chand at Barath is further described in the *Sri Guru Tirath Sangreh* (1884), a Sikh pilgrimage manual composed by Pandit Tara Singh Narotam (1822–89), a Sikh-Sanskrit scholar of the Nirmala sect.[85] The manual explains:

> Barath village is located in district Gurdaspur. After Guru Arjan composed 16 *astapadis*, he went to Barath to see Sri Chand. Sri Chand listened to the 16 *astapadis* and said he should compose 8 more. Guru Arjan composed 8 more to make a total of 24 *astapadis*.[86]

Most significantly, Giani Gian Singh (1822–1921) – an associate of Pandit Tara Singh Narotam[87] – provides a detailed account of Guru Arjan's meeting with Sri Chand at Barath in the *Tawarikh Guru Khalsa* (1891):

> 1657 *sambat* [1600 CE]. Guru Arjan visited Sri Chand at Barath village. At that time, Guru Arjan had completed 16 *astapadis*. Sri Chand was delighted with the composition, and said 'there should be 8 more *astapadis*. A person needs 24,600 breaths per day. If a person recites 24 *astapadis*, each breath will be fruitful, and the angel of death will not harm.' Upon hearing these wise words, Guru Arjan requested Sri Chand to complete the composition. Sri Chand then provided the *salok*: *adi sachu jugadi sachu hai bhi sachu nanak hosi bhi sachu*. Sri Chand only provided this *salok* by Guru Nanak and stopped. Sri Chand altered the *salok*, changing the *bhī* to *bhi* to show that he was not equal to Guru Nanak. Then Guru Arjan completed the remaining 8 *astapadis* in Sri Chand's presence. Sri Chand was delighted and said, 'no one will speak ill of you. And your gurbani will multiply in respect day by day and will benefit humanity.' After hearing this, Guru Arjan returned to Amritsar.[88]

This particular narrative about Sri Chand helping Guru Arjan, when the latter was composing the *Sukhmani*, has to be understood in its historical and sectarian context (see Table 2.1): While the narrative is written through a Nirmala lens, its content is also highly problematic since it is inconsistent with, and contradictory to, the *Guru Granth Sahib* (the highest authority) and also to the Bhai Gurdas's

Table 2.1 Earlier sources on Guru Arjan's meetings with Sri Chand: From mid-1800s to early 1900s

Citations	Narrative	Location of meeting	Sri Chand gives advice	Guru Arjan asks for assistance	Guru Arjan receives assistance
Bhai Gurdas (1551–1636), *Varan* 26.33	Describes Sri Chand, one of the Guru's progeny, as having displayed ego.	Not applicable	No	No	No
Bhai Santokh Singh, *Gur Pratap Suraj* (1849) *raas* 4.28	Sri Chand sends his disciple to collect his annual stipend from Guru Arjan.	Amritsar	No	No	No
Pandit Tara Singh Narotam, *Sri Guru Tirath Sangreh* (1884), 50, 209.	Guru Arjan goes to visit Sri Chand (1602–03); Guru Arjan recites 16 *astapadis*.	Barath	To write *astapadis* 17 to 24	No	No
Giani Gian Singh, *Tawarikh Guru Khalsa* (1891), 42.	In 1600, Guru Arjan requests Sri Chand for assistance.	Barath	To write *astapadis* 17 to 24	To help complete the *Sukhmani*	To use the modified *Japji salok* **MOTIF**: 24 *astapadis* & 24,600 breaths
M.A. Macauliffe, *The Sikh Religion*, vol. 3 (1909), 27–8.	Guru Arjan travels to preach *Sikhi* & consults the wishes of Sikhs in the Punjab.	Barath	No	No	No

Varan (a secondary text in the Sikh canon, discussed further in Chapter 3). First and foremost, one specific hymn in the *Guru Granth Sahib* contradicts the legitimacy of Sri Chand as a possible contributor to the *Sukhmani*. In lyrical verse (*var*), Rai Balwand and Satta significantly and explicitly describe the sons of Guru Nanak (Sri Chand and Lakhmi Das) as having been defiant and having turned their backs on Guru Nanak on account of his appointing Lehna as his successor (Guru Angad):

> Lehna's succession was earned,
>   thus proclaimed Nanak.
> United by the same Light,
>   only the body had changed.
> With a spotless umbrella swaying above,
>   seated on a throne, he attended to the Guru's shop with care.
> He followed the Guru's command,
>   and tasted the tasteless yoga stone.
> The *langar* of *shabad-Guru*
>   is never at a loss.
> He spent whatever the Beloved gave,
>   distributed to and consumed by all.
> The Beloved was praised,
>   the light descended from the celestial realms.
> A vision of the True King cuts away
>   the filth of countless past lives.
> The True Guru gave the True command,
>   why hesitate to proclaim this?
> The sons did not accept his words,
>   and turned their backs on the Guru.
> These impure hearts wandered in defiance,
>   carrying a heavy load on their backs.
> Whatever the Guru said, it was done,
>   thus Lehna came to be.
> Who lost, who won? (2)[89]

Balwand and Satta explicitly discredited Sri Chand, who had not only objected to Guru Nanak's appointment of Guru Angad as successor, but had also founded the Udasi sect that preached world renunciation and celibacy,[90] which are in direct contradiction of Guru Nanak's teachings about social involvement. While this hymn describes the situation that followed Guru Angad's succession, it reflects the tension that had existed between the Sikh Panth and Sri Chand, even though there was a change in perceptions after Guru Ram Das's meeting with Sri Chand and some reconciliation by the time of Guru Arjan. It is critical to underscore here that Guru Arjan incorporated the Ramkali *var* composed by Balwand and Satta in the middle section of the *Adi Granth*. Not only did Guru Arjan include the hymn against Sri Chand late in his life, since the *Adi Granth* was installed in 1604, but he simultaneously also included the *Sukhmani* in the same canon, which explicitly denounces those who malign or have disdain for the *sants*.[91]

A second critical source that also contradicts the narrative about Sri Chand helping Guru Arjan, when the latter was composing the *Sukhmani*, is found in Bhai Gurdas's *Varan*. As aforementioned, Bhai Gurdas (1551–1636) was both a scribe for the *Adi Granth* and the author of the *Varan*. While Bhai Gurdas's *Varan* does not have the status of being of the highest authority, Guru Arjan designated it as being the key to the *Guru Granth Sahib*. Significantly, in the *Varan*, Bhai Gurdas describes Sri Chand as one of the Gurus' progeny who displayed ego:

> Sri Chand, a celibate since childhood, made a centre [attributed to] Baba Nanak.
> Dharam Chand, son of Lakhmi Das, made a show of himself.
> Dasu installed [himself] on the seat of authority and Datu learned to sit in the *siddh* posture.
> Mohan went mad, and Mohari was celebrated.
> Prithi Chand, the rascal, with his hidden agenda, spread madness.
> Mahadev was egotistical and was led astray.
> Living amid the sandalwood, yet without its fragrance.[92]

Sri Chand is included among the other Sikh Gurus' progeny who, while 'living amid the sandalwood' (i.e. Guru), are 'without its fragrance' (i.e. eternal light of *shabad-Guru*). The preceding verse of Bhai Gurdas describes how such progeny, who did not possess or attain the spiritual stature of Guru, attempted to be elevated and revered as leaders. While Sri Chand is grouped with Prithi Chand in this verse, it is important to emphasize that their relationship with the Sikh Gurus was treated differently. That is, the Sikh Panth never expelled Sri Chand or the Udasis, as it did in the case of the Minas.[93]

Despite the ambiguous relations that Sri Chand had with the Panth, the above-mentioned scriptural references from the *Guru Granth Sahib* and Bhai Gurdas's *Varan* undermine the validity of the narratives about the *Sukhmani* that are contained in Nirmala texts like the *Tawarikh Guru Khalsa*. On the other hand, notwithstanding the canonical references against Sri Chand, Guru Arjan is also said to have added, according to Pashaura Singh, the introductory verse to Guru Nanak's *Japji*, which he then repeated in the *Sukhmani*.[94] The editorial addition of the *salok* to the *Japji* further strengthens the case that the Sikh textual tradition as established by Guru Arjan does not concur with the Nirmala narrative about the *Sukhmani*. Moreover, the notion that Sri Chand advised Guru Arjan to write eight more *astapadis* when the latter was composing the *Sukhmani* is not convincing, given the spiritual significance of the text's entire structure (see Chapter 4).

There are also later renditions of the *Tawarikh Guru Khalsa* narrative that differ on Sri Chand's contribution (see Table 2.2). For example, Gurbachan Singh Bhindranwale (1902–69), the twelfth leader of the Damdami Taksal, discusses the narrative.[95] According to him, Guru Arjan went to Barath, where he asked Sri Chand to contribute to the composition of the *Sukhmani*. Sri Chand replied, 'You have the Guru-seat, not me.' Guru Arjan then insisted that Sri Chand contribute. Out of respect for the *gur-gaddi*, Sri Chand gave him the modified *salok* of Guru Nanak.

Gurbachan Singh then discusses how there is a *sampraday* (sect) that has its own version of the story: When Sri Chand visited Guru Arjan at Ramsar, the latter had a 'mental block' while writing the *Sukhmani*, and subsequently asked Sri Chand if he would contribute to the composition. Sri Chand then gave him the modified *salok*. While acknowledging the two different versions (about whether the meeting occurred in Ramsar or Barath), Gurbachan Singh emphasizes how the core of the story demonstrates Guru Arjan's humility and display of respect for Sri Chand.[96] Significantly, Gurbachan Singh was the last Taksali leader to have received his initial education from Nirmala Sikhs, thus reflecting an ideological shift towards Sikh orthodoxy within the Damdami Taksal.[97]

Such explanations about Guru Arjan's meeting with Sri Chand reflect the Nirmala sectarian perspective on the reconciliation that may have occurred between the Sikh Panth and the Udasis. That is, with the passage of time, Sri Chand accepted the Sikh Panth's line of successors even as Guru Arjan showed respect for Sri Chand, since the latter was both an elder and the son of Guru Nanak. Despite the apparent reconciliation, however, composing *gurbani* is not a mere intellectual undertaking. Rather, it is a process wherein the human Guru is the medium through which *shabad* is revealed. As stated by Guru Arjan himself: 'Bani originated from the Primordial One (*dhurki bani*), and removes all anxiety.'[98] Consequently, the narrative about how Guru Arjan requested Sri Chand to participate in the composition of the *Sukhmani* contradicts the *shabad-Guru* perspective on *gurbani*.

Moreover, these alternative renditions about the *Sukhmani* suggest that Guru Arjan is subordinate to Sri Chand. Following one of the main functions of *sakhis* (which is to illustrate the spiritual stature of a religious figure), other

Table 2.2 Later sources on Guru Arjan's meetings with Sri Chand: From mid-1900s to the present

Citations	Narrative	Location of meeting	Sri Chand gives advice	Guru Arjan asks for assistance	Guru Arjan receives assistance
Giani Ishar Singh Nara, *Itihas Baba Sri Chand Ji Sahib Ate Udasin Sampradaie* (1959), 384–386.	Guru Arjan visits Sri Chand, who blesses Guru for taking care of the *dharam*; Guru Arjan then recites sixteen *astapadis* of the *Sukhmani*.	Barath	To write *astapadis* 17 to 24	To help complete the *Sukhmani*	To use the modified *Japji salok* **MOTIF**: 24 *astapadis* & 24,600 breaths
Gurbachan Singh Bhindranwale (1902–69), leader of Damdami Taksal, *katha*	Reiterates the narrative in the *Tawarikh Guru Khalsa*; explains why Guru Arjan gave respect to Sri Chand.	Barath	No	To help complete the *Sukhmani*	To use the modified *Japji salok*
Gurdwara Barath Sahib local story (n.d.)	For six months, Guru Arjan daily waits for Sri Chand to discourse with him.	Barath	To write *astapadis* 17 to 24	To help complete the *Sukhmani*	To use the modified *Japji salok*
Gobind Sadan Society, established in 1967 by Virsa Singh	In 1655 [1598 CE] Guru Arjan daily waits for Sri Chand to come out of meditation to discourse with him.	Barath (mentions that they also met at Ramsar)	To write *astapadis* 17 to 24	To help complete the *Sukhmani*	To use the modified *Japji salok*
Gurbachan Singh Talib (1911–86) in *Encyclopaedia of Sikhism* vol. 4 (1998), 263.	After composing the sixteenth *astapadi*, Guru Arjan requests Sri Chand to engage in its composition.	Ramsar	No	To help complete the *Sukhmani*	To use the modified *Japji salok*

renditions of the narrative further assert the superior status of Sri Chand, just as there are stories that establish the superiority of Guru Arjan. The narrative of Guru Arjan receiving Sri Chand's recommendations both to add the modified *salok* and to write eight more *astapadis*, when the former was composing the *Sukhmani*, has to be understood in its historical and sectarian context. That is, the narrative is sectarian in nature, with the aim to elevate the spiritual stature of Sri Chand and his Udasi sect (i.e. groups or factions other than the orthodox line of Sikh Gurus).[99] It is noteworthy that a more recent publication titled *The Miraculous Life of Baba Sri Chand Ji* reiterates the narrative about the *Sukhmani*:

> Guru Arjan Devji visited Babaji at Barath in 1655 [1598 CE]. Two sites still commemorate their meeting. Where the Gurdwara stands today, Guru ji used to wait each day for Babaji to come out of meditation. A second site, a mile away in what was then a jungle, marked the place of compiling *Guru Granth Sahibji*, Babaji gave whatever handwritten *bani* he still had, and suggested that Guruji obtain the other portions from Baba Mohanji. Guruji recited 16 *astapadis* of the *Sukhmani Sahib*. Babaji suggested that he increase the bani to 24 verses. On Guruji's request, Babaji provided the line to resume the 17th *astapadi*. He respectfully chose Guru Nanak Devji's verse: 'aad sach, jugaad sach, hoebi sach, nanak hosebi sach'.[100]

It is evident that *The Miraculous Life of Baba Siri Chand Ji*, published on behalf of the Gobind Sadan Society for Interfaith Understanding,[101] has been written from the perspective of the assumed superior spiritual stature of Sri Chand and his influence on the Sikh Gurus and their Panthic activities. The extract quoted above also describes Guru Arjan as waiting daily for Sri Chand to come out of his meditation, as if the former is the latter's disciple, thus emphasizing the spiritual superiority of Sri Chand. Besides, the drawings contained in the book complement the *sakhi* with its depictions of Sri Chand as leader and teacher in relation to the first five Sikh Gurus as if they were his disciples.

Similarly, the website for Gurdwara Barath Sahib (also known as Gurdwara Tap Asthan Baba Sri Chand Ji) at Barath[102] reiterates the Sri Chand sectarian perspective:

> After sometime Baba Shri Chand Ji sent Bhai Kamalya Ji to Amritsar to invite Fifth Sikh Guru, Shri Guru Arjun Dev Ji to Barath Sahib.[103] When Guru Arjun Dev Ji reached Barath Sahib, Baba Ji was meditating. Everyday Guru Ji used to come to this place, where Baba Ji was meditating and kept waiting for Baba Ji to complete his meditation. This continued for 6 Months. The place

where Guru Ji kept standing every day [is where the] Pillar known as Thamm Sahib is constructed. When Baba Ji opened his eyes, he received Guru Ji with respect. Guru Ji had discussions with Baba Ji. Guru Ji recited his 16 Ashtpadis. Baba Ji asked Guru Ji to utter 24 Ashtpadis. Guru Ji asked Baba Ji to add to 'Sukhmani Sahib' Prayer. Baba Ji uttered this Shalok: '*Aaad Sach Jugad Such Hai Bhi Such Nanak Hosi Bhi Such*'. Guru Ji collected some Pothies (Holy books) from Baba Ji for compilation of '*Sri Adi Granth*'. Guru Arjun Dev Ji stayed for some time.[104]

Continuous with the Hindu literary genre of local temple stories, this narrative establishes the spiritual stature of a religious figure (i.e. Sri Chand) even as it authenticates the link that the religious figure had with the place of worship or local area (i.e. Barath).[105] While this rendition makes reference to how Sri Chand told Guru Arjan to place Guru Nanak's *salok* in the 17th *astapadi*, it also refers to Guru Arjan as having gone on a regular basis to Sri Chand for guidance, thus reinforcing the spiritual superiority of Sri Chand.

Overall, these renditions of the narrative about the *Sukhmani* not only contradict the words (*gurbani*) that have been included in the *Guru Granth Sahib* or Bhai Gurdas's *Varan*, but they have also been written and retold through an Udasi lens. Indeed, these narratives were made popular by the Udasis for sectarian ends. Some Sikh scholars or preachers may assert that, even though there had been tension between the early Sikh Gurus and the Udasi sect (e.g. Guru Amar Das kept the Udasis away from the Panth), by the time of Guru Hargobind some reconciliation seems to have occurred between the Udasis and the Sikh Panth.[106] For instance, Guru Hargobind sent his eldest son Gurditta (1613–38) – as a married man with two sons – to spend time with Sri Chand at Barath.[107] Interestingly, Giani Ishar Singh Nara (1898–1995), a traditional Sikh scholar, demonstrates the reconciliation between Sri Chand and Guru Arjan by interweaving both the *shabad-Guru* and Nirmala/Udasi sectarian perspectives on the narrative about Sri Chand assisting Guru Arjan in composing the *Sukhmani*:

Following the recitation of his *bani*, Sri Chand asked Guru Arjan to recite his own *bani*. Guru Arjan recited 16 *astapadis* and then concluded the service. Sri Chand studied the Vedas and Shastras. But, after hearing the *Sukhmani*, he said the composition is a straightforward way to liberate one from *sansar* in the Kali age. Sri Chand praised the *Sukhmani* as priceless, but then also advised Guru Arjan to complete it with more detail…. After listening to the 16 *astapadis*, he told Guru Arjan that there are 24,600 breaths in the eight watches. Sri Chand then said that he should have 24 *astapadis* and complete it with 24,000 letters. Thus, those who read the *Sukhmani* with love will have fruitful breaths day and night. Guru Arjan then requested Sri Chand to complete the *Sukhmani*. Sri Chand said Guru Arjan had the responsibility to spread Guru Nanak's *bani*. The *gurbani* recited from *gur-gaddi* is the authentic *bani*. Guru Arjan insisted. Sri Chand then contributed the modified *salok* from *Japji*. Sri Chand's power and esteem was infused in the *Sukhmani*. Sri Chand did not offer his own compositions because the *bani* must come from the *gur-gaddi*. Sri Chand told Guru Arjan to complete 8 more *astapadis*, thus totaling 24.[108]

Although somewhat contradictory, this rendition continues to bolster the spiritual stature of Sri Chand,[109] especially by highlighting how his mystical power infuses the *Sukhmani*, even as it emphasizes the importance of preserving the authentic *bani* that comes from the Guru-seat (*gur-gaddi*). Whether or not some reconciliation transpired between the Sikh Panth and the Udasis, the former never expelled the latter. While Sri Chand initially claimed guruship and began an ascetic order, he never aggressively opposed the Sikh Gurus, or attempted to influence the direction of the Panth, or tampered with the scripture in the manner that Prithi Chand and the Minas did.[110]

Another sectarian literary work worthy of mention here is titled the *Sukhmani Sahasranam* (The Thousand Names of *Sukhmani*) of the Mina sect.[111] Miharvan, Prithi Chand's son and successor in 1618, is the attributed author of the *Sukhmani Sahasranam*.[112] The *Sukhmani Sahasranam* is a devotional poem that is undeniably modelled after Guru Arjan's *Sukhmani*. Besides the use of the word *sukhmani* in the title, both texts (1) are structured in the form of *astapadis* (each *astapadi* comprising eight verses), (2) have each *astapadi* begin with a *salok* (couplet) and (3) are composed in the Gauri *rag*.[113]

Despite these similarities, however, there are significant differences between the two compositions: First, Guru Arjan's *Sukhmani* has twenty-four *astapadis*, while Miharvan's *Sukhmani Sahasranam* contains thirty *astapadis*. Given the fact that twenty-four *astapadis* correspond to the eight watches of the day – night cycle, Miharvan fails to capture the spiritual and poetic significance of the structure of Guru Arjan's *Sukhmani*.[114] Second, unlike Guru Arjan's *Sukhmani*, the *Sukhmani Sahasranam* follows the pan-Indian literary genre of the 'The Thousand Names of God', a popular genre praising the various epithets of a Hindu god like Vishnu.[115] Third, the *Sukhmani Sahasranam* begins with an invocation to Lord Krishna and praises Vishnu's *avataras*, which goes against the *Sikhi* doctrine of *Ek Oankar*. Based on both the similarities and differences, it can be concluded that the *Sukhmani Sahasranam* – while inspired by Guru Arjan's

Sukhmani – was composed from Miharvan's perspective on 'Sikh Bhakti'[116] (i.e. Guru Nanak's teachings fused with Vaishanav Bhakti) and as a means to legitimize the Mina tradition, in the same way Hindu literary genres (such as the Upanishad, Purana and Sahasranama) are used as a means to legitimize more local and sectarian developments within orthodox Brahmin circles.[117]

While Prithi Chand objected to the succession of Guru Arjan and considered himself and his son Miharvan as the sixth and seventh gurus, respectively, it was Harji (Miharvan's son and successor) who expanded the Miharvan literature.[118] In 1635, when Harji took ownership of the Harmandar Sahib after Guru Hargobind left Amritsar to relocate at Kiratpur in the Shivalik Hills, he was able to afford the development of literature to both undermine the Sikh Panth and establish the authority of the Mina sect. Harji accomplished this by demonstrating that (1) Miharvan's birth was similar to Guru Nanak's birth, (2) both Prithi Chand and Miharvan had the spiritual stature akin to Guru Arjan and (3) Miharvan had the ability to explain *gurbani*.[119] Significantly, Harji composed commentaries on Miharvan's *Sukhmani Sahasranam* under the symbol of *mahala* 8, signifying his status as the eighth guru.[120] Harji wrote the Vaishnav Puranic myth-based commentaries during the time when the Banno Bir (a later unauthorized version of the *Adi Granth*) was also being initially copied from the Kartarpur Bir (the original *Adi Granth*), prior to the inclusion of the additional works of the Mina sect.[121] In sum, the *Sukhmani Sahasranam* reflects both sectarian competition, and Miharvan's and Harji's use of literary means to legitimize the Mina sect.

The sectarian context of the narratives about the *Sukhmani* and the *Sukhmani Sahasranam* reinforces the need and importance of Guru Arjan in establishing the doctrinal aspect of the Sikh Panth. As the authoritative text of the Sikh Panth, the *Adi Granth* serves as the governing doctrinal standard to overcome contradictions and inconsistencies. From the perspective of *Sikhi*, when a *sakhi* or religious text contradicts the *Adi Granth*, the latter takes precedence. Indeed, the *Adi Granth* emerged as critical for the very survival of the Panth, especially following Guru Arjan's execution.

Guru Arjan's martyrdom

Guru Arjan was born and, for the most part, lived under the Mughal rule of Emperor Akbar, during which there was relative peace, religious tolerance and prosperity in the region.[122] While Guru Arjan had cordial relations with Akbar, there were nonetheless revivalists among the Islamic theologians of the time who opposed Akbar's worldview and policies.¹²³ Moreover, given the intolerant religious posture of Akbar's successor, Emperor Jahangir, it was inevitable that he would view Sikhs as infidels (*kafirs*) and would dislike Muslims converting to the Sikh Panth, as he expressed it:

> In Gobindwal, which is on the river Beas, a Hindu named Arjan used to live in the garb of a spiritual master and mystic guide, under the influence of which he had induced a large number of simple-minded Hindus and some ignorant and silly Muslims, to become attached to his ways and customs.... For three or four generations they (he and his precursors) had kept his business brisk. For a long time the thought kept coming to me of either putting an end to that shop of falsehood or to bring him into the fold of Islam.¹²⁴

Hence, following Emperor Akbar's death (October 1605), the Sikh Panth became vulnerable to Mughal hostility, especially given Jahangir's religious intolerance. As quoted above, Jahangir had two options: (1) to crush the Sikh Panth or (2) to convert Guru Arjan to Islam. And, within a year of Akbar's death, Guru Arjan was executed.

There are no Sikh scriptural sources explaining the reason for Guru Arjan's execution or the precise cause of his death (i.e. tortured, burnt on a hot plate or drowned in the Ravi River). Based on the limited, fragmented and contradictory sources from that period, there are various theories surrounding the reason for his execution. The basic claim about Guru Arjan's execution is that the reason for it was political: Guru Arjan was punished for having supported Prince Khusrau (1587–1622), just prior to his failed rebellion against his father Emperor Jahangir (i.e. treason).¹²⁵ One non-partisan source that documents Guru Arjan's execution comprises a letter written by Father Jerome Xavier to the Provincial – leading father of the Jesuit Order – in Goa (Lahore, 25 September 1606).¹²⁶ It states that Guru Arjan was imprisoned and fined for having blessed Prince Khusrau by placing a 'tiara' on his forehead. Since he was unable to pay the large fine of around 2 lakh rupees, Guru Arjan was tortured to death in prison.

A second source on Guru's death is the discussion in Jahangir's memoirs called *Jahangirnama* (*Tuzuk-i-Jahangiri*). It mentions how Emperor Jahangir accused Guru Arjan for having 'supported' his rebel son Prince Khusrau by 'placing a saffron mark on his forehead'.¹²⁷ Subsequently, he ordered for Guru Arjan to be put to death and for his property to be confiscated.¹²⁸

A third source, albeit written forty years after Guru Arjan's execution, is from Mohsin Fani's Persian work titled *Dabistan-i-Mazahab* (Study on

Religions, 1645–6). It states that Guru Arjan was tortured (and died) for not having paid a fine imposed by Jahangir:

> When after the capture of [Prince] Khusrau, His Majesty king Jannat Makani Nuruddin Muhammad Jahangir punished and mulcted [Guru] Arjan Mal, on account of his having prayed for the welfare of Prince Khusrau, the son of His Majesty king Jannat Makani, who had rebelled against his father, and a large amount was demanded from him [Guru Arjan], he found himself powerless to pay it. He was tied up and kept [in the open] in the desert around Lahore. He gave up his life there owing to the strong sun, summer heat and the injuries inflicted by the collectors. This happened in [A.H.] 1015 [AD 1606–07]. Similarly, His Majesty exiled Shaikh Nizam Thanesari from India for his joining, and uttering a prayer for the welfare of Khusrau.[129]

Although this was written forty years after Guru Arjan's execution, it sheds light on the Mughal Empire's memory of Guru Arjan's execution following his blessing of Prince Khusrau, especially since some of the subjects were sympathetic towards Khusrau, a prince said to be like Akbar. While Guru Arjan's execution is fundamentally explained on political grounds in this claim, the extent to which he had actually backed Khusrau's rebellion is debatable.[130]

As aforementioned, Sikh scriptural texts do not refer to Guru Arjan's execution. In fact, the earliest Sikh reference to Guru Arjan's execution is found in *Mahima Prakash Vartak* (1741 CE).[131] The eighteenth- and nineteenth-century narratives explain how Guru Arjan was arrested and fined for having welcomed rebel Prince Khusrau for a night's stay. They further describe Chandu Shah, a Hindu banker and revenue official (*diwan*) in Lahore for the Mughal Empire, as having claimed that Guru Arjan gave money to Prince Khusrau. More significantly, a story describes how Guru Arjan was unable to pay the fine and was subsequently tortured for many days under the supervision of Chandu;[132] another narrative also states that Chandu paid the fine in return for Guru Arjan's body.[133]

According to this later rendition, Chandu was vengeful towards Guru Arjan for having declined the marriage proposal for his daughter to wed Hargobind.[134] While this particular narrative emphasizes Chandu as the one who tortured Guru Arjan, it is unclear as to whether or not Chandu was simply working on the orders of Emperor Jahangir or actually playing a decision-making role in his execution. Regardless of these interpretations about Chandu's role in Guru Arjan's execution, Emperor Jahangir would have been uncompromising towards Guru Arjan and his activities, especially since Jahangir – as he stated in his memoirs – wanted to either close Guru Arjan's 'shop' or convert him to Islam. Surely, this was in part a reaction to the thriving Sikh Panth under Guru Arjan, the Guru or 'true king' (*saccha padshah*) who had received Muslim converts and had compiled the *Adi Granth*, a canon which critiqued the hypocrisy and institutional form of religions, including Islam.[135]

The ambiguity surrounding Guru Arjan's death is understandable given the fact that it was a concealed execution. While there are no Sikh scriptural sources about Guru Arjan's execution, some scholars hold that Bhai Gurdas described Guru Arjan's condition after having been tortured:[136]

> The Guru cannot live without the eternal river, like a fish cannot live without water.
> The light merges with the eternal light, like the moth is drawn to the flame.
> The Guru remains attuned to the *shabad*, like the deer is mindful of the danger.
> The Guru remains balanced amid pleasure and pain of the night,
>   like the bee savours the lotus nectar.
> The Guru's teaching is not to be forgotten, like a rainbird yearns for a droplet.
> The *gurmukh* attains the supreme fruit of happiness absorbed in the *sadh sang*.
> I am a sacrifice to Guru Arjan.[137]

Bhai Gurdas describes Guru Arjan's strength and composure of joyful acceptance as the result of his connection with *Nam*. Moreover, according to tradition, Guru Arjan – while undergoing torture – recited words close to *Asa* 93: 'Your doing is sweet to me.'[138] Similarly, there are a couple of lines from the *Sukhmani* that echo this theme:

> The devotee's nature is to accept what happens,
>   recognizing the Creator in everything.
> Whatever *Prabh* does is sweet to the devotee;
> Whatever is understood, that is then shown [by You]. (*Sukhmani* 14.8)

Bhai Gurdas's verse about Guru Arjan's composure and the story about Guru Arjan reciting *Asa* 93 underscore the belief that all must accept *Guru's* will with an attitude of joyful acceptance, a very important theme contained in the *Sukhmani* (see Chapter 4). The motif of joyful acceptance, especially at the time of persecution, bolsters Guru Arjan's spiritual stature in the Sikh Panth.

Guru Arjan's martyrdom is commemorated as an incredible sacrifice that he made for the Panth. Curiously, however, Guru Arjan is not referred to as a martyr (*shaheed*) in early Sikh literature, such as the *Dasam Granth* (early 1700s) or *Gurbilas* (*c.* 1751).[139] Perhaps, as suggested by Fenech, it was more important for the Panth – under the new harsh realities – to be oriented towards its survival.[140] Besides the fact that Guru Arjan's execution was not a public event, as Pashaura Singh has argued, the meta-narrative about Chandu's role in Guru Arjan's execution was the empire's strategic ploy to 'shift the blame' on to the Guru's enemy.[141] While the Sikh literature of the eighteenth and nineteenth centuries widely accepted the claim about Chandu's decisive role in Guru Arjan's execution,[142] by the early twentieth century, Sikh scholars – after becoming aware of Emperor Jahangir's hostile statements against Guru Arjan in the *Jahangirnama* – honed their own interpretation on Jahangir's actual role.[143] Despite the Mughal strategy to shift the blame, Guru Arjan's martyrdom emerged as a major rallying point for the Panth even as it represents a defining event in Sikh history.

Summary

Guru Arjan's *Sukhmani* needs to be read with an understanding of his life, work and martyrdom, all of which contributed to the consolidation of the Sikh Panth. Having established *gurdwaras* and the *masand* network, Guru Arjan successfully organized the community throughout the Punjab. At the same time, the events during Guru Arjan's life shed light on the historical reality of sectarian competition over succession to the Guru-seat (*gur-gaddi*) and on the rise in Mughal hostility towards the flourishing Sikh community, most profoundly expressed in the events leading up to the Guru's execution. Significantly, in line with his own existential situation, Guru Arjan's *Sukhmani* profoundly addresses various groups of society, including kings and religious figures, in order to expose apparent falsehood.

Besides his organizational initiatives, Guru Arjan strengthened the Panth by compiling the *Adi Granth*. This accomplishment not only established Sikh doctrine (which further consolidated the tradition), but it also served as a safeguard for the Panth, especially in the context of his martyrdom. It served as a safeguard for the Panth in the sense that the *Adi Granth* – as the eternal *Guru* – emerged as the governing doctrinal standard that could protect the Sikh Panth from potential disarray. The prospect of the threat of potential disarray lay internally in the experience of factionalism over succession to the Guru-seat (*gur-gaddi*) and externally in the manifest of socio-political hostility from the governing empire that had a dislike for religious pluralism.

The internal and external forces arrayed against Guru Arjan certainly reveal the enormously challenging religious, social and political circumstances in which he composed the *Sukhmani*. Before proceeding to an in-depth analysis of the *Sukhmani*, including its outlook on the world, it is necessary to first examine the literary context and ritual function of this devotional composition, both of which form the subject of the next chapter.

3

The ritual function of the *Sukhmani*

The *Sukhmani* is one of many devotional texts contained in the *Guru Granth Sahib*, the most revered scripture of the Sikh canon. As discussed in the previous chapter, Guru Arjan compiled the first edition of the scripture titled the *Adi Granth*, which was then installed in the Harmandar Sahib (the Golden Temple) in 1604. In doing so, Guru Arjan established a standardized and authentic scripture for the Sikh Panth. Later, after having included the hymns of Guru Tegh Bahadur (1622–75), the tenth and last human Guru of the Sikh lineage – Guru Gobind Singh (1666–1708) – brought the scripture to a close in 1706.[1] While it has been traditionally held that Guru Gobind Singh bestowed the status of *Guru* on the *Adi Granth* before his death in 1708,[2] critical historians maintain that this status was in fact subsequently decided by the Sikh Panth only after his passing.[3] Despite these two differing perspectives, the Sikh Panth accepted the scriptural authority of the *Guru Granth Sahib* when there was no longer a human Guru.[4]

Accorded the status of the living *Guru* in *Sikhi*, the *Guru Granth Sahib* is also regarded and revered as the source of spiritual inspiration. In fact, many Sikhs 'confide' in the scripture for guidance by saying a prayer (*Ardas*) in front of the *Guru Granth Sahib* and then randomly opening it to read a sacred passage (*vak*).[5] The scripture not only forms the basis for insight into cosmology and the human condition, but it also plays a central role in Sikh worship. In contrast to the *garbha-griha* (home of the womb, inner sanctum) where the presiding deity or icon (*murat*; Skt. *murti*) is located in a Hindu temple, Guru Arjan installed the *Adi Granth* as the focal point in the Harmandar Sahib. As explained by Bhai Gurdas, 'The image (*murat*) of *Guru* is the *Guru's shabad*, experienced within the *sadh sangat* at daybreak (*amrit vela*).'[6] With its status as the eternal and living *Guru*, the scripture is the focal point in every Sikh place of worship (*gurdwara* or *Guru's* door), where it is covered in a colourful cloth, placed on a raised platform and presides under a regal canopy. Indeed, the *gurdwara* is where a devotee meets with the True *Guru* (*Satgur*).

The compositions contained in the *Guru Granth Sahib* provide both the Sikh Gurus' teachings (*updes*) and the sacred sound (*nad*) to experience *Nam* – the word for the inner Essence of all existence. In the *Guru's* presence, Sikhs recite the scripture (*path*), listen to sermons (*katha*), sing devotional hymns accompanied by musical instruments (*kirtan*) and chant (*jap*) the various names of *Ek Oankar*. In contemporary times, a central part of Sikh practice has been to congregate and collectively sing. Like the *Guru Granth Sahib*, of which it is a part, the purpose of the *Sukhmani* is threefold: (1) to guide the seeker in experiencing *Nam* in all aspects of life; (2) to recite the text, with single-minded attention; and (3) to sing its hymns in the *sadh sangat* for spiritual upliftment.[7]

This chapter explores the religious place of Guru Arjan's *Sukhmani* in order to shed light on the location, purpose and ritual function of the text. First, the chapter provides background material on the *Sukhmani*'s place in the Sikh textual tradition and, more specifically, on the structure of the composition, continuities it shares with previous Sikh texts, and the intended audience of the text. Second, the chapter analyses the purpose and role of the *Sukhmani*, both as a sacred text meant to inculcate the Sikh worldview and as a devotional poem intended to be recited and sung to create a spiritual connection with *Nam*. In doing so, the chapter sheds light on the location of the *Sukhmani* in Sikh scripture and practice, as well as on the various material and spiritual benefits believed to come with its recitation.

Sikh canon and the *Sukhmani*

The entire Sikh canon consists of the *Guru Granth Sahib*, *Dasam Granth*,[8] Bhai Gurdas's *Varan*[9] and Bhai Nand Lal's *Diwan*.[10] Notwithstanding this larger Sikh canon, the *Guru Granth Sahib* is the only scriptural text that has the status of the eternal *Guru* and is, therefore, regarded as the highest authority. According to Sikh tradition, there are two versions of this scripture: first, the initial canonical form of the *Adi Granth* compiled by Guru Arjan and installed in the Harmandar Sahib at Amritsar in 1604; and second, the *Guru Granth Sahib*, which Guru Gobind Singh – after making some editorial additions – closed as the final text in 1706.

While the Sikh tradition recognizes the two aforementioned versions, modern scholarship has established that there are, in fact, three main recensions of the *Adi Granth*: First, the Kartarpur Bir is the authoritative text compiled by Guru Arjan, which is extant at Kartarpur in Jalandhar District of the Punjab.

Second, the Lahori Bir, compiled in c. 1610, was found at a shrine in Lahore, thus the name. While the Lahori Bir is quite similar to the earlier Kartarpur Bir, differences nonetheless exist in the order of the verses of the *bhagats* (devotional poets) and *bhatts* (Sikh bards) in the concluding section. Third, Banno Bir was prepared by Banno of Khara Mangat of district Gujrat in Pakistan in c. 1642. While the Banno Bir includes the contents of the Kartarpur Bir, it also significantly contains some unauthorized additions associated with the Mina sect (founded by Prithi Chand, Guru Arjan's eldest brother), which took control of Harmandar Sahib when Guru Hargobind shifted his headquarters to Kiratpur.[11]

In part to prevent the circulation of the three different versions (especially the Banno Bir, as it contains unauthorized compositions), Guru Gobind Singh – after adding the compositions of Guru Tegh Bahadur to the Kartarpur Bir at Damdama Sahib – closed the *Adi Granth* referred to as the Damdama Bir. The closing of the Damdama Bir established the text not only as authoritative, but also as 'unchangeable'.[12] Despite Guru Gobind Singh's action, the Banno Bir continued to be circulated by sectarian rivals in Punjab. The Damdama Bir was, however, revived during the rule of Maharaja Ranjit Singh, who was in the position to support the Sikh Panth.[13] There were two original copies of the Damdama Bir, dated 1682 (1739 *sambat*) and 1691 (1749 *sambat*), which were unfortunately destroyed on 7 June 1984,[14] when the Sikh Reference Library was burned down in the Golden Temple complex during Operation Bluestar.[15]

The Damdama Bir, the standard version of the *Guru Granth Sahib*, contains verses composed by six of the ten Sikh Gurus (Guru Nanak, Guru Angad, Guru Amar Das, Guru Ram Das, Guru Arjan and Guru Tegh Bahadur), as well as by fifteen *bhagats*,[16] eleven *bhatts*,[17] Bhai Mardana, Bhai Satta, Bhai Rai Balwand and Baba Sundar.[18] The scripture comprises 1,430 pages, which can be divided into three distinct sections: (1) introduction, (2) *rag* and (3) conclusion. The introductory section (pp. 1–13) opens with the *Mul Mantar*,[19] followed by *Japji* (To Meditate, a morning prayer), five hymns of the *So Dar* (That Gate) and four hymns of the *So Purakh* (That Being) that are used for the *Rehras* (evening prayer), and lastly, five verses that are used for the *Sohila* (bedtime prayer).

The *rag* section (pp. 14–1,353) is the scripture's longest section, which is organized according to musical measure (*rag*; Skt. *raga*). The *Guru Granth Sahib* includes hymns in thirty-one *rags*.[20] Each *rag* segment begins with a hymn composed by a Sikh Guru and ends with verses composed by one of the many *bhagats* collectively known as *bhagat bani*. Each *rag* segment is further divided according to the length of the composition; it begins with a shorter verse (*pad*), followed by other poetic forms (*astapadi*, *chhant* or lyrical song and other longer works) like Guru Nanak's *Siddh Goshth*, Guru Amar Das's *Anand*, Guru Arjan's *Sukhmani* and then ending with a longer *var* or ballad.[21] The hymns in each of these categories are arranged in such a manner that Guru Nanak's compositions are placed first and are followed by later Sikh Gurus in order of their succession (M.2, M.3, M.4, M.5, M.9). That is, the Sikh Gurus are identified as 'M' for *mahala* (palace or vessel) and their number in the line of succession.

The concluding section (pp. 1,354–1,430) consists of miscellaneous compositions that were not integrated into the *rag* section.[22] This section includes sacred texts composed by Guru Nanak, Guru Amar Das, Guru Arjan and Guru Tegh Bahadur, as well as various works composed by a couple of *bhagats* (Kabir and Farid) and the *bhatts* (like Kalh, Harbans and Mathura). The section concludes with Guru Arjan's *Mundavani* (Closing Seal) and a couplet (*salok*) of gratitude. Significantly, Guru Arjan's *Mundavani* establishes the *Adi Granth* as a platter on which three virtues reside:

> On this platter are placed three things:
> Truth, contentment and contemplation.
> Within it is also the Master's nectar *Nam*,
>   the support of all.[23]

Lastly, the text concludes with the *Ragmala* text, which is further discussed below in the section on the Gauri *rag*.

Along with Guru Arjan's editorial achievement in having compiled the authoritative *Adi Granth*, his own work comprises almost two-fifths of the *Guru Granth Sahib*, with the *Sukhmani* being the most highly regarded and celebrated devotional composition.

The *Sukhmani*

The title of the composition – *Sukhmani* – has been translated into the English language in many different ways. Some of the commonly translated titles include: the 'Jewel of Peace',[24] the 'Pearl of Peace',[25] the 'Jewel of Bliss',[26] the 'Hymns of Peace',[27] the 'Psalm of Peace'[28] or the 'Peace of Mind'.[29] According to W.H. McLeod, the title contains a pun since *mani* can mean either pearl or mind.[30] That is, the title can be read as either the 'Pearl of Peace' or the 'Peace of Mind'. Since *sukh* connotes happiness or peace and *mani* primarily refers to a jewel, pearl or precious stone,[31] we have translated the *Sukhmani* as 'The Pearl of Happiness'. In fact, the metaphor of the pearl and the oyster shell echoes the spiritual teachings found in the *Sukhmani*:

> Forsaking the pearl and infatuated with its shell,
> > truth is renounced and falsehood is embraced.
> That which is passing is believed to be permanent,
> > the inevitable is recognised as far away. (*Sukhmani* 4.4)

Suffering arises when one is consumed by the impermanent nature of the manifest world and is ignorant about *Nam*. Indeed, the pearl is a metaphor for *Nam*, as both the means to and the goal of happiness and peace. Furthermore, elsewhere in the *Sukhmani*, *Nam* is also referred to as a 'jewel'. For instance, 'In the company of the *sadhs*, the jewel of *Nam* is obtained' (7.1). *Nam* is also described as a treasure: 'In the company of the *sadhs*, the treasure of *Nam* is obtained' (7.4).

It is appropriate to mention here that the word *Sukhmani* should not be mistaken for *sukhmana* (Skt. *sushmana*), which – according to Indian yogic traditions – is the central pathway that runs from the base of the spine towards the head within which the energy centres (*cakras*) are located.[32] While the term *sukhmana* is found in the *Guru Granth Sahib*,[33] Guru Nanak reinterprets the word to advance his own understanding of yoga: meditation on *shabad-Guru* (Guru's words) dissolves the ego and awakens consciousness to *Ek Oankar*. This is very different from *hath-yoga*, which views a dormant *kundalini-shakti* (primal energy) and imbalanced *ida* and *pingala* pathways as the deficiency and has as its aim to raise the *kundalini-shakti* through each of the seven central *cakras* to ultimately unite with Shiva-consciousness.[34] On the other hand, in Guru Nanak's approach, the ego is viewed as the barrier that prevents one from experiencing *Ek Oankar*.[35]

Guru Arjan's *Sukhmani* is a lengthy text of thirty-five pages (GGS, 262–96). Although long, the *Sukhmani* is very well structured. It is divided into twenty-four parts (*astapadi*), with each part comprising eight verses (*pauri*). Each verse is made up of ten lines or five couplets. Besides, an introductory couplet (*salok*) of two to four lines precedes each *astapadi*. Each introductory couplet provides the theme of the *astapadi*, which is then explored in the subsequent eight verses. The eighth verse either sums up the *astapadi* or reiterates the overall theme of connecting with *Nam*. The theme of each *astapadi* is linked to the over-arching and unifying framework of the composition's exposition on *Nam* as the 'pearl of happiness'.

There are two variations in or exceptions to the *Sukhmani*'s structure. First, the opening verse of the poem consists of a four-line invocation verse (*mangala-charan*) paying obeisance to the personal yet formless *Guru*: 'Bow to the primal

Guru. Bow to the *Guru* of the ages. Bow to *Satgur*. Bow to the great divine *Guru*.' Following a pan-Indian literary genre, the *mangala-charan* is placed at the beginning of a text and is meant to invoke divine blessing.

The second variation in the structure of the *Sukhmani* involves the inclusion of an additional couplet between the first and second verses of *astapadi* 1: '*Sukhmani: Prabh Nam* is ambrosial happiness, and resides in the hearts of the *bhagats*. [Pause].' This is the only couplet in the *Sukhmani* hymn that uses *rahau* (pause); that is, one should pause in order to reflect. The *rahau* verse purposely represents the central theme or essence of the entire devotional poem and is repeated as the refrain when put to music. Significantly, the last line of the *Sukhmani* reinforces the *rahau* couplet; in that it reiterates the essential teaching that '*Nam* is *Sukhmani*' (24.8) – *Nam* is the pearl of happiness.

Worthy of note here are the similarities of a couple of Guru Arjan's verses in the *Sukhmani* with verses contained in Guru Nanak's works. Indeed, Guru Nanak's works were interpreted as well as used for inspiration by the succeeding Sikh Gurus.[36] Interestingly, Guru Arjan seemingly employed, in the *Sukhmani*, parallel verses from Guru Nanak's *Japji* composition. For instance, *Sukhmani* 10.1–2 coincides with *Japji* 17–18. Guru Arjan's *Sukhmani* 10.1–2 says:

Many a million are the worshippers;
Many a million perform religious rituals.
Many a million reside at pilgrimage places;
Many a million wander as renunciates in the wilderness.
Many a million hear the Vedas;
Many a million are the ascetics.
Many a million place their concentration within;
Many a million are the poets discussing poetry.
Many a million meditate on new names;
Nanak: No one can attain the limits of the Creator. (10.1)

Many a million have pride;
Many a million are blinded by ignorance.
Many a million are stone-hearted misers;
Many a million lack heartfelt empathy.
Many a million steal others' property;
Many a million slander others.
Many a million work hard amid the *maya*;
Many a million wander in foreign lands.
Whatever the placement, so is the engagement;
Nanak: Only the Creator understands the creation. (10.2)

Similarly, Guru Nanak's *Japji* had earlier stated:

> Countless recitation, countless love.
> Countless worship, countless austerities.
> Countless scriptures, readings of the Vedas.
> Countless yogis, with detached minds.
> Countless devotees, contemplating virtues and wisdom.
> Countless the truthful, countless benefactors.
> Countless warriors, bearing the brunt of steel on their faces.
> Countless in silence, attuned to the string.[37]
> Who can describe the creation?
> Not once can I be a sacrifice to You.
> To Your delight is the only good done.
> You are eternal, secure and formless. (17)
>
> Countless fools, blinded by ignorance.
> Countless thieves, devouring the forbidden.
> Countless the departed, who ruled with force.
> Countless cut-throats and murderers.
> Countless sinners, sinning until departed.
> Countless liars, wandering in their falsehood.
> Countless barbarians, eating filth as their sustenance.
> Countless slanderers, carrying burden on their heads.
> Nanak humbly offers this description.
> Not once can I be a sacrifice to You.
> To Your delight is the only good done.
> You are eternal, secure and formless. (18)[38]

While Guru Arjan uses the Punjabi word *kai koti*, translated as 'many a million', and Guru Nanak uses *asankh*, translated as 'countless', the verses are similar in their message and style. This is an explicit example of how Guru Nanak's works served as the spiritual foundation of, and inspiration for, the later Sikh Gurus.

In addition, the introductory couplet (*salok*) of *Sukhmani* 17 corresponds closely to the introductory verse of the *Japji*:

True in the beginning, True throughout the ages;	*adi sachu jugadi sachu*
True in the present, Nanak, True in the future.	*hai **bhi** sachu nanak hosi **bhi** sachu*

The only difference involves the word *bhi*: in the *Japji bhi* is written with a long *i*, whereas in the *Sukhmani* it appears with a short *i*.[39] As discussed earlier in Chapter 2, Guru Arjan had added, according to Pashaura Singh, the introductory *salok* to the *Japji*, which he then repeated in the *Sukhmani*.[40] This action not only accounts for the stark similarity between the verses in both texts, but it also further discounts the suspect narrative about the *Sukhmani* contained in the *Tawarikh Guru Khalsa* about how Sri Chand gave the modified introductory *salok* of *Japji* to Guru Arjan.

Guru Arjan's use of the introductory *salok* of the *Japji* in *astapadi* 17 of the *Sukhmani* can be more accurately understood as a bridge between *astapadis* 16 and 17. In verse 6 of *astapadi* 16, Guru Arjan introduces the concept of *Sat Purakh* (True Being) in the *Sukhmani* text and continues to elaborate on *Sat* (Truth) in verse 7. After the *salok* introducing *astapadi* 17, the first verse continues to elaborate on *Sat*. Guru Arjan's use of the introductory *salok* for the seventeenth *astapadi* was not inserted as a result of Sri Chand's advice, but rather it was included to systematically link the thematic structure of the two *astapadis*. Besides, the number 17 when seen as two digits can be read as *Ek Sat* meaning One Truth.[41]

Similar to the *Guru Granth Sahib* in general, the *Sukhmani* is universal in its spiritual teaching. More specifically, its intended audience are those with a genuine thirst to connect with *Nam* and to transcend suffering (*dukh*) and pleasure (*sukh*). In this sacred text, Guru Arjan addresses different strata of society, including kings, householders, and religious figures and practitioners (such as *pandits*, *sadhus* and *yogis*): 'Many a million are the worshippers; Many a million perform religious rituals.... Many a million wander as renunciates in the wilderness' (10.1), and 'Many a million are the *siddhs* [ascetics], celibates and yogis; Many a million are the kings indulging in pleasure' (10.3). While these various members of society are discussed in order to underscore falsehood, overall attention is primarily given to those aspiring to alleviate their suffering through spiritual awareness and meaningful social engagement.

While the *Sukhmani* is a composition that provides insights into the Sikh understanding of well-being, the text is also meant to be used as part of ritual practice.

Sikh ritual and the *Sukhmani*

The verses of the *Guru Granth Sahib*, including the *Sukhmani*, are composed according to the musical system that originated in ancient India around 1500 BCE. The lack of a unified structure in this musical system reflects its dependence on oral traditions throughout the Indian subcontinent.[42] *Rag* (melodic measure) forms one of the two major components of traditional Indian music, with the other being *tal* (rhythmic metre). Derived from both the ancient Vedic and folk melodies, *rags* are arranged in an ascending to descending scale. The scale is very complex due to its melodic nature. Every *rag* has a strict set of rules which govern the number and type of notes that can be used, albeit with variation in pitch and tones. There are also rules about the interplay of notes when composing a melody. *Rag–tal* facilitates memorization and evokes specific moods.

The Indian musical *rag* plays an important role in the Sikh tradition, especially with respect to the *Guru Granth Sahib*. Although proficiency in the *rags* is not regarded as a religious requirement in *Sikhi*, the *rags* are nonetheless regarded as 'effective carriers of the message'.[43] The *Guru Granth Sahib* contains compositions written in a total of thirty-one *rags*. Guru Nanak sang his hymns in nineteen specific *rags* in order to awaken deep emotions that corresponded to his actual spiritual experience. While the succeeding Sikh Gurus continued composing hymns in the nineteen *rags*, it was not until Guru Ram Das that eleven additional *rags* were added to the Sikh scriptural corpus.[44] Along with employing more *rags*, Guru Ram Das also beautifully and explicitly highlighted the critical relationship between *rag* and *gurbani*:[45]

> Plucking the strings with the hand,
>   O yogi, this is how the mind is played in vain.
> Chant the virtues of *Har* with the *Guru's* intellect,
>   O yogi, this is how the mind is imbued with love. (1)
>
> O yogi! Surrender your intellect and receive instruction from *Har*;
> Pervading throughout the ages, I bow to You. (1) [Pause]
>
> Singing many *rags*, a lot of talk,
>   the mind is only playing a game.
> Looking at the well to water the fields,
>   yet the oxen have left to graze. (2)
>
> In this body, plant [the seed of] effort, and from there
>   *Har* will sprout like a lush field.
> O mortal! Harness the unsteady mind like an ox,
>   with the *Guru's* intellect, water the field with *Har*. (3)
>
> The yogis, *jangams* and the creation is all Yours,
>   as is the intellect given, so is their ways.
> O *Prabh*, the inner knower of hearts, Nanak, the devotee
>   yearns to have the mind harnessed with *Har*. (4)[46]

That is, *rags* are not sacred in themselves. Rather, it is the mystical quality of sacred words (*gurbani*) that sanctifies the *rags*. In effect, *rags* only acquire sanctity in their use for both praising *Guru* and, more significantly, transforming one's mind and heart so that they connect with *Nam*.[47] As explained by Mansukhani: 'It is not enough that we understand the theme of *shabad*; it is equally essential that we enter into its spirit and partake of the feeling of the Guru when he sang that hymn.'[48] Praising (*kirtan*) *Nam* through singing and music is a devotional path for seekers to experience union with Ultimate Reality (*Ek Oankar*). Indeed, although the *rag–tal* dimension of classical Indian music is used in the Sikh tradition, *gurbani-kirtan* evolved as a distinct musical genre with elements that serve the particular religious orientation of the Sikh Gurus.[49]

The goal of *gurbani-kirtan* is to recreate or evoke the Sikh Gurus' spiritual experience, which they expressed through the medium of sacred words (*gurbani*) and in the form of songs. Accordingly, there are four pillars to *gurbani-kirtan*: (1) *rag* (musical measure), (2) *tal* (rhythmic balance), (3) *shabad* (sacred words) and (4) *chitt* (author's intention).[50] While the first three pillars are necessary for singing and making music, the last pillar *chitt* is of great importance because it can reveal 'how it has been said',[51] and ultimately aids devotees to connect with *shabad-Guru*. Indeed, *gurbani* is not only a vehicle for transmitting sacred teachings or devotion to *Nam* (Name of the One essence) but it is also a means to connecting devotees with *Har* (omnipresent One) as described by Guru Arjan himself:

> The eternal nectar flows from my Beloved,
>   not for a moment has *Guru* been held back from the mind. (1) [Pause]
> Joyful and delightful is the touch and feel of being imbued with the Creator's love. (1)
> At every moment and breath, I approach and chant upon *Guru*, the god of death is no more,
> *Har* has placed a garland around Nanak's neck and within his heart. (2)[52]

Just as musicians tune their instruments, the *rag* is meant to tune the mind inwardly. In contrast, 'light music' carries the mind outwardly with lofty emotions.[53] And, in the case of musicians performing *gurbani-kirtan*, the realization emerges that one is not a doer (*karta*), but rather one 'that is done to (*kita*)'.[54] That is, the musicians and singers perform *gurbani-kirtan* with effortless effort.

The Sikh practice of singing sacred texts to a particular *rag* has as its purpose the evoking of a specific spiritual mood (*bhav*). Each *rag* also has a specific time of the day–night cycle and season in terms of when it should be performed, since the time of day and season correspond to the cycle of life and the stages of spiritual development.[55] For instance, Asa – a popular *rag* in the Punjab during the time of the Sikh Gurus – is performed at dawn during the cold season to evoke a calm mystical mood. In the case of the *Sukhmani*, its title '*Gauri Sukhmani* M.5' indicates both the author of the sacred text and the *rag* to which it is composed.

Gauri *rag*

Gauri means style, connoting the style to remember. Guru Amar Das explains: '*Gauri rag* is auspicious if the Beloved is remembered.'[56] The Gauri *rag* is the third *rag* to appear in the *rag* section of the *Guru Granth Sahib*. The compositions in this *rag* appear from page numbers 151 to 347, totalling 196 pages. In fact, the Gauri *rag* is a major musical measure used in the *Guru Granth Sahib* as it has the largest number of compositions assigned to it. While Guru Arjan's larger liturgical works – the *Sukhmani* and the *Bavan Akhri* – were composed in the Gauri *rag*,[57] the *rag* was also used by Guru Nanak, Guru Amar Das, Guru Ram Das and Guru Tegh Bahadur. In addition, Gauri *rag* was used by Bhagats Kabir, Namdev and Ravidas. There are also a large number of variants combining the pure Gauri form with other regional notes, regional tunes and folk melodies. The *Guru Granth Sahib* includes only twelve of the twenty-two variants of Gauri *rag*.[58]

The recommended time to sing Gauri *rag* is in the late afternoon (around 3–6 pm).[59] In addition, the Gauri *rag* is assigned to the autumn-winter season, which coincides with its contemplative mood. Significantly, although the *Sukhmani* is about attaining happiness and peace, Guru Arjan did not compose this text in the *rags* associated with happiness, such as Bilaaval (delight) or Basant (spring), both of which are associated with the experience of bliss and spring. Rather, Guru Arjan composed the *Sukhmani* in the Gauri *rag*, a musical measure meant to evoke a contemplative mood that brings stability to the mind.

As a contemplative *rag*, the Gauri *rag* was used by the Sikh Gurus for their works that explain profound beliefs about the nature of Ek Oankar, the nature of the soul and *Nam* as the means to liberation.[60] Given the fact that the *Sukhmani*'s essential teaching is that '*Nam* is *Sukhmani*' (24.8) – that is, liberating oneself from the duality of suffering and pleasure – it seems fitting that the text was composed according to the Gauri *rag*. In fact, assigned to the autumn-winter season, the Gauri *rag* can be viewed as a metaphor for the function of the *Sukhmani* text: Just as a plant during the winter becomes dormant to conserve its vital energy for survival and eventual growth, those suffering in a cold and dark world need to journey within to be soothed and strengthened, and eventually to flourish.

Besides having been one of the *rags* used in the middle section of the *Guru Granth Sahib*, Gauri is also one of several *rags* that appears in the *Ragmala*, an appendix-like list classifying eighty-four *rags* in the standardized version of the *Guru Granth Sahib* (p. 1430). In the *Ragmala*, Gauri *rag* actually appears as a *ragini* (female *rag*) and the consort of Sri Raga (male *rag*). Significantly, while gender is assigned to the *rags* in the traditional Indian musical system, the Sikh Gurus did not fundamentally subscribe to the notion of gendered musical measures (i.e. whether the musical measure is male or female) since they referred to all musical measures as *rags*.

Despite this difference between the Sikh Gurus' use of gender-neutral *rags* and the gendered *rags* listed in the *Ragmala*, most Sikh followers and scholars contend that the *Ragmala* is part of the scripture. This assertion is based on both the importance that *rags* have in the Sikh tradition and the fact that the *Ragmala* was included in the standardized version of the *Guru Granth Sahib*.[61] Conversely, others speculate that the *Ragmala* was not primarily written for the *Guru Granth Sahib*, since the classification of the Indian *rags* does not directly correspond with the *rags* used in the *Guru Granth Sahib*. Moreover, the followers of Bhai Randir Singh (Akhand Kirtani Jatha sect) and several scholars contend that the *Ragmala* is not an authentic *gurbani* hymn of the *Guru Granth Sahib*, because it does not consist of Sikh teachings.[62] Besides the different perspectives on the status of the *Ragmala*, its authorship is also disputed. Opponents of the *Ragmala* argue that the text was composed by Alam, a Muslim poet and contemporary of Guru Arjan.[63]

Reciting the *Sukhmani*

Sikhs, individually or as members of the congregation (*sadh sangat*), partake in the oral recitation of scripture as part of their daily religious discipline. Many Sikhs prefer to go to a Sikh place of worship (*gurdwara*) to recite prayers (*path*) and sing devotional hymns (*kirtan*) as a member of the congregation (*sadh sangat*) in the presence of the *Guru Granth Sahib*. Oral recitation has been a central practice since the time of Guru Nanak and his establishment of the *sangat* and *dharamsal* institutions of the Sikh Panth at Kartarpur.[64] Since then, the Sikhs have recited *Japji* in the early morning and *Sodar* and *Arti* in the evening.[65] In fact, a scriptural definition of a Sikh is based on the discipline of waking early and mindfully remembering *Nam*:

> The one who calls oneself a *Sikh* of the *Satgur*
> wakes up in the early morning,
> and meditates on *Nam*.[66]

As aforementioned, the devotional compositions have been written in poetic form according to specific musical measures, which also makes them easy to remember and master by rote. The oral recitation of sacred texts from memory is considered to have a transformative effect on individuals. Likewise, at the community level, the oral recitation of sacred words (*gurbani*) with single-minded attention as part of the congregation is regarded as both inspirational and motivational. Indeed, like a water droplet in a river,[67] the devotee's resolve is strengthened when worshipping in the company of the *sadh sangat*.

According to Article IV of the Sikh Code of Conduct (*Sikh Reht Maryada*),[68] the minimal requirement for Sikhs is to recite: (1) *Japji*, *Jaap* and Ten *Sawayyas* in the early morning;[69] (2) *Sodar Rehras*[70] in the evening; and (3) *Kirtan Sohila* in the night before going to bed. The morning and evening recitations are concluded with the *Ardas*, a Sikh prayer of remembrance, gratitude and goodwill that is recited at the conclusion of any Sikh ritual. These various sacred texts are collectively referred to as the *nitnem bani* or daily prayers. Even though the *Sukhmani* is not listed as one of the daily Sikh prayers in the *Sikh Reht Maryada*, the *Sukhmani* is such a popular composition that many devout Sikhs still recite it as part of their daily routine. Even after migrating to a new residing country, Sikh women continued the religious observance of reciting the *Sukhmani* as part of their health-promoting routine.[71] Moreover, it is also common for non-Sikhs from the Punjab, such as Hindus, to recite the text for good health and prosperity.[72]

While the *Sukhmani* is not currently regarded as a hymn to be recited daily (*nitnem bani*), Sikhs were, however, required at one time to recite the devotional composition on a daily basis. This may explain why on some websites on the internet, the *Sukhmani* is classified as a *nitnem bani*.[73] In fact, the *Sukhmani* is one of the hymns included in one of the more traditional *Panj Granthis*, anthologies of Sikh daily prayers.[74] One of the extant *Panj Granthis* gathered by Bhai Vir Singh (1872–1957) includes ten texts (*banis*):[75]

1. *Japji*, composed by Guru Nanak
2. *Sabad Hazare*, compiled by Guru Arjan, which contains one of his verses, along with six verses composed by Guru Nanak
3. *Rehras*, a collection of verses composed by Guru Nanak, Guru Ram Das and Guru Arjan
4. *Kirtan Sohila*, a collection of verses composed by Guru Nanak, Guru Ram Das and Guru Arjan
5. *Dakhni Oankar*, composed by Guru Nanak
6. *Siddh Goshth*, composed by Guru Nanak
7. *Anand*, composed by Guru Amar Das
8. *Bavan Akhri*, composed by Guru Arjan
9. *Sukhmani*, composed by Guru Arjan
10. *Asa di Var*, composed by Guru Nanak

Significantly, *Sukhmani* is included in the *Panj Granthi*, indicating that the *Sukhmani* has traditionally been regarded as an important text to be recited on a daily basis.

Given its simple syntax and structure, the *Sukhmani* is easy to memorize. The text takes around ninety minutes to recite. If not daily, many Sikhs, especially women, gather at a home on a weekly or monthly basis to recite the *Sukhmani*. Despite the fact that the Gauri *rag* is traditionally meant to be played and sung in the late afternoon, the *Sukhmani* is popularly recited in the early hours of the morning, the most peaceful time of the day.[76] It is noteworthy to mention here that, since recitation is not limited to the time associated with any particular *rag*, Sikhs can recite a sacred text at any time of the day or season. In fact, Sikhs often recite the *Sukhmani* during the pre-monsoon summer (May and June) in order to commemorate Guru Arjan's martyrdom.

As a fundamental Sikh text, the *Sukhmani* may also be recited by families on special occasions either at home or at the *gurdwara*. If recited at home, the family can arrange for the *Guru Granth Sahib* to be temporarily brought to its residence. Sikhs may also have the *Guru Granth Sahib* kept permanently at home for daily prayers and the reading of scripture. On the other hand, many Sikhs prefer to assemble at the *gurdwara*, either to listen to the reader (*granthi*) recite the *Sukhmani* or to recite it collectively with the congregation. The recitation of the *Sukhmani* in the *gurdwara* is then followed by the *Ardas*, *hukam-nama*[77] and *langar*.

Besides the transmission of sacred teachings to help devotees connect with *Nam* – the ultimate source of happiness – the *Sukhmani* is also said to console or soothe the mind.[78] The *Sukhmani* conveys the message to devotees that a peaceful or stable mind can be attained with *Nam* 'by chanting the *Nam*, peace is attained' (2.3), 'O mind, loving the *Nam* of *Har* brings peace' (5.3) and 'In the company of the *sadhs*, a stable mind is attained' (7.2). Sikhs, however, extend this teaching about the calming effect of mindful remembrance of *Nam* to the recitation of the *Sukhmani* text itself. That is, many Sikhs recite this sacred text in the hope of attaining spiritual and material benefit.

Consistent with the Sikh Gurus' teaching in general, the *Sukhmani* places importance on the well-being of both the mind (*man*) and body (*tan*). In effect, the *Sukhmani* is believed to have healing qualities. Just as the '*Nam* is the panacea for all illnesses' (9.5), or 'Nanak: Fruitful is the body that has the *Nam* of *Har*' (5.5), the *Sukhmani* is also recited for mental and physical well-being. Many Sikhs believe that the recitation of the *Sukhmani* will eliminate mental and physical suffering: 'Attune the mind and body to chant the *Nam*, suffering, pain, and fear will leave the mind' (22.6), and 'Whoever *Prabh* protects, the suffering of such a one is alleviated; Chanting the *Nam*, the mind becomes happy' (22.7). Significantly, a 1978 medical study, conducted at the Medical College in Amritsar, showed that reciting the *Sukhmani* mitigated the problems of high blood pressure of patients with hypertension.[79]

The *Sukhmani* is recited in the belief that it strengthens and inspirits the devotee. Just as meditation and chanting have been found to improve physical well-being,[80] reciting the text can, indeed, have a calming effect on the individual, such as to help reduce high blood pressure. This fits in with the Indian understanding of the dynamic relationship between the mind (*man*) and body (*tan*). While the Western medical model is built on the separation of mind and body, there has been over the last several decades an increasing interest in the interrelationship between mind and body. As a consequence, attention has been given to holistic healing and wellness that incorporate yoga, meditation, and aroma and massage therapy, not only as a form of stress management but also as a treatment intervention to help patients living with chronic illnesses.[81]

Indeed, many Sikhs believe that the recitation of the *Sukhmani* can result in the cure of acute bodily diseases. The *Sukhmani* text itself concludes references to *Nam*'s curative benefits: '*Nam* is the panacea for all illnesses; With good fortune, happiness is obtained by singing praises' (9.5), and 'The devotee of *Har* is immune to all illnesses. Only the praises [of *Har*] are sung night and day'

(14.4). In addition, there are miracle stories that are told about Sikhs and non-Sikhs who have been cured from serious bodily diseases because they recited or listened to the recitation of the *Sukhmani*.[82] For many Sikhs, miracle stories are not mere coincidences, but rather evidence of the healing power of the *Sukhmani*. Therefore, they hold to the belief that the regular recitation of the sacred text can result in miraculous cures and restoration of mental and physical wellness. The belief in the curative quality of the *Sukhmani* may be, in part, related to one popular narrative about how Wazir Khan (a Mughal governor)[83] – upon hearing Bhai Buddha recite the text – was cured from dropsy; convinced by the curative qualities, Wazir Khan employed Sikhs to daily recite the *Sukhmani* before daybreak.[84]

It is important to note here that there are various beliefs, interpretations and customs surrounding the recitation of the *Sukhmani*. Interpretations, for example, can depend on one's sectarian orientation or even as to whether one is reading the text from an orality, literacy or analytics perspective.[85] Some may interpret the verses as a form of metaphorical learning, whereas others may take a more literal approach to understanding the text. For example, in the case of *Sukhmani* 14.1, some aspirants may take the words 'Keep *Nam* strung around the neck' literally and actually wear *Nam* as an amulet for protection. Others may, however, understand the notion of wearing *Nam* around the neck as a metaphor to express the desire that one should be imbued with *Nam*. Another example is a verse that some may understand to be a guideline as to how one can become prosperous:[86]

> If the banker lends money,
>   the fool uses it for eating, drinking, joy and pleasures.
> But if some of the money is taken by the banker,
>   the ignorant mind becomes angry, [thus resulting in]
>   loss of credibility,
>   and trust.
> When one's possessions are placed before the One,
>   and the command of *Prabh* is obeyed on the forehead,
>   such a one will be happy fourfold;
> Nanak: *Sahib* is forever merciful. (*Sukhmani* 5.2)

However, other Sikhs, who read the text as a form of metaphorical learning, may interpret the verse as a description of how humans relate to the material world in general, and wealth in particular. They may even understand the verse to be an illustration of how humans tend to relate to God in terms of whether or not they receive what they desire.

Various Sikhs believe that the recitation of the *Sukhmani* helps devotees obtain all their desires because the text contains 24,000 letters, which is the number of breaths necessary for life for an entire day.[87] This may be, in part, related to Sri Chand's assertion that – if the text consists of 24 *astapadis* and 24,000 letters – those who read the *Sukhmani* with love will have fruitful breaths day and night, since there are 24,600 breaths in the eight watches.[88] Despite this *pranayam* yogic position, the *Sukhmani* does teach that *Nam* offers supernatural benefits: 'When mindful of *Prabh*, the spiritual, the supernatural and the nine treasures are attained' (1.3). Indeed, some Sikhs hold the belief that reciting the *Sukhmani* also results in the acquisition of supernatural or occult powers:

> Eternal peace, miracles, nine treasures,
>   intelligence, wisdom and supernatural powers.
> Learning, penance, yoga, concentration on *Prabh*,
>   supreme wisdom and purifying baths. ...
> These are the fruits when the mouth recites [*Nam*],
>   Nanak, and the mind listens to the Guru's *Nam* and teachings. (*Sukhmani* 24.6)

The *Sukhmani* states that *Nam* helps one attain the nine treasures (1.3, 4.3, 23.1 and 24.6). Even though there are a number of references to the nine treasures, the *Sukhmani* does not actually describe the nine treasures or explain what they are. The references may be an allusion to the nine treasures (*nau nidhi*) found in Hindu mythology and,[89] therefore, be a motif to express 'everything' or 'abundance' that one shall receive from *Ek Oankar*. In effect, some Sikhs recite the *Sukhmani* for good luck.

While the *Sukhmani* does not describe the nine treasures, Bhai Guriqbal Singh, a charismatic sectarian preacher,[90] provides a detailed description of the nine treasures that he believes one can attain with the recitation of the sacred text: (1) success with each breath, (2) protection from the five evils and other vices, (3) cure from bodily and mental disease, (4) liberation from *sansar*, (5) change in one's destiny, (6) change in one's disposition, (7) elimination of one's demerits, (8) protection against evils spirits and (9) removal of one's disguises.[91]

According to Bhai Guriqbal Singh, the eighth treasure of the *Sukhmani* is that 'the scripture of *Shri Sukhmani Sahib* protects one from witchcraft, black magic, ghosts and spirits, superstitions and from others being envious of you.'[92] Although the Sikh Gurus spoke against thoughtless ritualism and preoccupation with acquiring occult powers (also expressed in the *Sukhmani*),[93] some Sikhs may interpret the text more literally and recite it accordingly.[94] That is, when under emotional or psychological distress, they may recite the *Sukhmani* for protection. Alternatively, mainstream preachers – like Giani Sant Singh Maskeen – recommend Sikhs to read the *Sukhmani* mindfully through the lens of the *rahau* (pause or refrain),[95] which is '*Sukhmani: Prabh Nam* is ambrosial happiness, and resides in the hearts of the *bhagats*' (*Sukhmani* 1.1–2).

More recently, on 19 July 2016, San Francisco lawyer and vice president of the California Republican Party, Harmeet Kaur Dhillon, recited the *Ardas* as the invocation at the start of the second day of the Republican Nomination Convention in Cleveland.[96] While it was stated that Dhillon had delivered the *Ardas*, she had, in fact, recited a verse from the *Sukhmani*:

> To You, Master, this *ardas* is offered;
> The soul and body are all Your property.
> You are the mother and father, we are the children;
> With Your grace, there are many joys.
> No one knows Your end,
>   *Bhagwant* is the highest of the high.
> The whole creation is strung on Your thread,
>   that which You make happen, abides in Your will.
> You alone know Your state and extent;
> Nanak, the servant, is forever Your sacrifice. (*Sukhmani* 4.8)

Following the recitation of the above verse, Dhillon offered only the concluding portion of the standard *Ardas* prescribed in the *Sikh Reht Maryada*.[97] The selection of the passage was appropriate, given the rise in xenophobia and racial violence during Donald Trump's 2016 presidential election.

Chanting the sacred words of the *Sukhmani*

Along with oral recitation and listening to the scripture (*path*), the singing or chanting of devotional compositions (*kirtan*) is equally at the heart of Sikh spiritual practice. *Gurbani-kirtan* is believed to tune the mind to the resonance of the sacred words. The *rag* assigned to a sacred Sikh text is an instruction to the musician (*ragi*), not the Sikh devotee. As aforementioned, the fourth pillar of *gurbani-kirtan* – *chitt* (author's intent) – is of primary importance because the Sikh Gurus sang and wrote their compositions to help Sikhs attain the transformative experience of union with *Ek Oankar*.[98] Hence, musicians not only were customarily skilled in music but they also had the deep spiritual sensibility necessary for creating *gurbani-kirtan*. Initially, this musical tradition was transmitted orally through professional musical family lineages. Since the turn of the twentieth century, however, *kirtan* has been taught using the Indian musicologist V.N. Bhatkhande's modern treatise on Indian classical music.⁹⁹ As underscored by several scholars, Bhatkhande's system is based on newer forms of music and instruments that arrived after the Sikh Gurus.¹⁰⁰

By the late nineteenth and early twentieth centuries, Sikh *kirtan* began to incorporate Western music, including the use of the harmonium and the practice of congregational singing.¹⁰¹ More consequentially, the Sikh tradition of *gurbani-kirtan* was disrupted due to social and political turmoil in the Punjab over the last one and a half century, which was marked by the arrival of Christian missionaries and British rule (mid-1800s), the subsequent Singh Sabha movement (1870s–1920s),¹⁰² followed by the Gurdwara reform movement (1920s), and the partition of the Punjab (1947).¹⁰³ As Baldeep Singh explains:

> This [congregation singing] also accords with the changing social order and the newer crop of Sikh saints, probably in response to Christian missionaries, who went from village to village singing not *gurbani* but *sidhian dharnavan*, message that is, in simple language – a language that poor people easily understood. Bhai Attar Singh of Mastuana was famously given the title 'sant' by the organizers of the Chief Khalsa Diwan, and this started the new generation of saints who have played quite an influential role, even as massive as vote banks in political campaigns, since the partition of Punjab.¹⁰⁴

Subsequent to changes in the social and political environment of the Punjab, congregational singing has replaced *gurbani-kirtan*:

> Initially the music represented individual excellence as performers strove for it, as if they were constantly evolving living books…. This process was broken…. the introduction of congregational singing constituted a major blow to the aesthetical excellence of *gurbani kırtan* and its peaking performers. A greater blow still was the newly introduced 'tradition' that making everyone sing is a greater act than individual singing.¹⁰⁵

In the context of the break in the transmission of *gurbani-kirtan*, with its ideal of re-creating the sacred sound set by the Sikh Gurus, it is now congregational singing that predominates, as it engages with the masses, regardless of where they may be in their spiritual journey. Having said that, it needs to be acknowledged that there exists a strong sentiment among some Sikhs that contemporary worship is not in keeping with the standard set by the Sikh Gurus, since it is more concerned with the preference of the congregation.

Contemporary Sikh worship primarily involves the singing of scriptural verses put to music with musical instruments (harmonium, *tabla* and hand cymbals).¹⁰⁶

Kirtan is now typically led by a group of three musicians and/or singers (*ragis*, *kirtaniye*) who are joined by the congregation in a form of call-and-response style of chanting. Although Guru Arjan composed the *Sukhmani* in the Gauri *rag* in order to encourage a contemplative mood and to evolve a stable disposition, in contemporary times the text is rarely sung in its entirety or sung according to the Gauri *rag*. Instead, select verses are taken from the *Sukhmani* and are used for *kirtan*. One example of such a selection is the *mangala-charan* (introductory invocation) *salok* of the *Sukhmani*, which may be either recited (such as before a sermon or *hukam-nama*) or sung as part of contemporary Sikh worship. Since the *mangala-charan* is a very familiar and easy-to-remember *salok*, it is often included in various *kirtan* programmes.[107] Similar to the *Sukhmani* in general, 'Aad Guray Namah' is regarded as a sacred chant that, when sung, invokes spiritual blessings, including protection and clarity of mind.

aad guray namah	Bow to the primal *Guru*.
jugaad guray namah	Bow to the *Guru* of the ages.
satguray namah	Bow to *Satgur*.
sri gurudevay namah	Bow to the great divine *Guru*.

Ideally, the melody to which the *mangala-charan* is sung should evoke the emotions of both *dukh* and *sukh*. Moreover, it should also inspirit the feeling of 'hope amid the despair' – an important teaching of the *Sukhmani*.

Summary

The *Sukhmani* is a fundamental text located in the Sikh canon. It is not only included in the *Guru Granth Sahib*, but is also contained in the anthology of hymns (*Panj Granthi*) that was traditionally meant to be recited daily. While the *Sukhmani* teaches that *Nam* is the panacea for all illnesses, Sikhs often recite the *Sukhmani* for spiritual and material benefit. The *Sukhmani* addresses various members of society; however, it gives primary attention to those aspiring to enhance their spiritual well-being. Curiously, Guru Arjan composed 'The Pearl of Happiness' in the Gauri *rag*, a musical measure meant both to evoke a contemplative mood and to bring peace to the mind. Significantly, this serious *rag* matches the function of the *Sukhmani* because the text is for those suffering in a cold and dark world and are in need of an inward journey to be soothed and strengthened, and to eventually flourish. Similarly, the Gauri *rag* fits in well with the *Sukhmani*'s spiritual teachings on the pursuit of happiness, which is the focus of the next chapter.

4

The *Sukhmani*: Teachings and practice

In view of the *Guru Granth Sahib*'s status as the highest authority in the Sikh canon, much reverence is given to scriptural texts included in it, like the *Sukhmani*. Even though the devotional compositions of the *Guru Granth Sahib* belong to the literary genre of poetry, they also embody the Sikh spiritual perspective. As found in other Indic religious traditions,[1] the Sikh tradition regards poetry as a legitimate vehicle not only for religious expression, but also for spiritual discourse. Unsurprisingly, then, the transformative Sikh worldview is contained in such compositions. In fact, while the *Sukhmani* – Guru Arjan's most celebrated work – builds on Guru Nanak's perspective on the individual pursuit of liberation, it also reveals Guru Arjan's own distinctive spiritual and doctrinal contributions to the Sikh tradition.

Besides offering a particular worldview, religious beliefs are ultimately meant to be put into practice for spiritual upliftment and development. In line with Guru Arjan's pragmatic character, the *Sukhmani* not only offers philosophical teachings on the pursuit of wellness and happiness, but it also provides valuable insights into *how* one can apply *gurmat* values (or values taught by the Sikh Gurus) while navigating through the illusions of the material world. In doing so, the text guides the seeker in experiencing *Nam* – the expression for the inner essence of all existence (*Ek Oankar*) – in all aspects of life. This application of religious beliefs is reinforced by the way Guru Arjan creatively organized the *Sukhmani*. That is, the structure of the text *inspirits* hope in the seeker even as it also reinforces Sikh teachings.

In order to fully understand Guru Arjan's application of spiritual beliefs to actual living, it is necessary to also incorporate additional religious sources. Such inclusion is important when the followers of a religious tradition – like the Sikh one – are often rooted in oral culture. While Sikhs may remember their scriptural hymns by rote, they – more often than not – depend on the traditional narratives (*sakhis*) as part of oral transmission and sermons (*katha*) to learn about their beliefs and practices. Therefore, the inclusion of these traditional modes of learning is also helpful in offering a holistic approach to understanding *Sikhi* as a lived tradition.

Drawing on Guru Arjan's various hymns, religious discourses by Sikh *gianis*, the narrative accounts about Guru Arjan, and contemporary scholarship on the Sikh tradition, this chapter specifically examines the *Sukhmani* and its place in the development of Sikh thought. First, the chapter demonstrates how the structure of the *Sukhmani* – according to the eight *pehars* or watches of day and night (*din-rat*) – guides the seeker in experiencing non-duality. Second, the chapter provides a thematic analysis of the spiritual teachings of the *Sukhmani*. In doing so, the analysis underscores the key concept of *Nam*, the central role of the *sadh sangat*, the dynamic conception of *Sat Purakh* (True Being), and the Sikh way of 'detached engagement' for attaining *sukh*. Last, the chapter explores the *Sukhmani*'s teachings about the *sadh sangat* and demonstrates how Guru Arjan's spiritual understanding of the *sadh sangat* serves as a bridge between his doctrinal and his institutional contributions to the Sikh Panth.

Before commencing the analysis, it is important to clarify the terminology used for Ultimate Reality in *Sikhi*. The introductory *salok* of the *Sukhmani* begins with the invocation '*Ek Oankar*, realised by *Satgur*'s grace' (*Ek Oankar, Satgur prasad*). *Ek Oankar* literally means the One creator-creation. That is, the Creator is represented by the sound *Oan*,[2] which is the unstruck sound resounding throughout creation. Therefore, the Sikh understanding of Ultimate Reality involves the One creator as resonating throughout creation. Namely, the Creator and creation are One and the same.[3] While the phrase *Ek Oankar* appears only this one time in the *Sukhmani*, Guru Arjan uses *Sat Purakh* (True Being) and *Guru* to connote Ultimate Reality throughout the *Sukhmani*, even as he praises *Sat Purakh* by way of epithets, such as *Prabh*, *Har* and *Gobind* to name a few. *Satgur* (True *Guru*), on the other hand, refers to the embodiment of Ultimate Reality or *Ek Oankar*. While the word *Guru* is italicized when connoting Ultimate Reality, it is not italicized when used as a title (e.g. Guru Arjan).

The structure of the *Sukhmani*: Eight watches of the day and night cycle

In ancient Indian culture, time was arranged according to eight watches (*pehar*; Skt. *pahar*) of the day and night (*din-rat*) – or in modern terms, the twenty-four-hour clock – with the allocation of four watches to the day and four watches to the night. While the first watch or onset of the day begins at sunrise (dawn), the first watch of the night begins at sunset (dusk). At the time of the summer and winter solstices, the eight watches are equal in duration (i.e. three hours in length). But, since days are longer and nights are shorter in the summer months, a watch can range from three and a half hours for each watch in the day to two and a half hours for each watch in the night. Similarly, since days are shorter and nights are longer in the winter months, the length for each watch can range from two and a half hours for each watch in the day to three and a half hours for each watch in the night.[4]

This ancient arrangement of time is often referred to in the *Guru Granth Sahib* and appears in the *Sukhmani* eight times.[5] While the *Sukhmani* refers to the eight watches (*aath pehar*), it employs the term figuratively, signifying 'all day and all night'. Along with this metaphorical use of the term, the *Sukhmani* text can also be viewed as structured according to the eight watches, with three parts or *astapadis* (each part comprising eight verses), for a total of twenty-four *astapadis*. Astapadis 1–12 correspond to the four watches of the day (around 6 am to 6 pm), while *astapadis* 13–24 correspond to the four watches of the night (around 6 pm to 6 am).[6]

The structure of the *Sukhmani*, in terms of the eight watches of the day-night cycle, creates a medium through which the seeker can rise above dualities. That is, the *Sukhmani* guides the seeker in the non-dual experience of light and darkness as well as of *dukh* and *sukh*. While the four watches of the day – during which there is an abundance of light – provide a dark conception of the illusions of the material world, the four watches of the night – during which there is an absence of light – offer the Sikh perspective on *Sat Purakh* (True Being).[7] Indeed, where there is light there is also darkness, and where there is darkness there is also light. More specifically, the first twelve *astapadis*, associated with the four watches of the day, offer insights into the Sikh conception of the material world and also into *Nam* from the standpoint of overcoming *dukh*. On the other hand, the last twelve *astapadis*, associated with the four watches of the night, inculcate 'the way of a Sikh' with a view to attaining *sukh*.

Four watches of the day (*astapadis* 1–12): The Sikh conception of the world

The four watches of the day are covered by the first twelve *astapadis*, with each watch comprising three *astapadis*. The four watches of the day include (1) the first watch or early morning marked by sunrise (around 6 am to 9 am), (2) the second watch or late morning (around 9 am to 12 noon), (3) the third watch or early afternoon (around 12 noon to 3 pm) and (4) the fourth watch or late afternoon (around 3 pm to 6 pm). Overall, the four watches of the day – when people are awake and there are many distractions – provide the Sikh outlook on the illusions of the material world and lay the foundation for the Sikh practice necessary for spiritual inspiration and growth.

The first watch: *Dukh* and its cure

The first watch (*astapadis* 1–3), or the beginning of the day, sets the stage for the entire composition. It outlines the main sources of suffering and provides hope through its description of *Nam* as the cure. The first watch reminds the seeker of the spiritual and material benefits of mindful remembrance of *Nam*, especially its role in removing the human condition of suffering (*dukh*). As aforementioned in Chapter 1, while suffering in general terms is seen in *Sikhi* as the result of bondage to *sansar*, Guru Nanak had identified four main sources of human suffering: (1) separation, primarily from *Nam*, which results in anxiety and fear; (2) physical deprivation, such as hunger and thirst; (3) bodily ailments, like disease and infection; and (4) oppression and death.[8]

Like Guru Nanak, Guru Arjan gives a lot of attention to suffering. In fact, the overall orientation of the *Sukhmani* is to examine the sources of both affliction (*kalesh*) and suffering (*dukh*) as well as the means towards peace and happiness (*sukh*): 'Remember mindfully, mindfully, and attain happiness, tension and *kalesh* vanish from the body' (1.1). Consistent with the teachings of Guru Nanak's view of the sources of suffering and its cure,[9] Guru Arjan's *Sukhmani* also examines the various sources of suffering and prescribes *Nam* as the cure. While the entire *Sukhmani* text is about how to overcome suffering (*dukh*) and attain happiness (*sukh*), the watches of the day specifically provide the Sikh perspective on the sources of *dukh* in the transitory world. More specifically, *astapadi* 2 opens up with a *salok* in which three types of suffering are listed:

> Poverty, pain and suffering are destroyed, by the Master of hearts who has no master.
> In the sanctuary of *Prabh*, Nanak seeks help. (2.*salok*)

While the *salok* states that human suffering is a result of poverty (*deen*), physical or emotional pain (*dard*), and existential suffering (*dukh*), verses 1–4 of *astapadi* 2 provide a more detailed description of the human condition.

Guru Arjan explains *dukh* in terms of the experience of suffering that comes with mundane existence, including the illusions and disappointments that humans have in respect of people they depend on for their wellness, such as family, friends and clan. Accordingly, since people cannot solely rely on one another for comfort, they have to contend with the inevitable reality of aloneness when those whom they had trusted are unable to console them in their moments of despair. For instance, people (1) depend on their family for support, yet family members are unable to fully sustain their bodies and minds (2.1); (2) expect just governance from the king, and fair distribution of wealth from the tax collector, but they are not treated as such (2.2); (3) seek protection from the army, but they are ultimately trapped in the 'heat' of *sansar* (2.3); and (4) hope in achieving the prescribed worldly goals, which are meant to bring happiness, but in actuality their achievements are ineffective in alleviating the suffering that comes with mundane existence (2.4).

While the three Indic cultural goals of humans involve fulfilling social and religious duty (*dharam*), acquiring wealth and status (*arth*) and enjoying sensual-pleasures (*kam*), the fulfilment of these goals alone does not bring *sukh* or constitute wellness. Moreover, one cannot always rely on the family for sustenance, the king for good governance or the army for effective protection. In addressing those who suffer, Guru Arjan advises that *Nam* alone nourishes as the 'true' family, governs as the 'true' king and protects as the 'true' army:

> This path upon which miles cannot be counted,
>   the *Nam* of *Har* will offer sustenance.
> On this path of total darkness,
>   the *Nam* of *Har* will provide light.
> On this journey where you are anonymous,
>   the *Nam* of *Har* will be your identity.
> Where there is immense and unbearable heat,
>   the *Nam* of *Har* will be your shade.
> O mind, when thirst torments you,
>   Nanak, only *Har* showers ambrosial nectar. (2.4)

Thus, in Guru Arjan's understanding, without an awareness of *Nam*, one's identification with family, clan and social class or caste group is false.

When navigating through the darkness of the material world, one has to connect with *Nam* in order to swim across the ocean of *sansar*. The path for spiritual experience of *Ek Oankar* depends on the practice of remembering *Nam* (*Nam simran*), which is accessible to anyone and everyone regardless of their social standing. Leading a movement of the common people, the Sikh Gurus also taught the accessible practice of *Nam simran*, especially since the people at the time were, for the most part, illiterate, while those with non-*dvija* status were not permitted to learn the Vedas.

As part of their challenge to religious elitism and the hypocrisy associated with it, the Sikh Gurus explained that one is not bound to religious institutions or subject to rites and rituals. It is important to underscore here that, although Guru Arjan is celebrated for having consolidated the organizational and administrative aspects of the Sikh Panth – such as building *gurdwaras* and developing the *masand* system throughout the Punjab – he simultaneously composed verses that critique the institutional form of religion when explaining how to navigate through the world. McLeod reminds us that, while Guru Nanak had rejected all institutional forms of religion, one of his later successors, Guru Amar Das, in 'a different and more difficult circumstance [was] compelled to return to them', especially since the Sikh Panth was spreading throughout North India.[10] Certainly, in his explicit effort to break away from Hindu rituals, Guru Amar Das did begin distinctive Sikh rituals and customs.

Similarly, Guru Arjan's initiatives, like compiling the *Adi Granth* and installing it in Harmandar Sahib, strengthened the organizational and doctrinal aspects of the expanding Panth. However, Guru Arjan significantly continued to be critical of the hypocrisy that often comes with religious institutions and thoughtless ritualism:

> Known as a *pandit*, yet wandering many paths and hard as uncooked beans.
> Attachment within, always engrossed in doubt, and unable to hold the body still.
> Comes in falsehood, goes in falsehood, always looking for *maya*.
> When the truth is spoken, there is agitation and a lot of anger within.
> Engrossed in foul intellect, fallacious thinking and mental attachments.
> The deceiver resides with the [five] thieves, they are of the same company.
> With *Satgur's* appraisal, the goldsmith clearly sees the iron.
> Mixing and mingling in many places, but when the veil lifts he is exposed in front of all.
> By entering *Satgur's* sanctuary, iron is transformed into gold.
> *Satgur* has no enemies, sees friend and foe as alike, and purifies the body by removing faults.
> Nanak: Whoever had it inscribed on their forehead from the beginning are in love with *Satgur*.[11]

Indeed, Guru Arjan critiqued Hindu *pandits* and Brahminical ritualism. The *Sukhmani*, which was composed during the later years of Guru Arjan's life, is a testimony to this point: 'You will not swim across by performing countless rituals, the *Nam* of *Har* will remove millions of sins' (2.1). In fact, Guru Arjan not only critiques thoughtless ritualism, but he also highlights the illusions of religious practice, including how the outward display of virtue cannot and will not bring happiness. Moreover, he challenges the human propensity to elevate and worship another: 'In the company of the *sants*, good fortune is secured, serve the *sants* by concentrating on *Nam*' (2.8).

Along with his critique of thoughtless religious practice, Guru Arjan's actions also reveal his understanding of how power and politics can manifest in religion. For instance, when family members contested the *gur-gaddi* title (as Sri Chand, Dasu, Datu, Mohan and Prithi Chand did), Guru Arjan and the preceding Gurus did not fight over control of territory.[12] Rather, in response to the rivalry over the *gur-gaddi* for economic benefit and political control, the Sikh Gurus preferred to avoid clan-related conflicts and to instead move their centres of activity elsewhere. Notably, Guru Arjan did not leave Amritsar; rather it was Prithi Chand who moved to Heran, a village of his in-laws, near Lahore to seek the support of Mughal authorities.

Guru Arjan maintained that people are blinded not only by the illusions of what brings comfort and happiness, but also by their misconceptions of the cure for suffering. Contrary to these illusions, including those of a religious nature, one has to be mindful of *Nam*:

> Chanting, meditation, knowledge and concentration,
> > sermons about the six Shastras and Simritis.
> Yoga, *karam*, *dharam* and *kirya*,
> > renouncing everything and wandering in the wilderness.
> Participating in all sorts of rituals,
> > virtue, charity and the burning of purified butter.
> Cutting the body into pieces and offering them,
> > keeping fasts and taking many vows.
> Nothing equals contemplating *Ram Nam*;
> Nanak: Try chanting *Nam* as a *gurmukh*. (3.1)

In the light of Indic religious practices like puja, pilgrimage and renunciation, the *Sukhmani* describes *Nam* as the superior and legitimate means to alleviate suffering:

> If a person wants to erase one's suffering,
> > sing the *Nam* of *Har* within the heart.
> If a person wants to be honoured,
> > abandon the ego in the company of the *sadhs*.
> If a person fears birth and death,
> > seek refuge in the company of the *sadhs*. (3.5)

As the panacea for suffering, *Nam* can be experienced with the practice of *Nam simran* and support of the *sadh sangat* (congregation of the *sadhs*), the topics of the next two watches, respectively.

The second watch: Reciting, listening and internalizing *Nam*

The second watch of the day (*astapadis* 4–6), or the late morning, focuses on the practice of *Nam simran* as the only means to be rid of all suffering. It teaches that besides *Nam*, all else is impermanent (5.3–6). Therefore, without *Nam* even acts of a religious nature can be hollow. For instance, beliefs, rituals and practices can shroud one in darkness, as the ego uses them either to provide temporary moments of solace or to form a rigid exterior religious identity:

> Behaving like an animal, yet of the human species;
> Preaching to others day and night.
> Outer facades, yet the filth of *maya* within,
>   trying to hide this, but it cannot be hidden.
> Outer knowledge, concentration and bathing,
>   yet the dog of greed clings within.
> Ashes on the body, yet fire within;
> With stones around the neck, can one swim the bottomless ocean?
> Within whom *Prabh* resides,
>   Nanak, those devotees are spontaneously absorbed. (4.5)

The outer expression or display of religion for ego-gain does not address existential suffering or provide spiritual awakening. In fact, attaining goals of the impermanent world – regardless of the rituals one performs – results in a dark inner state that makes humans behave like hedonistic animals. While disconnectedness from *Nam* often results in an attachment to *maya*, it also misguides humans so that they identify with the unreal:

> Working hard for that which will be left behind,
>   and letting go of inner support.
> Washing off sandalwood paste
>   is like a donkey loving the mud.
> Fallen and afraid in a dark well,
>   Nanak, the merciful *Prabh* can rescue them. (4.4)

That is, the ritual of both applying sandalwood paste and then washing it off is equal to cleansing oneself with the filth of mud. Indeed, rituals are a distraction from one's 'inner support'. Besides, the absence of remembering and chanting *Nam* further results in one being completely consumed by *maya* or illusion: 'But the foolish mind is disconnected.... The fool is unaware, always making mistakes' (4.3).

Separation from *Nam* is the original and most intense form of *dukh* that affects both the mind and the body. Therefore, the cure for existential suffering comprises both the connection with, and realization of, *Nam*. In order to connect with *Nam*, one needs to remember *Nam*, which is taught in the *rehau* of the *Sukhmani*: '*Sukhmani: Prabh Nam* is ambrosial happiness, and resides in the hearts of the *bhagats* [Pause]'. The *rehau*, the central theme or refrain, of the entire *Sukhmani* reinforces the essential teaching that '*Nam* is *Sukhmani*'.

Nam simran is central to Sikh practice because it is viewed as the legitimate means to self-realization. In contrast to the significance placed on the iconic form of God (Skt. *arca-avatara*) in Hindu (Vaishanava) Bhakti, the Sikh Gurus give central importance to *Nam*. And, just as *darshan* or visual experience of the *arca-avatara* is central to Hindu Bhakti,[13] mindful remembrance of *Nam* is fundamental to the Sikh experience because it brings about a profound inner and outer awareness of *Ek Oankar*. While *Nam* can be literally translated as name, such a loose translation does not capture the philosophical importance of the term, even as it understates its experiential qualities. *Nam* is not a mere label to identify a person, object or phenomenon. Rather, it is an ontological category denoting the mystical presence and experience of *Ek Oankar*. Specifically, *Nam* binds the entire creation into one integral whole.

While the *Adi Granth* refers to the various forms of *bhakti* metaphorically,[14] only four of the nine forms are relevant to Sikh practice: (1) *suna* (listening to *sakhis*, *katha* and *kirtan*), (2) *nam-sankirtan* (reciting the names of *Ek Oankar*), (3) *simran* (i.e. remembering *Nam*) and (4) *archa* (worshipping *Sat Purakh*).[15] Significantly, all these four forms of devotion are addressed to *Nam* and *Sat Purakh*. While *kirtan* and *simran* are listed as the second and third modes in Hindu Bhakti, respectively, the Sikh Gurus viewed them as central to spiritual advancement towards the goal of immersion in Truth (*mukti*) or union with *Sat Purakh*.[16] Guru Arjan explains:

> Happiness is attained through mindful remembrance;
> The *Guru's* lotus feet are enshrined in the heart.
> *Guru Gobind Parbraham* is perfect;
> Meditating upon this, my mind is steady. [Pause][17]

The word *simran* is derived from the Sanskrit verb root *smr*, which literally means to remember or to bring back to attention. While *Nam simran* is widely translated as remembering or meditating on *Nam*, the practice actually involves three distinct stages. Consistent with the words of Guru Nanak that 'by singing, listening and love within the heart, suffering is shed and happiness is taken home',[18] the three stages of *Nam simran* involve (1) reciting *Nam*, (2) listening to *Nam* and (3) internalizing *Nam*. Significantly, these three stages of *Nam simran* reflect the transformation from the audible to the inner subtle experience of *Nam*.

Reciting or chanting *Nam* is the initial stage of spiritual practice. According to *Sikhi*, the mind is distracted by the ego and the four vices,[19] as well as by the illusions of the world. The unsteady mind therefore requires *Nam* in order to cultivate single-minded concentration. An initial step towards spiritual development therefore involves the actual chanting or uttering of *Nam* out loud with the 'mouth and tongue' in a rhythmic pattern:

> By whose grace is respect given?
> Sing the praises with the mouth and tongue.
> By whose grace have you mastered *dharam*?
> O mind, always and only meditate on *Parbraham*.
> Chanting *Prabh*, honour is attained in the heavenly court,
>   Nanak, the real home is entered with honour. (6.2)

The oral recitation of *Nam* (or *gurbani* in general) is considered to have a transformative effect as the rhythmic sound pattern of epithets and *mantars* helps tune the mind to be more stable and focused. In contemporary times, more often than not, the chanting of *Nam* is emphasized in *kirtan* programmes at the *gurdwara*. However, this concrete practice of chanting is only the beginning stage of *Nam simran*. Once the mind becomes stabilized with the chanting of *Nam*, the mind can then be more attentive to the inner experience of *Nam*.

The second stage of *Nam simran* – listening to *Nam* – not only involves concentrating on *Nam* and listening to the chanting of *Nam* or *kirtan*, but it also entails listening to *Nam* as the subtle sound of *Ek Oankar*: 'In the mind where the love of listening to *Nam* resides, that devotee continuously remembers *Prabh*' (24.8). With the practice of mindful listening, the mind increasingly becomes more and more connected with the unstruck sound (*anhat nad*) of *Ek Oankar*. With the greater ability to connect with *Nam*, the heart and mind gradually begin to open up to the experience of *Nam*.

The third and last stage of *Nam simran* – internalizing *Nam* – involves opening the heart with love to experience *Nam*. In experiencing *Nam*, the heart and mind begin to internalize *Nam*. That is, the connection to, and the experience of, the unstruck sound of *Ek Oankar* eventually leads to the superimposition of *Nam* on the self:

> You make the chanting of *Nam* happen;
> You make the qualities of *Har* be sung.
> With *Prabh's* blessing, there is enlightenment;
> With *Prabh's* kindness, the lotus blooms in the heart.
> When pleased, *Prabh* resides in the mind;
> With *Prabh's* kindness, the intellect is perfect. (6.8)

With *Prabh's* blessing (*kirpa*), one internalizes *Nam*, whereby one becomes imbued with the characteristics of *Ek Oankar*, such as fearlessness (*nirbhau*) and without enmity (*nirvair*).

In view of the three stages of *Nam simran*, the practice can be more accurately and profoundly translated as the 'mindful remembrance of *Ek Oankar*'. That is, *Nam simran* involves mindful chanting of *Nam*, mindful listening to *Nam* and mindful absorption in *Nam*. Unlike in Buddhism, where mindfulness is awareness of the present moment without judgement (i.e. practice is the medicine and awareness is liberation), the Sikh practice of mindful remembrance involves the awareness and experience of *Nam* resonating in the present moment. Indeed, *Nam* is the medicine, and the experience of *Nam* is liberation: 'The world is ill, *Nam* is the medicine. Filth sticks without the Truth.'[20]

Significantly, the entire *Sukhmani* is structured to reflect spiritual development that comes with the practice of *Nam simran*. While the *Sukhmani* begins with inculcating the importance of chanting *Nam*, the text ends stating that happiness is achieved by those absorbed in *Nam*: 'One's fame is pure, one's words are ambrosial, the mind is only absorbed with *Nam*' (24.8). However, those absorbed in *Nam* do not stop reciting, or listening to, *Nam*. Rather, they joyfully continue with all three stages.

In setting the stage for the entire text, the first watch describes *Guru's* grace – the spontaneous flow of compassion and mercy – as a catalyst for the pursuit of happiness: 'Bestowed with grace (*diala*), mindfulness begins' (1.5). Then, *astapadi* 6, in the form of rhetorical questions and answers, enhances the seeker's belief that liberation depends on *Guru's* grace (*prasad*) (see 6.2 and 6.8 above). Similar to Bhakti, the concept of grace is central in *Sikhi*.[21] This notion of grace appears throughout the *Sukhmani* since it emboldens the devotee to go further along the spiritual journey towards selfless effort.[22] It is, however, only when the ego is completely dissolved that one experiences the flow of grace as continuous. One gets rid of the ego with the practice of *Nam simran*.

While human nature is described as an obstacle to experiencing *Nam*, the practice of *Nam simran* helps one dissolve the ego and acquire the qualities of *Sat Purakh*. However, since proceeding through the three stages of *Nam simran* can prove to be challenging, Guru Arjan also teaches that the *sadh sangat* is a vital source of support.

The third watch: The *sadh sangat*

The third watch of the day (*astapadis* 7–9), or the early afternoon, underscores the fundamental role of the *sadh sangat*. Although the *sadh sangat* is popularly translated as the holy congregation, it is more accurate to translate it as the congregation of the *sadhs*. While *sadh* generally refers to someone who practises a technique to attain truth (*sadhan*), for Guru Arjan, *sadh* specifically refers to one who practises *Nam simran* (see section below on 'The congregation of the *sadhs*'). Although *sadh sangat* was not a new or an exclusively Sikh concept,[23] it was further developed by Guru Arjan in view of its significance for the Sikh tradition. In fact, he dedicates the entire seventh *astapadi* to explain its nature and role.

The Sikh practice of *sangat* dates back to Guru Nanak and reveals the formation of the community. As Guru Nanak primarily focused on spiritual development with *Nam simran* as an individual practice,[24] he used *satsang* (spiritual gathering or company) to connote a spiritual 'meeting' for the purpose of enquiry or practice with others in order to further their spiritual growth.[25] This use of *satsang* fits in with Guru Nanak's *udasis* or journeys to the four directions of the world, during which he sought out religious figures and teachers for the purpose of religious discourse (*vichar*).[26] For Guru Nanak, it is also important to keep the company of like-minded individuals (*sadhus, bhagats, sants, fakirs*), as their company can help mitigate the influence of self-centred thoughts and worldly attachments:[27]

> Even with a hundred thousand clever thoughts,
>   and love from a hundred thousand people,
>   without the company of the *sadhs*, one is unfulfilled,
>   and suffers in sorrow without *Nam*.
> By chanting *Har*, the *gurmukh* is released and has self-understanding.[28]

The *gurmukh* (one who follows the Gurus' teachings) is encouraged to seek the company of, and associate with, others journeying on a similar path because that can have a positive spiritual effect on the *gurmukh*,[29] and as well provide guidance and support. Indeed, the *gurmukh* can rely on the *satsang* for inspiration and motivation to help navigate through the difficult moments on the spiritual path. Guru Nanak also valued the practice of reciting *Nam* in the company of the *satsang*, which fits in with his practice of having members of the Panth congregate at the *dharamsal* (religious sanctuary or resting place), especially during the latter part of his life in Kartarpur.[30]

With Guru Angad's establishment of the *langar* (community dining), the *sangat* became connected with it. That is, the *sangat* was no longer only a place where followers meet to chant *Nam*, but it was also a community that provides food.[31] Building on Guru Nanak's teachings and Guru Angad's custom of *langar*, Guru Amar Das added new significance to *satsang* in his devotional poetry: There is a shift from Guru Nanak's *satsang* as the meeting for religious discourse to Guru Amar Das's use of the term *sat sangat* to signify a sacred place to meet the *Guru*.[32] Indeed, the *sat sangat* is a place where the virtuous go to remember *Nam* as well as to unite with *Guru* in order to attain happiness.[33] More significantly, the *sangat* is where people congregate to single-mindedly sing the praises of *Guru*,[34] and to find peace of mind through the worship of *Nam*: 'O *Prabh*, may I meet the *sat sangat*, and may *Har Nam* reside within the mind.'[35] Significantly, Guru Amar Das's verses about the role of the *sangat* were composed at the time when he built Goindval Sahib as a *tirath* (pilgrimage place) and also established the *manji* system of 'seats', where appointed representatives spread *Sikhi* throughout North India. Consistent with his effort in spreading the teachings and promoting *langar* through the *masands*, Guru Ram Das continued with Guru Amar Das's conception of the *sat sangat* as a place where one can meet *Guru*,[36] learn about the path of *Har*,[37] sing *Guru*'s praises and chant the name of *Har*.[38]

Building on the previous Sikh Gurus' practice of the *sat sangat*,[39] Guru Arjan's *Sukhmani* further advances the concept of the *sadh sangat*: While one journeys through life alone at the personal level, the *sadh sangat* gives positive value to the maintenance of a connection with those who are also striving to connect with *Guru*. More specifically, *sadh sangat* connotes the spiritual connectivity of the congregation in the mystical presence of one of the Sikh Gurus or the *Adi Granth*. While the oral recitation of *shabad-Guru* with single-minded attention in the congregation (*sadh sangat*) is regarded as both inspirational and motivational, there is also an important communal component to Guru Arjan's concept of the *sadh sangat*.

Unlike Guru Nanak's use of the word, Guru Arjan expanded the meaning of *sadh sangat* to include *sadhs*, or Sikhs congregating and singing as One in the presence of *Satgur*, in order to connect with *Nam*. On a mystical level, praising *Prabh* as a unified congregation inspirits and imbues one with the characteristics associated with *Prabh* so that one both realizes *Prabh* and breaks free from the ego: 'In the company of the *sadhs*, the fever of ego is no more; In the company of the *sadhs*, all "I am-ness" is driven away' (7.3). When there is dissolution of the ego, there is no difference between the perfected one and the eternal One:

> The *sadhs'* glory is not known to the Vedas,
>   the Vedas only describe what the sages heard.
> Praises about the *sadhs* are above the three qualities;[40]
> Praises about the *sadhs* are present everywhere.
> The *sadhs'* glory has no end;
> The *sadhs'* glory is forever limitless.
> The *sadhs'* glory is the highest of the high;
> The *sadhs'* glory is the greatest of the great.
> The *sadhs'* glory is their own;
> Nanak: There is no difference between the *sadhs* and *Prabh*. (7.8)

The *sadh sangat* not only functions as a vehicle that inspirits the devotee, but given its intricate relation with *Satgur*, it also significantly connects the devotee with *Prabh* or *Sat Purakh*. That is, from the perspective of Sikh doctrine on reality, the *sangat* shares the essence of *Satgur* (see section below on 'The sixth watch: *Sat Purakh*, *Satgur* and a *Sikh*').

For Guru Arjan, this practice of mindful remembrance of *Nam* is enhanced with the support of the *sadh sangat*. And, staying in the company of the *sadhs* has a positive effect on an individual, in that it helps get rid of mental defilements, delusional thinking, ego and pride:

> In the company of the *sadhs*, the face begins to glow;
> In the company of the *sadhs*, all filth is removed.
> In the company of the *sadhs*, pride is erased;
> In the company of the *sadhs*, wisdom appears.
> In the company of the *sadhs*, *Prabh* is immanent;
> In the company of the *sadhs*, everything becomes resolved.
> In the company of the *sadhs*, the jewel of *Nam* is obtained;
> In the company of the *sadhs*, efforts are for the One.
> Can a mortal describe the glory of the *sadh*?
> Nanak: The *sadh's* glory merges with *Prabh*. (7.1)

Along with ridding the ego of defilements and delusions, the practice of keeping the company of the *sadhs* is believed to cure suffering. When in the company of the *sadhs*, one also realizes and obtains the jewel of happiness – *Nam*. The attainment of happiness is expressed through *Nam* possessing the four aims of life (*purusartha*):

> In the company of the *sadhs*, one is firm in *dharam*; (7.4)
>
> In the company of the *sadhs*, wealth is acquired; ...
> In the company of the *sadhs*, all pleasures are within reach;
> Nanak: In the company of the *sadhs*, birth is fruitful. (7.5)

In effect, Guru Arjan redefines the traditional Hindu concepts of the four goals of the individual: (1) social and religious duty (*dharam*), (2) wealth and prosperity (*arth*), (3) pleasure (*kam*) and (4) liberation (*mukti*), by transforming the accomplishment of these goals in the company of the *sadhs*. While some may interpret the above verse literally, the context of the entire hymn suggests its function as a metaphor urging reflection on how the *sadh sangat* is an effective support that inspires the devotee to let go of worldly desires and attain happiness through *Nam simran*. Similarly, while Guru Arjan recognizes various familiar religious figures (like the *vaishnav*, *bhagauti* and *pandit*), he modifies their descriptions so that they fit in with his definition of a *sadh* (9.1–4).

Along with the concept of *sadh sangat*, the third watch begins to describe the material world that all have to journey through. The world is described as comprising different forms of creation and all types of people, although attention is primarily given to those aspiring to enhance their wellness through spiritual awareness:

> The seed mantra imparts wisdom to all,
>   anyone of the four classes can chant the *Nam*.
> Whoever chants shall be saved;
> Only a few obtain [*Nam*] in the company of *sadhs*.
> With blessings, there is concentration within the heart;
> Brutes, ghosts, fools and the stone-hearted will cross over.
> *Nam* is the panacea for all illnesses;
> With good fortune, happiness is obtained by singing praises.
> [*Nam*] cannot be secured through religious ritual;
> Nanak: Received by those whom it was written for in the beginning. (9.5)

Indeed, regardless of one's social standing, *Nam simran* is the practice and the *sadh sangat* is the supportive conduit for those inspirited to recite and remember *Nam* with a pure heart. While the *sadh sangat* is meant to be both inspirational and motivational, one has to still learn how to navigate through the darkness of the material world.

The fourth watch: Navigating the illusions of the material world

The fourth watch of the day (*astapadis* 10–12), or the late afternoon, offers Guru Arjan's outlook on the world. Building on Guru Nanak's position on pursuing liberation while living as a householder (*grahasti*),[41] significantly Guru Arjan provides insights on how to navigate the world that is both diverse and transitory in nature. Guru Arjan describes creation, humans, animals, plants and inanimate objects as embodying different qualities (*gun*), including goodness (*sat*), passion (*raj*) and darkness (*tam*). Just as there are beautiful mountains, creation also consists of dirty and greedy pigs, fierce tigers and evil spirits:

> Many a million live in passion, darkness and purity;
> Many a million are the Vedas, Simritis, Shastras and Puranas.
> Many a million are the pearls created in the ocean;
> Many a million are the various kinds of creatures.
> Many a million are made with long lives;
> Many a million are the hills and beautiful mountains.
> Many a million are the *yakhshas*, *kinnars* and *pisaach*;
> Many a million are the zombies, ghosts, pigs and tigers.
> All are near, all are far.
> Nanak: You are all-pervasive, yet unaffected. (10.4)

Such diversity is all part of *Guru's* worldly drama (*lila*). It is intentionally made by, and under the control of, *Ek Oankar*. Just as *sadhs* sit with their rosary moving one bead at a time, the Creator, too, is at play moving creation: 'All creation is strung on Your thread' (10.3). That is, many a million – whether land, animals or humans – are moving around in a cyclical manner in the web of *sansar*. *Maya* in *Sikhi* should not be confused with the concept of *maya* in Advaita Vedanta (philosophical school of non-dualism), where it refers to the illusory or unreal nature of the material world.[42] Distinctively, in the *Sukhmani*, Guru Arjan uses *maya* to connote the transitory nature of creation even as that creation is real since it is an extension of *Ek Oankar* (17.*salok* and 23.1–8). While creation is the manifest form (*sargun*) of *Ek Oankar*, the Creator also employs vices such as greed (*lobh*) and ego (*ahankar*):

> Many a million have pride;
> Many a million are blinded by ignorance.
> Many a million are stone-hearted misers;

Many a million lack heartfelt empathy.
Many a million steal others' property;
Many a million slander others.
Many a million work hard amid the *maya*;
Many a million wander in foreign lands.
Whatever the placement, so is the engagement;
Nanak: Only the Creator understands the creation. (10.2)

Although creation is transitory, it manifests under the *hukam* or will of *Ek Oankar*. However, humans guided by greed and ego lose sight of the fact that *Ek Oankar* is the true player of creation – not only in terms of what manifests itself in the universe, but also in terms of what happens:

> The One is competent to be the cause of all causes,
>   everything that happens, pleases the One.
> In an instant, there is creation and dissolution,
>   there are no boundaries.
> The *hukam* supports without any other support,
>   *hukam* creates, *hukam* absorbs.
> Through *hukam* there is high and low work;
> Through *hukam* there are countless colours.
> Creating the creation, the One sees Its own greatness;
> Nanak: The One pervades everything. (11.1)

When humans fail to recognize *Ek Oankar* as the true player, they are blinded by the illusions of the world and are bound to *sansar*. On the other hand, those who are aware of the *hukam* of *Ek Oankar* unite with *Nam*:

> Say, what can a person do?
> Whatever delights You will happen.
> If it was in their hands, everything would be taken;
> Whatever delights You will happen.
> The ignorant ones are drawn to poison,
>   if they understood, they would save themselves.
> Misled by doubt, running in ten directions,
>   in an instant, one returns from wandering the four quarters.
> Blessed is the one on whom devotion is conferred,
>   Nanak, such a devotee unites with *Nam*. (11.3)

Since people living in the world may possess good and/or negative qualities, significance does not lie in an individual's particular role. Rather, importance lies in their orientation towards *Ek Oankar*. Just as a dog can be either a greedy scavenger or loyal at the master's feet, some humans can partake of falsehood while others may be imbued with virtue. Indeed, Guru Arjan differentiates those humans who are ego-centred from those who are imbued with the qualities associated with the eternal One, which is most frequently referred to as *Prabh* or *Har*.

Those who are under the influence of their ego (*manmukh*), and distracted by worldly illusions, will be disappointed and suffer in their search for wealth, power and status because these offer only a false sense of permanence. While the *manmukh* is inclined to acquiring power of influence, this inclination provides an illusory sense of empowerment. According to Guru Arjan, humans have very little power or control over the worldly drama (*lila*), whereas true empowerment and contentment comes from the realization of one's own true nature in relation to *Ek Oankar*. That is, instead of journeying through life guided by the ego, one needs to recognize that all that happens is but a manifestation of *Ek Oankar*:

> Power is not in one's own hands,
>   the Cause of all causes is the master of all.
> The helpless live according to Your will,
>   whatever delights You will happen.
> Sometimes the placement is high or low;
> Sometimes anxious or laughing joyfully.
> Sometimes behaviour is slanderous or anxious;
> Sometimes high in the sky or in the nether lands.
> Sometimes discourses about *Braham* are understood;
> Nanak: It is You who unites. (11.5)

In accepting *hukam*, one still has to be familiar with, and be able to navigate, the joys and sorrows of *sansar*, whether it be types of people, experiences, or feelings and the like. Since the universe contains both good and evil, energy and lethargy, beauty and ugliness, one needs to acknowledge and accept mundane existence as such.

In contrast to the *manmukh*, the *gurmukh*, who is guided by the teachings of *shabad-Guru*, steadily gains insight into the world's illusions. Insight into one's true place and role in the universe, such as that *Ek Oankar* is the cause of all causes, engenders contentment. Not only is there acceptance of *Ek Oankar*'s *hukam* in the play of life, but also humility – freedom from pride or arrogance – is an important virtue that helps one attain happiness. In fact, the *salok* for *astapadi* 12 states: 'The humble reside in happiness, "I am-ness" is beneath them, Nanak, very big egos rot in pride.' Humility is a virtue that comes with the awareness of *Nam*, and it carries one across the ocean of *sansar*:

> Becoming wealthy and full of pride,
>   not even a piece of straw will accompany you.
> Putting hope in a large army of men,
>   in an instant they can be destroyed.
> Identifying oneself as more powerful than all others,
>   instantly turning into ashes.
> The egotistical cares for no one,
>   the god of justice will punish such a one.
> Through *Guru's* grace, pride is erased,
>   Nanak, such a devotee is accepted in the heavenly court. (12.2)

One can better navigate the world through humility and by keeping a balanced outlook on the world and life, where the pleasant and adverse aspects of mundane existence are accepted and happiness is not dependent on worldly accomplishments. The awareness of *Nam* allows for the qualities of humility and indifference to guide the *gurmukh* without falling prey to worldly influences:

> Earning a thousand, then running after a hundred thousand,
>   never satisfied, collecting more wealth.
> In illusions, one seeks countless pleasures,
>   never satisfied, dying a disgruntled death.
> Without contentment, no satisfaction, and,
>   as in a dream, all efforts are meaningless.
> Coloured in *Nam*, one attains total happiness,
>   fortunate is whoever obtains this.
> You, Yourself, are the cause of causes;
> Nanak: Forever, forever chant *Har*. (12.5)

While *astapadi* 12 describes human nature and human tendencies in the course of interacting with mundane existence, *astapadis* 12 and 13 also serve as a bridge that transitions the seeker from journeying through the day to travelling during the night. This is achieved by Guru Arjan differentiating between two types of people: those who are guided by their ego and desires (*manmukh*) and those who are connected with *Nam* and imbued with *Ek Oankar* (*gurmukh*). While those who are ego-centred remain dissatisfied and restless, those with humility open up to, and internalize, *Nam* and can attain happiness (*sukh*). In order to regain oneself, one has to journey through the night and connect with *Ek Oankar*.

Four watches of the night (*astapadis* 13–24): The way of the Sikh

The four watches of the night are covered by the last twelve *astapadis*, which provide a critical examination into 'the way of the Sikh'. The four watches of the night include (1) the fifth watch or evening marked by sunset (around 6 pm to 9 pm), (2) the sixth watch or early night (around 9 pm to 12 midnight), (3) the seventh watch or the middle of the night (around 12 midnight to 3 am) and (4) the eighth watch or the hours of the night just before dawn (around 3 am to 6 am). The four watches of the night – when people are sleeping and there is greater peace and fewer distractions – provide the *Sikhi* conception of reality even as it guides the seeker through the Sikh journey towards peace and happiness (*sukh*).

The fifth watch: A balanced view of the world

The fifth watch (*astapadis* 13–15), or the evening, echoes some of the themes contained in the fourth watch, especially Guru Arjan's outlook on the fleeting nature of the material world. Following *astapadi* 12 (which distinguishes the *manmukh* from those imbued with *Prabh*), the bridging *astapadi* 13 focuses entirely on differentiating those who are dissatisfied from those who are blessed. Moreover, Guru Arjan revisits the overarching theme of the entire *Sukhmani* outlined in the first watch: *Nam simran* as the sole means to eliminating the suffering that comes with feeling alone in a dark and cold world.

People are strengthened by the practice of *Nam simran*, because mindful remembrance of *Nam* removes different forms of suffering, like separateness, ego-centredness, physical deprivation and psychological distress (14.3). In order to attain happiness, it is necessary for a person to turn to *shabad-Guru* (*Guru's* words): 'Just as a pillar supports a house, *Guru's shabad* supports the mind.... Just as the lamp turns darkness into light, the mind blossoms upon seeing *Guru*' (15.3). With *Nam* one is able to stabilize the mind and recognize the One:

> The goods you came to purchase,
>   *Ram Nam*, can be attained in *Sant's* [i.e. *Guru's*] home.
> Renounce pride, and receive profit in the mind;
> Imbibe *Ram Nam* within the heart.

> Load the goods, and walk in the company of the *sants*;
> Detach from being entangled in vice.
> Everyone will proclaim you as very blessed,
>> and your face will shine in *Har's* heavenly court.
> Rare is the trader in this trade (i.e. of *Ram Nam*),
>> Nanak, I am a sacrifice to that one. (15.5)

Along with attaining his outlook on the world and people, Guru Arjan also introduces, in the fifth watch, the value of faith (*parteet, biswas*), namely the placing of complete trust or confidence in someone or something. While faith is first mentioned in the second watch of the day, there it pertains merely to how one easily loses a 'false' sense of faith: 'Having and caring for ten possessions, if one possession is withheld, one loses faith (*bikhoot*)' (5.1). On the other hand, the fifth watch (or the first watch of the night) explains how 'true' faith is something to aspire for in the pursuit of happiness:

> The one whose heart has faith (*parteet*) in *Guru*,
>> such a devotee always remembers *Prabh*.
> One is known as a *bhagat* in the three worlds,
>> within whose heart is the One. …
> The one who understands *Parbraham* as the truth,
>> Nanak, such a devotee will be absorbed in the truth. (15.8)

This affirmative understanding of faith – the complete trust and confidence in *Guru* – continues throughout the subsequent watches of the night. For example: 'Nanak: True faith (*biswas*) is acquired from *Guru*' (16.6) and 'In the hearts where there is faith (*biswas*), *Prabh* enters, quintessential wisdom emerges in the mind' (17.2).[43] Indeed, the concept of faith in *Guru* sets the stage for the Sikh journey through the night.

The fifth watch also provides the important message of hope – the confident expectation of fulfilment – amid despair. While hope (*aas*) is mentioned sporadically throughout the *Sukhmani*, it is especially emphasized in the fifth watch. There are two types of hope that are specified: (1) hope in what is false, which will likely prove to be a source of suffering (12.2) and (2) hope in what is true (i.e. *Nam*), which will bring peace (8.4). The fifth watch states that hope in the true One rids us of all suffering:

> Through *Guru's* grace one becomes self-aware;
> Recognize such a one as having extinguished desire.
> In the company of the *sadhs*, *Har* is praised;
> The devotee of *Har* is immune to all illnesses.

> Only the praises [of *Har*] are sung night and day,
> without other desires within the household.
> The devotee who places hope in the One,
> will have the noose of death cut.
> Whose heart is hungry for *Parbraham*,
> Nanak, such a one will not suffer. (14.4)

Indeed, a forward-looking or evolving attitude towards life and the future not only generates courage to overcome hardship and despair, but it also makes room for *Nam*. In order to proceed through the night, one needs hope amid the darkness,[44] as hope provides the vital space for one to open up to the experience of *Sat Purakh*.

The sixth watch: *Sat Purakh*, *Satgur* and the *Sikh*

The sixth watch (*astapadis* 16–18), or the early night, highlights the Sikh perspective on Ultimate Reality, which involves the triadic relation among *Sat Purakh*, *Satgur* and the *Sikh*. In crystallizing and honing the Sikh perspective on Reality, Guru Arjan also provides an explicit description of a Sikh in relation to both *Satgur* and *Sat Purakh*. In fact, the introductory *salok* of *astapadi* 18 states: 'The one who recognises *Sat Purakh* is called *Satgur*; In [*Satgur's*] company, the Sikh is saved by singing the qualities of *Har*' (18.*salok*).

While Guru Arjan introduces *Sat Purakh* (True Being) to connote Ultimate Reality in the sixth watch, *Ek Oankar* (the One creator-creation) only appears in the introductory *salok*. The best way of looking at the Sikh perspective on the true nature of Reality is by way of the *mul-mantar* (root mantra; Skt. *mula-mantra*), which is the preamble attributed to Guru Nanak and found at the beginning of the *Adi Granth*. While the numeral *Ek* in front of *Oankar* denotes the oneness of the Creator and creation, *Oankar* has three aspects or qualities: (1) *akar* (creative), (2) *okar* (sustaining) and (3) *mokar* (dissolving). These three qualities attributed to *Oankar* are regarded as one and the same. *Ek Oankar* is followed in the *mul-mantar* by a listing of the qualities that reflect its essence. The qualities of *Ek Oankar* include truth (*satnam*), creatorship (*karta purakh*), fearlessness (*nirbhau*), without enmity (*nirvair*), timelessness (*akal murat*), self-existing (*ajuni saibang*) and one that is realized by the grace of *Guru* (*gur prasad*).[45] Therefore, while *Ek Oankar* is primarily understood as the formless source of all creation, it is also manifest in all of creation as *sargun*:

> True form, true place;
> Only *Sat Purakh* is in command.

True actions, true word;
Sat Purakh is manifest in all.
True deeds, true creation;
True origin, true burgeoning.
True doing, purest of the pure;
Whoever understands this is conferred with nobility.
Happiness from *Prabh's* true *Nam*.
Nanak: True faith is acquired from *Guru*. (16.6)

This conception of *Ek Oankar* allows reconciliation between the absolute and the finite in *Sikhi*.

While *Sat Purakh* is the term used to denote Ultimate Reality, Guru Arjan also uses many epithets for the latter in order to illustrate the qualities of *Ek Oankar*. As mentioned earlier, *Nam* is not a label or a proper name for Reality, but an ontological category denoting the mystical presence and experience of *Ek Oankar* and its qualities or attributes (*gun*) described in the *mul-mantar*. While *Prabh* (all-pervasive One) and *Har* (omnipresent One) are the most common epithets used in the sixth watch, Guru Arjan also uses other names like *Gobind* (Preserver of the world) (16.1), *Parbraham* (highest Reality) (16.1, 18.3, 18.4) and *Paramesar* (supreme God) (16.1, 18.3). Such epithets are often employed to reflect the contents of the verse. For example, 'in the congregation, the praises of *Ram* are sung, reaching *Parbraham's* court' (18.4), which means *Ram* – permeating throughout all existence – is praised, and these praises reach *Parbraham*, the highest Reality.

As the ineffable One essence, *Sat Purakh* also manifests as *Satgur* (True *Guru*), which can be understood as the embodiment of *Sat Purakh* as in *shabad-Guru*. While *shabad-Guru* is the guiding principle, *Satgur* can also refer to the ten human Sikh Gurus who share the same infinite light as well as to the *Adi Granth*.[46] Indeed, out of respect and reverence, Sikhs refer to Nanak and his nine successors as gurus (spiritual masters). However, their status as *Guru* is based on the belief that each human Guru shares the infinite light of *Satgur*. While the ten human Gurus are considered as *Satgur*, they are not to be worshipped as Ultimate Reality (i.e. *Sat Purakh*). Rather, they are to be revered as the embodiments of *shabad-Guru*:

Rare is the devotee who savours the attainment of *Har*,
    and becomes immortal by drinking nectar.
The devotee's heart shines with the treasure of goodness,
    such a devotee can never be destroyed.
[*Satgur*] has the *Nam* of *Har* throughout the eight watches,
    and gives true teachings to the servant.

> Unstained amid attachment and *maya*,
>> only *Har* is within the heart.
> The blind are enlightened by the lamp,
>> Nanak, doubt, attachment and suffering are destroyed. (18. 6)

Just as the human form of the Sikh Gurus is not to be worshipped as *Sat Purakh*, because it is a medium through which the sacred word or *gurbani* is revealed, the *Adi Granth* is likewise regarded as the scriptural medium that contains *shabad-Guru* and is also not to be worshipped as *Sat Purakh*.

Consistent with his predecessors – who regarded *shabad-Guru* as *Satgur* – Guru Arjan also distinctly links the *sadh sangat* with *Satgur*. Indeed, the doctrine of the *sadh sangat* is further developed here; Guru Arjan views the *sadh sangat* as the congregation of devotees who sing as a collective in the presence of *Satgur* and collectively connect with *Ek Oankar* through the practice of *Nam simran*. As Bhai Gurdas states in the *Varan*:

> The merciful *Satgur* bestows compassion on the home,
>> and the *shabad* of *Nirankar* is heard.
> The realm of birth is embodied in the *sadh sangat*;
> The true throne is formed and saluted.[47]

The *sadh sangat* as a collective is connected through *shabad-Guru*. This connection is also regarded as *Satgur*. The *sadh sangat* is ideally a realm where individual members are not in a state of worldly attachment, even to their own external religious identity. *Nam* is the identity of the *sadh sangat*, in which both the individual and group egos are absent. While ego is often understood at the individual level, Guru Arjan's father – Guru Ram Das – recognizes that the ego is not limited to the individual, but also extends to the collective (i.e. family, clan, religious denomination etc.) with his reference to 'group ego' (*dharra*):

> Some form alliances with friends, children and siblings.
> Some form alliances with in-laws and relatives.
> Some form alliances with governors and chiefs out of selfishness.
> My allegiance is to *Har*, permeating everywhere. (1)
> My allegiance is to *Har*, my only support.
> Other than *Har*, I have no other alliance, I sing countless praises of *Har*. (1) [Pause]
> Those whom you form alliances with will perish.
> You will regret these false alliances.
> Those who earn falsehood will not survive.
> My allegiance is to *Har*, the all-powerful. (2)[48]

While group ego or false attachments result in sorrow and ultimately death in the sea of *sansar*, allegiance to *Har* or *Satgur* provides support and refuge.

Astapadi 18 clearly explains the role of *Satgur* in the life of a *Sikh*. In line with the experiential meaning of the word *Sikh*, a learner or follower of the lived path of learning, Guru Arjan explicitly describes *Satgur* as a guide, teacher and support:

> *Satgur* cares for the *Sikh*,
> > *Guru* always has compassion for the servant.
> The *Sikh's Guru* removes the filth of foul intellect,
> > *Guru's* instruction is to repeat the *Nam* of *Har*.
> *Satgur* breaks the *Sikh's* bondage,
> > *Guru's Sikh* refrains from vice.
> *Satgur* gives the wealth of *Nam* to the *Sikh*,
> > *Guru's Sikh* is fortunate.
> *Satgur* comforts the *Sikh* here and hereafter,
> > Nanak, *Satgur* takes care of the *Sikh's* life. (18.1)

Satgur instructs the *Sikh* to engage in selfless service (*seva*) and to be mindful of *Nam* (*simran*) to attain contentment and enlightenment:

> The *Sikh* who lives in *Guru's* home
> > faithfully obeys *Guru* in the mind.
> Recognizing oneself as nothing,
> > the *Nam* of *Har* is contemplated in one's heart.
> Having given the mind to *Satgur*,
> > the endeavours of such a servant are successful.
> Serving without desire,
> > *Swami* is attained.
> Whosoever You bless,
> > Nanak, such a servant attains *Guru's* intellect. (18.2)

While 'Guru's home' can be interpreted literally as a physical space or *gurdwara*, from a theological perspective it is understood as a spiritual connection with *shabad-Guru* in the mind and heart as well as with the *sadh sangat*. By means of *Satgur* the bonds of duality are broken, and oneness is experienced with *Sat Purakh*. However, while the ultimate goal is of union between a *Sikh* and *Sat Purakh*, the triadic relationship between *Sat Purakh*, *Satgur* and the *Sikh* sets the stage for understanding the various forms of *sukh* specifically and spiritual development more generally.

The seventh watch: The six forms of *sukh*

The seventh watch (*astapadis* 19–21), or the middle of the night, sheds light on the different forms of *sukh*. While the *Sukhmani*'s overarching theme is *Nam* as the panacea for suffering (*dukh*), happiness is not merely the result of removing or overcoming *dukh*. Rather, there are six forms of *sukh* that can be deduced from the *Sukhmani*: (1) pleasure and comfort, (2) physical and mental relief, (3) acceptance, (4) meaningful living, (5) contentment and fulfilment and (6) experience of oneness with *Sat Purakh*. While the text refers to the various forms of *sukh* randomly, for clarity's sake, they are discussed here in this section in ascending order, beginning with the most basic and superficial form of *sukh* and leading up to the more lasting notion of *sukh*.

Guru Arjan's description of the various forms of *sukh* can be seen as reflecting different stages of spiritual development. The first and most basic form of *sukh* is pleasure and comfort, which provides immediate gratification of sensual-pleasures, including the most rudimentary ongoing needs for survival in the face of hunger, thirst and threat to security. While this form of *sukh* involves the meeting of basic survival needs, it can also be regarded as the pleasure derived from the satisfaction of one's desires having been met. In cases where it is ego driven, this form of *sukh* is also considered a source of suffering that further runs the risk of entrapping one in the cycle of vices.[49] Regardless of the nature of the desire, this form of *sukh* is very fleeting in nature. That is, when ego-driven desires are fulfilled, they do not provide a stable or long-lasting sense of happiness or peace.

The second form of *sukh* consists of physical and mental relief. This type of *sukh* refers to the removal or alleviation of any type of distress, whether it be physical ailments like disease and infection or mental affliction, including anxiety or fear. Physical and mental relief is important for acquiring well-being. However, since separation from *Nam* affects both the mind and the body, the cure for existential suffering requires connecting with *Nam*. It is important to note here that there is a difference between relief and maladaptive coping. While relief entails attenuating psycho-emotional stress or distress, maladaptive coping, like overeating or alcohol misuse, only temporarily relieves or reduces stress symptoms, for in the long term it is likely to exacerbate the problem.[50]

The third type of *sukh* is the experience of acceptance, that is, the action of consenting to receive something offered, as in agreeing to follow *Guru's hukam* or will. Thus, one accepts one's life situation instead of living under the influence of one's own attachment to a preferred outcome. In fact, the first six verses of *astapadi* 21 are in the form of rhetorical questions and answers that remind the seeker that experiences like fear and anxiety, along with their opposites, are but two sides of the same coin, all of which emerge from *Sat Purakh*:

> When no form was visible,
>   who performed virtuous or sinful deeds?
> When the Upholder was absorbed in *sunn*,
>   who was one hostile to or against?
> When the qualities of the One were not chanted,
>   who experienced joy or grief?
> When *Parbraham* was all alone,
>   where was attachment and doubt?
> You alone orchestrate Your play,
>   Nanak, there is no other Creator. (21.1)

Acceptance of one's existential situation and the events that occur during one's life are approached with impartiality and equanimity, thus allowing room for the experience of joy, no matter what the outcome. That said, acceptance of one's life situation does not entail resigning to self-deprivation, or neglecting physical ailments and psychological distress, or surrendering to abuse. As aforementioned in Chapter 1, the Sikh Gurus taught that external sources of suffering need to be acknowledged and addressed, as made evident by their social actions, including *langar*, education and speaking out against discriminatory practices. Along with requiring acceptance of *Guru's hukam*, Guru Arjan teaches that one is at the same time accountable for one's actions.[51]

In the case of the first two forms of *sukh*, which relate to the meeting of basic human needs and comfort, *sukh* is experienced more immediately in time but is short-lived. The third form of *sukh* – acceptance of one's life situation – functions as a transitional stage that allows for the cultivation of the last three types of *sukh* (see below), where deeper forms of peace and happiness emerge from being increasingly connected with *Sat Purakh*. In effect, the gradual development of *sukh* is integrated into one's being. That is, *sukh* deepens as one internalizes *Nam* and is imbued with the characteristics of *Sat Purakh*.

The fourth type of *sukh* is meaningful living, with which one experiences happiness (*sukh*) from performing service and noble actions and keeping the company of the *sadhs*:

> The wealth for which you run in the four directions,
>   that wealth can be obtained only in the service of *Har*.

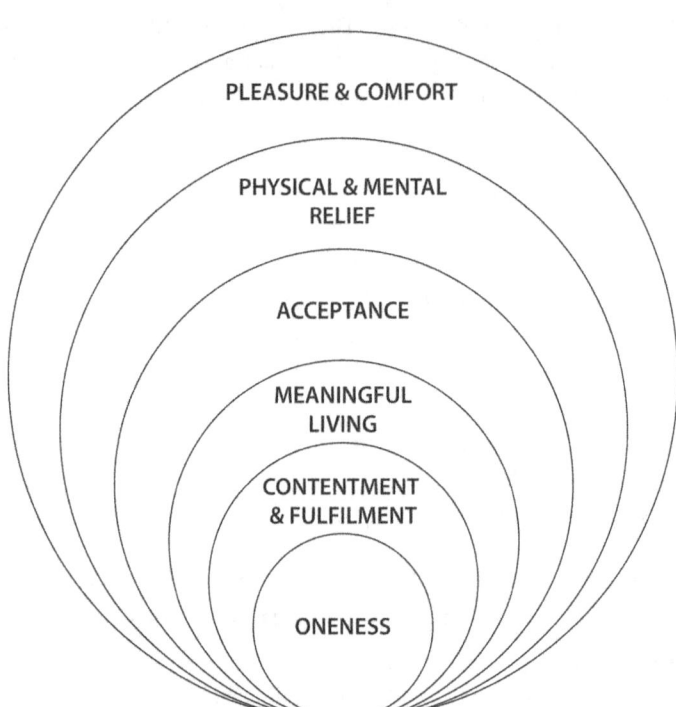

Figure 4.1 The six forms of happiness.

> O friend, the happiness that you always yearn for,
>   that happiness is the love experienced with the *sadhs*.
> The glory of performing noble actions,
>   that glory is in seeking the sanctuary of *Har*.
> Countless remedies cannot make maladies go away,
>   maladies disappear by applying the medicine of *Har*.
> *Nam* is the treasure of all treasures;
> Nanak: Chant and be present in the heavenly court. (19.2)

Of course, 'noble actions' refer to selfless acts that enhance the welfare of humanity (*sarbat da bhalla*), as manifest in one's community or society. With the orientation towards improving the condition of society or the betterment of humanity, the practice of *seva* (selfless service) affects the *gurmukh* by

(1) cultivating compassion and (2) connecting the *gurmukh* to society.[52] As a social being, one has not only the moral responsibility to contribute to society, but the resulting connection with humanity also provides a sense of meaningful living.

The fifth form of *sukh* is the experience of contentment and fulfilment. This experience is most often expressed as a state of not desiring or wanting anything. While the state of not desiring or wanting anything may reflect the mental state in which one has got rid of ego, it may also lead to the experience of completion: 'Be mindful, mindful, and attain everlasting happiness. Fear is destroyed, and aspirations are fulfilled, with loving devotion, there is enlightenment' (19.3). And, the more one is content and fulfilled, the more one may inspire or help others in need.

The sixth and highest form of *sukh* is the peace and happiness that comes with the experience of oneness with *Sat Purakh*. This unifying experience and connection with *Sat Purakh* also involves transcending duality or a dualistic mode of thinking:

> The servant's aspirations are fulfilled,
>   when *Satgur* bestows pure intellect. ...
> Cutting off bondage, the devotee is liberated,
>   suffering and duality of birth and death vanish.
> Wishes are fulfilled, and faith is complete,
>   always in the company of the omnipresent One.
> The devotee is reunited and belongs to the One,
>   Nanak, with devotion, one merges with *Nam*. (20.3)

In the highest form of *sukh*, one experiences the dissolution of 'me' and 'I' while engaging in selfless service for the betterment of humanity. It is commonly believed that once *sadhs* have attained the highest state, they are susceptible to slowly withdrawing from worldly responsibilities and humanitarian efforts, and becoming disconnected from the world. To sit alone in an absorbed state of tranquillity is, however, discouraged in the Sikh tradition. Rather, the *sadh* is required to be dispassionate about, and detached from, material endeavours while at the same time working for the betterment of humanity. That is, a *sadh* practises 'detached engagement'.

The three latter types of *sukh* are more reflective of joy and peace being integrated into one's being, especially since they are directly the result of connecting with *Nam*. In addressing both the individual and social dimensions of life, Guru Arjan illustrates the importance of transcending dualities. Indeed, life is simultaneously both bitter and sweet. Transcending duality also includes transcending the duality of *dukh* and *sukh*. That is, lasting happiness is attained when one accepts or transcends the existential reality of both *dukh* and *sukh* so that they are experienced as alike. While the various meanings of *sukh* reflect the stages of spiritual development, they also point to the ingredients of wellness and happiness.

The eighth watch: The Sikh formula for happiness

The eighth watch (*astapadis* 22–24) – the hours of the night just before dawn (*amrit-vela*) – is revered as the most mystical time of the day-night cycle. As the final watch, it leads to a new day, which can also be metaphorically understood as a 'new beginning'. While the eighth watch may be viewed as summing up the overarching teachings of the entire composition, it also underscores the ingredients of happiness. That is, participating in the *sadh sangat* inspires one to perform service (*seva*) and to be mindful of *Nam* (*simran*), all of which are the constituents of *sukh*.

Continuing the Sikh practices of *seva* and *simran*, Guru Arjan also includes the personal and community dimensions of the *sadh sangat* in the pursuit of *sukh*. In doing so, he underscores how the *sadh sangat* serves as a 'launching pad' for the way of the Sikh. In effect, with the inspiration of the *sadh sangat*, spiritual practice begins with *seva*, the act of selfless service:

> *Seva* is a blessing, the servant is accepted,
>> the Chief knows the hearts of all.
>
> Within whose heart resides the One, such a one will flourish,
>> and death will not come.
>
> The servant attains the eternal state,
>> Nanak, concentrate on *Har* in the company of the *sadhs*. (22.8)

Seva in the *sadh sangat* fosters the spirit of compassion. In turn, the *sadh sangat* serves as an inspirational and strengthening medium through which happiness can be attained. As Bhai Gurdas explains:

> *Gursikhs* inspire a *gursikh* to serve;
> Serving the *sadh sangat*, the fruit of happiness is obtained.
> By dusting and spreading out the carpets, one is cleansed of the dirt.
> Empty pots are filled with water,
>> and sacred food is distributed and eaten.[53]

With selfless service, the ego slowly begins to lose its grip on the mind. As the mind becomes free and untainted by mental defilements, one is able to enshrine the teachings of *Satgur* within the heart and experience *Nam* as a member of the *sadh sangat*:

> Join the company of the *sadhs*, and experience bliss,
> > sing the praises of *Prabh*, the supreme bliss.
> Contemplate the essence of *Ram Nam*,
> > and save this precious body.
> Sing the praises of *Har*, the ambrosial words,
> > in this way, the soul swims across [*sansar*].
> Throughout the eight watches, when you see *Prabh* near,
> > ignorance will be removed and darkness will dissipate.
> Listen to the teachings, and enshrine them in the heart,
> > Nanak, obtain the fruit of your heart's desire. (22.5)

Along with *seva*, congregating with the *sadhs* to collectively practise the mindful remembrance of *Nam* unites one with *Sat Purakh*:

> The devotee is attached to the *Nam* of *Har*,
> > such a one's aspirations will not go in vain.
> For the servant, service is the purpose,
> > understanding *hukam*, the supreme state is attained.
> Nothing higher can be contemplated,
> > in whose heart where *Nirankar* resides.
> Bondage is broken, and enmity is gone,
> > *Guru's* feet are worshipped night and day.
> Happiness in this world, and joy in the next,
> > Nanak, *Prabh* unites the devotee unto Itself. (22.4)

This unifying experience with *Sat Purakh* results in *sukh*, where the mind and body are at ease and the heart is content. And, with the dissolution of ego, grace is experienced as the continuous flow of *Guru's* mercy and compassion. Consistent with Guru Nanak's perspective about ego-renunciation in the larger context of

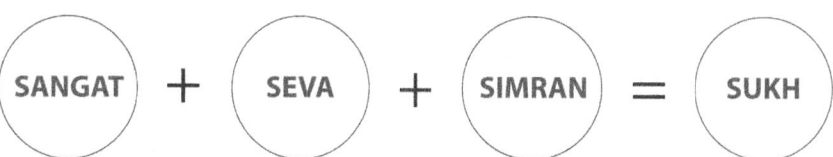

Figure 4.2 The Sikh formula of happiness.

social involvement, Guru Arjan teaches 'detached engagement'. Having attained the highest form of *sukh*, one performs noble deeds while living in the world. As Bhai Gurdas states:

> *Gursikh jogis* are awake and detached amid the *maya*.
> *Guru's mantar* is their earrings, and the dust of the *sants'* feet is the ashes.
> Forgiveness is their worn-out blanket, love their begging bowl, and devotion their food.
> *Shabad* awareness is their conch shell, wisdom their staff, and serving *Guru* their concentration.
> Seated in the *sadh sangat* is their *Guru's* cave, where they reside immersed in profound tranquility.
> The disease of ego is cured, and they are released from union and separation.
> *Guru's* wisdom is applauded in the *sadh sangat*.[54]

In order to maintain peace and joy, one needs to continue the practice of *sangat*, *seva* and *simran* in the play of life. When there is no ego involvement, there is no actor in the performance of noble actions. Rather, there is only effortless effort and goodness. That is, the realized one experiences that one is not the doer (*karta*), but rather one through whom action is done (*kita*). There is only action. A very rare quality.

The congregation of the *sadhs*

In the *Sukhmani*, Guru Arjan's conception of Ultimate Reality (i.e. *Sat Purakh*) supports his doctrinal and organizational contributions to the Sikh Panth. That is, the *sadh sangat* functions as both a conduit for spiritual development and a vehicle to strengthen the community aspect of the Panth. In describing the *sadh sangat* as an extension of *Satgur*, Guru Arjan advances Sikh doctrine on the triadic relationship between *Sat Purakh*, *Satgur* and a *Sikh*. In addition, Guru Arjan also built the Harmandar Sahib and other centres networked through the *masand* system and compiled the initial *Adi Granth*, all of which are central in terms of the Sikh practice of *sadh sangat*. Bhai Gurdas acknowledges Guru Arjan's contribution not only as building the actual Sikh centres to house *shabad-Guru* (Guru's words) but also in terms of developing the role of the *sadh sangat*:

> The light of his father, grandfather and forefathers is within Guru Arjan.
> The throne was attained through the trade of *shabad* awareness.

The treasure of *gurbani*, *kirtan* and *katha* imbues one with love.
Attuned to the unstruck vibration, ambrosial love is savoured.
The *sadh sangat* is *Guru's* assembly, where jewels and gems are traded.
The flag hoisted in [Guru Arjan's] true court was attained with strength and esteem.
[His] rule is eternal and indescribable.[55]

Certainly, the *sangat* forged a communal identity even as it emerged as a critical institution that was placed under the stewardship of the *masand* system. And, just as the *masand* network spread throughout Punjab and beyond, so did the closely knit system of *sangats*,[56] thus consolidating the expanding Sikh Panth and bolstering its economic base.

While the *sadh sangat* is a central concept described in the *Sukhmani*, *sadh* should not be misunderstood as a special status given to an individual Sikh who is part of the *sangat*. In fact, Guru Arjan ends the *Sukhmani* with a clear and concise explanation about the constituents of a *sadh*:

In the mind where the love of listening to *Nam* resides,
    that devotee continuously remembers *Prabh*.
The sufferings of birth and death end,
    and this precious body is instantly saved.
One's fame is pure, one's words are ambrosial,
    the mind is only absorbed with *Nam*.
Suffering, illness, fear and doubt have disappeared,
    one is called a *sadh*, performing pure action.
Such a one has the most exalted fame,
    Nanak, with these qualities, *Nam* is *Sukhmani*. (24.8)

In providing a definition of the *sadh*, Guru Arjan leaves no room for confusion. While the concept of the *sadh sangat* refers to the congregation of the *sadhs*, a *sadh* is specifically one who – through the mindful remembrance of *Nam* – is connected with *Sat Purakh*. In connecting with *Sat Purakh*, the *sadh* is imbued with the qualities of *Prabh*, where suffering disappears and actions are pure. *Satgur's* light both lifts the veil of ignorance and exposes the ego and its clever schemes. In effect, *Guru's* light guides the *sadh* across the ocean of *sansar*. And the way of the *sadh* or Sikh becomes a beacon of hope for others in search of light amid the darkness. Indeed, Guru Arjan's spiritual and communal understanding of the *sadh sangat* serves as a bridge between his contributions to the doctrinal advance and institutional development of the Sikh Panth.

Summary

The *Sukhmani* is a poem that has been creatively composed not only to inculcate the Sikh worldview, but also to guide the seeker in experiencing the non-duality of *dukh* and *sukh*. Through the eight watches of the day-night cycle, the *Sukhmani* guides the seeker in experiencing the journey towards spiritual development. As one reads through the 'watches of the day', one attains insight into the source of suffering (*dukh*) even as the poem provides the 'sign posts' of practices that can help one navigate through the diverse and transient nature of the material world. The 'watches of the night', on the other hand, guide the seeker in experiencing *Nam* even as the poem inculcates 'the way of the Sikh' towards meaningful living and happiness (*sukh*).

Not only does the *Sukhmani* provide insights into eliminating suffering and into the pursuit of wellbeing and happiness, but it further advances *Sikh* doctrine. First, Guru Arjan provides a community dimension to his understanding of the *sadh sangat* as a place where people collectively chant. Second, he clearly relates *sadh sangat* to being an extension of *Satgur*, that is, a medium through which one can experience *Sat Purakh*. Third, Guru Arjan lucidly expounds on the dynamic relationship of *Sat Purakh*, *Satgur* and a *Sikh*, in which he underscores how a Sikh performs noble actions, like *sangat*, *seva* and *simran*, in a state of 'detached engagement' while joyfully living amid the world's illusions. In line with his pragmatic character, Guru Arjan's values can be put into daily practice for meaningful living, the focus of the next chapter.

5

A path towards meaningful living

The quest for happiness has been the subject of profound enquiry since time immemorial. From the Athenian philosophers in the West to Confucius in the East, humanity as a whole has endeavoured to understand the constituents of a good life and the means to attain happiness.[1] In the Indian subcontinent, religious texts, such as the *Bhagavad Gita* and the *Dhammapada*, offer insights about the existential quest for meaning, purpose and happiness.[2] Similarly, Guru Arjan's *Sukhmani* provides the Sikh perspective on what makes people happy and how people can lead meaningful and fulfilling lives. In fact, the term *Sikhi* (experiential or lived path of learning) – the original Punjabi word to refer to the traditions established by the Sikh Gurus – reveals the religion's purpose as providing a path for seekers.[3] This orientation towards offering a path for seekers is a distinguishing characteristic of the religious traditions born out of the Indian subcontinent, as opposed to the salvation-oriented religions born out of West Asia, like Christianity and Islam.[4]

Given the nature of Indic religions, their perspectives on happiness and well-being are grounded in spirituality. In fact, Indic traditions generally differentiate between two main sources of happiness: (1) extrinsic, the fulfilment of desires and the avoidance of displeasure or suffering and (2) intrinsic, the spiritual experience of oneness as a result of transcending the ego.[5] While the former source is regarded as fleeting or impermanent, the latter source is considered essential to the attainment of happiness and the cultivation of wellness. Modern understandings of happiness, on the other hand, emphasize the mental and emotional dimensions of the human condition.[6] According to modern psychology, including positive psychology, happiness involves meaningful engagement, an optimistic outlook and pleasant emotions, accompanied by the understanding that life comes with its ups and downs.[7]

The terms 'happiness' and 'wellness' are used interchangeably. However, there are subtle differences. While happiness is the emotional experience of optimism and fulfilment, wellness refers to the state of being well.[8] Indeed, wellness is a multidimensional concept that reflects the interconnections of physical, mental and social well-being that goes beyond the modern definition of health.[9] Given its process of enhancing awareness about, and making choices towards, a healthy and meaningful life, wellness includes choices and activities intended for attaining (1) physical vitality, (2) mental acuity, (3) social satisfaction, (4) a sense of accomplishment and (5) personal fulfilment.[10]

Wellness studies differ from the medical model in that, while the latter focuses on pathology, the former is centred on well-being. Although wellness studies do not ignore suffering, they do not exclusively focus on disease, disorder and distress. Rather, wellness studies aim to enhance balance and fulfilment amid the ups and downs of life. Such an approach can serve as a bridge between Western helping professionals and various Asian communities as it lends itself to a more holistic approach to well-being.

On the other hand, the Western model of psychiatric illness and mental health is premised on a mind–body dichotomy, and a rigid adherence to a classification system that separates psychology, religion, medicine and spirituality.[11] Since South Asian culture traditionally integrates the different disciplines to form a more synergistic system, its understanding of happiness and wellness has to be understood from both a holistic and a spiritual framework. For practising Sikhs, the *Sukhmani* offers a holistic approach to alleviate suffering as well as to make people happier and to live healthier and more meaningful lives.

That said, this chapter explores how *Sikhi* addresses the existential problem of suffering and the pursuit of happiness from within the tradition itself. In doing so, it highlights Sikh wellness concepts and healing practices, along with the overlap of Sikh teachings with Western psychotherapy. In the light of the Sikh view of both the person and the source of distress and suffering, this chapter delineates the *Sukhmani*'s teachings about the human pursuit of happiness or 'the way of the *brahamgiani* (the enlightened one)', which is grounded in the spiritual dimension of the human condition. In doing so, the chapter examines the *Sukhmani*'s pragmatic teachings in terms of their therapeutic value in helping seekers or adherents to improve their physical, mental, emotional and spiritual well-being. Lastly, the chapter compares Sikh teachings with existential psychotherapy with respect to the human condition and the alleviation of suffering.

Before examining the therapeutic aspects of the *Sukhmani*, it is necessary to first explore the Sikh perspective on the multi-layered person and the nature of psychological distress.

The multi-layered person

According to Sikh cosmology, the entire universe both emerges from and revolves around *Ek Oankar* (the One creator-creation). Indeed, *Ek Oankar* resounds and permeates throughout all of creation. *Ek Oankar* is not separate from, or governing over, creation, but is rather interwoven within it, like how the dancer is fully present in dance. All existence flows from *Ek Oankar*, where its formless form creates, sustains and dissolves. The human body is viewed as the microcosm of the universe. That is, the body is contained in the universe, and the universe is contained in the body.[12] Just as *Ek Oankar* is at the centre of creation, *Ek Oankar* resounds deep within the sacred space of each and every human being.

Sikhi regards human life as a precious gift as it has the inherent capacity to introspect and to peel away the outer layers of human existence and discover *Nam*. At the core of the human person lies the *atma*, which shares the same qualities as those of *Ek Oankar*, including the fact that it has no form, shape, colour or gender. As it pertains to human life, *Nam* is also referred to as the *atma* (eternal soul or self), which is metaphorically described as a ray of light (i.e. creation) from the sun (i.e. creator). The eternal soul is understood as

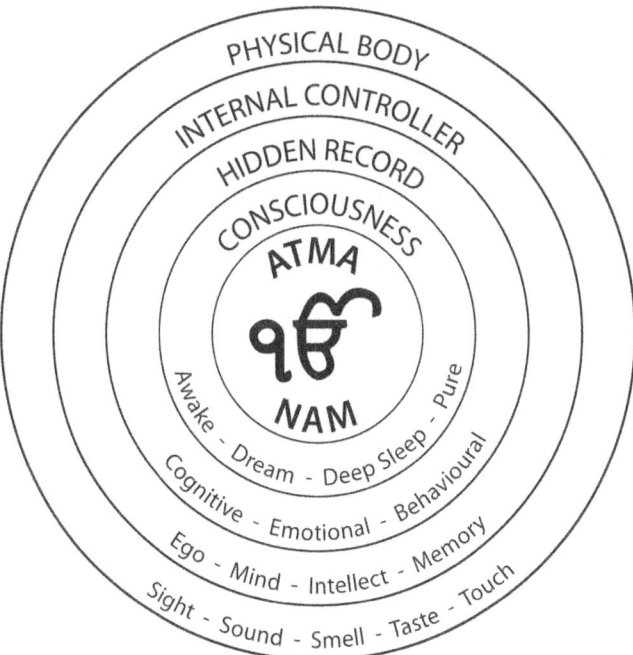

Figure 5.1 The multi-layered person.

impersonal because it is ultimately part of the cosmic essence of *Ek Oankar*. And, it is through the *atma* that *Nam* or the sound of *Ek Oankar* resounds. This core is clothed with an outer psychic and physical dress. From the innermost to the outermost layer, the multi-layered person consists of (1) consciousness (*chit*), (2) the hidden record (*chitr gupt*), (3) the internal controller (*antahkaran*) and (4) the physical body (*sarir*).[13]

Chit (consciousness, awareness or memory) is regarded as the dynamic sphere of awareness. There are four different conscious states, including the awake state (*jagrat*), the dream state (*supan*), the deep-sleep state (*sushupti*) and the fourth or pure consciousness state (*turiya avasta*).[14] The first three states of consciousness relate to the mind (*man*), whereas the fourth state pertains to the transpersonal realm of experience. During the awake state, the mind collects information about the material world through the sense organs. While the sense and motor organs are at rest during the dream state, the impressions engraved on the hidden record during the awake state give rise to dreams. In the deep-sleep state, the mind is in a state of absolute stillness. As there are no thoughts or dreams, consciousness gradually experiences *Nam* resonating from the core of one's being. The deep-sleep state leads to the fourth state, wherein consciousness is totally immersed in *Ek Oankar*. This fourth state or pure consciousness is metaphorically referred to as a jewel because its attainment is rare. In fact, the masses are generally considered to be in a slumber state of awareness, where consciousness is subconsciously influenced by the hidden record (*chitr gupt*) and under the grip of the internal controller (*antahkaran*).

The hidden record (*chitr gupt*) is regarded as the subconscious sphere, which stores cognitive, emotional and behavioural impressions (*sanskar*) that have accumulated both in the past and in current life.[15] Impressions imprinted on the hidden record in previous life forms are more instinctual in nature. For instance, infants with no experience of depth are reluctant to explore near the edge of a cliff. This instinctive knowledge about the dangers of cliffs has been imprinted on the hidden record from previous life forms. In addition, physical traits and psycho-social behaviour that fall outside the spectrum of cultural norms are commonly understood from the framework of past life impressions manifesting themselves in the present birth. This approach is similar to the Western study of human genetics, wherein individual differences are attributed to genetic predispositions.[16]

The hidden record in the present birth acquires three types of impressions: mental (*mansakh*), verbal (*vashakh*) and physical (*sarirak*).[17] Every thought, word and physical action creates an impression on the hidden record, which in turn leads to further experiences and behaviours that match the original ones. The accumulation of impressions on the hidden record makes it difficult for a person to think, feel and behave in any other manner. As a result, the person is bound by habitual behavioural consequences or *karam* (Skt. *karma*). This view of causality is seen as a function of the cosmic order or *hukam*. That said, while the Sikh perspective on *karam* indicates importance given to accountability for one's actions, there is, however, an intricate relationship between effort and *Guru's* grace. As Bhai Gurdas explains, 'By taking a single step towards *Guru*, *Satgur* takes a million steps to receive you.'[18] Both effort and grace are necessary to proceed in the spiritual journey. While grace emboldens the adherent to make effort along the spiritual journey towards selfless effort, it is when the ego is completely dissolved that one experiences the flow of grace as continuous. Having said that, the Sikh view of causality allows for the person to wipe away the karmic debris on the hidden record by awakening consciousness and controlling the ego.

The internal controller (*antahkaran*) is comprised of four parts: (1) mind (*man*), (2) memory (*chit*), (3) intellect (*buddhi*) and (4) ego (*ahankar*).[19] The mind is often portrayed as a wanderer because it is easily distracted by the colours, sounds, tastes, smells and textures of the phenomenal world. The mind or the general thinking faculty is the receptacle that organizes sense impressions into precepts and stores them in memory. Knowledge arises from the intellect and the experiences that arise out of the ego. The intellectual aspect of the internal controller functions to bring about certainty and definitiveness in knowledge that come from either discriminative intellect (*bibek buddhi*) or self-centred thinking (*aham buddhi*).

Of the four parts of the internal controller, the ego or 'I' (*ahankar*) is the most dominating, as a result of which it falsely experiences the phenomenal world as its own. The ego in the Sikh perspective should not be confused with the ego in the Freudian psychoanalytical discipline, where it functions as a mediator between the conscious and the unconscious. Quite distinctively, in the Sikh perspective, the ego creates a fixed sense of identity based on worldly roles and persistently tries to distinguish itself from others. Indeed, the ego in *Sikhi* is viewed as an obstacle to the intrinsic form of happiness. Unable to recognize the impermanent nature of the phenomenal world, the ego struggles for permanence in life. As Guru Arjan expounds:

> That which is passing is believed to be permanent,
>   the inevitable is recognized as far away.
> Working hard for that which will be left behind,
>   and letting go of inner support. (4.4)

When under the grip or misguidance of the ego, people endure chronic suffering as they anxiously run away from sources of stress and seek solace from transitory pleasures.

The outer shell of the person is the body (*sarir*), which is regarded as ephemeral in nature. And, when the last breath departs, the body merges back into the five original elements (Skt. *panch tattva*) – ether, air, fire, water and earth.[20] Therefore, without the breath, the body is a lifeless corpse. The breath (*pran*) is the life-force energy that allows the heart to beat, giving life to every cell of the body. It is for this reason that meditation practices often involve the breath as the focus or object of meditation. The Sikh Gurus cherished every breath as a precious gift, and encouraged mindfulness towards both the breath and the Creator who supports it. As Guru Arjan explicates, 'The jewel of human birth will be saved; Being mindful of *Har* supporting the breath' (19.4).

The distress cycle

In the Sikh view, the primary source of distress or suffering arises from the ego's desire to be a permanent entity that is separate from others. Suffering or *dukh* (Skt. *duhkha*) literally means the space in which distress is experienced. Mental and bodily spaces become distressed when the mind is directionless and is lured by the ego. It is for this reason that the Sikh Gurus' teachings primarily focus on the mind and treat the mind like a friend, child or fool in need of guidance.[21] The mind struggles with befriending consciousness because it involves an inner journey in which undesirable impressions on the hidden record have to be confronted. Therefore, the mind runs the risk of becoming easily swayed by worldly distractions and falling prey to the five thieves (*panj chor*). Guru Arjan describes the five thieves in the *Sahaskriti saloks* as:[22]

> O attachment, knowing no defeat,
>   you crush the bravest warriors.
> You captivate soldiers, gods, people,
>   animals, birds and beasts.
> Salutations to the cause of all,
>   Nanak seeks refuge in *Jagdish*. (45)
>
> O lust, you place mortals in hell,
>   making them wander through many births.

You rob consciousness and pervade the three worlds,
> destroying chanting, austerity and virtue.

The pleasure you give is short-lived,
> making the poor weak,
> as you pervade among the high and low.

Your fear is removed in the company of *sadhs*,
> Nanak seeks shelter in *Narayan*. (46)

O anger, the root of all strife,
> kindness does not arise in you.

The foul-minded are under your control,
> making them dance like monkeys.

People are degraded in your company,
> and punished by the messenger of death.

O merciful *Prabh*, the destroyer of suffering,
> Nanak prays for all to be saved. (47)

O greed, the mighty drown in your company,
> and your waves assault them.

You make them run, wavering
> unsteadily in their ways.

You have no respect for friends, mystics,
> relatives, mothers or fathers.

You favour that which should not be done,
> eaten or accomplished.

Help, help! Nanak seeks refuge
> in *Swami's* sanctuary. (48)

O ego, the root of birth and death,
> you are the very soul of sin.

Friends are abandoned, enemies are made stronger,
> and illusions are spread.

You cause exhaustion through birth and death,
> giving both suffering and pleasure.

You guide one to wander fearfully in the forest of doubt,
> where one contracts harsh incurable diseases.

The only physician is *Parbraham Paramesar*,
> Nanak meditates on *Har Har Hare*. (49)[23]

Guru Arjan spares the mind by calling out the ego as the source of sin and suffering. These five thieves are similarly listed in the *Sukhmani* as lust (*kam*), anger (*karodh*), greed (*lobh*), attachment (*moh*) and ego (*ahankar*) (*Sukhmani* 6, salok).²⁴ Sikh *gianis* in *gurdwara* sermons describe the five thieves as robbing and assaulting the mind in a cyclical manner.²⁵ They advise that the list of five thieves in the *Sukhmani* can be better understood if read backwards. That is, the distress cycle originates with the ego and is then followed by its companions of attachment, greed, anger and lust.

The ego seeks to fulfil certain core needs. Depending on the nature of the person, these needs can range from humanistic (i.e. security, love, respect and freedom) to materialistic (i.e. wealth, status, power and fame). To satisfy these needs, the ego relies upon worldly roles where each role has a prescribed script for accomplishing its goals. Over time, the ego consolidates the various roles to create a fixed sense of identity and aims to validate and assert itself in the world. Success and happiness are measured by the fulfilment of the aforementioned needs. This understanding of the ego goes beyond that of the stereotypical interpretation of it where the man is merely seen as greedy and lustful, while the woman is seen as obsessed with beauty and youthfulness. That is to say, even the humanistic needs can be a function of the ego and, when these needs are not fulfilled, they too become a source of distress.

The ego (*ahankar*) attempts to fulfil its core needs by first being attached (*moh*) to the needs in and of themselves, and then becoming attached to the

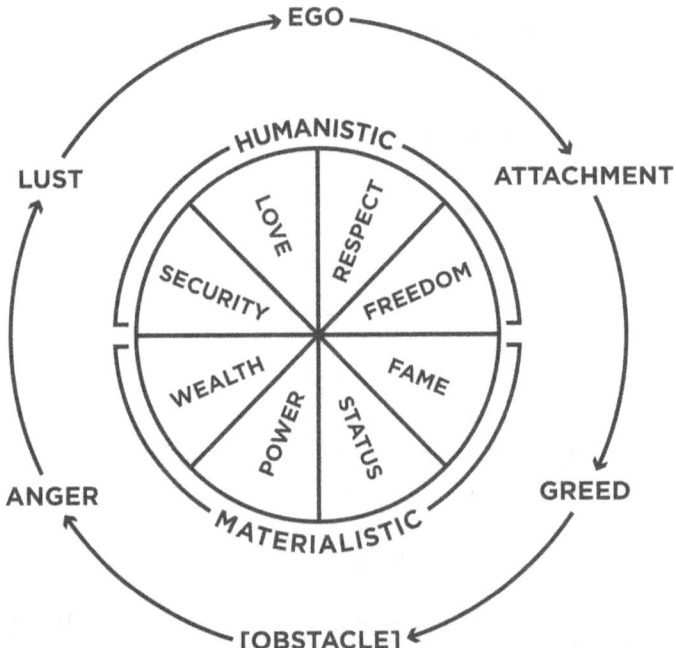

Figure 5.2 The distress cycle.

people, places, things and activities that can fulfil those needs. As the attachment intensifies, it transforms into greed (*lobh*), which is the unquenchable desire to possess and control. However, the desire to possess and control is almost always beset with obstacles that block the ego from fulfilling its core needs. These obstacles inevitably lead to anger (*karodh*), where the mind is impulsive and the body is agitated. Anger manifests itself on a spectrum ranging from internalized anger to anger expressed verbally and physically. Internalized anger results in doubt and depression in which there is lower self-esteem, whereas externalized anger involves blaming and lashing out at the obstacles perceived to be blocking the fulfilment of core needs. The expression of anger is influenced by a person's nature, which in turn is influenced by the impressions on the hidden record.

To subdue this anger, the ego resorts to lustful indulgence (*kam*), such as gratuitous sex, mood-altering substances, gambling, food and other forms of sensory excess. Satisfying the craving associated with lust is short-lived as the ego, along with attachment, greed and anger, resumes its quest for permanence through the fulfilment of the core needs. As a consequence, the mind, controlled by the ego (*ahankar*), remains habitually caught in the cycle of distress where exposure to anxiety-producing situations leads to a generalized condition of anxiety. The *Sukhmani*'s explanation of the source of anxiety or worry (*chinta*) is twofold: it is either described as (1) being the result of attachment of the ego to a preferred outcome or (2) the symptom of a profound existential separation from *Nam*:

> Performing a million actions, but in ego,
>   anxiety results from such efforts.... (12.3).

And again:

> Humans make a lot of effort,
>   but these efforts are done out of anxiety.... (17.5)

The understanding of anxiety as an underlying symptom of human suffering is consistent with contemporary research on how an anxious temperament is an important predictor of mental disorders.[26] Moreover, anxiety can also elevate the stress hormone cortisol,[27] which may increase the risk of bodily ailments and slower recovery due to lowered immune functioning.[28] Essentially, the ego's anxious desire to fulfil its core needs results in mental and physical distress, where the person is trapped in a roller-coaster ride of emotions ranging from excitement to despair.[29]

While the *Sukhmani* acknowledges that these ups and downs are an inevitable part of life, it offers practical guidance to help engage the seeker or adherent in an active process of being aware of *Nam* and living a balanced, healthy and meaningful life. Moreover, the karmic (genetic and behavioural) influences on temperament are not considered immutable, since – according to the Sikh perspective on wellness – humans also possess the resilience to break free from self-defeating behavioural patterns.

The way of the *brahamgiani*

Happiness in the Sikh tradition is not merely a mental or emotional state of well-being which is influenced by positive or pleasant emotions ranging from comfort to joy. Rather, it also involves the transpersonal experience, during which the 'I' or ego (*ahankar*) is dissolved and the eternal resonance flowing from *Ek Oankar* extinguishes desire and brings about sweetness to life. This sweetness is savoured by the *brahamgiani* (enlightened one) amid the joys and sorrows of human existence. As the *Sukhmani* states, '*Brahamgiani* is eternally unstained, just as the lotus remains clean in [muddy] water' (8.1). Drawing upon the way of the *brahamgiani*, the discussion below delineates key healing practices and character strengths that can be of therapeutic benefit to the adherent's wellness.

Simran: Mindful remembrance of *Nam*

Nam as the panacea for human suffering is the key teaching that Guru Arjan expounds throughout the *Sukhmani*. As the panacea for suffering, *Nam* or the spiritual experience of *Ek Oankar* can be achieved with the practice of *Nam simran*. As mentioned in the previous chapter, the word *simran* is derived from the Sanskrit verb root *smr*, which literally means to remember or to bring back to attention. Remembrance is therefore not merely a mental exercise where adherents construct a cognitive schema of *Ek Oankar* from their intellect. Rather, adherents are encouraged to be mindful of the experience of *Ek Oankar* at the present moment. *Simran* involves the mind and body being fully engaged in the practice of mindful remembrance. However, this is easier said than done as the mind has to both bear witness to the many impressions accumulated on the hidden record and resist being enticed by the ego. Prior to the practice of *simran*, adherents are often advised to first sit at the edge of their inner world of experiences and to simply observe.

For many, observing the karmic debris on the hidden record can be overwhelming and may feel like a form of punishment, such as solitary confinement. To help adherents look within, they can use simple breathing exercises, which are commonly found in pan-Indian spiritual traditions like *pranayama* yoga (the discipline of the breath or life force) or *vipassana* meditation (Buddhist meditation for insight). In the Sikh tradition, the human body is metaphorically described as a musical instrument that the Creator infuses with the breath or life force energy.[30] Breathing is a natural process, but becomes disrupted when the mind is anxious and the body is agitated.

A simple breathing technique is to let go of the notion that 'I am breathing' and to let breathing just happen, when the inhalations and exhalations through the nostrils or the rise and fall of the navel are mindfully observed. Adherents are advised not to cling or react to the various thought waves that emerge during meditation. Rather, adherents should let those distractions pass without judgement or reactivity, especially since these thought waves stem from the ego's wants, worries, regrets and/or resentments. As the mind becomes more stable and still, the adherent can slowly venture within to observe the karmic debris, all the while using the mindful breathing technique as an anchor.

It is here that the adherent gains insight into how one is bound by habitual behavioural patterns (*karam*) and how one can break free from karmic debris. The hidden record is like a glass window while karmic debris is the dirt that accumulates on it over time, thus making the home of the mind and body a dark dwelling place. *Simran* is the solution that wipes away the karmic debris and allows for the resonance of *Ek Oankar* to vibrate within the mind and body. Similarly, *kirtan* (singing of praise) can also benefit mental and physical wellness.

Kirtan

As mentioned in Chapter 3, *gurbani-kirtan* is believed to tune the mind into the resonance of the sacred words. In re-creating the sacred sound of the Sikh Gurus, *gurbani-kirtan* aids adherents to connect with *shabad-Guru* or *Nam* flowing from *Ek Oankar*. In addition to being a form of Sikh religious worship, *kirtan* can also be of therapeutic benefit when performed according to the classical Indian music system of *rag*. In fact, there have been several medical studies on the calming effect and/or healing quality of listening to classical

Indian *rag* music. For instance, in a 2012 medical study, classical Indian music therapy was shown to have effectively reduced intraoperative stress related to cardiopulmonary bypass surgery (as evidenced in a decrease in cortisol levels), resulting in a reduction in the requirement for drugs (such as Fentanyl, Propofol and Vecuronium).[31]

Furthermore, a 2014 medical study of forty patients, who had been diagnosed with clinical depression, found that there was a significant decrease in the level of depression with classical Indian music therapy.[32] Lastly, a 2015 study on the relationship between *rag* and emotional responses to it among 122 participants – recruited online from across the world – found that the various *rags* used in the study had marked distinct emotional responses,[33] ranging from happy and calm to tense and sad. Overall, the *rags* had a calming effect on the participants, while unpleasant emotions, such as anger, remained low in the participants.

The use of the emotive qualities of *rag* for healing is an example of the holistic nature of Eastern therapeutic approaches. That is, such treatment is not limited to cognitive interventions that refute irrational thoughts and beliefs, but it also involves giving serious consideration to the role of emotions in human behaviour. That said, the therapeutic role of emotions on wellness has more recently gained popularity in the West, since contemporary research suggests that neurons in the emotional centres of the brain are activated before the neurons in the cognitive centres.[34] Indeed, this research puts forward the proposition that cognitive functions (like 'logic') accessible to the conscious mind are actually under the influence of prior subconscious emotional responses. In light of these research findings, it can therefore be inferred that the performance of *kirtan* in the classical Indian music system of *rag* can benefit mental and physical wellness.

While *simran* and *kirtan* are regarded as practices that both wipe away karmic debris and allow for the experience of resonance of *Ek Oankar*, such practices can still be unsettling and overwhelming if the impressions accumulated on the hidden record are of a disturbing or traumatic nature. When the mind cannot connect with *Nam* through *simran* and *kirtan*, the adherent is advised to engage in *seva* for inner cleansing.

Seva: Service for inner cleansing

Seva and *simran* are regarded as the two wings of *Sikhi* and are also reflected in the manner in which *gurdwara* buildings are designed. The main prayer hall or *darbar sahib* (divine court that contains the *Guru Granth Sahib*) is for the practice of *simran*, whereas the *langar* or communal dining hall is for *seva*. Common activities in the *langar* are food preparation, cooking, serving and cleaning. Adherents are encouraged to be mindful of the *Waheguru* mantra while practising *seva*.[35] For instance, the mantra can be rhythmically recited when cutting vegetables, stirring food, rolling dough, scrubbing pots or when cleaning the floor. Such mindful service is believed to simultaneously wipe away karmic debris from the hidden record and, in turn, also to make it easier for the mind to attune itself to the practice of *Nam simran* and *gurbani-kirtan* while seated in the *darbar sahib*.

Seva: Service for humanity

Throughout the *Sukhmani*, Guru Arjan highlights the importance of *seva* and *simran* for living a meaningful life. *Seva* has a twofold function where it both cleanses the adherent within and enhances the betterment of humanity (*sarbat da bhalla*). As aforementioned, *seva* for inner cleansing is usually performed at the *gurdwara*. *Seva* for the betterment of humanity, however, extends beyond the *gurdwara* setting where the individual or the collective engages in selfless service.[36]

Seva for the betterment of humanity in the Sikh tradition involves addressing both the problem and its cause. For instance, social issues like poverty are tackled through a two-pronged approach where basic necessities are provided at the grassroots while advocacy for the poor is carried out at the political and policy levels, even if it entails sacrificing one's own comfort and security. In effect, *seva* sanctifies and dignifies manual labour in a way that is unique to the Sikh tradition. Contrary to traditional Indian society, wherein societal work involving manual labour was regarded with disdain and traditionally has mostly been confined to the lower castes,[37] Guru Nanak institutionalized *seva* as an integral part of the Sikh tradition when he created the *langar* (community kitchen).[38]

A crucial aspect of *seva* is that it is to be carried out in such a manner that the act of giving results in the dissolution of the ego rather than inflating it. That is, such actions or efforts are not to be done out of self-interest, but rather for the welfare of humanity. Therefore, *seva* in its true spirit must be essentially performed with humility, purity of intention and sincerity. Such selfless service instils *gurmat*-oriented values that also assist the adherent in navigating the world's illusions. Overall, *Nam simran*, *gurbani-kirtan* and *seva* enable the adherent to cultivate a greater sense of awareness and equilibrium, which, in turn, allows for harmonious social engagement.

Navigating *sansar*: *Gurmat* values

Gurmat values (or values taught by the Sikh Gurus) are relied upon to stay balanced amid the ups and downs of life. The *Sukhmani* espouses a value system to help the adherent engage with the world, which is metaphorically described as a chaotic sea or dark forest that one has to journey through. Just as a sailor or hiker uses a compass as a navigation tool, the *Sikh* uses *gurmat* values to travel through the world of *sansar*.

Interdependence

A common metaphor used in the *Sukhmani* is that of creation being strung on the Creator's string. As Guru Arjan explains, 'With Your thread, the whole world is strung, without You, nothing happens' (22.1). Although appearing as separate on the surface, the entire creation is, in fact, interconnected: 'All matter originates from the One heart, although it appears in countless colours' (23.1). Indeed, *Nam* is the inner essence that binds all of creation. Without the awareness of *Nam*, there develops a sense of separateness and division. This sense of separateness can lead to social comparison where success of one is measured in relation to the other. A *Sikh* ought to be mindful that success is not the result of individual effort, rather it entails the help of others and favourable circumstances for which one ought to be grateful. The *Sukhmani* highlights the importance of gratitude, which is the feeling of appreciation after receiving a gift or being the beneficiary of an act of kindness. Guru Arjan explicates thus: 'All wealth is obtained through You, *Prabh*, nothing can be independently acquired' (6.8). One ought to be appreciative of the gifts that one receives from the Creator and to enjoy these gifts with modesty and humility.

Acceptance

Acceptance of life circumstances is a recurring teaching in the *Sukhmani*. Guru Arjan describes the enlightened one as having an accepting disposition since the Creator's hand is viewed as being in everything: 'The devotee's nature is to accept what happens, recognizing the Creator in everything' (14.8). Accepting the Creator's will is welcomed with joy: 'Whatever happens, accept it joyfully' (15.4). That said, acceptance does not mean surrendering to adverse life circumstances where one succumbs to hardships and suffering.[39] Only the ego is to be surrendered. It is from the ego that negative emotions like resentment, bitterness and anger arise. Conversely, when the ego is not one's internal frame of reference, one can be aware of, and accept, the dualities of joy and suffering in life. Just as one is mindful of the thorns while enjoying the beauty and fragrance of a rose, the enlightened one skilfully navigates through difficulties while staying mindful of the nectar of *Nam* within.

Accepting the dualities of joy and suffering enables one to approach life without being attached to preferred outcomes. Conversely, the ego-driven individual suffers when preferred outcomes are not achieved, because unmet goals give rise to feelings of disappointment and failure. That said, such unpleasant emotions can also be a catalyst for change, and encourage personal growth and development. In fact, the Sikh tradition reframes suffering as the cure, where it forces one's hand to press *pause* in the game of life, accept the predicament one finds oneself in and commit to a new game plan. For the *Sikh*, *shabad-Guru* is like a 'life coach' who shines a guiding light for those who feel lost, abandoned and directionless in life. As Guru Arjan explains, 'Just as the lamp turns darkness into light, the mind blossoms upon seeing *Guru*' (15.3) and 'On this path of total darkness, the *Nam* of *Har* will provide light' (2.4). Having the wisdom to accept the Creator's hand in everything, along with being detached from ego-centred goals, helps an adherent cultivate the values of forgiveness, compassion and mercy.

Impermanence

Acceptance of joy and suffering also enables one to gain insight into the impermanent nature of existence. Both material and immaterial phenomena – including mental and emotional states – are transitory experiences. In contrast to the Buddhist view of impermanence (Pali *anicca*) as a marker of existence (along with suffering and the non-self), according to Guru Arjan, the world is ever-changing but real because of its connection with *Ek Oankar*. In the Sikh perspective, creation is in a continuous cyclical flow of change involving becoming, being and dissolving. Human life is subject to decay and death. Similarly, lived experiences – though appearing as permanent at the moment – are like dreams which come and go. All that appears to be permanent inevitably becomes a subjective memory. Just as human birth is accompanied by eventual death, all experiences – positive or negative – are subject to their own births and deaths. Attachment to the material and immaterial aspects of creation as if they were permanent leads to suffering and being caught in the cycle of birth and death. As Guru Arjan states:

> Impermanent is the body, wealth and entire family;
> Impermanent is the ego, attachment and *maya*.
> Impermanent is power, youth, wealth and capital;
> Impermanent is lust and frightening anger.
> Impermanent are chariots, elephants, horses and clothes;
> Impermanent is enjoyment in the love of *maya*.
> Impermanent is deceit, attachment and pride;
> Impermanent is your overconfidence.
> Permanence is devotion in the sanctuary of the *sadhs*;
> Nanak: Chanting at the feet of *Har* is to be alive. (5.4)

The ego is ignorant of this underlying reality of impermanence, and rigorously tries to accomplish role-related goals for a solidified sense of self and identity. The fulfilment of goals can create inner unrest since the goals of one role can conflict with those of another role. For instance, one's ambition to be a politician may conflict with one's role as a spouse or parent. Such conflict is resolved by the ego demoting roles incongruent with its core needs, and expending more energy on roles that it believes can strengthen its ability both to be validated and to assert itself in different social contexts. Lastly, the fulfilment of any role-related goal is short-lived. However, since the initial goal is shortly replaced by another goal, the ego subsequently becomes caught in a roller-coaster ride of emotional states ranging from excitement to anxiety.

Guru Arjan advises one to be mindful of the fact that *Nam* permeates all existence. Worldly roles – such as spouse, parent, sibling, friend, worker or citizen – are not to be renounced. Rather, these roles ought to be mindfully played on the worldly stage but with unwavering awareness of *Nam* and indifference towards success or failure. In essence, *Nam* is one's true identity, with all other social roles revolving around *Nam*. As Guru Arjan explains: 'On this journey where you are anonymous, the *Nam* of *Har* will be your identity' (2.4).

Just as there is equilibrium and harmony among the planets as they orbit around the sun, one experiences inner harmony when one's social roles are synchronic with *Nam*. Such inner and outer harmony cultivates contentment, a mental and emotional state of satisfaction where the mind and body are at ease, regardless of life circumstances. Contentment is an integral component of life satisfaction. Guru Arjan states: 'Without contentment, no satisfaction, and, as in a dream, all efforts are meaningless' (12.5).

Temperance

One's ability to be content amid the joys and sorrows of human life requires a certain degree of temperance. Key aspects of temperance include prudence (being careful about one's choices), self-regulation (the ability to control instinctual responses, such as aggression and impulsivity) and social intelligence (being aware of the motives and feelings of others as also those of one's own).[40] In the *Sukhmani*, Guru Arjan attributes the virtue of temperance to the enlightened ones (*brahamgiani*). On the other hand, in the case of the ego-driven personality – beneath the outer facade – lie impulsive and hedonistic tendencies. The virtue of temperance allows one to control the five vices or thieves, those being lust, anger, greed, attachment and ego. While lust and anger are more instinctual in nature, greed, attachment and ego relate to the psycho-emotional dimension of the person.

As stated in Chapter 4, *seva*, *simran* and *sangat* are key ingredients of happiness, all of which increase one's ability to exercise temperance. Contemporary neurobiological research has found meditative practices improve frontal brain cortex functioning.[41] The frontal cortex is more developed in humans, and is responsible for planning, decision making and self-regulation. It also makes sense of the perceptions created by the back brain cortex which is more concrete, instinctual and immediate in time.[42] Significantly, the modern scientific understanding of the brain, as having evolved from instinctual and concrete functioning to abstract thinking and self-awareness, can be used as a template for making sense of the metaphors used in the *Sukhmani*, where humans are described as hedonistic yet possessing the capacity to exercise temperance and experience transcendence.

Transcendence

Transcendence in the *Sukhmani* involves a twofold process where one (1) rises above egotistical desires and (2) experiences a sense of belonging, harmony and unity with *Nam* – the inner essence that binds all creation together. Transcendence or the awareness of *Nam* is the intrinsic source of happiness even as it provides the vital space for personal enhancement and spiritual growth. As mentioned earlier in Chapter 4, Guru Arjan puts forward a spiritual path that is free of thoughtless ritualism. In fact, throughout the *Sukhmani*, ritualistic practices for enlightenment and liberation are critiqued, while preference is given to an authentic inner experience of *Nam*. As Guru Arjan explains:

> Of all *dharams*, the best *dharam* is
> to chant the *Nam* of *Har*, the purest of actions.
> Of all *kiryas*, the best *kirya* is
> to remove the filth of foul intellect in the company of the *sadhs*.
> Of all efforts, the best effort is
> to continuously chant the *Nam* of *Har*.
> Of all speech, the best speech is
> to hear and sing the praises of *Har*.
> Of all places, the best place is
> Nanak, the heart where the *Nam* of *Har* resides. (3.8)

That is to say, against the canvas of Hindu practice, Guru Arjan describes mindful remembrance and the inner experience of *Nam* as central to the pursuit of happiness and well-being.

The awareness of *Nam* is described as a state of emptiness (*sunn*), resonance and awe. Guru Arjan explains thus: 'Absorbed in *sunn*, one connects with the unstruck sound, but this wondrous awe is indescribable' (23.1). Emptiness (*sunn*) refers to that which is to be filled with the resonance.[43] It is only in this state of *sunn* that one can experience the cosmic resonance of *Ek Oankar*. This inner experience of *Nam* involves a sensitivity to greatness and being overwhelmed by its greatness: 'Wonderstruck, in the awe of the Wonderful, the one who understands this, savours it' (16.8). And, savouring the inner experience of *Nam* allows one to flourish and transcend the cycle of birth and death. As Guru Arjan explains: 'Within whose heart resides the One, such a one will flourish, and death will not come' (22.8).

To flourish or bloom – where one grows and develops in a healthy way – is a common metaphor in the *Sukhmani*. As discussed in Chapter 3, the *Sukhmani* is set to the Gauri *rag* – a serious and contemplative musical measure that is assigned to the autumn/winter season – one that can also be viewed as a metaphor for the function of the text (i.e. to guide the seeker). That is, just as a plant conserves its energy during the cold season and flourishes in the spring with nourishment, one journeys within during hardships and flourishes with the love and warmth experienced in a *Guru*-centred *sangat*. According to the *Sukhmani*, love is a virtue that entails kindness, compassion and empathy, and flows from the enlightened one's heart unconditionally. As Guru Arjan states: '*Brahamgiani* shows kindness to all' (8.3). And, '*Gobind's* virtues and *Nam* are the pearls of happiness (*Sukhmani*), the heart in which *Nam* resides is a treasure chest' (24.5).

By exploring the way of the *Brahamgiani*, the *Sukhmani* makes evident that personal development and growth entails a value system that is oriented towards meaningful living. The values espoused throughout the *Sukhmani*, such as wisdom, courage, love, justice, temperance and transcendence, are consistent with the core values that have been identified by moral philosophers and religious thinkers throughout history.[44]

Meaningful living amid materialism

Guru Arjan describes meaningful values as virtuous and the basis for good character, whereas he critiques materialistic values and equates them with suffering. Indeed, while humans seek core needs (like security and respect), the ego's desire for, and pursuit of, core needs, especially materialistic ones (like wealth, power, status and fame), is a source of suffering. The link between materialism and suffering has also been confirmed by contemporary research in positive psychology and happiness economics. The general finding is that there is no direct relationship between the level of economic development of a society and the overall happiness of its members. This finding is referred to as the Easterlin Paradox, which puts forward the proposition that life satisfaction does increase with the rise in average incomes, but after a certain point the extent of gain in happiness goes down.[45] The notion of wealth as a determinant of happiness and life satisfaction is more of a myth when a person earns above the poverty line. The correlation between happiness and income is only strong when income is low, but the connection is weak when income is high.[46] Once a person is above the poverty line, higher income has only a minimal effect on happiness levels.[47] In fact, proponents of the Easterlin Paradox suggest individualism and an expanding free market economy, where money and material wealth are important life values, lead to life satisfaction at a diminishing rate.[48]

Materialistic values undermine the life values considered beneficial for personal development and growth, and give rise to less life satisfaction and increase the risk for the development of psychological disorders.[49] These disorders are possibly the result of the inner tension that individuals experience when suppressing inherent collective values, while expending their energy on materialistic pursuits that leave them unfulfilled.[50] Moreover, in individualistic societies, there is an erosion of family solidarity and community integration as individuals become more competitive and distrustful of one another.[51]

On the other hand, happiness and life satisfaction improve when a person has loving relationships, meaningful social engagement and a sense of purpose.[52] Happiness is a by-product of finding meaning and purpose in life, while material benefits are secondary to achieving it. Meaning and purpose are common themes found in religious traditions, and perhaps it is for this reason that religion – excluding religious extremism – is positively correlated with subjective well-being.[53] Religion provides social contacts, support, consolation – the ingredients for a good life – and a connection with something greater than oneself.

Parallels with existential psychotherapy

By exploring the ingredients for a happy life as elaborated in the *Sukhmani*, it becomes apparent that the text offers answers to existential concerns commonly held by humans, irrespective of the culture to which they belong. Universal existential experiences, such as fear, guilt, responsibility, dread or despair, are common themes found in Sikh teachings. Contemporary researchers have increasingly been investigating the link between existential psychotherapy and Eastern philosophy. While their work has mostly emphasized exploring the parallels between existential psychotherapy and Buddhism, especially in relation to the Four Noble Truths, little seems to have been done in regard to the Sikh tradition. That said, the exploration of the link between existential psychotherapy and Eastern philosophy is most often understood in terms of the framework of Yalom's four existential concerns: (1) the inevitability of death, (2) isolation, (3) groundlessness and (4) meaninglessness.[54] These four concerns, if left unaddressed, lead to suffering, thus making 'suffering as a condition of life' – a key principle in existential psychotherapy.

'Suffering as a condition of life' is echoed in the teachings of the Sikh Gurus. Sikhs, when experiencing hardship, often quote Guru Nanak's words: 'Nanak: The whole world suffers' (*Nanak dukhia sabh sansar*).[55] Moreover, Sikhs find meaning in their suffering by reframing it as remedy or maintaining that 'suffering is medicine' (*dukh daru*).[56] Essentially, such acceptance of suffering relieves one of the expectation that they are obligated to be happy. While melancholy and sadness are normal emotions during unsettling life events, they are unhealthy when depressive states of mind become debilitating personality traits. That said, suffering provides an opportunity to stop doing those things that bring about unhappiness, and also to cultivate resilience when having to endure pain and suffering.

The ability to bounce back from unsettling life events strengthens one's sense of coherence. A strong sense of coherence (SOC) is the degree to which a person perceives life as:

1. *comprehensible*, a belief that things happen in an orderly and predictable fashion and a sense that one can understand events in one's life and reasonably predict what will happen in the future;
2. *manageable*, a belief that one has the skills or ability, the support, the help, or the resources necessary to take care of things, and that things are within one's control and manageable; and
3. *meaningful*, a belief that things in life are interesting and a source of satisfaction, that things are really worthwhile and that there is good reason or purpose for caring about what happens.[57]

This approach fits in well with the Salutogenesis model of health, which espouses the position that individuals can attain a good quality of life despite disease, disability and distress by developing meaning out of their experiences through their worldview, beliefs, values and practices.[58]

Religion and spirituality can serve as a lens or framework through which one can make sense of one's existential situation,[59] and subsequently influence the formation of one's goals and determine one's actions.[60] While resilience may be a process inherent in all societies, there is specificity in socio-cultural practices and experiences of resiliency building.[61] In the Sikh context, the resilience-building activities include attending the *gurdwara*, reciting sacred texts on a regular basis, listening to *kirtan* and engaging in *seva*.[62] And, the suffering that stems from existential concerns, including death, isolation, groundlessness and meaninglessness, is alleviated by transcending mental and physical anguish through an inner journey to discover the underlying essence of all existence – Nam – that is, the way of the *brahamgiani*. As Guru Arjan describes it:

Brahamgiani places hope in the One;
Brahamgiani will never perish.
Brahamgiani is steeped in humility;
Brahamgiani enjoys helping others.
Brahamgiani is not entangled [in *maya*];
Brahamgiani no longer wanders.
Brahamgiani sees that everything is for the best;

Brahamgiani blooms with fulfilment.
Brahamgiani saves others in his/her company;
Nanak: *Brahamgiani* helps the whole world meditate. (8.4)

Besides espousing the getting rid of suffering (*dukh*) and the building of resilience, Guru Arjan's *Sukhmani* provides a description of the way of the *brahamgiani*, a path that fundamentally provides meaning and purpose, human connection and social involvement, all of which are key to the healing process, the cultivation of well-being and the attainment of happiness (*sukh*).

6

Understanding Guru Arjan's *Sukhmani*: Summary and conclusions

The growing theoretical discussion in Sikh studies – around (1) interpreting the tradition through *Sikhi* frames, (2) the fluidity in the development of Sikhism, (3) the heterogeneity in the tradition and (4) the complexity of identity – has contributed to greater value being accorded to the impact of the Singh Sabha movement and colonial influence on previous historical reconstructions of the Sikh tradition. The present study on Guru Arjan's *Sukhmani* (The Pearl of Happiness) vividly demonstrates the value of employing the earlier *Sikhi* frames in translating and interpreting the text. Particularly striking is the important part that the *Sikhi* perspective plays in our specific understanding of the sectarian context of the nineteenth-century and twentieth-century narratives about the *Sukhmani* and Miharvan's *Sukhmani Sahasranam*. As well, our analysis further illustrates Guru Arjan's doctrinal contributions and his conception of Ultimate Reality, and the key Sikh psychological concepts delineated in the *Sukhmani*.

Instead of solely employing Western philosophical categories and theories to deconstruct the tradition or of simply using modern psychological concepts to frame its spiritual teachings, this study offers an analysis of how *Sikhi* addresses the existential problem of suffering and the pursuit of happiness from within the tradition itself, and as well from within the larger framework of Indic religions. Such advancing of the inclusion of the *Sikhi* perspective on wellness significantly adds, at the same time, to the contributions made by other Indic spiritual traditions, such as Patanjali's Yoga and Theravada Buddhism. The important differentiating point to note here is that these earlier religious and philosophical systems were meant primarily for the world-renunciate. The *Sikhi* spiritual path, on the other hand, is meant for all those living in the world as householders.[1] This distinction is best illustrated through Gautama Buddha's concept of the *sangha* (i.e. the monastic community of monks and nuns)[2] in comparison to the Sikh Gurus' understanding and practice of the *sadh sangat* (i.e. the congregation of those who practise *Nam-simran*).³ Moreover, while the later Bhakti traditions are oriented towards the accessibility of intrinsic religious practice for the common people, with concepts like God's grace and the world as an extension of God, they do not provide a pragmatic approach as to how one can live in the world and navigate through the trials and turbulence of the material world while simultaneously pursuing liberation. Indeed, *Sikhi* is unique in the way it integrates and balances the personal pursuit of liberation and social involvement.

Continuous with other Indic religions, the Sikh tradition views human bondage to *sansar* as the major source of suffering. Besides this understanding of human bondage, the Sikh tradition explicitly identifies four other sources of suffering: (1) separation, primarily from *Nam*, resulting in anxiety and fear; (2) physical deprivation, such as hunger and thirst; (3) bodily ailments, like disease and infection; and (4) oppression and death.[4] Since humans are caught in a continual cycle of suffering, pain is taken to be inevitable. Notwithstanding the inevitability of suffering, one can still escape or avoid suffering (*dukh*) by addressing its internal and external causes. However, since the attainment of happiness (*sukh*) is not merely the result of removing or overcoming *dukh*, Guru Arjan's *Sukhmani* positively offers valuable insights into human nature, the cultivation of wellness and the pursuit of *sukh*, for seekers living as householders in the world.

In advancing an analysis of the *Sukhmani* through a *Sikhi* lens, it is important to systematically explore four essential dimensions of the text: (1) Guru Arjan's life-situation, (2) the ritual purpose of the text, (3) the spiritual perspective provided by the *Sukhmani* and (4) the implications of the text for the cultivation of well-being and the attainment of happiness.

Guru Arjan's life-situation

Guru Arjan was introduced to the Sikh religion and the community's activities from a very young age, since he was not only the first Sikh Guru to have been born in a Sikh family, but also both his father and maternal grandfather had been Sikh Gurus. As the youngest son, however, Guru Arjan had to contend with the antagonism of his eldest brother, Prithi Chand, since the latter did not inherit the Guru-seat (*gur-gaddi*). Despite this antogonism, Guru Arjan successfully organized the Sikh community throughout the Punjab, by way of establishing places of worship (*gurdwaras*) and the network of community officials (*masand*). Besides his organizational initiatives, Guru Arjan also strengthened the community (Panth) by compiling the initial canonical text called the *Adi Granth*.

Arjan's guruship (1581–1606) had begun and, for the most part, continued in the reign of Mughal Emperor Akbar (1556–1605), during which there had prevailed relative peace, religious tolerance and prosperity in the region. However, his guruship came to a tragic end during Mughal Emperor Jahangir's reign (1605–27) and his evident religious intolerance towards the Sikh Panth.

Certainly, the actual events of Guru Arjan's life shed light on the historical reality of competition over succession to the Guru-seat (*gur-gaddi*) and also on the rise in Mughal hostility towards the flourishing Sikh community, most profoundly evident in the events leading up to the Guru's execution. These internal and external forces arrayed against Guru Arjan reveal the trying religious, social and political circumstances during which he composed the *Sukhmani*. And, in line with his own existential situation, Guru Arjan's *Sukhmani* significantly and profoundly addresses various strata of society, including religious figures and kings, in order to expose falsehood.

The *Sukhmani* through sectarian lenses

Historical context is undoubtedly important in looking at religious development. But, a mere historical reconstruction may well fall far short in advancing our understanding of matters relating to religious beliefs and practices. This is made evident by an examination of the nineteenth-century and twentieth-century Nirmala narratives regarding Guru Arjan receiving Sri Chand's recommendations about both adding a modified *salok* and writing eight more *astapadis*, when the former was composing the *Sukhmani*. This Nirmala narrative and its many renditions have, however, to be understood in their historical and sectarian context. That is, the narrative and its various renditions are sectarian in nature, with the essential aim of elevating the spiritual stature of Sri Chand and his Udasi sect (i.e. a group or faction other than the orthodox line of Sikh Gurus), even as they contradict the words (*gurbani*) that have been included in the *Guru Granth Sahib* or Bhai Gurdas's *Varan*.

Likewise, Miharvan's *Sukhmani Sahasranam* – while, no doubt, inspired by Guru Arjan's *Sukhmani* – was composed from the Mina perspective of Sikhism as a means to legitimize that sectarian tradition. While the two compositions share some similarities (such as both texts have *sukhmani* in the title, are structured in the form of *astapadis*, with each *astapadi* beginning with a *salok*, and are composed in the Gauri *rag*), there are significant differences between the two compositions. For instance, Guru Arjan's *Sukhmani* has twenty-four *astapadis*, while Miharvan's *Sukhmani Sahasranam* contains thirty *astapadis*. Given the fact that twenty-four *astapadis* correspond to the eight watches of the day-night cycle (i.e. each watch comprises three *astapadis*), Miharvan fails to capture the spiritual and poetic significance of the structure of Guru Arjan's *Sukhmani*. Moreover, the *Sukhmani Sahasranam* follows the pan-Indian literary genre of 'The Thousand Names of God', a popular genre praising the various epithets of a Hindu god like Vishnu, even as it specifically begins with an invocation to Lord Krishna and praises Vishnu's *avataras*, all of which go against the *Sikhi* doctrine of *Ek Oankar* (see 'Guru Arjan's Conception of Ultimate Reality' in this chapter).

The context of the sectarian narratives and the *Sukhmani Sahasranam* underpins the need and importance of Guru Arjan in establishing the *Adi Granth*. As the authoritative text of the Sikh Panth, the *Adi Granth* serves as the governing doctrinal standard to overcome contradictions and inconsistencies. From the *Sikhi* perspective, when a *sakhi* or religious text contradicts the *Adi Granth*, the latter takes precedence. In this manner, the *Adi Granth* emerged as critical to the very survival of the Panth, especially after Guru Arjan was executed.

The ritual function of the *Sukhmani*: For the seeker, for the masses

The original Punjabi word to refer to the traditions established by the Sikh Gurus is *Sikhi* (experiential or lived path of learning), which reflects the religion's purpose of providing a path for the seeker. This orientation towards offering a path for the seeker is a distinguishing characteristic of the religious traditions born out of the Indian subcontinent, since the primary goal of liberation from the cycle of birth, death and rebirth (*sansar*) is attainable by way of self-realization and/or God-realization. Certainly, then, the *Sukhmani* is a text meant for seekers.

The *Sukhmani* is a text that is also contained in the Sikh canon – the *Guru Granth Sahib* – which is regarded as the highest doctrinal authority in Sikhism.

From a Western perspective, it may be assumed that scriptural texts are meant to be read and studied. However, according to *Sikhi*, the *Guru Granth Sahib* is regarded as the living *Guru* and is, therefore, ultimately meant to be heard with the mind and heart. Moreover, the Sikh Gurus – in leading a movement of the common people – taught the accessible practice of *Nam simran*, since the masses at the time were illiterate and/or considered as not socially and religiously pure enough to study the Hindu scripture known as the Vedas. One cannot therefore assume that the *Sukhmani* text is automatically meant to guide the reader. Rather, to be more precise, the *Sukhmani* is intended to guide the seeker, who may read the text, or remember and recite/chant the text by rote, or listen to the recitation of the text.

While the *Sukhmani* addresses various strata of society, attention is primarily given to seekers aspiring to alleviate suffering. Curiously, Guru Arjan did not compose the *Sukhmani* to a *rag* that evokes happiness or joy. Rather, he composed the text in the Gauri *rag*, a musical measure meant both to evoke a contemplative mood and to bring peace to the mind. Significantly, this serious *rag* matches the primary function of the *Sukhmani* since the text is meant for those seekers undergoing suffering in a cold and dark world, and are in need of an inner journey to be soothed and strengthened, and to eventually flourish.

As one of the more popular Sikh texts, the recitation of the *Sukhmani* is also central to Sikh practice. Given its simple syntax and structure, the *Sukhmani* is easy to memorize. While the *Sukhmani* teaches that *Nam* is the panacea for all illnesses, Sikhs nevertheless often extend this teaching about the calming effect of mindful remembrance of *Nam* to the recitation of the *Sukhmani* text itself. That is, many Sikhs recite this sacred text in the hope of attaining spiritual and material benefit.

Some Sikhs may interpret the text more literally and recite it in accord with their literal understanding. For instance, Sikhs may recite the text for good luck because the *Sukhmani* states that *Nam* helps one attain 'everything'; or, when under emotional or psychological distress, Sikhs may recite the *Sukhmani* for protection, for cure of an illness, for health and well-being, and the like. On the other hand, mainstream preachers recommend Sikhs to read the *Sukhmani* mindfully through the medium of the *rahau* (pause or refrain): '*Sukhmani: Prabh Nam* is ambrosial happiness, and resides in the hearts of the *bhagats*' (1.1–2). The *Sukhmani* can, therefore, be regarded as a text for both the seeker and the masses. That is, the *Sukhmani* may be interpreted according to, or regardless of, where one may be in one's spiritual journey.

The spiritual journey of the *Sukhmani*

The *Sukhmani* is a poem that has been creatively composed to guide seekers on their spiritual journey towards experiencing the non-duality of *dukh* and *sukh*. It guides them in experiencing the journey towards spiritual development through the eight watches of the day-night cycle. As one reads through the 'watches of the day' (*astapadis* 1–12) – when people are awake and there are many distractions – one attains insight into the source of suffering (*dukh*) even as the watches provide the 'sign posts' of *Nam-simran* (the mindful remembrance of *Nam*) and the *sadh-sangat* (the congregation of practitioners) that can help one navigate through the transitory nature of the material world.

In contrast to Buddhism – where mindfulness is awareness of the present moment without judgement (i.e. the practice is the medicine, and awareness is liberation) – the Sikh concept of mindful remembrance involves the awareness and experience of *Nam* resonating in the present moment (i.e. *Nam* is the medicine, and the state of being immersed in *Nam* is liberation). *Nam simran* is the ultimate practice that helps one dissolve the ego and connect with *Ek Oankar*. However, since proceeding through the three stages of *Nam simran* (i.e. reciting, listening and internalizing *Nam*) can prove to be challenging, Guru Arjan also teaches that the *sadh sangat* is a vital source of support in navigating through the world that is both diverse and transitory in nature.

Subsequently, the 'watches of the night' (*astapadis* 13–24) – when people are sleeping and there is greater peace and fewer distractions – guide seekers in experiencing *Nam* even as they provide the way of the *Sikh* towards meaningful living and happiness (*sukh*). In fact, there are six forms of *sukh* that can be deduced from the *Sukhmani*: (1) pleasure and comfort, (2) physical and mental relief, (3) acceptance, (4) meaningful living, (5) contentment and fulfilment and (6) experience of oneness with *Sat Purakh*. In ascending order, these forms reveal the stages of spiritual development. While the first and second forms of happiness are more immediate in time but not long lasting, the third form – joyful acceptance – makes room for the cultivation of the fourth, fifth and sixth forms of *sukh*, which are more integrated into one's being. The ultimate goal is the intrinsic experience of ego dissolution and connecting to *Ek Oankar*, resulting in one's enlightened performance of noble action. Hence, according to the *Sukhmani*, the formula for happiness involves *seva* (selfless service), *simran* (mindful remembrance) and *sadh sangat* (the congregation of the *sadhs*).

Guru Arjan's doctrinal contributions

Guru Arjan's key spiritual and philosophical teachings that are contained in the *Sukhmani* contribute to a greater understanding of the development of Sikh thought. Not only does the *Sukhmani* provide valuable insights into eliminating suffering and pursuing happiness, but it further advances Sikh doctrine. In describing the *sadh sangat* as an extension of *Satgur*, Guru Arjan advances Sikh doctrine on the triadic relationship between *Sat Purakh*, *Satgur* and a *Sikh*. That is, the *sadh sangat* is a medium through which one can experience *Sat Purakh*. Guru Arjan views the *sadh sangat* as the congregation of devotees who sing as a collective in the presence of *Satgur* and collectively connect with *Ek Oankar* through the practice of *Nam simran*.

In providing a definition of the *sadh*, Guru Arjan leaves no room for confusion. While the concept of the *sadh sangat* refers to the congregation of the *sadhs*, a *sadh* is specifically one who – through the mindful remembrance of *Nam* – is connected with *Ek Oankar*. In connecting with *Ek Oankar*, the *sadh* is imbued with the qualities of *Prabh*, where suffering disappears and actions are pure. *Satgur's* light both lifts the veil of ignorance and exposes the ego (*ahankar*) and its clever schemes. In effect, *Guru's* light guides the *sadh* across the ocean of *sansar*. And, the way of the *sadh* or Sikh becomes a beacon of hope for others in search of light amid the darkness. Indeed, Guru Arjan's spiritual and communal understanding of the *sadh sangat* serves as a bridge between his contributions to the doctrinal advance and his contributions to the institutional development of the Sikh Panth.

Guru Arjan's conception of Ultimate Reality

Based on the *Sikhi* perspective, the *Sukhmani* ultimately points to the Sikh spiritual goal of connecting with *Ek Oankar* (Ultimate Reality) as it manifests in all of creation. Fundamentally, the Sikh understanding of Ultimate Reality involves the One Creator as resonating throughout creation. Namely, the Creator and creation are One and the same.[5] The introductory *salok* of the *Sukhmani* begins with the invocation '*Ek Oankar*, realized by *Satgur's* grace' (*Ek Oankar, Satgur prasad*). While *Ek Oankar* literally means 'the One creator-creation', it appears only this one time in the *Sukhmani*. Instead, Guru Arjan uses *Sat Purakh* (True Being) and *Guru* to connote Ultimate Reality throughout the *Sukhmani* even as he also praises *Sat Purakh* by way of epithets, such as *Prabh* (all-pervasive One), *Har* (omnipresent One) and *Gobind* (Preserver of the world) to name a few, in order to illustrate the qualities of *Ek Oankar*. Furthermore, *Ek Oankar* is gender neutral, since the inner dimension of a person is genderless. And, going beyond gender, Guru Arjan's verses at the same time embody the masculine and feminine qualities of *Ek Oankar*.

Application of the *Sukhmani*

Traditionally, religious texts have offered insights about the existential quest for meaning, purpose and happiness. Likewise, Guru Arjan's *Sukhmani* provides the Sikh view on what makes people happy and live a meaningful life. It underpins the existential and psychological insights into the human problem of suffering. The root cause of suffering in the *Sukhmani* is the ego's struggle for permanence in the material world. The *manmukh* (one who is guided by the ego) is believed to be in a slumber state of awareness as the ego constructs a sense of self by taking on worldly roles to fulfil its core needs. Depending on the nature of the person, which is said to be influenced by both current and past life impressions on the hidden record or subconscious sphere, core needs can range from humanistic (i.e. security, love, respect and freedom) to materialistic (i.e. wealth, status, power and fame). The fulfilment of these needs is directly related to the goals associated with the roles that the ego has taken on. These roles are like 'robes' that the ego wears to validate and assert itself in the material world.

The manner in which the *manmukh* suffers while under the grip or influence of the ego involves a cyclical process, beginning with attachment (*moh*), which is followed by greed (*lob*), anger (*karodh*) and lust (*kam*). Attachments are formed with those people, places, things and activities that the ego believes can fulfil its core needs. Over time, the ego's attachment intensifies and transforms into greed, which is then inevitably beset with obstacles and ultimately leads to anger. The ego temporarily subdues this anger with lustful indulgences, and shortly afterwards falls back into the cycle of vices, wherein the mind becomes anxious and the body is prone to illness.

Simran and *seva* are the key ingredients in the Sikh view on attaining happiness, as they are believed to wipe away the karmic debris in the hidden record, and allow one to be fully awake amid the joys and sorrows of the material world. This notion of contentment or happiness amid the ups and downs of life overlaps with Western wellness studies (in contrast to the medical model), where there is not an exclusive focus on pathology and a rigid adherence to a classification system that separates psychology, religion, medicine and spirituality. Indeed, these different disciplines are integrated in South Asian wellness models to form a more synergistic system. In the Sikh view, spirituality involves the experience of oneness through transcending the ego while at the same time navigating the material world with meaningful values derived from *gurmat*, such as interdependence, acceptance, impermanence, temperance and transcendence. Wakefulness amid the dualities of life (i.e. birth and death, joy and sorrow) is the way of the *brahamgiani* or enlightened one.

Summing up

In the Indian subcontinent, religious texts, such as the *Bhagavad Gita* and the *Dhammapada*, have long guided seekers in the pursuit of happiness. The pursuit of happiness in Indic spiritual traditions generally involves both extrinsic and intrinsic experiences, where the former includes the fulfilment of desires and the avoidance of pain, while the latter involves transcending the ego and attaining an enlightened state of awareness. The *Sukhmani* (The Pearl of Happiness), regarded as Guru Arjan's most celebrated work, offers the Sikh existential, psychological and spiritual perspective on well-being and happiness.

While the *Sukhmani* acknowledges that worldly happiness provides pleasure, it views it, however, as an impermanent experience that ultimately leaves the *manmukh* unfulfilled and entangled in *maya*. The temporary nature of worldly happiness is seen as resulting in suffering, where the *manmukh* feels anxious, agitated and directionless when having to contend with existential realities, such as death, loneliness and meaninglessness. During such suffering, the mind and body become agitated and distressed, and the *manmukh* has to endure a generalized condition of misery. However, such misery can be a catalyst for personal growth and development.

That said, healing in the Sikh tradition involves a trajectory that begins with *misery*, then progresses through *recovery* and finally concludes with *discovery*. Not only is recovery merely about recovery from misery, but it also entails a process of discovery during which material and immaterial facades are pealed back and the inner essence – *Nam* – is discovered. Healing is facilitated by the inter-connective relation that the Sikh has with *Satgur* and *Sat Purakh*, and as well by key practices, such as *sangat*, *seva* and *simran*. These practices, which involve social action, human connectivity and meaningful effort, are holistic in nature and fundamentally reflect a multidimensional approach to health and well-being.

However, unlike the Theravada Buddhist and Patanjali's Yogic paths – which are to be pursued within the context of renouncing mundane existence – the *Sukhmani* explicitly offers an approach to happiness for those who are actually navigating through the trials and turbulence of the world. Indeed, healing and happiness through the discovery of *Nam* involve neither retreating from worldly affairs nor pursuing an inward journey in seclusion. Rather, the way of the *brahamgiani*, or enlightened one, encompasses both social involvement and meaningful engagement in the world. That is, the *brahamgiani* is one who has mastered navigating both the dualities of human existence and the transitory nature of the material world. The *brahamgiani* is thus one who is mindful of *Nam* and who skilfully puts *gurmat* values into action.

The values espoused by Guru Arjan in the *Sukhmani*, such as wisdom, courage, love, justice, temperance and transcendence, are oriented towards meaningful living and detached engagement. These values were personally exemplified in Guru Arjan's spiritual leadership by the manner in which he contributed to the evolving Sikh Panth. During his guruship, Guru Arjan galvanized the collective identity of the Sikh Panth, even as he had to contend with both internal factionalism over succession to the Guru-seat (*gur-gaddi*) and external socio-political hostility towards the expanding Sikh community, most poignantly expressed in his own martyrdom. Guru Arjan's scriptural and administrative initiatives served to safeguard the Panth even as they provided a structure for the Sikhs to learn, practise and experience the teachings of *shabad-Guru*. Most of all, the *Sukhmani*'s insights into the attainment of happiness came from Guru Arjan, a man who was both spiritually and socially engaged amid the joys and sorrows of life.

The *Sukhmani: The Pearl of Happiness*
(An English Translation)

Gauri Sukhmani M: 5
Salok
Ek Oankar
Realized by *Satgur's* grace.

Bow to the primal *Guru*.
Bow to the *Guru* of the ages.
Bow to *Satgur*.
Bow to the great divine *Guru*. (1)

Astapadi
Remember mindfully, mindfully, and attain happiness,
    tension and *kalesh* vanish from the body.
Be mindful of the One who cares for the universe,
    and whose *Nam* is chanted by countless people, in a myriad of ways.
The Vedas, Simritis and Puranas accept the pure word,[1]
    Ram Nam was created by the One.
The hearts where the essence of the One resides,
    their praises cannot be described.
Those yearning for a vision of Your Oneness,
    Nanak, I can be saved in their company. (1)

Sukhmani: Prabh Nam is ambrosial happiness,
    and resides in the hearts of the *bhagats*. [Pause]

When mindful of *Prabh*, one is not reborn in the womb;
When mindful of *Prabh*, the suffering of death disappears.

When mindful of *Prabh*, death is far away;
When mindful of *Prabh*, adversaries are in retreat.
When mindful of *Prabh*, obstacles are overcome;
When mindful of *Prabh*, there is awareness night and day.
When mindful of *Prabh*, fear is not experienced;
When mindful of *Prabh*, the sorrow of suffering is no more.
Be mindful of *Prabh* in the company of the *sadhs*;
Nanak: All treasures are attained in the love of *Har*. (2)

When mindful of *Prabh*, the spiritual, the supernatural and the nine treasures are attained;[2]
When mindful of *Prabh*, there is wisdom, concentration and pure intellect.
Be mindful of *Prabh* in chant, devotion and worship;
When mindful of *Prabh*, there is no duality.
Being mindful of *Prabh* is like bathing on pilgrimage;
When mindful of *Prabh*, there is honour in the court.
When mindful of *Prabh*, one becomes wholesome;
When mindful of *Prabh*, one reaps fruit.
Be mindful of the One who makes you mindful;
Nanak: I want to touch the feet of the mindful ones. (3)

Be mindful of *Prabh* as the highest;
When mindful of *Prabh*, many are saved.
When mindful of *Prabh*, desires are extinguished;
When mindful of *Prabh*, everything is understood.
When mindful of *Prabh*, the fear of death vanishes;
When mindful of *Prabh*, aspirations are fulfilled.
When mindful of *Prabh*, mental defilements are removed;
When mindful of *Prabh*, the ambrosial *Nam* is absorbed in the heart.
Prabh resides on the *sadhs'* tongue;
Nanak: I want to serve the servants who serve. (4)

When mindful of *Prabh*, one is wealthy;
When mindful of *Prabh*, one is honoured.
When mindful of *Prabh*, one is accepted;
When mindful of *Prabh*, one is in command.
When mindful of *Prabh*, one is independent;
When mindful of *Prabh*, one rules over all.

When mindful of *Prabh*, one resides in happiness;
When mindful of *Prabh*, one is everlasting.
Bestowed with grace, mindfulness begins;
Nanak: I want the dust of the devotee's feet. (5)

Those mindful of *Prabh* help others;
Those mindful of *Prabh*, I am forever indebted to them.
Those mindful of *Prabh*, their faces radiate;
Those mindful of *Prabh* live in happiness.
Those mindful of *Prabh* are victorious within;
Those mindful of *Prabh* are absorbed in purity.
Those mindful of *Prabh* have many joys;
Those mindful of *Prabh* dwell close to *Har*.
Blessed by the *sants*, they are awake night and day;
Nanak: With mindfulness, fortunes are complete. (6)

When mindful of *Prabh*, endeavours are completed;
When mindful of *Prabh*, there is no grief.
When mindful of *Prabh*, the qualities of *Har* are uttered;
When mindful of *Prabh*, there is spontaneous engagement.
When mindful of *Prabh*, one's posture is unmovable;[3]
When mindful of *Prabh*, the lotus flower blooms.
When mindful of *Prabh*, the unstruck sound resonates;
With mindfulness, happiness has no end.
Blessed by *Prabh*, one is mindful;
Nanak: Seek refuge among the devotees. (7)

When mindful of *Har*, *bhagats* become known;
When mindful of *Har*, the Vedas were composed.
When mindful of *Har*, one becomes a *siddh*, a celibate and a giver;
When mindful of *Har*, the lowly become known in all four directions.
Be mindful of *Har*, the supporter of the whole earth;
Be mindful of *Har*, the cause of all causes.
Be mindful of *Har*, the creator of all forms;
Be mindful of *Har*, the formless one (*Nirankar*).
Those blessed receive this understanding;
Nanak: The *gurmukh* mindfully attains *Har*. (8) [1]

Salok

Poverty, pain and suffering are destroyed, by the Master of hearts who has no master.
In the sanctuary of *Prabh*, Nanak seeks help. (1)

Astapadi

Where there is no mother, father, son, friend, or brother,
    O mind, *Nam* will help you.
Where the great and scary messenger of death wants to crush you,
    only *Nam* will accompany you.
Where there are heavy burdens,
    the *Nam* of *Har* will instantly rescue you.
You will not swim across by performing countless rituals,[4]
    the *Nam* of *Har* will remove millions of sins.
The *gurmukh* chants *Nam* with the mind;
Nanak: All sorts of happiness will be attained. (1)

A king ruling over the whole world suffers,
    chanting the *Nam* of *Har* brings happiness.
Desires are not blocked by collecting hundreds, thousands, or millions,
    chanting the *Nam* of *Har* provides release [from the cycle].
Thirst is not quenched by the countless colours of *maya*,[5]
    chanting the *Nam* of *Har* satisfies this thirst.
The path is tread upon alone,
    the *Nam* of *Har* provides comfort.
O mind, concentrate on such a *Nam*;
Nanak: The *gurmukh* attains a high state. (2).

Hundreds, thousands and millions of arms are of no help,
    chanting the *Nam* ferries one across.
When countless obstacles harass one,
    the *Nam* of *Har* quickly comes to the rescue.
Countless are the births, lives and deaths,
    by chanting the *Nam*, peace is attained.
The ego is filthy and can never be cleansed,
    only the *Nam* of *Har* erases millions of sins.
O mind, chant such a *Nam* with love,
    Nanak, this is acquired in the company of the *sadhs*. (3)

This path upon which miles cannot be counted,
    the *Nam* of *Har* will offer sustenance.
On this path of total darkness,
    the *Nam* of *Har* will provide light.
On this journey where you are anonymous,
    the *Nam* of *Har* will be your identity.
Where there is immense and unbearable heat,
    the *Nam* of *Har* will be your shade.
O mind, when thirst torments you,
    Nanak, only *Har* showers ambrosial nectar. (4)

Nam is a necessity for the *bhagats*;
The *sants* have a peaceful mind.
The *Nam* of *Har* shelters the devotees;
The *Nam* of *Har* saves millions.
Har is praised day and night by the *sants*;
Har is the healing remedy used by the *sadhs*.
Nam is treasured by the devotees of *Har*;
Parbraham blesses the devotee with this gift.
Mind and body are imbued with the love of the One;
Nanak: The devotee has insight and discernment. (5)

The *Nam* of *Har* liberates the devotee;
The *Nam* of *Har* satisfies the devotee's hunger.
The *Nam* of *Har* is the devotee's form and colour;
Chanting the *Nam* of *Har*, the devotee overcomes obstacles.
The *Nam* of *Har* brings praise to the devotee;
The *Nam* of *Har* brings glory to the devotee.
The *Nam* of *Har* brings enjoyment and unity;
Chanting the *Nam* of *Har*, there is no separation.
The devotee is dedicated to the service of *Har*;
Nanak: *Har* is the God to be worshipped. (6)

The devotee of *Har* has a treasure of wealth,
    Prabh confers this wealth.
The devotee of *Har* has powerful support;
The devotee of *Har* does not recognize any other power.

The devotee of *Har* is interwoven with love,
   ecstatic from being absorbed in *sunn*.
The devotee of *Har* chants throughout the eight watches;[6]
The *bhagat* of *Har* appears, and is never hidden.
The *bhagat* of *Har* liberates many others;
Nanak: In the devotee's company, many more swim across. (7)

The *Nam* of *Har* grants wishes;
Singing the praises of *Har* fulfils desires.
Discourses about *Har* is above all;
Listening to *Nam*, pain and suffering are removed.
The grandeur of *Nam* resides in the *sants'* hearts;
Sins depart with the *sants'* kindness.
In the company of the *sants*, good fortune is secured;
Serve the *sants* by concentrating on *Nam*.
There is nothing equal to *Nam*;
Nanak: Rare is the *gurmukh* who attains *Nam*. (8) [2]

Salok
Many Shastras, many Simritis, I have searched them all;
Nanak: Nothing equals the priceless *Nam* of *Hare Har*. (1)

Astapadi
Chanting, meditation, knowledge and concentration,
   sermons about the six Shastras and Simritis.
Yoga, *karam*, *dharam* and *kirya*,
   renouncing everything and wandering in the wilderness.
Participating in all sorts of rituals,
   virtue, charity and the burning of purified butter.
Cutting the body into pieces and offering them,[7]
   keeping fasts and taking many vows.
Nothing equals contemplating the *Nam* of *Ram*;
Nanak: Try chanting *Nam* as a *gurmukh* (1).

Wandering the nine regions of the land and living forever,
   becoming a great renunciate and ascetic.
Burning yourself in fire;
Making many gifts of gold, horses and land;
Performing *naoli* and many *asans*;

The Jain path of self-restraint and its many methods,
    cutting the body piece by piece,
    yet the filth of the ego will not go away.
Nothing equals the *Nam* of *Har*;
Nanak: Chant *Nam* as a *gurmukh* and secure deliverance. (2)

The mind desires to leave the body at a pilgrimage place,
    ego and pride will not leave the body.
Bathing day and night,
    mental filth will not leave the body.
Putting this body through many yogic techniques,
    the mind is not rid of illusions.
Washing this impermanent body with loads of water,
    but how can a mud wall be cleansed?
O mind, the *Nam* of *Har* is the highest praise;
Nanak: Many of the fallen have been saved by *Nam*. (3)

Many schemes, yet the fear of death pervades;
Many endeavours are made, yet desires remain unquenched.
Many facades, yet the fire remains inextinguishable;
Millions of techniques, yet access to the heavenly court is denied.
Reaching the sky and nether regions, but there is no escape;
Attachment spreads and *maya* entangles.
All clever schemes result in death;
Nothing is accepted, except the praise of *Govind*.
By chanting the *Nam* of *Har*, suffering departs;
Nanak says: There is spontaneous love. (4)

If a person wants the four blessings,[8]
    engage in the service of devoted *sadhs*.
If a person wants to erase one's suffering,
    sing the *Nam* of *Har* within the heart.
If a person wants to be honoured,
    abandon the ego in the company of the *sadhs*.
If a person fears birth and death,
    seek refuge in the company of the *sadhs*.
The devotee who thirsts for a vision of *Prabh*,
    Nanak, I sacrifice myself to such a devotee. (5)

Among all people, the One is in command;
In the company of the *sadhs*, pride is erased.
Recognizing oneself as low
    is taken to be of the highest account.
The one whose mind becomes the dust of everyone's feet,
    is able to see the *Nam* of *Har* in all.
When negativity is erased from the mind,
    there is friendship with the whole world.
The devotee views pleasure and suffering as alike,
    Nanak, and is uninfluenced by sin or virtue. (6)

To the poor, Your *Nam* is wealth;
To the homeless, Your *Nam* is home.
To the dishonoured, *Prabh* is honour;
You bear gifts to all.
Swami, the cause of all causes,
    knows the secrets of all hearts.
You alone know Your state and extent,
    Prabh, You are absorbed within Yourself.
Only You can praise Yourself,
    Nanak, no one else understands. (7)

Of all *dharams*, the best *dharam* is
    to chant the *Nam* of *Har*, the purest of actions.
Of all *kiryas*, the best *kirya* is
    to remove the filth of foul intellect in the company of the *sadhs*.
Of all efforts, the best effort is
    to continuously chant the *Nam* of *Har*.
Of all speech, the best speech is
    to hear and sing the praises of *Har*.
Of all places, the best place is,
    Nanak, the heart where the *Nam* of *Har* resides. (8) [3]

Salok
O characterless and ignorant ones, always cherish *Prabh*;
Nanak: Remember your Creator forever. (1)

Astapadi
Remember the qualities of beautiful *Ram*,
    from whom you originated and got your appearance.

You were made, decorated, adored,
    and saved from the womb's fire.[9]
Nursed with milk in infancy;
Given nourishment, comfort and guidance in youth.
Friends and relatives provide care in old age,
    putting food in your mouth, and keeping you seated.
The characterless are unaware of everything,
    Nanak, pardon them, and may they understand. (1)

With blessings, there is happiness on earth,
    laughter with sons, brothers, friends and women.
With blessings, there is cool water to drink,
    soothing air, and precious fire.[10]
With blessings, pleasures are enjoyed,
    the necessities of life are obtained.
Given hands, feet, ears, eyes and tongue,
    why abandon [*Prabh*] and attach to others?
The bad are foolish, blind and stuck,
    Nanak, only *Prabh* can save the bad. (2)

Cared for in the beginning and the end,
    the ignorant one does not love You.
In Your service, the nine treasures are attained,
    but the foolish mind is disconnected.
The Master is always present,
    but the blind one thinks You are far away.
Through service, there is honour in the heavenly court;
The fool is unaware,
    always making mistakes.
Nanak: The Infinite is the caregiver. (3)

Forsaking the pearl and infatuated with its shell,
    truth is renounced and falsehood is embraced.
That which is passing is believed to be permanent,
    the inevitable is recognized as far away.
Working hard for that which will be left behind,
    and letting go of inner support.
Washing off sandalwood paste
    is like a donkey loving the mud.[11]

Fallen and afraid in a dark well,
   Nanak, the merciful *Prabh* can rescue them. (4)

Behaving like an animal, yet of the human species;
Preaching to others day and night.
Outer facades, yet the filth of *maya* within,
   trying to hide this, but it cannot be hidden.
Outer knowledge, concentration and bathing,
   yet the dog of greed clings within.
Ashes on the body, yet fire within;
With stones around the neck, can one swim the bottomless ocean?
Within whom *Prabh* resides,
   Nanak, those devotees are spontaneously absorbed. (5)

How can the blind find the path by listening?
By holding someone's hand, the destination is reached.
How can the deaf solve a riddle?
Say it is night, one understands it as day.
How can the mute sing a verse?
Making an attempt, the voice breaks.
How can the crippled climb a mountain?
Such a one will not be able to reach there.
O merciful Creator, the meek prays;
Nanak: With Your grace, one swims across. (6)

Inner support is forgotten,
   and love is given to enemies.
Living in a sandhouse,
   enjoying the games, pleasures and love of *maya*.
The foolish mind believes this to be permanent,
   and does not remember death.
Hate, enmity, lust, anger, attachment,
   falsehood, misdeeds, intense greed and deceit;
In this way, many births are wasted.
Nanak: Save such a one with Your mercy. (7)

To You, Master, this *ardas* is offered;
The soul and body are all Your property.

You are the mother and father, we are the children;
With Your grace, there are many joys.
No one knows Your end,
>   *Bhagwant* is the highest of the high.
The whole creation is strung on Your thread,
>   that which You make happen, abides in Your will.
You alone know Your state and extent;
Nanak, the servant, is forever Your sacrifice. (8)[4]

Salok
Letting go of *Prabh*, the provider, and going after other tastes;
Nanak: Without *Nam*, there is no success and respect disappears. (1)

Astapadi
Having and caring for the ten possessions,[12]
>   if one possession is withheld, one loses faith.
But if one possession is not given or the ten are taken away,
>   what would the fool then say or do?
The Master cannot be moved by force,
>   so forever bow.
All pleasures reside in the mind,
>   which seems sweet to *Prabh*.
The devotee who abides by Your command,
>   Nanak, acquires everything. (1)

If the banker lends money,
>   the fool uses it for eating, drinking, joy and pleasures.
But if some of the money is taken by the banker,
>   the ignorant mind becomes angry, [thus resulting in]
>   loss of credibility,
>   and trust.
When one's possessions are placed before the One,
>   and the command of *Prabh* is obeyed on the forehead,
>   such a one will be happy fourfold;
Nanak: *Sahib* is forever merciful. (2)

Attachment to the many aspects of *maya*,
>   understand that in the end they are all impermanent.

The shade of the tree is loved,
   but the mind suffers as it disappears.
The visible is impermanent,
   yet the blindest of the blind clings to it.
Giving love to a traveller,
   leaves one empty-handed.
O mind, loving the *Nam* of *Har* brings peace;
Nanak: With blessings, such a one unites with the One. (3)

Impermanent is the body, wealth and entire family;
Impermanent is the ego, attachment and *maya*.
Impermanent is power, youth, wealth and capital;
Impermanent is lust and frightening anger.
Impermanent are chariots, elephants, horses and clothes;
Impermanent is enjoyment in the love of *maya*.
Impermanent is deceit, attachment and pride;
Impermanent is your overconfidence.
Permanent is devotion in the sanctuary of the *sadhs*;
Nanak: Chanting at the feet of *Har* is to be alive. (4)

Impermanent are the ears that listen to the slander of others;
Impermanent are the hands that steal the wealth of others.
Impermanent are the eyes that gaze at the beauty of another's woman;
Impermanent is the tongue that savours food and other flavours.
Impermanent are the feet that run to mistreat others;
Impermanent is the mind that covets another's wealth.
Impermanent is the body that is not thoughtful towards others;
Impermanent is the nose that smells vice.
Without understanding, everything is impermanent;
Nanak: Fruitful is the body that has the *Nam* of *Har*. (5)

Useless, the life of the materialist;
Without Truth, how can anyone be pure?
Useless, the blind body without *Nam*,
   foul smell comes from its mouth.
Without mindfulness, day and night pass in vain;
Without clouds, the crop withers away.
Without praising *Gobind*, all work is done in vain;

Like the wealth of a miser, it is useless.
Blessed, blessed is the devotee whose heart is filled with *Nam*.
Nanak, I am a sacrifice to such a devotee. (6)

Professing one thing, but doing something else,
    the mind lacks love and misleads with talk.
The all-knowing *Prabh* is wise,
    and is not impressed by outer facades.
Preaching to others, but not following it,
    one comes, goes, and is born and dies.
Within the devotee's heart *Nirankar* dwells,
    such a one's teachings can save the world.
Pleasing the One, *Prabh* is recognized;
Nanak lays at such a devotee's feet. (7)

When a prayer is offered, *Prabh* knows,
    creatures are given esteem by You alone.
You, Yourself alone make decisions;
You are known to some as far, and to others as near.
Beyond all schemes and disciplines,
    You are all-knowing and aware of the inner conditions of all.
Those with love, You attach them to Yourself,
    dwelling in every place.
The blessed servants,
    Nanak, chant *Hari* every moment. (8) [5]

Salok
Lust, anger, greed, attachment and ego vanish;[13]
Nanak: Through the divine *Guru's* grace, *Prabh's* sanctuary is entered. (1)

Astapadi
By whose grace are thirty-six kinds of delicacies eaten?[14]
Keep the Master in the mind.
By whose grace is perfume applied to the body?
Be mindful and attain the supreme condition.
By whose grace is there comfort at home?
Always attune the mind within.
By whose grace is there comfort of family?

Throughout the eight watches, mindfully chant with the tongue.
By whose grace are colours, tastes and pleasures enjoyed?
Nanak: Concentrate and merge with that which is worthy of concentration. (1)

By whose grace are silk and satin worn?
Let go of attachment to others.
By whose grace is there comfortable sleep in bed?
O mind, sing the praises [of *Prabh*] throughout the eight watches.
By whose grace is respect given?
Sing the praises with the mouth and tongue.
By whose grace have you mastered *dharam*?
O mind, always and only meditate on *Parbraham*.
Chanting *Prabh*, honour is attained in the heavenly court,
    Nanak, the real home is entered with honour. (2)

By whose grace is this golden body healthy?
Attune yourself to the lovable *Ram*.
By whose grace is your image maintained?
O mind, attain happiness by singing about *Har*.
By whose grace have your defects remained hidden?
O mind, seek the sanctuary of *Prabh*, the master.
By whose grace is no one able to harm you?
O mind, with every breath be mindful of *Prabh*, the highest.
By whose grace was this precious body given?
Nanak: Perform devotion to the One. (3)

By whose grace are ornaments worn?
O mind, why do you procrastinate being mindful?
By whose grace are horses and elephants ridden?
O mind, never forget *Prabh*.
By whose grace are gardens, property and wealth possessed?
Connect the mind with *Prabh*.
O mind, acknowledge the Creator;
Always concentrate [on *Prabh*] while standing and sitting.
Concentrate on the indescribable One;
Nanak: You will be protected in this world and the next. (4)

By whose grace is plenty of charity given?
O mind, concentrate on the One throughout the eight watches.

By whose grace can you perform duties?
Remember *Prabh* with every breath.
By whose grace do you have a beautiful form?
Always be mindful of *Prabh*, the unique One.
By whose grace do you have a good caste?
Always be mindful of *Prabh*, day and night.
By whose grace is your honour maintained?
Nanak: With *Guru's* grace, sing praises. (5)

By whose grace do the ears hear sound?
By whose grace are wonders seen?
By whose grace does the tongue say sweet words?
By whose grace is there spontaneous happiness?
By whose grace do the hands perform work?
By whose grace is one fulfilled?
By whose grace is the supreme state attained?
By whose grace are you absorbed in spontaneous happiness?
Why forsake such a God (*Prabh*) and attach yourself to another?
Nanak: The mind awakens through *Guru's* grace. (6)

By whose grace are you known in the world?
Accept *Prabh* in the mind as your source.
By whose grace do you attain prestige?
O foolish mind, you ought to chant [the *Nam*].
By whose grace are your endeavours completed?
O mind, always understand the One is omnipresent.
By whose grace, do you attain the Truth?
O my mind, remain connected.
Through grace, everyone is saved;
Nanak: Mindfully chant the chant. (7).

You make the chanting of *Nam* happen;
You make the qualities of *Har* be sung.
With *Prabh's* blessing, there is enlightenment;
With *Prabh's* kindness, the lotus blooms in the heart.
When pleased, *Prabh* resides in the mind;
With *Prabh's* kindness, the intellect is perfect.
All wealth is obtained through You, *Prabh*,
    nothing can be independently acquired.

O *Har*, the master, under Your direction everything happens;
Nanak: There is nothing in one's hand. (8) [6]

Salok
Parbraham is inaccessible and unfathomable,
    whoever recites [*Nam*] will be liberated.
Nanak requests, listen friend,
    sermons about the *sadhs* are awesome. (1)

Astapadi
In the company of the *sadhs*, the face begins to glow;
In the company of the *sadhs*, all filth is removed.
In the company of the *sadhs*, pride is erased;
In the company of the *sadhs*, wisdom appears.
In the company of the *sadhs*, *Prabh* is immanent;
In the company of the *sadhs*, everything becomes resolved.
In the company of the *sadhs*, the jewel of *Nam* is obtained;
In the company of the *sadhs*, efforts are for the One.
Can a mortal describe the glory of the *sadh*?
Nanak: The *sadhs*' glory merges with *Prabh*. (1)

In the company of the *sadhs*, there is transcendental awareness;
In the company of the *sadhs*, one forever flourishes.
In the company of the *sadhs*, the five are controlled;
In the company of the *sadhs*, the ambrosial nectar is savoured.
In the company of the *sadhs*, one becomes the dust of all feet;
In the company of the *sadhs*, speech is beautiful.
In the company of the *sadhs*, there is no directionless wandering;
In the company of the *sadhs*, a stable mind is attained.
In the company of the *sadhs*, one detaches from *maya*;
Nanak: In the company of the *sadhs*, *Prabh* is delighted. (2)

In the company of the *sadhs*, all adversaries become friends;
In the company of the *sadhs*, there is utmost purity.
In the company of the *sadhs*, no one is hated;
In the company of the *sadhs*, the feet do not sway.
In the company of the *sadhs*, no one is seen as bad;
In the company of the *sadhs*, supreme bliss is experienced.

In the company of the *sadhs*, the fever of ego is no more;
In the company of the *sadhs*, all 'I am-ness' is driven away.
You know the *sadhs*' greatness,
    Nanak, the *sadhs* and *Prabh* have a solid bond. (3)

In the company of the *sadhs*, there is no wandering;
In the company of the *sadhs*, happiness is everlasting.
In the company of the *sadhs*, the transcendent One can be seen;
In the company of the *sadhs*, the unbearable is bearable.
In the company of the *sadhs*, the One resides on an exalted platform;
In the company of the *sadhs*, the palace is reached.
In the company of the *sadhs*, one is firm in *dharam*;
In the company of the *sadhs*, there is only *Parbraham*.
In the company of the *sadhs*, the treasure of *Nam* is obtained;
Nanak: I am a sacrifice to the *sadhs*. (4)

In the company of the *sadhs*, the entire family is saved;
In the company of the *sadhs*, acquaintances, friends and family are saved.
In the company of the *sadhs*, wealth is acquired;
In the company of the *sadhs*, everyone benefits from the wealth.
In the company of the *sadhs*, the god of justice engages in service;[15]
In the company of the *sadhs*, the gods sing praises.
In the company of the *sadhs*, sins vanish;
In the company of the *sadhs*, the ambrosial qualities of the One are sung.
In the company of the *sadhs*, all pleasures are within reach;
Nanak: In the company of the *sadhs*, birth is fruitful. (5)

In the company of the *sadhs*, there are no strenuous practices;
The gift of their vision is joyful.
In the company of the *sadhs*, sins are distant;
In the company of the *sadhs*, hell is far away.
In the company of the *sadhs*, peace is here and hereafter;
In the company of the *sadhs*, the separated are united.
Yearning for the fruit, they acquire it;
In the company of the *sadhs*, no one goes empty-handed.
Parbraham resides in the *sadhs*' hearts;
Nanak: One is saved upon hearing the *sadhs*' sweet words. (6)

In the company of the *sadhs*, the name of *Har* is heard;
In the company of the *sadhs*, the praises of *Har* are sung.
In the company of the *sadhs*, the mind is not forgetful;
In the company of the *sadhs*, liberation is for sure.
In the company of the *sadhs*, the experience of *Prabh* is sweet;
In the company of the *sadhs*, the One is seen in the hearts of all.
In the company of the *sadhs*, one abides by the Will;
In the company of the *sadhs*, I have good health.
In the company of the *sadhs*, all diseases are washed away;
Nanak: The *sadhs* are met with good fortune. (7)

The *sadhs'* glory is not known to the Vedas,
    the Vedas only describe what the sages heard.
Praises about the *sadhs* are above the three qualities;[16]
Praises about the *sadhs* are present everywhere.
The *sadhs'* glory has no end;
The *sadhs'* glory is forever limitless.
The *sadhs'* glory is the highest of the high;
The *sadhs'* glory is the greatest of the great.
The *sadhs'* glory is their own;
Nanak: There is no difference between the *sadhs* and *Prabh*. (8) [7]

Salok
True mind, true mouth,
    besides the One, nothing else is seen;
Nanak: These are the qualities of a *brahamgiani*. (1)

Astapadi
Brahamgiani is eternally unstained,
    just as the lotus remains clean in [muddy] water.
Brahamgiani is always free from negativity,
    just as the sun dries up everything.
Brahamgiani looks upon all as equal,
    just as the wind blows on the king and beggar alike.
Brahamgiani is steadfast with the One,
    like the earth, either dug or anointed with sandalwood paste.[17]
These are the qualities of the *brahamgiani*;
Nanak: The *brahamgiani's* inherent nature purifies like fire. (1)

Brahamgiani is the purest of the pure,
    like water to which filth cannot stick.
Brahamgiani has an enlightened mind,
    like the sky above the earth.
Brahamgiani treats friends and foes alike;
Brahamgiani has no pride.
Brahamgiani is the highest of the high,
    yet such a one's mind is humble.
Only those are *brahamgianis*,[18]
    Nanak, who *Prabh* makes so. (2).

Brahamgiani is the dust of everyone's feet;
Brahamgiani knows how to savour the soul.
Brahamgiani shows kindness to all;
Brahamgiani is never negative.
Brahamgiani is always impartial;
Brahamgiani's glance is like a shower of ambrosia.
Brahamgiani is released from entanglement;
Brahamgiani has a pure way.
Brahamgiani has wisdom for nourishment;
Nanak: *Brahamgiani* concentrates on *Braham*. (3)

Brahamgiani places hope in the One;
Brahamgiani will never perish.
Brahamgiani is steeped in humility;
Brahamgiani enjoys helping others.
Brahamgiani is not entangled [in *maya*];
Brahamgiani no longer wanders.
Brahamgiani sees that everything is for the best;
Brahamgiani blooms with fulfilment.
Brahamgiani saves others in his/her company;
Nanak: *Brahamgiani* helps the whole world meditate. (4)

Brahamgiani has one love;
Brahamgiani resides in the company of *Prabh*.
Brahamgiani has the support of *Nam*;
Brahamgiani has *Nam* as family.
Brahamgiani is always and forever awake;

Brahamgiani renounces egotistical thinking.
Brahamgiani experiences supreme bliss in the mind;
Brahamgiani always has bliss in his/her heart.
Brahamgiani lives in spontaneous happiness;
Nanak: *Brahamgiani* never perishes. (5)

Brahamgiani understands *Braham*;
Brahamgiani loves the company of the One.
Brahamgiani is spontaneous;
Brahamgiani has pure teachings.
Brahamgiani does whatever *Prabh* makes happen;
Brahamgiani has great glory.
Brahamgiani is seen with good fortune;
Brahamgiani is to whom sacrifices are made.
Brahamgiani is sought by Shiva;
Nanak: *Brahamgiani* is *Paramesar*. (6)

Brahamgiani is priceless;
Brahamgiani is mindful of everything.
Brahamgiani, who can know your secrets?
Brahamgiani, to whom one bows forever.
Brahamgiani cannot be described with words;
Brahamgiani is the Master of all.
Who can estimate *Brahamgiani*'s measure?
Brahamgiani is all-knowing.
Brahamgiani is limitless;
Nanak: Forever salute the *brahamgiani*. (7)

Brahamgiani is the Creator of the world;
Brahamgiani lives forever and never dies.
Brahamgiani provides the way to liberation;
Brahamgiani is the perfect Being, orchestrating everything.
Brahamgiani is the helper of the helpless;
Brahamgiani extends a hand to everyone.
Brahamgiani has all form;
Brahamgiani is *Nirankar*.
Brahamgiani alone knows the *brahamgiani*'s glory;
Nanak: *Brahamgiani* is the Master of all. (8) [8]

Salok

The one who keeps *Nam* within the heart,
   sees *Bhagwan* pervading in all,
   and bows to the Master every moment;
Nanak: Such a one is an *aparas* (puritan) and saves others. (1)

Astapadi

Whose tongue does not touch falsehood,
   whose mind is filled with love and sees *Niranjan*,
   whose eyes do not gaze upon the beauty of another's woman,
   who serves the *sadhs* and joins the *sants* with love,
   whose ears do not hear the slander of others,
   who recognizes oneself as the worst of all,
   whose illusions are removed with *Guru's* grace,
   whose desires of the mind vanish from the mind,
   who conquers the senses and is above the five evils,
Nanak, such an *aparas* is one in a million. (1)

The *vaishnav*, who has delighted [Vishnu],
   is separate from Vishnu's *maya*,
   and performs deeds without reward,
   such a *vaishnav* has a pure *dharam*.
[The *vaishnav* has] no desires for the fruit of his/her deeds,
   only absorbed in devotion and singing the praises.
Mindful of *Gopal* within the mind and body,
   [such a one] is merciful;
Firm within, and inspiring others to chant the *Nam*,
   Nanak, such a *vaishnav* attains the supreme state. (2)

The *bhagauti* (devotee) of *Bhagwant* is devoted with love,
   and renounces the company of all the wicked.
All doubt is eradicated from the mind,
   worshipping the totality of *Parbraham*.
In the company of the *sadhs*, filthy sin is washed away,
   such a *bhagauti* has a high intellect.
Constantly serving *Bhagwant*,
   offering the mind and body to Vishnu with love.

Enshrining the feet of *Har* in the heart,
    Nanak, such a *bhagauti* attains *Bhagwant*. (3)

The *pandit* (priest) who awakens the mind
    searches for *Ram Nam* within,
    and savours the essential drink of *Ram Nam*,
    from such a *pandit's* teachings, the world survives.
Teaching about *Har* within the heart,
    such a *pandit* will not take birth again.
Understanding the origin of the Vedas, Simritis and Puranas,
    recognizing the invisible within the visible,
    and giving teachings to the four classes,[19]
    Nanak, forever bow to such a *pandit*. (4)

The seed mantra imparts wisdom to all,
    anyone of the four classes can chant the *Nam*.
Whoever chants will be saved;
Only a few obtain [*Nam*] in the company of the *sadhs*.
With blessings, there is concentration within the heart;
Brutes, ghosts, fools and the stone-hearted will cross over.
Nam is the panacea for all illnesses;
With good fortune, happiness is obtained by singing praises.
[*Nam*] cannot be secured through religious ritual;
Nanak: Received by those whom it was written for in the beginning. (5)

In whose mind resides *Parbraham*,
    such a one can be called the true servant of *Ram*.
In whose mind is able to see *Ram* in everything,
    such a one is liberated by serving the servant's servant.
Recognizing *Har* as forever near,
    such a servant is recognized in the heavenly court.
Your servant is blessed by You,
    such a servant understands everything.
In the company of all, yet detached within,
    Nanak, such is the way of the servant of *Ram*. (6)

Abiding in the will of *Prabh* with inner sincerity,
    such a one is liberated.
As is joy, so is despair;

Always blissful, never separated.
As is gold, so is clay;
As is nectar, so is bitter poison.
As is esteem, so is pride;
As is the beggar, so is the king.
Whoever the One ordains,
    Nanak, such a one is called *jiwan mukat*. (7)

All places belong to *Parbraham*,
    according to their environments, creatures are placed and named.
You are the Creator, the cause of all causes,
    whatever pleases *Prabh* will happen.
You are all-pervading, like an endless wave,
    the colours of *Parbraham* are indescribable.
As is the intellect given, so is enlightenment;
Parbraham is the indestructible creator.
Forever, forever, forever merciful,
    Nanak, with mindful remembrance, one flourishes. (8) [9]

Salok
Countless people praise the One, but You have no end or boundaries;
Nanak: *Prabh* created the creation, in many ways and with countless varieties. (1)

Astapadi
Many a million are the worshippers;
Many a million perform religious rituals.
Many a million reside at pilgrimages;
Many a million wander as renunciates in the wilderness.
Many a million hear the Vedas;
Many a million are the ascetics.
Many a million place their concentration within;
Many a million are the poets discussing poetry.
Many a million meditate on new names;
Nanak: No one can attain the limits of the Creator. (1)

Many a million have pride;
Many a million are blinded by ignorance.
Many a million are stone-hearted misers;

Many a million lack heartfelt empathy.
Many a million steal others' property;
Many a million slander others.
Many a million work hard amid the *maya*;
Many a million wander in foreign lands.
Whatever the placement, so is the engagement;
Nanak: Only the Creator understands the creation. (2)

Many a million are the *siddhs* [ascetics], celibates and yogis;
Many a million are the kings indulging in pleasure.
Many a million are the birds and snakes created;
Many a million are the stones and trees created.
Many a million are the elements of air, water and fire;
Many a million are the lands and regions.
Many a million are the moons, suns and stars;
Many a million are the gods, demons and canopied *Indras*.
All creation is strung on Your thread;
Nanak: Those who love You, will be saved. (3)

Many a million live in passion, darkness and purity;
Many a million are the Vedas, Simritis, Shastras and Puranas.
Many a million are the pearls created in the ocean;
Many a million are the various kinds of creatures.
Many a million are made with long lives;
Many a million are the hills and beautiful mountains.
Many a million are the *yakhshas, kinnars* and *pisaach*;
Many a million are the zombies, ghosts, pigs and tigers.
All are near, all are far;
Nanak: You are all-pervasive, yet unaffected. (4)

Many a million inhabit the nether regions;
Many a million take residence in hell and heaven.
Many a million are born, live and die;
Many a million wander through many births.
Many a million eat while seated;
Many a million work hard and are exhausted.
Many a million are created with wealth;
Many a million are anxious amid *maya*.

Whatever the Will, so is the placement;
Nanak: Everything is in *Prabh*'s hands. (5)

Many a million are the detached ascetics,
    deeply absorbed in the *Nam* of *Ram*.
Many a million are in search of *Prabh*,
    and discover *Parbraham* within their inner being.
Many a million thirst for a vision of *Prabh*,
    and *Prabh*, the indestructible one, meets them.
Many a million want the company of Truth,
    and *Parbraham* gives them love.
Those who have delighted the One,
    Nanak, such devotees are forever blessed. (6).

Many a million are the four types of creation;[20]
Many a million are the skies and worlds.
Many a million are the births;
Many methods are used for expansion.
Many times the expansion has spread,
    the Creator only exists forever.
Many a million are created in many forms,
    from *Prabh* they originated, and in *Prabh* they merge;
No one knows Your end,
    Nanak, only You, *Prabh*, exist. (7)

Many a million are the servants of *Parbraham*,
    their inner beings shine.
Many a million realize the essence,
    their eyes gaze forever on the One.
Many a million savour the drink of *Nam*,
    they become immortal, living forever.
Many a million sing the qualities of *Ram*,
    spontaneously immersed in savouring inner happiness.
You remember Your servants with every breath,
    Nanak, they are loved by *Paramesar*. (8) [10]

Salok
Only *Prabh* is the cause of all causes, there is no other;
Nanak: I am a sacrifice to that which pervades water, land and space. (1)

Astapadi
The One is competent to be the cause of all causes,
    everything that happens, pleases the One.
In an instant, there is creation and dissolution,
    there are no boundaries.
The *hukam* supports without any other support,
    hukam creates, *hukam* absorbs.
Through *hukam* there is high and low work;
Through *hukam* there are countless colours.
Creating the creation, the One sees Its own greatness;
Nanak: The One pervades everything. (1)

When *Prabh* is delighted, a person attains liberation;
When *Prabh* is delighted, stones swim across [the ocean].
When *Prabh* is delighted, the breathless are restored;
When *Prabh* is delighted, the qualities of *Har* are chanted.
When *Prabh* is delighted, the fallen are saved;
You act according to Your own judgement.
You are the master of both worlds;
The play is enjoyed by the inner-Knower of hearts.
Whatever delights You will happen;
Nanak: See no other. (2)

Say, what can a person do?
Whatever delights You will happen.
If it was in their hands, everything would be taken;
Whatever delights You will happen.
The ignorant ones are drawn to poison,
    if they understood, they would save themselves.
Misled by doubt, running in the ten directions,[21]
    in an instant, one returns from wandering through the four quarters.[22]
Blessed is the one on whom devotion is conferred,
    Nanak, such a devotee unites with *Nam*. (3)

In an instant, the lowly worm becomes a king,
    Parbraham protects the poor.
The one who has not been seen
    is instantly recognized in the ten directions.

The one upon whom blessings are conferred,
    accounts of such a one are not called upon by *Jagdish*.
The soul and body are Your property;
The light of *Braham* fills every heart.
Your structure was built by You;
Nanak lives by seeing Your greatness. (4)

Power is not in one's own hands,
    the Cause of all causes is the master of all.
The helpless live according to Your will,
    whatever delights You will happen.
Sometimes the placement is high or low;
Sometimes anxious or laughing joyfully.
Sometimes behaviour is slanderous or anxious;
Sometimes high in the sky or in the nether lands.
Sometimes discourses about *Braham* are understood;
Nanak: It is You who unites. (5)

Sometimes one dances in many ways;
Sometimes one sleeps day and night.
Sometimes one frightens with extreme anger;
Sometimes one is the dust of everyone's feet.
Sometimes one sits as a colossal king;
Sometimes one wears the clothes of a beggar.
Sometimes one acquires an evil reputation;
Sometimes one is spoken of as very noble.
However placed by *Prabh*, that is how one lives;
Nanak: Through *Guru's* grace, truth is spoken. (6)

Sometimes teaching as a *pandit*;
Sometimes sitting in silent concentration.
Sometimes bathing at pilgrimage places;
Sometimes a *siddh*, a seeker, speaking wisdom.
Sometimes an insect, elephant, or moth;
Many living in delusion.
In various forms, the actors appear,
    and dance to *Prabh's* delight.
Whatever delights You will happen;
Nanak: There is no other. (7)

Sometimes the company of *sadhs* is attained,
>   their space should not be left for the outside world.

The inner being shines with wisdom,
>   this place will never perish.

Mind and body are imbued with only the colour of *Nam*,
>   always residing in the company of *Parbraham*.

As water blends with water,
>   so does light merge with light.

Released from wandering, peace is attained;
Nanak: Forever a sacrifice to *Prabh*. (8) [11]

Salok
The humble reside in happiness, 'I am-ness' is beneath them,
>   Nanak, very big egos rot in pride. (1)

Astapadi
The one in whose heart exists the pride of kingship,
>   falls into hell, and becomes a dog.

Recognizing oneself as youthful,
>   only to become an insect in excrement.

Calling oneself virtuous,
>   such a one takes birth and dies, wandering through many lives.

Proud of one's land and wealth,
>   the fool is blinded by ignorance.

Bless that heart where humility resides,
>   Nanak, liberated here, and attain happiness hereafter. (1)

Becoming wealthy and full of pride,
>   not even a piece of straw will accompany you.

Putting hope in a large army of men,
>   in an instant they can be destroyed.

Identifying oneself as more powerful than all others,
>   instantly turning into ashes.

The egotistical cares for no one,
>   the god of justice will punish such a one.

Through *Guru's* grace, pride is erased,
>   Nanak, such a devotee is accepted in the heavenly court. (2)

Performing a million actions, but in ego,
>   anxiety results from such efforts.

Performing countless penances, but in ego,
    born over and over again in hell and heaven.
Countless efforts, yet the heart is not softened,
    how can one then enter the heavenly court of *Har*?
Calling themselves noble,
    but nobility does not come near them.
When the mind becomes the dust of everyone's feet,
    Nanak, then there is purity. (3)

As long as the 'me' thinks it can do something,
    then it will not have peace.
As long as the 'me' thinks it can make something happen,
    then the 'me' wanders being born in wombs.
As long as someone is seen as foe or friend,
    the mind is unsteady.
As long as one is enmeshed in the company of attachment,
    the god of justice will punish.
The blessings of *Prabh* break bondage;
Nanak: *Guru's* grace extinguishes pride. (4)

Earning a thousand, then running after a hundred thousand,
    never satisfied, collecting more wealth.
In illusions, one seeks countless pleasures,
    never satisfied, dying a disgruntled death.
Without contentment, no satisfaction, and,
    as in a dream, all efforts are meaningless.
Coloured in *Nam*, one attains total happiness,
    fortunate is whoever obtains this.
You, Yourself, are the cause of causes;
Nanak: Forever, forever chant *Har*. (5)

The Creator is the cause of causes;
What decision is in one's hands?
Whatever You envision, that will happen,
    You, Yourself, *Prabh* are everything.
Whatever has been created is Your play,
    away from all, yet within all.
Understanding, watching and discerning,
    You are One, You are many.

Deathless, permanent, and not coming and going,
   Nanak, always absorbed in Yourself. (6)

You instruct, You understand,
   You are within everything.
You created Your own expanse,
   everything is Yours, You are the creator.
Without You, what can happen?
At every place, there is the One.
You the creator, Your drama,
   many colours in this spectacle.
You reside in the heart, and the heart resides in You;
Nanak: Your worth cannot be described. (7)

True, true, true, *Prabh Swami*;
Through *Guru's* grace, the truth can be described.
True, true, true, the entire creation;
Among a million, it is rare for anyone to understand.
Excellent, excellent, excellent is Your form;
Exquisite beauty, infinite and unique.
Pure, pure, pure is Your *bani*;
Spoken and heard, through the ears, within every heart.
Sacred, sacred, sacred is the sacred [*Nam*];
Nanak: Chant the *Nam* with a loving mind. (8) [12]

Salok
The devotee is saved in the sanctuary of the *sants*;
Nanak: Slandering the *sants* results in many rebirths. (1)

Astapadi
Those who have disdain for the *sants*, their lives will be shortened.
Those who have disdain for the *sants*, the god of death does not let them go.
Those who have disdain for the *sants*, all their happiness will vanish.
Those who have disdain for the *sants* go to hell.
Those who have disdain for the *sants*, their intellect becomes tainted.
Those who have disdain for the *sants* are deprived of glory.
Those [who have been] reproached by the *sants*, no one can protect them.
Those who have disdain for the *sants*, their place becomes polluted.

If the blessed *sants* give blessings,
  Nanak, the slanderer can swim across [the ocean] in the *sants*' company. (1)

Those who have disdain for the *sants* are crooked.
Those who have disdain for the *sants* moo like a cow.
Those who have disdain for the *sants* are reborn as a snake.
Those who have disdain for the *sants* are reborn as a worm.
Those who have disdain for the *sants* burn in desire.
Those who have disdain for the *sants* deceive everyone.
Those who have disdain for the *sants* lose all their clout.
Those who have disdain for the *sants* are the lowest of the low.
Those who have disdain for the *sants* have no support,
  Nanak, but if it delights the *sants*, liberation can still be attained. (2)

Those who slander the *sants* are great oppressors.
Those who slander the *sants* do not have a moment's rest.
Those who slander the *sants* are great killers.
Those who slander the *sants*, *Paramesar* strikes out at them.
Those who slander the *sants* are without a kingdom.
Those who slander the *sants* shall suffer from poverty.
Those who slander the *sants* contract all diseases.
Those who slander the *sants* are forever separated [from *Nam*].
Slandering the *sants* is the worst of actions,
  Nanak, but if it delights the *sants*, the slanderer can be liberated. (3)

Those who malign the *sants* are forever impure.
Those who malign the *sants* are no one's friend.
Those who malign the *sants* will be punished.
Those who malign the *sants* are abandoned by everyone.
Those who malign the *sants* have big egos.
Those who malign the *sants* are forever evil.
Those who malign the *sants* are born and die.
Those who malign the *sants* lose their happiness.
Those who malign the *sants* have no support,
  Nanak, but if it delights the *sants*, they can be united [with the One]. (4)

Those who malign the *sants* break down along the way;
Those who malign the *sants*, their endeavours remain unfulfilled.

Those who malign the *sants* wander in the wilderness;
Those who malign the *sants* become lonely.
Those who malign the *sants* are hollow within,
   like a breathless corpse.
Those who malign the *sants* have no roots;
They eat what they sow.
Those who malign the *sants*, no one protects them,
   Nanak, but if it delights the *sants*, they will be saved. (5)

Those who malign the *sants* cry out loud,
   just as a fish struggles without water.
Those who malign the *sants*, their hunger is never satisfied,
   just as fire is not satisfied with wood.
Those who malign the *sants* are abandoned,
   just as the dried up sesame withers in the field.
Those who malign the *sants* are void of *dharam*.
Those who malign the *sants*, their words are forever false.
These are the slanderers' deeds from the beginning,
   Nanak, whatever delights You will happen. (6)

Those who malign the *sants* have a damaged demeanour.
Those who malign the *sants* will receive punishment in the heavenly court.
Those who malign the *sants* are forever perplexed.
Those who malign the *sants* are neither dead nor alive.
Those who malign the *sants*, their hopes remain unfulfilled.
Those who malign the *sants* live without hope.
Those who malign the *sants* are never satisfied.
As is the disposition, so is the outcome.
No one can erase their misdeeds.
Nanak: The true One understands. (7)

Everybody belongs to You, the creator,
   forever, forever, they bow to You.
Praise *Prabh* day and night,
   meditate with every breath.
All that happens is done by You,
   whatever is done is done by You.
Your worldly drama, You are the creator,
   who else can offer an opinion?

Whoever is blessed receives Your *Nam*,
   Nanak, such a devotee is fortunate. (8) [13]

Salok
O noble one, abandon your cleverness, and be mindful of *Har*, the king;
Nanak: With one aspiration in the heart, suffering, doubt and fear vanish. (1)

Astapadi
Understand dependence on another is useless;
Bhagwan alone is the provider,
   by whose offerings we are satisfied,
   and our desires do not return.
Harm and protection come from You,
   nothing is in anyone's hand.
By understanding Your *hukam*, happiness occurs;
Keep *Nam* strung around the neck.
Be mindful, mindful, mindful of *Prabh*,
   Nanak, and no obstacle will come. (1)

O mind, praise *Nirankar*;
O mind, engage in truthful work.
Drink the pure nectar with the tongue,
   and forever live in joy.
See the Master's worldly drama with the eyes;
In the company of the *sadhs*, all other divisions disappear.
Make the feet walk the path of *Gobind*;
Sins are erased by chanting *Har* for a moment.
Perform actions for *Har*, listen to the sermons about *Har*,
   Nanak, the forehead shines in the heavenly court of *Har*. (2)

Those devotees are fortunate in this world,
   forever, forever singing the praises of *Har*.
Contemplating on *Ram Nam*,
   they are wealthy and fulfilled in the world.
Chanting *Har* with the heart, body and mouth,
   forever, forever, recognize those devotees as happy.
Recognizing the One as the only One,
   the here and hereafter are understood.

Whose mind accepts the company of *Nam*,
   Nanak, recognizes *Niranjan*. (3)

Through *Guru's* grace one becomes self-aware;
Recognize such a one as having extinguished desire.
In the company of the *sadhs*, *Har* is praised;
The devotee of *Har* is immune to all illnesses.
Only the praises [of *Har*] are sung night and day,
   without other desires within the household.
The devotee who places hope in the One,
   will have the noose of death cut.
Whose heart is hungry for *Parbraham*,
   Nanak, such a one will not suffer. (4)

Whoever remembers *Prabh* in the heart
   is a *sant*, both joyous and unwavering.
Whoever *Prabh* blesses,
   what will that servant be afraid of?
Whatever is understood, has been shown [by You];
You are absorbed in Your own creation.
By examining, examining, examining, there is success;
Through *Guru's* grace the essence of all is realized.
When looking, the root of all is seen,
   Nanak, the invisible is in the visible. (5)

Nothing is born, nothing dies,
   You are the director of the worldly drama.
Coming, going, the visible, the invisible,
   the whole of creation abides by You.
You, Yourself, are within everything,
   many methods in making and unmaking creation.
The indestructible One cannot be destroyed;
Keeping the universe stable.
Invisible, without appearance, and glorious Being,
   Nanak, You inspirit the chanter to chant. (6)

The one who realizes *Prabh* becomes glorious;
The whole world is saved by such a one's counsel.

The servant of *Prabh* can save us all;
The servant of *Prabh* makes suffering disappear.
You, the merciful One, unite the servant with Yourself;
With the chanting of *Guru's shabad*, one flourishes.
Inspirited to serve the One,
    such a one is fortunate and blessed.
Chanting the *Nam*, steadfastness is attained,
    Nanak, such a one is given high esteem. (7)

Whatever the devotee does is out of love for *Prabh*;
Forever, forever in the company of *Har*.
The devotee's nature is to accept what happens,
    recognizing the Creator in everything.
Whatever *Prabh* does is sweet to the devotee;
Whatever is understood is then shown [by You].
From where all have sprung is where the devotee returns,
    such a one is a treasure of happiness, and made thus.
You, Yourself give esteem;
Nanak: Recognize *Prabh* and the servant as one. (8) [14]

Salok
The all-powerful and complete *Prabh*, knower of sorrow;
Nanak: I am a sacrifice to *Prabh* and saved through remembrance. (1)

Astapadi
Gopal ties the broken string,
    the Nurturer takes care of all living beings.
The worries of all are in the One's heart,
    no one is turned away.
O my mind, always meditate on *Har*,
    Prabh, You, Yourself are indestructible.
Your creatures cannot do anything on their own,
    even though they desire to do so a hundred times.
Without You, nothing is of any use,
    Nanak, saved by only chanting the *Nam* of *Har*. (1)

If one is beautiful, there should be no attachment to such beauty,
    the light of *Prabh* is in the hearts of all.

If one is wealthy, there should be no pride over it,
    all wealth is given by You.
If one is called a warrior,
    without *Prabh's* power, what can the warrior break?
If one sits as a philanthropist,
    the fool should recognize the Giver of all.
By *Guru's* grace the disease of ego is removed,
    Nanak, the devotee will be forever healthy. (2)

Just as a pillar supports a house,
    Guru's shabad supports the mind.
Just as a stone floats in a boat,
    the one attached to *Guru's* feet is saved.
Just as the lamp turns darkness into light,
    the mind blossoms upon seeing *Guru*.
Just as the lost ones find a path in the great wilderness,
    the light appears in the company of the *sadhs*.
I want the dust of such a *sant's* feet,
    Nanak, fulfil this yearning for *Har*. (3)

O foolish mind, why the anguish?
These are the consequences of past recorded deeds.
Prabh gives sorrow and joy;
Detach from others, and remember [*Prabh*].
Whatever happens, accept it joyfully;
O mistaken one, why wander in ignorance?
What possessions accompanied you at birth?
Enmeshed in pleasures, like a greedy moth.
Chant *Ram Nam* with the heart,
    Nanak, and go home with honour. (4)

The goods you came to purchase,
    Ram Nam, can be attained in *Sant's* [i.e. *Guru's*] home.
Renounce pride, and receive profit in the mind;
Imbibe *Ram Nam* within the heart.
Load the goods, and walk in the company of the *sants*;
Detach from being entangled in vice.
Everyone will proclaim you as very blessed,
    and your face will shine in *Har's* heavenly court.

Rare is the trader in this trade (i.e. of *Ram Nam*),
    Nanak, I am a sacrifice to that one. (5)

Wash *Sadh's* [i.e. *Guru's*] feet, and drink the water;
Entrust your life to *Sadh*.
Bathe in the dust of *Sadh's* feet;
Become a sacrifice to *Sadh*.
Serving *Sadh* is secured through good fortune;
In the company of the *sadhs*, sing the praises of *Har*.
Sadh protects you from countless obstacles;
Praise the attributes of *Har*, taste the nectar.
Whoever takes refuge at *Sant's* [i.e. *Guru's*] doorway,
    Nanak, such a one attains total happiness. (6)

Competent to restore the dead;
Giver of support to the hungry.
Receive the consequences of past recorded deeds,
    yet all treasures are in the glance of the One.
Everything is Yours, O competent creator,
    without You, there is nothing else.
O devotee, forever, forever, chant day and night,
    this is the highest and purest activity.
Blessed is the one who receives *Nam*,
    Nanak, such a devotee becomes pure. (7)

The one whose heart has faith in *Guru*,
    such a devotee always remembers *Prabh*.
One is known as a *bhagat* in the three worlds,
    within whose heart is the One.
Truthful actions, truthful behaviour;
Truthful heart, truthful words spoken from the mouth.
Truthful vision, truthful form;
Using truth, spreading truth.
The one who understands *Parbraham* as the truth,
    Nanak, such a devotee will be absorbed in the truth. (8) [15]

Salok
Prabh has no form, mark, or colour, and is beyond the three qualities.[23]
Nanak: When one pleases the One, there is understanding. (1)

Astapadi
Keep the indestructible *Prabh* in your heart,
    and detach yourself from the love of others.
There is nothing beyond Your reach, *Prabh*,
    the One exists within all.
You are aware, You are wise,
    deeply profound, deeply intuitive.
Parbraham, Paramesar, Gobind,
    a treasure of blessings, a compassionate forgiver.
To fall at Your *sadhs'* feet,
    Nanak, this is my yearning. (1)

Fulfiller of desires, competent to protect,
    whatever is placed in one's hand, that will happen.
In the blink of an eye, creation and dissolution,
    no one knows Your power.
A blissful form, always joyful;
Your house is known to have everything.
A King among kings, a Yogi among yogis,
    an Ascetic among ascetics, a Householder among householders.
The *bhagat* attains happiness by concentrating, concentrating.
Nanak: No one has found the limits of this [True] Being. (2)

Your play is beyond measure,
    all the gods are lost in their search.
How can a son know about his father's birth?
Everything is strung on Your string.
O good friend, given wisdom and concentration,
    the devoted servant concentrates on *Nam*.
Confused by the three qualities,
    the ignorant ones are born and die over and over again.
High and low are Your places;
Nanak: A person knows what one is destined to know. (3)

Various forms, various colours,
    various appearances, yet of one colour.
Various ways in expanding creation,
    only the indestructible *Prabh* is the creator.

Various dramas are played in an instant,
   but [*Prabh*] stays perfect in all places.
Various ways to build the universe;
You alone know Your value.
All hearts are Yours, all places are Yours;
Nanak: One lives by chanting the name of *Har*. (4)

Nam supports all creatures;
Nam supports the regions and the universe.
Nam supports the Vedas, Simritis and Puranas;
Nam supports listening, wisdom and concentration.
Nam supports the sky and nether lands;
Nam supports all forms.
Nam supports the worlds and spheres;
In the company of *Nam*, one is saved by listening with the ears.
Those blessed with Your *Nam*,
   Nanak, such devotees attain the fourth state.[24] (5)

True form, true place;
Only *Sat Purakh* is in command.
True actions, true word;
Sat Purakh is manifest in all.
True deeds, true creation;
True origin, true burgeoning.
True doing, purest of the pure;
Whoever understands this is conferred with nobility.
Happiness from *Prabh's* true *Nam*;
Nanak: True faith is acquired from *Guru*. (6)

True are *Sadh's* (*Guru's*) words and teachings,
   true is the devotee's heart where they enter.
If one comes to know the love of Truth,
   such a one is saved by chanting *Nam*.
You are Truth, the entire creation is Truth,
   You know Your own extent and state.
You the creator, Yours the creation;
Never think of another as the Creator.
No one knows the extent of the Creator;
Nanak: Whatever pleases You will happen. (7)

Wonderstruck, in the awe of the Wonderful,
    the one who understands this, savours it.
The devotee remains absorbed in *Prabh's* love,
    Guru's words provide sustenance,
    and cut away suffering.
In the devotee's company, everyone swims across.
Fortunate is the servant of the devotee,
    in the devotee's company, the servant becomes absorbed in the One.
The devotee sings the praises of *Gobind*,
    Nanak, through *Guru's* grace one is fulfilled. (8) [16]

Salok
True in the beginning, True throughout the ages;
True in the present, Nanak, True in the future.[25] (1)

Astapadi
True feet, true the one who touches them;
True worship, true the servant.
True vision, true the seer;
True *Nam*, true the one concentrating.
You are true, and all Your support is true;
You are virtuous, bestowing virtues.
True *shabad*, true the *bhagat* of *Prabh*;
True awareness, true hearing the praises.
The realized one understands everything as true,
    Nanak, *Prabh* is true, true. (1)

Whoever accepts the true form of *Prabh* in the heart,
    recognizes the Cause of causes as the root.
In the hearts where there is faith, *Prabh* enters,
    quintessential wisdom emerges in the mind.
From fear to fearless, that is how one lives;
Absorbed in the One, from where one originated.
Blending the same materials,
    they cannot be called separate.
The one with understanding can discern,
    Nanak, and becomes one with *Narayan*. (2)

The Master's servant is dutiful;
The Master's servant is always a worshipper.
The Master's servant has faith in the heart;
The Master's servant has a pure lifestyle.
The Master's servant realizes the One within;
Prabh's servant is imbued with *Nam*.
The servant is nurtured by *Prabh*;
Nirankar cares for the servant.
The servant to whom compassion flows from *Prabh*,
    Nanak, that servant remembers *Prabh* with every breath. (3)

You protect the devotee with a curtain,
    You surely safeguard the devotee.
You give glory to the servant;
You inspirit the servant to chant the *Nam*.
You protect the honour of Your servant;
No one knows Your state and extent.
No one can harm *Prabh's* servant,
    Prabh's servant is the highest of the high.
The one *Prabh* inspirits to serve,
    Nanak, such a servant becomes known in the ten directions. (4)

A small ant, infused with power,
    can reduce an army of a million to ashes.
Whosoever's breath You do not want to take away,
    they are protected and given a hand.
Humans make a lot of effort,
    but these efforts are done out of anxiety.
No one can harm or protect,
    You are the only protector of all creatures.
O mortal, what are you thinking?
Nanak: Chant the imperceptible wonder of *Prabh*. (5)

Chant *Prabh* again, again and again,
    drink the nectar and satisfy the mind and body.
The *gurmukh* attains the jewel of *Nam*,
    there is none other to be seen.

Nam is wealth, *Nam* is beauty and love,
   happiness comes from the company of *Nam*.
The satiated devotee savours *Nam*,
   the mind and body are absorbed in *Nam*.
Standing, sitting and sleeping in *Nam*,
   Nanak says, this is the devotee's work. (6)

Uttering praises with the tongue day and night,
   Prabh, You gave this gift to Your servants.
The *bhagats*' hearts yearn
   to remain absorbed in *Prabh*.
Understanding that whatever happens had to happen,
   Prabh's hukam is recognized.
How can the *bhagats*' grandeur be described?
Difficult to comprehend a single virtue.
Throughout the eight watches, they are in *Prabh's* presence,
   Nanak says, such devotees are perfect. (7)

O my mind, seek the devotee's shelter,[26]
   give your mind and body to the devotee.
The devotee who recognizes *Prabh*
   becomes the giver of all things.
Attain total happiness in the devotee's sanctuary;
Upon seeing the devotee, all sins are erased.
Let go of all clever thoughts,
   serve and connect with the devotee.
You will not come and go;
Nanak: Forever worship the devotee's feet. (8) [17]

Salok
The one who recognizes *Sat Purakh* is called *Satgur*;
In [*Satgur's*] company, the *Sikh* is saved by reciting the qualities of *Har*. (1)

Astapadi
Satgur cares for the *Sikh*,
   Guru always has compassion for the servant.
The *Sikh's Guru* removes the filth of foul intellect,
   Guru's instruction is to repeat the *Nam* of *Har*.

Satgur breaks the *Sikh's* bondage,
   Guru's Sikh refrains from vice.
Satgur gives the wealth of *Nam* to the *Sikh*,
   Guru's Sikh is fortunate.
Satgur comforts the *Sikh* here and hereafter,
   Nanak, *Satgur* takes care of the *Sikh's* life. (1)

The *Sikh* who lives in *Guru's* home
   faithfully obeys *Guru* in the mind.
Recognizing oneself as nothing,
   the *Nam* of *Har* is contemplated in one's heart.
Having given the mind to *Satgur*,
   the endeavours of such a servant are successful.
Serving without desire,
   Swami is attained.
Whosoever You bless,
   Nanak, such a servant attains *Guru's* wisdom. (2)

Accepting *Guru* one hundred per cent in the mind,
   such a servant knows the state of *Paramesar*.
The heart that has *Har Nam* is *Satgur*,
   and forever sacrifices to *Guru*.
The Treasure of all gives *Parbraham's* love for
   the living throughout the eight watches.
Braham within the devotee, the devotee within *Braham*,
   they are one, no doubt about it.
A thousand clever thoughts do not bring realization,
   Nanak, with good fortune, one meets with such a *Guru*. (3)

A vision of [*Satgur*] is fruitful and pure,
   touching *Satgur's* feet, one's behaviour is no longer filthy.
In the congregation, the praises of *Ram* are sung,
   reaching *Parbraham's* court.
Hearing [*Satgur's*] words is satisfying to the ears,
   the mind is content and the heart is consoled.
The perfect *Guru's* mantra is everlasting,
   Guru's ambrosial glance transforms one into a *sant*.
[*Satgur*] has countless qualities, and is priceless,
   Nanak, to [*Satgur's*] delight, one attains unity. (4)

One tongue, countless praises.
Sat Purakh has perfect insight.
A person cannot describe the One in words,
    Prabh is inaccessible, transcendent and *nirban*.
Without sustenance, without enmity and giver of happiness,
    no one has appraised [*Sat Purakh's*] value.
Everyday countless *bhagats* bow,
    mindful of the lotus-like feet in their hearts.
Forever a sacrifice to *Satgur*,
    Nanak, by whose grace *Prabh* is chanted. (5)

Rare is the devotee who savours the attainment of *Har*,
    and becomes immortal by drinking nectar.
The devotee's heart shines with the treasure of goodness,
    such a devotee can never be destroyed.
[*Satgur*] has the *Nam* of *Har* throughout the eight watches,
    and gives true teachings to the servant.
Unstained amid attachment and *maya*,
    only *Har* is within the heart.
The blind are enlightened by the lamp,
    Nanak, doubt, attachment and suffering are destroyed. (6)

Amid the heat, coolness is deployed,
    bliss is attained and suffering flees, brother.
Worries about births and deaths are erased,
    with perfect teachings from *Sadh* [i.e. *Guru*].
As fear lifts, one lives without fear,
    all maladies crumble and flee from the mind.
Upon whom blessings are bestowed,
    Nam is chanted in *Sadh's* company.
Calmness is attained, and confusion and wandering are lifted;
Nanak: Listen to the praises of *Har* with the ears. (7)

You are *nirgun*, You are also *sargun*,
    the Beholder of power fascinates all.
Your worldly drama is made by You, *Prabh*,
    You alone know Your worth.
Besides *Har*, there is no other,
    the One is within all.

Interwoven in all forms and colours,
    in *Sadh's* company comes this enlightenment.
After creating the creation, Your power sustains it;
Nanak: Is always a sacrifice to You. (8) [18]

Salok
Besides devotion, nothing accompanies [in the end] and everything turns into ashes;
Nanak: Earning the *Nam* of *Har* is splendid wealth. (1)

Astapadi
Meeting the *sants*, engage in contemplation,
    be mindful of the One *Nam* supporting all.
O friend, forget all other means,
    place the lotus feet firmly in the heart.
The cause of causes is *Prabh*, the powerful one,
    firmly hold on to *Nam*, the only reality.
Gather this wealth, and become fortunate,
    this is the pure counsel given by the *sants*.
Have only one aspiration in the heart,
    Nanak, all maladies will then disappear. (1)

The wealth for which you run in the four directions,
    that wealth can be obtained only in the service of *Har*.
O friend, the happiness that you always yearn for,
    that happiness is the love experienced with the *sadhs*.
The glory of performing noble actions,
    that glory is in seeking the sanctuary of *Har*.
Countless remedies cannot make maladies go away,
    maladies disappear by applying the medicine of *Har*.
Nam is the treasure of all treasures;
Nanak: Chant and be present in the heavenly court. (2)

Running in the ten directions, but when the [*Nam*] of *Har*
    awakens the mind, a resting place is reached.
No obstacles will block one
    in whose heart *Har* resides.
The dark age is hot, and the [*Nam*] of *Har* cools;
Be mindful, mindful, and attain everlasting happiness.

Fear is destroyed, and aspirations are fulfilled,
    with loving devotion, there is enlightenment.
In that home resides the indestructible One,
    Nanak says, and the noose of death is cut. (3)

The devotee who contemplates the essence will be known as true;
Birth and death are for the raw and unripe.
Serving *Prabh* will erase one's coming and going;
Renounce 'I am-ness', and seek the divine *Guru's* sanctuary.
The jewel of human birth will be saved;
Being mindful of *Har* supporting the breath.
Many practices will not release one,
    nor by contemplating the Vedas, Simritis or Shastras.
Worship *Har* with the heart,
    Nanak, and the heart's desires will be fulfilled. (4)

Your wealth will not accompany you,
    O foolish mind, why are you so wrapped up in it?
Sons, friends, family and wife,
    tell us which one will accompany you?
The kingdom, the joys and immense wealth,
    tell us which one will help you escape [*sansar*]?
Horses, elephants, chariots and pageantry,
    a false show displays a false person.
The ignorant one does not recognize the Giver,
    Nanak, forgetful of *Nam*, one repents. (5)

O ignorant one, take *Guru's* advice;
Without devotion, many clever ones have drowned.
Dear mind, devote yourself to *Har*,
    and you will have pure consciousness.
Place the lotus feet in the heart,
    and the transgressions of many births will go away.
Chant yourself, and inspire others to chant;
Attain liberation by listening, speaking and abiding.
The true [*Nam*] of *Har* is the highest element;
Nanak: Sing the praises with spontaneous love. (6)

By singing *Har's* praises, your filth is removed,
    and the ego's poisonous spread will be destroyed.
Become worry-free, and live in happiness;
With every breath cherish the *Nam* of *Har*.
O mind, let go of all clever thoughts,
    and obtain the true wealth in the company of the *sadhs*.
Collecting the wealth of *Har* is the true trade,
    happiness here, and glory in the heavenly court.
The One is seen within all,
    Nanak says, those upon whose forehead it is so written. (7)

Chant the One, praise the One;
Be mindful of the One, let the One enter the mind.
Sing the praises of the infinite One,
    meditate only on *Bhagwant* with mind and body.
Har is the One and only One;
Prabh, the perfect One, pervades all.
Many creations from the One;
Meditate on the One, and sins will go away.
Those whose mind and body are fully imbued with *Prabh*,
    Nanak, with *Guru's* grace the One is realized. (8) [19]

Salok
O *Prabh*, after wandering astray, I have come to Your sanctuary;
Nanak requests *Prabh*: May I be devoted to You. (1)

Astapadi
As a beggar, I beg for a gift from *Prabh*,
    with whose blessing, the *Nam* of *Har* is given.
I ask for the dust of the devoted *sadhs'* feet;
O *Parbraham*, fulfil my wish.
Forever, forever, singing praises of *Prabh*,
    concentrating on *Prabh* with every breath.
Attach me to Your lotus feet with love;
May I always be devoted to *Prabh*.
There is only one shelter and one support;
Nanak wants the supreme *Nam* of *Prabh*. (1)

With *Prabh's* glance, the devotee is content;
Rare is the one who savours *Har*.
Having tasted it, the devotee is fulfilled;
The devotee is perfect and never wavers.
The devotee is filled to the brim with sweetness and love;
In the company of the *sadhs*, yearning sprouts [for the One].
Forsaking all others, and arriving at the sanctuary,
    the devotee is absorbed in the inner light every day.
Fortunate are those who meditate on *Prabh*,
    Nanak, imbued with *Nam*, happiness occurs. (2)

The servant's aspirations are fulfilled,
    when *Satgur* bestows pure intellect.
Prabh is kind to the devotee,
    and makes the servant flourish forever.
Cutting off bondage, the devotee is liberated,
    suffering and duality of birth and death vanish.
Wishes are fulfilled, and faith is complete,
    always in the company of the omnipresent One.
The devotee is reunited and belongs to the One,
    Nanak, with devotion, one merges with *Nam*. (3)

Why forget the One who does not allow labour to go fruitless?
Why forget the One who recognizes whatever is done?
Why forget the One who gives everything?
Why forget the One who gives life to creatures?
Why forget the One who cares within the fire [womb]?
With *Guru's* grace, rare is the enlightened one.
Why forget the One who removes poison?
Those separated by repeated births are united with the One.
The perfect *Guru* makes one understand this reality;
Nanak: The devotee concentrates on *Prabh*. (4)

O friendly *sants*, perform this work,
    let go of others, and chant the *Nam* of *Har*.
Remember mindfully, mindfully, and attain happiness,
    chant yourself, and inspire others to chant.
With devotional love, swim across the worldly ocean,
    without devotion, the body turns into ashes.

Nam is the treasure of happiness and good fortune;
Those drowning will be rescued.
All sufferings will be destroyed,
    Nanak, by chanting the *Nam*, the treasure of virtues. (5)

A yearning to savour affectionate love emerges,
    the mind and body enjoys its taste within.
The eyes seeing the One gives one happiness;
The mind blossoms by washing *Sadh's* [i.e. *Guru's*] feet.
The minds and bodies of the *bhagats* are imbued with love;
Rare is the one who gets their company.
Receive the blessing of *Nam*,
    and by *Guru's* grace, *Nam* is chanted.
No one can narrate Your praises enough;
Nanak: *Nam* always permeates all. (6)

Prabh forgives, and is kind towards the poor,
    loves the *bhagats*, and is forever merciful.
Gobind Gopal helps the helpless,
    and nurtures all living creatures.
Adi Purakh created the creation,
    and supports the breath of the *bhagats*.
Whoever chants *Nam* will become pure;
With devotional love, the heart becomes affectionate.
I am without virtues, lowly and ignorant;
Nanak: O *Bhagwan*, I seek Your sanctuary. (7)

Liberation and celestial realms are all attained,
    when the *Nam* of *Har* is chanted for a moment.
Countless kingdoms, pleasures and praises,
    for the one who loves the *Nam* of *Har*.
Forever chanting *Har* [is like]
    enjoying many delicacies, clothes and music.
With noble actions, one becomes glorious and wealthy;
The perfect *Guru's* counsel dwells within the heart.
O *Prabh*, give me a place in the *sadhs'* company,
    Nanak, where total happiness shines. (8) [20]

Salok
Absorbed in *sunn*, *Nirankar* is both *sargun* and *nirgun*,
 Nanak, Your creation is what You meditate upon. (1)

Astapadi
When no form was visible,
 who performed virtuous or sinful deeds?
When the Upholder was absorbed in *sunn*,
 who was one hostile to or against?
When the qualities of the One were not chanted,
 who experienced joy or grief?
When *Parbraham* was all alone,
 where was attachment and doubt?
You alone orchestrate Your play,
 Nanak, there is no other Creator. (1)

When there was only *Prabh*, the master,
 who was considered entangled or liberated?
When the inaccessible and boundless *Har* was alone,
 who was born in hell or heaven?
When *Prabh* was without form, and innately pleasing,
 where was the place of Shiva and Shakti?
When You held Your own light,
 who was fearless, who was afraid?
You direct Your own drama;
Nanak: The Master is inaccessible and boundless. (2)

When the indestructible One sat at ease,
 where was birth, death and dissolution?
When there was only *Prabh*, the perfect creator,
 who was afraid of the god of death?
When there was only the invisible and inaccessible *Prabh*,
 how was one's hidden record taken into account?[27]
When there was only *Niranjan*, the inaccessible and unfathomable One,
 who was released, who remained in bondage?
Equal to only Yourself, You are wonderful,
 Nanak, You created Your own form. (3)

When there was only pure Being, the master,
  where was the filth, and what was to be washed?
When there was only *Niranjan*, *Nirankar* and *Nirban*,
  who had esteem, who had pride?
When there was only the form of *Jagdish*,
  who committed fraud or vice?
When the form of Light was immersed in Itself,
  who was hungry, who was fulfilled?
The Creator is the cause of all causes,
  Nanak, no one knows the Creator's extent. (4)

When You were only in the company of Your glory,
  where was mother, father, friend or brother?
When only the all-pervasive One existed,
  who understood the Vedas and *kitab*?[28]
When You were absorbed within the One heart,
  who thought of good or bad omens?
When You were transcendent, when You were immanent,
  who was the master, who was the servant?
The astonished ones remain wonderstruck,
  Nanak, You alone know Your own state. (5)

When the omniscient, indivisible and indistinguishable One was absorbed within,
  who was attached to *maya*?
When You bowed to Yourself,
  who was influenced by the three qualities?
When there was only *Bhagwant*,
  who was worry-free, who was anxious?
When only You believed in Yourself,
  who spoke, who listened?
The wholly boundless One is the highest of the high,
  Nanak, only You can reach Yourself. (6)

When You made the phenomenal creation,
  and infused the three qualities,
    then emerged the talk of sin and virtue.
Some went to hell, some yearned for heaven.

Entangled and trapped in the snares of *maya*,
    ego, attachment, doubt, love and the burden of fear.
Suffering and pleasure, honour and dishonour,
    many dualities were described.
You direct and watch Your own play,
    Nanak, when the play wraps up, You are all alone again. (7)

Wherever the invisible One is, so is the *bhagat*,
    the creation was expanded for the *sants'* glory.
You are the Master of the two sides,
    Your praise is to You alone.
You are delighted by Your worldly play,
    savouring pleasures, yet uninfluenced by them.
To Your delight, one is attached to Your *Nam*;
To Your delight, one plays the game.
O incalculable, unfathomable, immeasurable and unparalleled One,
    however spoken to, so Nanak, the servant, speaks. (8) [21]

Salok
O Master of beings and creatures, You are omnipresent,
    Nanak, besides the all-pervasive One, what else can be seen? (1)

Astapadi
You speak, You listen,
    You are the One, You are all-pervasive.
Absorbed in Your own will,
    when delighted, You created the world.
With Your thread, the whole world is strung,
    without You, nothing happens.
To whom *Prabh* gives awareness,
    that devotee obtains the true *Nam*.
Seeing all as equal, one understands reality,
    Nanak, such a one is victorious in the whole world. (1)

All beings and creatures are in Your hand;
You are kind to the poor, the helper of the helpless.
The protected cannot be harmed;
The forgetful are taken as dead.
Leaving the One, where can one go?

Only *Niranjan* is the king and the head of all.
In Your hand are the ways of all beings;
Recognize the One's support in the inner and outer [worlds].
The Treasure of virtues is infinite and boundless,
    Nanak, the servant, is forever Your sacrifice. (2)

The perfect One pervades with compassion,
    and bestows mercy upon all.
You understand Your own ways;
The Knower of all hearts is omnipresent.
The One nurtures living beings in various ways;
All created things are connected to the One.
Whoever delights, blends with the One;
The *bhagat* sings the praises of *Har*.
Accepting faith within the heart,
    Nanak, only the Creator is recognized. (3)

The devotee is attached to the *Nam* of *Har*,
    such a one's aspirations will not go in vain.
For the servant, service is the purpose,
    understanding *hukam*, the supreme state is attained.
Nothing higher can be contemplated,
    in whose heart where *Nirankar* resides.
Bondage is broken, and enmity is gone,
    Guru's feet are worshipped night and day.
Happiness in this world, and joy in the next,
    Nanak, *Prabh* unites the devotee unto Itself. (4)

Join the company of the *sadhs*, and experience the bliss,
    sing the praises of *Prabh*, the supreme bliss.
Contemplate the essence of *Ram Nam*,
    and save this precious body.
Sing the praises of *Har*, the ambrosial words,
    in this way, the soul swims across [*sansar*].
Throughout the eight watches, when you see *Prabh* near,
    ignorance will be removed and darkness will dissipate.
Listen to the teachings, and enshrine them in the heart,
    Nanak, obtain the fruit of your heart's desire. (5)

Change this life and the next,
    by placing *Ram Nam* within the heart.
The perfect *Guru's* teachings are complete,
    in whose heart they reside, Truth is realized.
Attune the mind and body to chant the *Nam*,
    suffering, pain and fear will leave the mind.
O trader, conduct the true trade,
    your goods will be valued in the heavenly court.
Keep the support of the One within the heart,
    Nanak, you will not come and go again. (6)

When one is saved by concentrating on the Protector,
    where else can one go?
Meditating on the fearless One, all fears vanish;
With *Prabh's* blessings, one will be released [from the cycle].
Whoever *Prabh* protects, the suffering of such a one is alleviated;
Chanting the *Nam*, the mind becomes happy.
Anxiety departs, and the ego is destroyed,
    no one can harm such a devotee.
Guru courageously stands above the devotee's head,
    Nanak, and the affairs of such a devotee are completed. (7)

With a perfect intellect, and an ambrosial vision,
    the Divine glance saves the creation.
The lotus feet are unique,
    fruitful is the vision of the beautiful *Har*.
Seva is a blessing, the servant is accepted,
    the Chief knows the hearts of all.
Within whose heart resides the One, such a one will flourish,
    and death will not come.
The servant attains the eternal state,
    Nanak, concentrate on *Har* in the company of the *sadhs*. (8) [22]

Salok
When *Guru* gives the collyrium of wisdom,[29] the darkness of ignorance is shattered.
Nanak: With *Har's* blessing, one meets *Sant* (*Guru*), and the mind is illuminated. (1)

Astapadi
In *Sant's* company, *Prabh* is experienced within,
    and the *Nam* of *Prabh* tastes sweet.
All matter originates from the One heart,
    although it appears in countless colours.
The nine treasures are in the ambrosial *Nam* of *Prabh*,
    which rests deep within the body.
Absorbed in *sunn*, one connects with the unstruck sound,
    but this wondrous awe is indescribable.
One sees what You reveal,
    Nanak, such a devotee attains awareness. (1)

The Infinite exists inside and outside,
    Bhagwant permeates every heart.
Manifest in the earth, sky and nether lands,
    the perfect One nurtures all regions.
Parbraham is in the forest, grass and mountains;
As is the command, so is the action.
Manifest in air, water and fire,
    pervading in the four quarters and the ten directions.
There is no place without the One;
Nanak: With *Guru's* grace one attains happiness. (2)

See the One in the Vedas, Simritis and Puranas,
    and in the moon, sun and stars.
Everyone speaks the language of *Prabh*,
    Prabh is steady, never wavering.
The All-powerful performs the play;
Your value cannot be estimated, Your attributes are invaluable.
All light is manifest in Your light;
Swami's support stays interwoven [with the creation].
With *Guru's* grace doubt is destroyed,
    Nanak, and such a one is faithful. (3)

Devoted *sants* see *Braham* in all,
    the totality of *dharam* is in their hearts.
Devoted *sants* listen to good words,
    they are absorbed in the all-pervading *Ram*.

Realization is the way,
   the *sadhs* only speak the truth.
Whatever happens is accepted happily,
   Prabh, the cause of causes, understands everything.
The One resides inside and outside,
   Nanak, everyone is fascinated by Your vision. (4)

You are truth, and all creation is truth,
   Prabh created the creation.
To Your delight, Your creation expands;
To Your delight, You become One again.
Countless powers, beyond comprehension;
To Your delight, one is united with the One.
Say, who is near? Who is far?
Only You pervade all.
Whoever realizes the inner state,
   Nanak, You give such a devotee understanding. (5)

You function in all elements;
You see through the eyes of all.
The entire creation is Your body;
You listen to Your own praises.
Coming and going is merely Your play,
   even *maya* is under Your command.
Within all, yet remaining untouched,
   whatever is said, is said by You.
By Your will, one comes and goes,
   Nanak, when the One is delighted, all of creation is united. (6)

Whatever You do is not bad,
   say, who else can do anything?
You are noble, and Your actions are good,
   You know Your own Being.
You are true, and Your support is true,
   You are interwoven with the creation.
No one can describe Your state and extent,
   only Your equivalent could understand.
All Your actions are to be accepted,
   Nanak, with *Guru's* grace one has understanding. (7)

Whoever realizes the One is forever happy,
   such a one is united with *Prabh*.
One may be wealthy, of good family and honourable,
   but is only a *jiwan mukat* with *Bhagwant* in the heart.
Blessed, blessed, blessed is the arrival of the devotee,
   by the devotee's grace, the whole world can be saved.
The devotee came for this purpose,
   in the devotee's company, *Nam* is remembered.
Such a one is liberated, and liberates the world,
   Nanak, forever bow to such a devotee. (8) [23]

Salok
Meditate upon *Prabh*, whose *Nam* is perfect;
Nanak: Attain perfection by singing the praises of the perfect One. (1)

Astapadi
Listen to the teachings of the perfect *Guru*,
   see *Parbraham* as near.
With every breath, be mindful of *Gobind*,
   worries within the mind will depart.
Renounce the waves of transitory aspirations,
   O mind, ask for the dust of the devoted *sants'* feet.
Abandon 'I am-ness', make this the request,
   in the company of the *sadhs*, swim across the ocean of fire.[30]
Fill the storehouse with the wealth of *Har*;
Nanak: Bow to the perfect *Guru*. (1)

Forever cheerful, composed and joyful,
   in the company of the *sadhs*, meditate on supreme bliss.
Drink the nectar of *Gobind's* virtues,
   and escape hell and be saved.
Consciously focus on *Narayan*,
   One form, yet of many colours.
Gopal Damodar has compassion for the poor;
The Merciful is perfect and destroys suffering.
Mindfully remember *Nam* again and again;
Nanak: *Nam* supports the living being. (2)

The highest *salok* is *Sadh's* (*Guru's*) words,
  these are priceless red jewels.
Listening and acting upon these words liberates,
  one swims across and saves others.
A fruitful life, a fruitful fellowship,
  for the mind imbued with love.
Hail to the *shabad* that resonates with the unstruck sound,
  listening in bliss, the thunderous sound of *Prabh*.
Gopal radiates from the *mahant's* forehead,
  Nanak, also saving those accompanying the *mahant*. (3)

Hearing the capable One offers refuge, I arrive at the sanctuary;
With blessings, one is united with *Prabh*.
Loving the dust of the feet of all, hatred disappears;
Receive ambrosial *Nam* in the company of the *sadhs*.
The divine *Guru* is pleased,
  and the servant's service is complete.
Beyond the snares and entanglements of vice,
  hearing the tongue say *Ram Nam*.
With blessings, *Prabh* bestows compassion,
  Nanak, my merchandise has been secured.[31] (4)

O friendly *sants*, praise *Prabh*,
  with single-minded concentration.
Gobind's virtues and *Nam* are the pearls of happiness (*Sukhmani*),[32]
  the heart in which *Nam* resides is a treasure chest.
All desires are fulfilled,
  the devotee is known as a chief by all.
The highest place is attained,
  no more coming and going.
The devotee leaves with the wealth of *Har*,
  Nanak, this is what is obtained. (5)

Eternal peace, miracles, nine treasures,
  intelligence, wisdom and supernatural powers.
Learning, penance, yoga, concentration on *Prabh*,
  supreme wisdom and purifying baths.

The four blessings,[33] the unfolding lotus,
   in the midst of all, yet detached.
Beautiful, smart, realized,
   impartial and seeing everything as One.
These are the fruits when the mouth recites [*Nam*],
   Nanak, and the mind listens to *Guru's Nam* and teachings. (6)

The mind chanting this treasure
   is saved throughout the ages.
Praise *Gobind*, whose *Nam* vibrates in *bani*,
   the Vedas, Shastras and Simritis speak of this.
Only the *Nam* of *Har* is fundamental,
   Gobind resides in the *bhagat's* heart.
In the company of the *sadhs*, millions of misdeeds are erased,
   with *Sant's* (*Guru's*) blessing, the god of death lets go.
Upon whose forehead *Prabh* has bestowed such destiny,
   Nanak, such a one arrives at *Sadh's* sanctuary. (7)

In the mind where the love of listening to *Nam* resides,
   that devotee continuously remembers *Prabh*.
The sufferings of birth and death end,
   and this precious body is instantly saved.
One's fame is pure, one's words are ambrosial,
   the mind is only absorbed with *Nam*.
Suffering, illness, fear and doubt have disappeared,
   one is called a *sadh*, performing pure action.
Such a one has the most exalted fame,
   Nanak, with these qualities, *Nam* is *Sukhmani*. (8) [24]

Summary of the four watches of the day (*Astapadis* 1–12)

Astapadi	Spiritual teaching
1	Summarizes the spiritual and material benefits of the mindful remembrance of *Nam*, including obliterating suffering and achieving wellness.
2	The practice of *Nam* rids all forms of suffering, including separation, physical deprivation and psychological distress. When *Nam* resides in the heart, happiness and peace are attained.
3	Learning religious texts and performing external forms of worship are inferior to mindfully remembering *Nam*, which purifies the mind.
4	Those who are disengaged from *Nam*, and are ignorant of their true support, are blinded by the illusions of the world and are caught in the cycle of the five 'thieves'.
5	Without awareness of *Nam*, one takes the material world as permanent and real, when in fact it is all impermanent. All actions are meaningless without the understanding of, and gratitude for, the eternal and all-pervasive One (*Prabh*).
6	One's existence, life-situation and experiences are all the result of *Guru's* grace. This realization results in the dissolution of the ego. Conversely, without this realization, one suffers.
7	Staying in the company of the *sadhs* serves both as a critical practice and as a form of support to a seeker, especially since the seeker becomes imbued with the qualities of *Prabh* in the *sadhs*' presence.
8	Differentiates those imbued with *Prabh* from those who are not. The *brahamgiani* is the knower of the formless and timeless One.
9	The qualities of those who keep *Nam* in their hearts are equated with the realized *vaishnav*, *bhagat* and *pandit*, and differentiates those imbued with *Nam* from those who are not.
10	Describes various types of people (such as a king, householder, ascetic and yogi) and creation (such as the elements, regions and animals), and differentiates those imbued with *Nam* from those who are not.
11	Happiness and peace arise only when one (1) realizes that all is under the control of *Prabh* and (2) follows the will (*hukam*) of *Prabh*.
12	Those who are ego-centred remain dissatisfied and restless, whereas those imbued with *Nam* experience happiness and peace.

Summary of the four watches of the night (*Astapadis* 13–24)

Astapadi	**Spiritual teaching**
13	Those who do not recognize and slander the *sants* are dissatisfied, whereas those who recognize the *sants* are blessed.
14	People cannot rely on others; rather, people can only rely on *Har*. Those mindful of *Nam* are strengthened even as they are rid of suffering, doubt and fear.
15	Mindful remembrance of *Nam* removes different forms of suffering like separateness, ego-centredness, physical deprivation and psychological distress.
16	*Sat Purakh* is described as the Creator and Inner-Controller of all, including being the remover of suffering and provider of happiness. Focused on *Nam*, one attains such fruits.
17	Single-minded devotion of *Nam* results in nourishment, protection, connection, acceptance and compassion.
18	Sikhs who sing the praises of *Guru* in the company of the *sadhs* are saved.
19	Mindful remembrance of *Har* not only heals physical ailments, psychological distress and existential suffering, but it also purifies the body and mind. This results in the experience of fulfilment and joy.
20	When devotees seek refuge with humility, they attain happiness. Lasting happiness and peace, however, emerge with the experience of oneness as a result of the dissolution of duality.
21	Absorbed in emptiness, one realizes *Har* is both manifest and unmanifest. With the support of *Nam*, dualities are viewed as alike.
22	Devotees should be focused on alleviating internal suffering as well as helping others in need. Importance of *seva* for the betterment of humanity.
23	Devotees firm in *Har* speak and act in truth, which also inspirits others.
24	Devotees achieve wellness and perfection with mindful remembrance of *Nam*.

Glossary of Punjabi terms

Adi Granth sacred scripture of the Sikhs compiled by Guru Arjan in 1604
ahankar ego or the sense of being separate from others; one of the five thieves or **panj chor** in *Sikhi* (Skt. *ahamkara*)
Akal Purakh Timeless Being; epithet frequently used for **Ek Oankar**
Akal Takhat Timeless Throne; the seat of temporal and spiritual authority within the Sikh **Panth**
amrit deathless, nectar, ambrosia; sacred water prepared during initiation into the Khalsa
anhat nad unstruck sound; eternal sound
antarajami Indweller of the heart; inner *Guru* in *Sikhi*, regarded as a full form of Vishnu in Sri Vaishnava Bhakti (Skt. *anataryamin*)
aparas puritan; person who does not touch anything
Ardas supplication or request; a prayer recited at the conclusion of every Sikh ceremony
asan posture; yogic physical postures (Skt. *asana*)
astapadi an *Adi Granth* hymn of eight verses
atma self or eternal soul (Skt. *atman*)
bani speech, utterances; sacred utterances of the Gurus and Bhagats in the *Adi Granth*
Bhagat devotee; one who practises devotion (Skt. *bhakta*)
bhagat bani utterances of poet-saints from the Bhakti and Sufi traditions recorded in the *Adi Granth*
Bhagauti one who knows **Bhagwant**; one imbued with **bhagti**
bhagti devotion of a personal god (Skt. *bhakti*)
Bhagwant One whose heart is full of devotion; epithet used for **Ek Oankar**; name used for Hindu god, especially Vishnu and his incarnations (Skt. *Bhagavan*)
Bhatt bard who sings ballads of praise in the Sikh court
Braham Ultimate Reality or the Absolute described in the Upanishads (Skt. *Brahman*)
brahamgiani knower of **Braham**
brahmin highest of the four Hindu classes described in the **Vedas**
Brahmin member of the priestly class
chinta anxiety or worry
Damodar God; he who has the universe in his stomach; epithet for **Ek Oankar**
dan gift; charity (Skt. *dana*)
darshan vision; visual witnessing of an eminent person or divine object; an Indian philosophical system (Skt. *darshana*)
dasvand to distribute a tenth of one's earnings
dharam duty, righteousness or way of life; one of the five **panj khand** in *Sikhi* (Skt. *dharma*)

dharamsal place of worship in the early Sikh **Panth** (Skt. *dharamsala*)
dukh suffering or pain (Skt. *duhkha*)
Ek Oankar One creator-creation; primary reference to Ultimate Reality in *Sikhi*; see also **Guru**
gauri a contemplative *rag* in which the largest number of compositions are found in the **Adi Granth**
gian knowledge or wisdom; one of the ***panj khand*** in *Sikhi* (Skt. *jnana*)
giani learned one; religious teacher or Sikh scholar
Gobind preserver of the world; epithet for **Ek Oankar**; name for Vishnu or Krishna in Hinduism
Gopal epithet for *Ek Oankar*; name (cow protector) for Vishnu or Krishna in Hinduism
Govind preserver of the world; epithet for ***Ek Oankar***; name for Vishnu or Krishna in Hinduism
grahasti a householder
granth book or religious scripture
granthi reader of the **Guru Granth Sahib**; one who performs daily prayers in the ***gurdwara***
gurbani *Guru's* word; utterances or compositions of the Sikh Gurus
gurdwara door to *Guru*; Sikh place of worship; place in which the **Guru Granth Sahib** is installed
gur-gaddi **Guru**-seat; refers to the installation of Guruship to the succeeding Sikh Gurus
gurmat Sikh Gurus' teachings or viewpoint
gurmukh one who follows the will or teachings of **Guru**
guru a spiritual teacher or master
Guru Ultimate Reality or the embodiment of that Reality, such as ***shabad-Guru***, the ten human Gurus and the scripture
Guru Granth Sahib Adi Granth in its role as ***Guru***
Har epithet for **Ek Oankar**; the omnipresent One in the Sikh tradition; name (the green one) for Vishnu or Krishna in Hinduism (Skt. *Hari*)
hath-yog forceful, rigourous; a branch of yoga that emphasizes physical exercises (Skt. *hatha-yoga*)
hukam order or command; the cosmic order emanating from **Ek Oankar** in *Sikhi*
Indra Hindu Vedic god responsible for the atmosphere, including lightning, thunder and storms
Jagdish epithet for **Ek Oankar**; Hindu name for the lord of the world
janam-sakhi traditional biography or hagiography of Guru Nanak
jat agricultural peasantry; a caste group; a non-indigenous group of peasants settled in the Punjab; a peasant or farmer
jiwan mukat liberated life; self-realized person still living in the world (Skt. *jivan mukti*)
kalesh affliction; there are five types in Patanjali's *Yoga Sutras* (Skt. *klesha*)
kaliyug dark age; age of degeneracy; the fourth and last age of the cosmic cycle (Skt. *kaliyuga*)

kam sensual-pleasures or lust; one of the five evils or *panj chor* in *Sikhi*; one of the householder goals in Hinduism (Skt. *kama*)

Kanphat yogi split-ear yogi; follower of Gorakhnath and member of the Nath tradition

karam action; destiny determined by deeds performed in one's present and past existences; one of the **panj khand** in *Sikhi* (Skt. *karma*)

kinnar mythological singers in Indra's court; class of demi-gods

kirtan singing of praise

kirya technique; practice within yoga meant to achieve a specific physical result (Skt. *kriya*)

karodh anger; one of the five thieves or **panj chor** in *Sikhi*

kundalini-yoga a branch of yoga that focuses on awakening **shakti** (psycho-spiritual) energy through meditation, yogic postures and chanting of mantras so that it merges with Shiva or cosmic consciousness

langar communal dining or the communal dining hall attached to every **gurdwara** where food is served to all regardless of caste or creed

lila play or sport; **Ek Oankar's** play with creation in *Sikhi*

lobh greed; one of the five thieves or **panj chor** in *Sikhi*

Mahala palace; code word used with a number to distinguish works by the successive Sikh Gurus in the **Adi Granth**

mahant respectable; caretaker; in mid-eighteenth century managed *gurdwaras* even though many of them belonged to the **Udasi** sect and who had strayed away from *Sikhi*

man mind, heart or psyche (Skt. *manas*)

manmukh one who faces the mind; one who is turned away from *Guru* and follows the ego

mantar sacred syllable (Skt. *mantra*)

masand administrative official serving the Sikh **Panth**; established by Guru Ram Das but later discontinued by Guru Gobind Singh due to corruption

maya illusion; a Vedantic notion of the world as illusory and unreal; transient nature of the world in *Sikhi*; also written as *maia* in the **Guru Granth Sahib**

Mina rascal; a follower of Prithi Chand (eldest son of Guru Ram Das)

moh emotional attachment; one of the five evils or **panj chor** in *Sikhi*

mukat liberation from the cycle of rebirth (Skt. *mukti*)

nad sound wave; sacred sound (Skt. *nada*)

Nam Name; all names used to express the One essence in all existence

Nam jap chanting an epithet of **Ek Oankar**

Nam simran mindful remembrance of **Ek Oankar**

naoli one of the **kiryas**; circular movement of the central abdominal muscles in classical **hath-yog** (Skt. *nauli*)

Narayan an epithet for **Ek Oankar**; Supreme God in Vaishnava Hinduism

Nath master; a yogic sect, which practises **hath-yog**, founded by Gorakhnath and had considerable influence in the Punjab prior to and during the time of the Sikh Gurus; also called **Kanphata**

Niranjan pure or untainted; epithet for *Ek Oankar*; name for the Hindu god Shiva
Nirankar without form; epithet for *Ek Oankar*
nirban cooling or blowing out (i.e. of desire, vices, *kleshas*); without desire (Skt. *nirvana*; Pali *nibbana*)
nirgun without qualities or form; un-incarnated God (Skt. *nirguna*)
nirgun bhagti devotion that emphasizes the realization of *nirgun* is attained by remembering *Nam* (Skt. *nirguna bhakti*)
nishan mark; marker or flag of the Sikh court
Pandit a Hindu priest; title used for **Brahmins**
panj chor five thieves or evils (*kam, karodh, lobh, moh* and *ahankar*) that rob the mind from awareness in *Sikhi*
panj khand five spheres of spiritual development (*dharam, gian, saram, karam* and *sach*) in *Sikhi*
panth way or path; system of religious belief or practice
Panth the Sikh community at large
Paramesar Supreme God; epithet for *Ek Oankar* (Skt. *Parameshvara*)
Parbraham Highest Reality; epithet for *Ek Oankar* (Skt. *Parabrahman*)
parkrama circumambulation of the *Adi Granth* in the Darbar Sahib
pisaach ghost
pothi small book; religious text
Prabh all-pervasive One; epithet for *Ek Oankar*; name for God in Hindu Bhakti
pranayam breath control; breathing exercises (Skt. *pranayama*)
Puranas of ancient times; ancient Hindu texts praising various Hindu gods
rag Indian musical measure; a series of five or more notes on which a melody is based (Skt. *raga*)
Rag-mala garland of musical measure; a controversial hymn at the end of the *Adi Granth*, which describes eighty-four *rags*
Ram immersed in all; epithet for *Ek Oankar*; name for an incarnate form of God in Hinduism
sach Truth; one of the *panj khand* in *Sikhi*
sadh someone who practises a technique to attain truth (Skt. *sadhu*); in *Sikhi*, one who practises *Nam simran*
sahaj/sahej innate or effortless; ultimate bliss experienced with the practice of *Nam simran*; yogic term for the ultimate goal of union, during which one transcends all duality
salok a short poetic composition; a couplet from the *Adi Granth*
sangat congregation or companionship; a fellowship of Sikh devotees, especially in the presence of the **Guru Granth Sahib**
sansar transmigration; cycle of rebirth (Skt. *samsara*)
sant a saintly person
Sant embodiment of truth
santokh contentment; fulfilment (Skt. *santosh*)
sargun with qualities or form; an incarnate form of God (Skt. *saguna*)

sarovar sacred pool
Sat Purakh True Being; Ultimate Reality
Satgur True *Guru*; embodiment of Ultimate Reality
Satnam True *Nam*; the expression for the One essence in all existence
seva selfless service
SGPC Shiromani Gurdwara Prabandhak Committee; the chief Sikh organization that governs the main *gurdwaras* in the Punjab and Haryana
Shabad Sacred Word; hymn in the **Adi Granth** (Skt. *shabda*)
shabad kirtan singing of hymns
shabad-Guru *Guru's* sacred word
shakti power; feminine creative energy
shastras treatises; socio-religious law books in Hinduism (such as *Manusmriti, Dharmashastras*)
Shiva Hindu god of destruction
siddh an ascetic; an accomplished one
Sikh a learner; follower of the lived path of learning
Simritis that which is remembered; body of authored Hindu literature containing traditional religious teachings, including the Epics (*Ramayana, Mahabharata*) and the socio-religious law books (*Manusmriti, Dharmasastras*) (Skt. *smrti*)
Singh Sabha Sikh reform movement started in 1873
sukh pleasure or happiness (Skt. *sukha*)
Sukhmani the jewel or pearl of happiness
sunn empty; mental state in which one can experience the cosmic resonance of **Ek Oankar**; mental state or experience of being devoid of an intrinsic nature in Buddhism (Skt. *shunya*)
swami a holy person
Swami epithet for **Ek Oankar**
takht throne; seat of spiritual or royal authority
tirath a sacred place; a pilgrimage place (Skt. *tirtha*)
Udasi follower of the Udasi sect, an order of ascetics who revere Guru Nanak's son, Sri Chand, as their founder
Vaishnav devotees of the Hindu god Vishnu (Skt. Vaishnava)
vak saying; passage from the Sikh scripture
varna colour; the four Hindu social divisions or classes, that is, priestly class (*brahmin*), warrior and ruler class (*kshatriya*), agriculturalist and trader class (*vaishya*), and servant class (*shudra*)
Vedas Hindu scripture; highest authority in Hinduism
vismad immense awe; bliss experienced with the practice of **Nam simran**
Vishnu Hindu god who preserves creation; Supreme Lord in Vaishnav Hinduism
Waheguru wondrous light that dispels all darkness; epithet for **Ek Oankar** popularly used in Sikh practice
yakshas mythological spirits dwelling in trees and earth; class of nature spirits in the **Vedas**

Notes

Note on translation

1. Kamala Elizabeth Nayar and Jaswinder Singh Sandhu, *The Socially Involved Renunciate: Guru Nanak's Discourse to the Nath Yogis* (Albany: State University of New York Press, 2007), xv–xvi.
2. For an in-depth discussion on *Ek Oankar*, see Chapter 4.

Chapter 1

1. *Guru* is Ultimate Reality or embodiment of that reality, such as the Sacred Word (*shabad-Guru*), the ten human Gurus who uttered the Sacred Word, and the scripture (*Guru Granth Sahib*) that contains the Sacred Word.
2. *Sikhi* is the original Punjabi word to refer to the religion as taught by the Sikh Gurus. While the term 'Sikhism' is more popularly used, that term was coined by the British in the nineteenth century and it inaccurately objectifies the religion and its teachings. Arvind-Pal Mandair, *Sikhism: A Guide for the Perplexed* (London: Bloomsbury Academic, 2013), 3–14.
3. Ancient ascetic traditions belong to the late Vedic period (*c.* 700–500 BCE), during which there emerged three important religious streams – the Upanishadic, Theravada Buddhist and Jaina traditions.
4. Various devotional traditions – including Mahayana Buddhism (*c.* 100 CE), Hindu (Vaishnava) Bhakti (*c.* 500 CE), *nirgun* Bhakti (1400 CE) and *Sikhi* (1500 CE) – emerged across the Indian subcontinent as challenges to the earlier more socially conservative and elitist forms of religion, which had contended that world renunciation was a prerequisite for liberation. These traditions, in effect, made religion more accessible to the masses.
5. In *Sikhi*, the ego negatively creates a fixed sense of identity that functions to distinguish itself from others. The Sikh perspective on the ego should not be confused with the Freudian psychoanalytical understanding of the ego, where the ego functions as a mediator between the conscious and the unconscious. For further discussion, see Chapter 5.
6. For example, see Khushwant Singh, *A History of the Sikhs, 1469–1838*, vol. 1 (Princeton: Princeton University Press, 1963), 41–2; Daljeet Singh, *The Sikh*

Ideology (Amritsar: Singh Brothers, 1990), 74–7; Surinder Singh Kohli, *Yoga of the Sikhs* (Amritsar: Singh Brothers, 1991), 10.

7   While Guru Nanak views world renunciation as a form of escape from social responsibility, he also critiques the socio-religious norms associated with the traditional role of the householder, especially in regard to its ego-oriented goals of acquiring the 'fruits' of (1) wealth (*arth*), (2) sensual-pleasures (*kam*) and (3) religious merit (*dharam*). See Kamala Elizabeth Nayar and Jaswinder S. Sandhu, *The Socially Involved Renunciate: Guru Nanak's Discourse to the Nath Yogis* (Albany: State University of New York Press, 2007), 107–9.

8   While *maya* (illusions of the transient material world) is frequently written as *maia* in the *Guru Granth Sahib*, we write *maya* for consistency and readability.

9   Nayar and Sandhu, *The Socially Involved Renunciate*, 109–10.

10 In his rejection of the first three types of religious lifestyles – (1) the renunciate living outside society, (2) the householder living in society and (3) the householder living in the larger context of eventual withdrawal from society – Guru Nanak differentiates his distinctive path of (4) self-renunciation in the larger context of social involvement. For a description of the four religious lifestyles, see Nayar and Sandhu, *The Socially Involved Renunciate*, 3–16.

11 'Axial age' (from the German word *achsenzeit*) is a term coined by the philosopher Karl Jaspers for the 'pivotal' period in ancient history (900–200 BCE) during which, throughout the inhabited world, sophisticated philosophical and religious systems emerged that drastically shaped human, cultural and societal development. See Karl Jaspers, *The Origin and Goal of History* (London: Routledge Revivals, 2011).

12 Burjor Avari, *India: The Ancient Past: A History of the Indian Subcontinent from 7000 BC to AD 1200* (New York: Routledge, 2007), 66–9.

13 Avari, *India*, 86–8. According to *RigVeda* 10.90, the four *varnas* are: (1) *brahmin* (priestly) class, (2) *kshatriya* (warrior) class, (3) *vaishya* (agriculturalist) class and (4) *shudra* (serving) class.

14 While *samsara* (wandering or world) is mentioned in earlier Vedic texts, it is first discussed as a concept in the later Upanishadic texts, such as *Brhadaranyaka Upanishad* 4.4.6; *Katha Upanishad* 1.3.7; *Maitri Upanishad* 1.4, 6.34; and *Svetasvatara Upanishad* 6.16.

15 *Brhadaranyaka Upanishad* 4.3.21. Passage taken from Patrick Olivelle (trans.), *Upanisads* (New York: Oxford University Press, 2008), 61.

16 George Weston Briggs, *Gorakhnath and the Kanphata Yogis* (1938; Delhi: Motilal Banarsidass, 2001), 259.

17 For example, *Katha Upanishad* 2.12, 3.4, 6.1; *Svetasvatara Upanishad* 2.11, 6.13; and *Taitiriya Upanishad* 2.4.

18 For example, *Katha Upanishad* 6.10–11.

19 The six orthodox Hindu philosophical schools are: Purva Mimamsa, Vedanta (Advaita, Visistadvaita and Dvaita), Nyaya, Vaisesika, Samkhya and Yoga. The Hindu philosophical systems (except for Purva Mimamsa) are based on the condensed version of the Upanishads in the form of aphorisms called the *Vedanta Sutras*.
20 Klaus Klostermaier, *A Survey of Hinduism* (Albany: State University of New York Press, 1989), 358–67.
21 The three *gunas* are *sattva* (being, true, purity, illumination), *rajas* (passion, excitement, activity) and *tamas* (darkness, inertia).
22 The classical Yoga School is often grouped with the Samkhya philosophical system because of the inter-connectedness between the two. There is, however, one critical difference between the Samkhya and Yoga schools: In addition to the twenty-five elements of reality that are delineated in the Samkhya system, the Yoga School recognizes a twenty-sixth essential one – a distinct *purusha* – that is, the omnipresence of God. Unlike the Samkhya schema of reality, the Yoga School allows for belief in God (*Yoga Sutras* 1.23–9).
23 Mircea Eliade, *Yoga: Immortality and Freedom* (Princeton: Princeton University Press, 1969); Georg Feuerstein, *The Philosophy of Classical Yoga* (Manchester: University of Manchester Press, 1982).
24 Patanjali, *Yoga Sutras* 2.1–9. Passage taken from Barbara Stoler Miller (trans.), *Yoga: Discipline of Freedom: The Yoga Sutra Attributed to Patanjali* (New York: Bantam Books, 1998).
25 Patanjali, *Yoga Sutras* 2.4–5.
26 Patanjali, *Yoga Sutras* 2.15.
27 Patanjali, *Yoga Sutras* 2.6.
28 Patanjali, *Yoga Sutras* 2.7.
29 Patanjali, *Yoga Sutras* 2.8.
30 Patanjali, *Yoga Sutras* 2.9.
31 Patanjali, *Yoga Sutras* 3.4.
32 According to Bronkhorst, Classical Yoga shares similar beliefs with Buddhism, because Classical Yoga was influenced by Buddhism several centuries after the Buddha's death. Johannes Bronkhorst, *Buddhism in the Shadow of Brahmanism* (Leiden: Brill, 2011), 11.
33 Brahmins viewed *aryavarta* (land of the Vedas) – which lies between the Thar Desert and the confluence of the Yamuna and Ganga rivers – as their land only by the second century CE. Therefore, Greater Magadha (the ancient region south of the Ganga River some of which is in present-day Bihar) was not under the influence of Brahmanism during the Buddha's life. Rather, the Jaina and Ajivika (fatalist and atheist) traditions were the initial and primary influences and rivals of Buddhism. Bronkhorst, *Buddhism in the Shadow of Brahmanism*, 2, 12.

34 *Dhammapada* 191. Verses taken from John Ross Carter and Mahinda Palihawadana (trans.), *Dhammapada: The Sayings of the Buddha* (Oxford: Oxford University Press, 2000). The *Dhammapada* is a Theravada Buddhist collection of the Buddha's utterances in Pali compiled *c*. first century BCE.
35 The Eightfold Path consists of: (1) Right View, (2) Right Intention, (3) Right Speech, (4) Right Action, (5) Right Livelihood, (6) Right Effort, (7) Right Mindfulness and (8) Right Concentration.
36 *Dhammapada* 1.
37 *Dhammapada* 2.
38 *Dhammapada* 192.
39 Bhikkhu Bodhi, *The Connected Discourses of the Buddha: A Translation of the Samyutta Nikaya* (Boston: Wisdom Publications, 2000), 27.
40 For instance, see *Samyutta Nikaya* 4.25, v. 518. Bodhi, *The Connected Discourses of the Buddha*, 220.
41 The *Pali Canon* was collected *c*. first century BCE and codified in Sri Lanka. There are three parts to the *Pali Canon*: (1) *Vinaya* Pitika, the 'Basket of Discipline' for monks and nuns about how they ought to live within the monastic community; (2) *Sutta Pitika*, the 'Basket of Discourse' of the Buddha and his close companions and disciples; and (3) *Abhidhamma Pitika*, 'Basket of Virtue', which comprises the reworking of the teachings found in the *Sutta*, and includes the rules and regulations of the community, accounts of how the Buddhist community continued after the Buddha died, and the revoking or making of rules following the Buddha's death.
42 Majjhima Nikaya 27.18–19. Bhikkhu Bodhi, *Teachings of the Buddha: Middle Length Discourses of the Buddha: A Translation of the Majjhima Nikaya* (Boston: Wisdom Publishers, 1995), 274–5.
43 *Vibhanga* (Nanavibhanga, Pancavidhena) XVI.4. Carline Augusta Rhys Davids, *The Vibhanga: Being the Second Book of the Abhidhamma Pitaka* (1904; London: The Pali Text Society, 1978), 341.
44 *Visuddhimagga: The Path of Purification by Bhadantacariya Buddhaghosa*, trans. Bhikkhu Nanamoli (1975, 1991; Onalaska, WA: Pariyatti Publishing, Buddhist Publication Society, 1999), xxiii.
45 *Visuddhimagga* III.74. *Visuddhimagga*, Nanamoli (trans.), 101.
46 *Visuddhimagga* IV.85–7. *Visuddhimagga*, Nanamoli (trans.), 138–9.
47 *Dhammapada* 9–10.
48 Wendy Doniger, *The Hindus: An Alternative History* (New York: Penguin, 2010), 208.
49 Doniger, *The Hindus*, 207–9.
50 During the period of Classical Hinduism, the pan-Indian socio-religious law books – *Dharmasastras* (*c*. 200 BCE) and *Manusmrti* (*c*. 200 BCE–100 CE) – prescribe religious and social duty (*dharma*) based on gender, social class (*varna*)

and stage-in-life (*ashrama*). The four stages of life are: (1) studenthood stage (*brahmana-ashrama*), (2) householder stage (*grihastha-ashrama*), (3) forest-dweller stage (*vanaprastha-ashrama*) meant for the married couple and (4) renunciation stage (*samnyasa-ashrama*). The texts stipulate different stages in life for the action-oriented path of living-in-this-world for worldly pursuits prior to the path of renouncing-this-world for self-realization.

51 Interestingly, contrary to the *Manusmrti*, the *Kama Sutra* writes of three aims (*dharma*, *artha* and *kama*), attaching *moksha* onto *dharma*, but it does not mention the four stages of life (*ashramas*). Doniger, *The Hindus*, 208.

52 The males of the three higher classes are referred to as *dvija* (twice-born). Having received Vedic learning during the first stage of life (*brahmana-ashrama*), they are eligible to renounce mundane existence in the pursuit of liberation during the *samnyasa-ashrama*. Therefore, while there is an important orientation to pursuing material goals as a householder, there is nevertheless the notion that the ultimate goal of liberation is attainable only by those with the ascriptive status of *dvija*, who are in a position to take on the traditional renunciate lifestyle of withdrawal from society during the last stage of life. *Moksha* is, therefore, open only to the privileged males belonging to the three upper-Hindu classes (*dvija*).

53 Doniger, *The Hindus*, 208.

54 'Nor shall he be passionately attached to any of the sensory objects out of lust, but using his mind he should stamp out any excessive attachment to them' (*Manusmrti* 4.16). Passage taken from *The Law Code of Manu*, trans. Patrick Olivelle (New York: Oxford University Press, 2009).

55 *Mahabharata* 1.187; *Arthasastras* 1.17.35–8.

56 The *Bhagavad Gita* is a section of the *Mahabharata* (c. 500–100 BCE), one of the two great Hindu epics. The epics are of primary importance as they are in fact at the heart of Hindu belief and devotional ritual practice. The *Bhagavad Gita* has twofold importance for Hindus: (1) the notion of Krishna revealing himself as an incarnation of God (*avatara*) (*Bhagavad Gita* 4.6.) and (2) Krishna's teachings to the warrior Arjuna, who does not want to fight in the battle (*Bhagavad Gita* 2).

57 In the *Bhagavad Gita*, Krishna outlines three different religious paths: *jnana-marga* (path of wisdom), *karma-marga* (path of action) and *bhakti-marga* (path of devotion).

58 Nayar and Sandhu, *The Socially Involved Renunciate*, 106–9.

59 Nayar and Sandhu, *The Socially Involved Renunciate*, 109–13.

60 M.1, *GGS*, 1256.

61 M.1, *GGS*, 722–3. By the time Guru Nanak had established his religious system, the Mughal Emperor Babur had commenced his rule in northern India. During Emperor Babur's rule, Guru Nanak was, in fact, temporarily imprisoned. Guru Nanak's 'Babar-bani', contained in the *Guru Granth Sahib*, provides an account of Babur's invasion that had occurred around 1521 CE, which resulted in the

establishment of Mughal rule over India (1526 CE). According to the 'Babar-bani', the invasion (or at least one of them) occurred in 'seventy-eight' (1578 *sambat*), which is 1521 CE. J.S. Grewal, *The Sikhs of the Punjab* (Cambridge: Cambridge University Press, 1998), 39; Harbans Singh, *The Heritage of the Sikhs* (New York: Asia Publishing, 1964), 19–20; Louis E. Fenech, *Martyrdom in the Sikh Tradition: Playing the 'Game of Love'* (Delhi: Oxford University Press, 2000), 81.

62 Jaswinder Singh Sandhu, 'The Sikh Model of the Person, Suffering, and Healing: The Implications for Counselors', *International Journal for the Advancement of Counseling* 26, no. 1 (2004): 39–40.
63 Fenech, *Martyrdom in the Sikh Tradition*, 64–7.
64 M.1, *GGS*, 142.
65 M.1, *GGS*, 1328.
66 The five evils include ego (*ahankar*), attachment (*moh*), greed (*lobh*), anger (*karodh*) and lust (*kam*).
67 M.1, *GGS*, 469.
68 M.1, *GGS*, 139.
69 M.1, *Japji* 5, *GGS*, 2.
70 M.1, *Siddh Goshth* 25, *GGS*, 940–1.
71 M.1, *GGS*, 149.
72 M.1, *Siddh Goshth* 49, *GGS*, 943.
73 M.1, *GGS*, 57; M.1, *GGS*, 598.
74 M.1, *Japji* 2, *GGS*, 1. See also M.1, *GGS*, 581–2.
75 Sandhu, 'The Sikh Model of the Person, Suffering, and Healing', 39–40.
76 M.1, *Japji* 16, *GGS*, 3.
77 M.1, *Siddh Goshth* 36, *GGS*, 942.
78 Pashaura Singh, 'Revisiting the "Evolution of the Sikh Community"', *Journal of Punjab Studies* 17, nos. 1–2 (2010): 51; Khushwant Singh, *A History of the Sikhs*, vol. 1, 47–8. *Nam-dan-ishnan* can also be interpreted as the purification of the mind and body by *nam-dan*, the twofold practice of remembering the Name (*nam*) and engaging in selfless service (*dan*).
79 M.1, *Siddh Goshth* 50, *GGS*, 943.
80 *Sikh Reht Maryada* (Amritsar: Shiromani Gurdwara Parbhandak Committee, 1982), Article III. The *Sikh Reht Maryada* is based on the *rahit-namas* (codes of discipline) of the eighteenth and nineteenth centuries. While its compilation commenced during the Gurdwara reform movement in the 1920s by the Shiromani Gurdwara Parbhandak Committee (SGPC), the *Sikh Reht Maryada* was approved and published only in 1950. For an analysis of the *rahit-namas* and *maryadas*, see W.H. McLeod, *Sikhs of the Khalsa: A History of the Rahit* (New Delhi: Oxford University Press, 2003).

81 *Sikh Reht Maryada* can be found in both Punjabi and English on the SGPC's official website (4 November 2017), retrieved from http://sgpc.net/sikh-rehat-maryada-in-punjabi/ and http://sgpc.net/sikh-rehat-maryada-in-english/
82 'Truth is above all, but higher is truthful living' (M.1, *GGS*, 62).
83 W.H. McLeod, *Guru Nanak and the Sikh Religion* (Delhi: Oxford University Press, 1988), 151–3; W. Owen Cole and Piara Singh Sambhi, *A Popular Dictionary of Sikhism: Sikh Religion and Philosophy* (London: Routledge, 1997), 22; J.S. Grewal, *Four Centuries of Sikh Tradition: History, Literature, and Identity* (New Delhi: Oxford University Press, 2011), 7–23.
84 Gurinder Singh Mann, 'Guru Nanak's Life and Legacy: An Appraisal', *Journal of Punjab Studies* 17, nos. 1–2 (2010): 9–11.
85 See Pashaura Singh, 'Revisiting the "Evolution of the Sikh Community"', 45–74; Mann, 'Guru Nanak's Life and Legacy', 9–12; Nayar and Sandhu, *The Socially Involved Renunciate*, 109–13; Khushwant Singh, *A History of the Sikhs*, vol. 1, 36.
86 Pashaura Singh, *Life and Work of Guru Arjan: History, Memory, and Biography in the Sikh Tradition* (New Delhi: Oxford University Press, 2006), 15.
87 According to *Manusmrti* 4.6 and 4.160, service is a dog's work that is meant for those belonging to the lowest of the four *varnas* – the *shudra* (serving) class – or even the outcastes of the *varna* system. Nayar and Sandhu, *Socially Involved Renunciate*, 87, 160 n.47.
88 Pashaura Singh, *Life and Work of Guru Arjan*, 16.
89 For a thorough analysis on the polarized nature of Sikh Studies, see J.S. Grewal, *Contesting Interpretations of the Sikh Tradition* (Delhi: Manohar Publishers, 1998); W.H. McLeod, 'Cries of Outrage: History versus Tradition in the Work on the Sikh Community', *Exploring Sikhism: Aspects of Sikh Identity, Culture and Thought* (Delhi: Oxford University Press, 2000), 269.
90 Ernest Trumpp, *The Adi Granth: The Holy Scripture of the Sikhs* (1877; New Delhi: Munisharam Manoharlal, 1989); Arthur Max Macauliffe, *The Sikh Religion: Its Gurus, Sacred Writings and Authors*, 6 vols. (1909; Delhi: DK Publishers, 1998); J.D. Cunningham, *A History of the Sikhs* (1849; Delhi: S. Chand, 1955).
91 Teja Singh, *Sikh Dharam* (1952; Amritsar: Singh Brothers, 1977); Professor Sahib Singh, *Sri Guru Granth Sahib Darpan*, 10 vols. (Jalandhar: Sahib Singh Ji, 1962–64).
92 For examples of the viewpoint of 'traditional historians', see Trilochan Singh, *Ernest Trumpp and W. H. McLeod as Scholars of Sikh History, Religion and Culture* (Chandigarh: International Centre of Sikh Studies, 1994); Daljeet Singh, *The Sikh Ideology*, 38.
93 For examples of the viewpoint of 'critical historians', see McLeod, *Guru Nanak and the Sikh Religion*; Harjot Singh Oberoi, *The Construction of Religious Boundaries: Culture, Identity, and Diversity in the Sikh Tradition* (Chicago: University of

Chicago Press, 1994); Pashaura Singh, *The Guru Granth Sahib: Canon, Meaning and Authority* (Delhi: Oxford University Press, 2000).

94 The main contentious issues surrounding Sikh studies are: (1) the application of the textual-critical method to Sikh literature (both scripture and religious literature, including the *Guru Granth Sahib*, *Dasam Granth* and *janam-sakhis*); (2) the correlation made between Jat cultural and Shakti religious patterns with the emergence of militancy in the Sikh tradition and the creation of the Khalsa; (3) the codification of the *Sikh Rahit Maryada*; and (4) the discrepancy between social equality in theory and the use of caste in practice. For an elaborate analysis of the debate surrounding these contentious issues, see Grewal, *Contesting Interpretations of the Sikh Tradition*.

95 For more recent theoretical perspectives on translating the Sikh tradition, see Balbinder Singh Bhogal, 'Postcolonial and Postmodern Perspectives on Sikhism', *The Oxford Handbook of Sikh Studies* (Oxford, UK: Oxford University Press, 2014), 282–97; Arvind-Pal Singh Mandair, *Religion and the Specter of the West: Sikhism, India, Postcoloniality, and the Politics of Translation* (New York: Columbia University Press, 2009). For a thorough treatment challenging a single linear and essentialist approach to the development of Sikhism, see Pashaura Singh, 'Revisiting the "Evolution of the Sikh Community"', 45–74.

96 For further elaboration of the pan-Indian genre of hagiography or 'sacred biography', see Chapter 2.

97 Of course, Abraham Maslow, founder of humanist psychology, later added 'self-transcendence' to his hierarchy of human needs, thus setting the stage for transpersonal psychology, which is regarded as a sub-field in psychology. See Abraham H. Maslow, *The Farther Reaches of Human Nature* (New York: The Viking Press, 1971).

98 See Susan A. David, Ilona Boniwell and Amanda Conley Ayers, *The Oxford Handbook of Happiness* (Oxford: Oxford University Press, 2013).

99 Kiran Kumar Salagame, 'Meaning and Well-Being: Indian Perspectives', *Journal of Constructivist Psychology* 30, no. 1 (2017): 67.

Chapter 2

1 Harmandar Sahib (temple of *Har*) is now popularly called the Golden Temple, as a result of its distinctive appearance after Maharaja Ranjit Singh in the early 1800s captured the region and rebuilt the temple by covering the upper exterior of the temple with gold leaf. While it was originally designed and built by Guru Arjan around 1601 CE, the temple and the surrounding complex have been constructed and re-constructed throughout the centuries.

2   Akbar is the popular and shortened version of Abu'l-Fath Jalal-ud-din Muhammad Akbar. And, Jahangir is the popular name for Nur-ud-din Muhammad Salim.
3   J.P.S. Uberoi, *Religion, Civil Society and the State: A Study of Sikhism* (Delhi: Oxford University Press, 1996), 91.
4   For an explanation of *Nam-dan-ishnan*, see 'Sikhi, Suffering, and Social Responsibility' in Chapter 1.
5   Paul Valliere, 'Tradition', in *The Encyclopedia of Religion*, ed. Mircea Eliade, vol. 13 (1st edn.; New York: Macmillan, 2005), 9271.
6   Hagiographies or 'sacred biographies' are stories about historical figures that mix fact with legend. Therefore, hagiographies relate historical events, even as they intertwine them with stories of supernatural births, miracles and the like. Although a narrative's kernel may be historical, it often reflects the religious or societal concerns of the times. Moreover, the many pan-Indian hagiographical motifs employed are common to stories about religious figures, leaders, philosophers and mystics in order to establish the spiritual status of the person along with offering a particular theological perspective. Kamala Elizabeth Nayar and Jaswinder Singh Sandhu, *The Socially Involved Renunciate: Guru Nanak's Discourse to the Nath Yogis* (Albany: State University of New York Press, 2007), 41.
7   Christian Lee Novetzke, 'The Theographic and the Historiographic in an Indian Sacred Life Story', *Sikh Formations* 3, no. 2 (2007): 169–84.
8   For instance, see Nikky-Guninder Kaur Singh, 'The Myth of the Founder: The Janamsakhis and Sikh Tradition', *History of Religions* 31, no. 4 (1992): 329–43.
9   For more information on the *bhatts*, see Chapter 3.
10 Bhai Gurdas (1551–1636) was a scribe who had a significant role in the writing of the *Adi Granth* under the supervision of Guru Arjan.
11 *Gur Pratap Suraj* was composed in Braj Bhasha (medieval Hindi) and written in the Gurmukhi script. While there are other earlier hagiographical sources, such as the Gurbilas (*c.* 1751), Kesar Singh Chhibbar's *Bansavalinama Dasan Patishahian Ka* (1769) and Sarup Das Bhalla's *Mahima Prakash* (1776), *Gur Pratap Suraj* is a text from which preachers frequently quote during their *gurdwara* sermons in the afternoon or early evening.
12 W.H. McLeod, *Textual Sources for the Study of Sikhism* (Manchester: Manchester University Press, 1984), 11–13; Sukhdial Singh, *Historical Analysis of Giani Gian Singh's Writings* (Jalandhar: UICS, 1996), 9, 29–30. For a postcolonial approach to historiography, see Arvind-Pal Singh Mandair, *Religion and the Specter of the West: Sikhism, India, Postcoloniality, and the Politics of Translation* (New York: Columbia University Press, 2009).
13 The Nirmala sect is an ascetic order that is believed to have emerged during the period of Guru Gobind Singh and gained political prominence in the nineteenth century. Some scholars contend that the Nirmala sect is a derivative of the Udasi

sect founded by Guru Nanak's son Sri Chand. Harjot Singh Oberoi, *Construction of Religious Boundaries: Culture, Identity, and Diversity in the Sikh Tradition* (Delhi: Oxford University Press, 1994), 124–35; Raijasbir Singh, 'Nirmala bekh da arambh', in *Nirmala Sampraday*, ed. Pritam Singh (Amritsar: Guru Nanak Dev University, 1981), 33–7.

14 The Nirmala sect established a network of seminaries for the creation and transmission of *Sikhi*. Paramjit Singh Judge, 'Taksals, Akharas, and Nihang Deras', in *The Oxford Handbook of Sikh Studies*, ed. Pashaura Singh and Louis Fenech (Oxford: Oxford University Press, 2014), 377; Oberoi, *Construction of Religious Boundaries*, 124–35.

15 Inter-faith dialogue is most evident through the actions of Guru Nanak during his travels in the four directions of the world, described in the *janam-sakhis*. See Nayar and Sandhu, *The Socially Involved Renunciate*, 44–5, 86.

16 As a poet and philosopher of the Singh Sabha movement, Bhai Vir Singh (1872–1957) edited the *Suraj Prakash* in order to remove its Hindu elements. Bhai Vir Singh, *Sri Gurpratap Suraj Granth*, 14 vols. (1927–35; Amritsar: Khalsa Samachar, 1963).

17 Bhatt Mathura, *GGS*, 1408.

18 Bhai Gurdas, *Varan* 24.18.1–4, 7.

19 Bhai Gurdas, *Varan* 24.19.1–2.

20 J.S. Grewal, *The Sikhs of the Punjab* (Cambridge: Cambridge University Press, 1998), 58.

21 Narratives describe Guru Nanak as testing Guru Angad's stature prior to appointing him as the successor. Max Arthur Macauliffe, *The Sikh Religion: Its Gurus, Sacred Writings and Authors*, vol. 2 (Delhi: DK Publishers, 1998), 3–12.

22 Grewal, *The Sikhs of the Punjab*, 47–8; Khushwant Singh, *A History of the Sikhs, 1469–1838*, vol. 1 (Princeton: Princeton University Press, 1963), 49; Macauliffe, *The Sikh Religion*, vol. 2, 11–12.

23 Bhai Gurdas, *Varan* 1.45–6, 24.8, and 39.2.

24 Surjit Singh Hans, *A Reconstruction of Sikh History from Sikh Literature* (Jalandhar: ABS, 1988), 42–8, 47.

25 Indubhusan Banerjee, *Evolution of the Khalsa*, vol. 1 (1936; Calcutta: University of Calcutta, 1972), 153–8.

26 Grewal, *The Sikhs of the Punjab*, 49; Khushwant Singh, *A History of the Sikhs*, vol. 1, 52 n.8; Macauliffe, *The Sikh Religion*, vol. 2, 63–70.

27 According to tradition, Datu, a celibate, also temporarily ousted Guru Amar Das from the guru-seat in Goindval.

28 Khushwant Singh, *A History of the Sikhs*, vol. 1, 53; Macauliffe, *The Sikh Religion*, vol. 2, 97–8; Pashaura Singh, *Life and Work of Guru Arjan: History, Memory, and Biography in the Sikh Tradition* (New Delhi: Oxford University Press, 2006), 66.

29 Grewal, *The Sikhs of the Punjab*, 51; Macauliffe, *The Sikh Religion*, vol. 2, 105, 106–11, 132–3.
30 Macauliffe, *The Sikh Religion*, vol. 2, 151. For a thorough discussion on the *manji* system, see Fauja Singh, *Guru Amardas: Life and Teachings* (New Delhi: Sterling, 1978), 116–29, 143–64.
31 M.3, *Anand*, GGS, 920. For information about the *Goindval Pothis*, see notes 73 to 76.
32 M.3, *Anand*, GGS, 917–22.
33 M.3, *Anand*, GGS, 917.
34 Jetha Sodhi's nephew was married to Guru Angad's daughter. Macauliffe, *The Sikh Religion*, vol. 2, 30–5.
35 Guru Amar Das's daughter, Bibi Bhani, requested that the *gur-gaddi* remain in her family. Bhai Gurdas explains that Guru Amar Das appointed Jetha Sodhi as the successor because it was only the Sodhi clan that could handle the responsibility (*Varan* 1.47). While Mohari, who desired a life of comfort, accepted his father's decision to appoint Ram Das as successor, Mohan, who became 'mad', established a parallel seat at Goindval even as he tried to assert his legal right based on being the eldest son (Bhai Gurdas, *Varan* 26.33). Macauliffe, *The Sikh Religion*, vol. 2, 144, 148; Pashaura Singh, *The Life and Work of Guru Arjan*, 66.
36 Pashaura Singh, *Life and Work of Guru Arjan*, 67; Grewal, *The Sikhs of the Punjab*, 51.
37 Khushwant Singh, *A History of the Sikhs*, vol. 1, 55; Macauliffe, *The Sikh Religion*, vol. 2, 253.
38 Bhai Gurdas, *Varan* 1.47.1–3.
39 Macauliffe, *The Sikh Religion*, vol. 2, 271–2; Grewal, *The Sikhs of the Punjab*, 52; Hans, *A Reconstruction of Sikh History from Sikh Literature*, 99–100.
40 M.4, GGS, 304.
41 For instance, see Bhai Gurdas, *Varan* 1.47.6, 13.25, 20.1, 24.18, 24.19; Bhatt Kalh, GGS, 1407–8; Bhatt Mathura, GGS, 1409; Bhatt Harbans, GGS, 1409.
42 Grewal, *The Sikhs of the Punjab*, 54; Macauliffe, *The Sikh Religion*, vol. 3, 1–3.
43 Macauliffe, *The Sikh Religion*, vol. 3, 1; K.S. Duggal, *Sikh Gurus: Their Lives and Teachings* (New Delhi: UBS Publishers, 1993), 111.
44 Pashaura Singh, *The Life and Work of Guru Arjan*, 71.
45 Bhai Gurdas, *Varan* 1.47.1–8. See also Bhai Gurdas, *Varan* 1.48, 24.19, 26.33; Bhatt Kalh, GGS, 1407; Bhatt Mathura, GGS, 1408–9; Bhatt Harbans, GGS, 1409.
46 Macauliffe, *The Sikh Religion*, vol. 2, 138.
47 Pashaura Singh, *Life and Work of Guru Arjan*, 65.
48 For more information about the *rags*, see the section on 'Sikh Ritual and the *Sukhmani* Text' in Chapter 3.
49 Alternatively, Kesar Singh Chhibbar's *Bansavalinama Dasan Patishahian Ka* states that Guru Arjan first married Ram Dei, but since she could not conceive a child,

Guru Arjan married Ganga Devi in 1589, after which she gave birth to Hargobind in 1590. Pashaura Singh, *Life and Work of Guru Arjan*, 67, 99n15.

50 Bhai Gurdas, *Varan* 24.20.1–3.

51 The specific practice of *dasvand* (distribute one-tenth) is found in later texts, like Bhai Nand Lal Goya's *Tankhah Nama* verse 24. Banerjee, *Evolution of the Khalsa*, vol. 1, 254; Khushwant Singh, *A History of the Sikhs*, vol. 1, 57; Teja Singh, *Sikhism: Its Ideals and Institutions* (1937; Bombay: Orient Longman, 2009), 45.

52 According to the *Dabistan-i-Mazahib*, the Sikh Panth grew with every succeeding guru until Guru Arjan, when the community expanded substantially with the *masand* network throughout the Punjab. Irfan Habib (trans.), '"Sikhism and the Sikhs," 1645-6: From Mobad, *Dabistan-i-Mazahib*', in *Sikh History from Persian Sources*, ed. J.S. Grewal and Irfan Habib (New Delhi: Tulika, 2001), 66–7. See also Banerjee, *Evolution of the Khalsa*, vol. 1, 258–61; Grewal, *The Sikhs of the Punjab*, 56–7. Irfan Habib, *The Agrarian System of Mughal India 1556–1707* (New Delhi: Oxford University Press, 1999), 397.

53 Pashaura Singh, *Life and Work of Guru Arjan*, 71.

54 Macauliffe, *The Sikh Religion*, vol. 2, 276–7.

55 Bhai Gurdas, *Varan* 26.33.5. According to Kesar Singh Chhibbar's *Bansavalinama Dasan Patishahian Ka*, 49–50, Guru Arjan began to use the name Mina for Prithi Chand after the latter's deceit.

56 Hans, *A Reconstruction of Sikh History from Sikh Literature*, 137.

57 Grewal, *The Sikhs of the Punjab*, 54; Pashaura Singh, *Life and Work of Guru Arjan*, 78–9; Khushwant Singh, *A History of the Sikhs*, vol. 1, 56–8; and Macauliffe, *The Sikh Religion*, vol. 3, 34–46.

58 Hardip Singh Syan, 'Sectarian Works', in *The Oxford Handbook of Sikh Studies*, ed. Pashaura Singh and Louis Fenech (Oxford: Oxford University Press, 2014), 177.

59 W.H. McLeod, *Exploring Sikhism: Aspects of Sikh Identity, Culture and Thought* (New Delhi: Oxford University Press, 2000), 55. More recently, Syan argues that the development of *Sikhi* is told from the orthodox perspective, overlooking splinter groups like Prithi Chand's son Miharvan, who claimed himself as seventh Guru. Hardip Singh Syan, 'Early Sikh Historiography', *Sikh Formations* 7, no. 2 (2011): 148.

60 Hans, *A Reconstruction of Sikh History from Sikh Literature*, 137–45.

61 Macauliffe, *The Sikh Religion*, vol. 3, 48; Pashaura Singh, *Life and Work of Guru Arjan*, 73.

62 For instance, Guru Arjan prayed for Prithi Chand's health when he fell ill, and then thanked Guru upon Prithi Chand's recovery. Pashaura Singh, *Life and Work of Guru Arjan*, 73–4.

63 Sukhdial Singh, *Historical Analysis of Giani Gian Singh's Writings*, 36–7.

64 Pashaura Singh, *Life and Work of Guru Arjan*, 81.

65 Emperor Akbar encouraged interfaith dialogue, which is expressed in his repeal of the Islamic tax on non-Muslims (*jizya*) (1568), his construction of the 'House of worship' (*Ibadat Khana*) at Fatehpur Sikri (1575), and his 'Sufi' conceptualization of a syncretistic religion (*Din-i-Ilahi*) based on the various religions practised by his subjects, including Islam, Hinduism, Jainism, Christianity and Zoroastrianism (1582). Emperor Aurangzeb (1618–1707), however, reintroduced *jizya* in 1679. Habib, *The Agrarian System of Mughal India*, 138–9, 285.

66 *Akbarnama* III, 746. Shireen Moosvi (trans.), 'Akbar Meets Guru Arjan, 1598, from Abu'l Fazl, *Akbarnama*', in *Sikh History from Persian Sources*, ed. J.S. Grewal and Irfan Habib (New Delhi: Tulika, 2001), 55.

67 The Mughal Empire employed a system whereby it collected land revenue tax from its subjects. While the *Khulasatu't Tawarikh* states that Guru Arjan made a plea for a reduction in the land tax, the *Akbarnama* does not mention this. *Khulasatu't Tawarikh*, 425; Iqbal Husain, (trans.), 'The Sikhs and The[ir] History, 1696: From Sujan Rai Bhandari, *Khulasatu't Tawarikh*', in *Sikh History from Persian Sources*, ed. J.S. Grewal and Irfan Habib (New Delhi: Tulika, 2001), 93–5.

68 W.H. McLeod, 'The Development of the Sikh Panth', in *Exploring Sikhism: Aspects of Sikh Identity, Culture and Thought* (New Delhi: Oxford University Press, 2000), 55; Sarup Das Bhalla, *Mahima Prakash*, part II, ed. Gobind Singh Lamba et al. (Patiala: Bhasha Bibhag, 1971), 358; Pashaura Singh, *Life and Works of Guru Arjan*, 93.

69 *Bansavalinama Dasan Patishahian Ka*, 81. Macauliffe, *The Sikh Religion*, vol. 3, 55; Pashaura Singh, *Life and Work of Guru Arjan*, 73; Pashaura Singh, *The Guru Granth Sahib: Canon, Meaning and Authority* (New Delhi: Oxford University Press, 2003), 38.

70 Syan, 'Early Sikh Historiography', 145–60. See also Habib (trans.), 'Sikhism and the Sikhs', 67–8.

71 Pashaura Singh, *Life and Work of Guru Arjan*, 137–40.

72 Santokh Singh equates the *Adi Granth* to the Vedas. *Sri Gur Pratap Suraj Granth*, vol. 6, 2083; Gurinder Singh Mann, *The Making of Sikh Scripture* (New York: Oxford University Press, 2001), 23; Pashaura Singh, *Life and Works of Guru Arjan*, 93.

73 There are two extant copies of the *Goindval Pothis* (Jalandhar and Pinjore). Pashaura Singh, *The Guru Granth Sahib*, 18–19. Gurinder Singh Mann, *The Goindval Pothis: The Earliest Extant Source of the Sikh Canon* (Cambridge, MA: Harvard University Press, 1996), 40–50.

74 Khushwant Singh, *A History of the Sikhs*, vol. 1, 58. The narratives about Guru Arjan obtaining the *Goindval Pothis* differ based on Mohan Bhalla's (un)willingness to share the collection with Guru Arjan. The discrepancy in the narratives reflects the struggle over leadership between the Sodhi and Bhalla clans. Besides, it illustrates how possession of the *Goindval Pothis* played a significant role in

claims to guruship. According to Mann, the struggle between the two clans ended with the Bhalla clan lending the *Goindval Pothis* to Guru Arjan. The *Goindval Pothis*, however, remain in the possession of the Bhalla clan. Mann, *The Goindval Pothis*, 2–14; Mann, *The Making of Sikh Scripture*, 47–50.

75 While Mann asserts that there was a single line of transmission beginning with a single source, which then developed into various strands with minor variations, Pashaura Singh argues that there have been other sources that Guru Arjan used in the compilation process of the *Adi Granth*. Pashaura Singh, *The Guru Granth Sahib*, 18–19; Mann, *The Making of Sikh Scripture*, 40–50; Pashaura Singh, *Life and Work of Guru Arjan*, 141–3.

76 Pashaura Singh, *Guru Granth Sahib*, 151–76.

77 The *Adi Granth* was installed in the Harmandar Sahib in 1604 during Emperor Akbar's rule. Guru Arjan established the Sikh divine court (*darbar sahib*) by installing the *Adi Granth* as the focal point in a Mughal-style courtly structure within the Sikh temple. In a sense, the *Adi Granth* (i.e. *shabad-Guru*) is the *murat* (image or icon) of *Guru*.

78 Khushwant Singh, *A History of the Sikhs*, vol. 1, 58; Pashaura Singh, *Life and Work of Guru Arjan*, 82.

79 McLeod, *Textual Sources for the Study of Sikhism*, 110.

80 For information about the Guru Nanak Dev University manuscript 1245, see Pashaura Singh, *Guru Granth Sahib*, chapter 2. According to Giani Gian Singh, the *Sukhmani* was composed in 1657 [1600 CE], whereas Pandit Tara Singh Narotam asserts that the text was written in 1660 [1602–03 CE]. Giani Gian Singh, *Tawarikh Guru Khalsa*, vol. 1 (Amritsar: Giani Gian Singh Ji, 1897), 42; Pandit Tara Singh Narotam, *Sri Guru Tirath Sangreh* (1884; Kankhal: Sri Nirmal Panchait Akhara, 1975), 209.

81 Gurbachan Singh Talib, 'Sukhmani', in *The Encyclopedia of Sikhism*, vol. 4, ed. Harbans Singh (Patiala: Punjabi University, 1998), 263.

82 When Sri Chand sends his disciple Kamalia to collect a yearly stipend from Guru Arjan, Sri Chand instructs him to be assertive when he meets with the Guru in order to obtain the stipend. Although Guru Arjan is hospitable and invites him for *langar*, Mata Ganga (Guru Arjan's wife) questions Kamalia why he is standing like a soldier in the *langar* hall. Upon receiving the stipend, Kamalia returns to Sri Chand and describes the meeting. In reaction to Mata Ganga's treatment of Kamalia, Sri Chand utters the statement that 'soldiers will then come', foreshadowing Guru Arjan's encounter with Mughal forces and his subsequent execution. Bhai Santokh Singh, *Gur Pratap Suraj* 4.28. Even though the narrative makes Sri Chand look dependent on the Sikh Panth, it also reflects the Nirmala outlook on Sri Chand's alleged possession of supernatural powers, by the way it emphasizes 'whatever Sri Chand utters becomes true' (i.e. the words that Sri Chand uttered that 'soldiers will then come'). The narrative also indicates that the Sikh

Gurus did not expel Sri Chand and that Sri Chand accepted the fact that the *tilak* belongs to the Sodhi clan.

83 Instead, Macauliffe provides many stories that establish Guru Arjan's superiority. For instance, there is the reference to a yogi who waited to see Guru Arjan after he was told that, if he meets the Guru, he will attain liberation. Macauliffe, *The Sikh Religion*, vol. 3, 2–3; *Sri Gur Pratap Suraj Granth*, vol. 6, 1785–93.

84 Macauliffe, *The Sikh Religion*, vol. 3, 27–8.

85 Pandit Tara Singh Narotam was trained and initiated into the Nirmala Dera of Sant Gulab Singh at Kurala. He continued learning and teaching in Amritsar and Varanasi, before establishing the Nirmala Dera at Patiala (known as Dharam Dhuja) under the patronage of Maharaja Narinder Singh. In 1875, Tara Singh became chief priest at the Nirmal Panchaiti Akhara at Kankhal (Haridwar).

86 Narotam, *Sri Guru Tirath Sangreh*, 50.

87 Under the patronage of Maharaja Narinder Singh, Giani Gian Singh was assigned to assist Pandit Tara Singh Narotam in his research for the *Sri Guru Tirath Sangreh*. For an overview of Giani Gian Singh's life, see Sukhdial Singh, *Historical Analysis of Giani Gian Singh's Writings*, 18–27.

88 Giani Gian Singh, *Tawarikh Guru Khalsa*, vol. 1, 42. The *Tawarikh Guru Khalsa* (1891) is Giani Gian Singh's first work which provides the life accounts of all the Sikh Gurus. While his aim was to simplify Santokh Singh's *Sri Gur Pratap Suraj* (with its difficult Braj verses) so that the common person could comprehend the stories, his historical approach nonetheless incorporated hagiographical elements and oral traditions. Sukhdial Singh, *Historical Analysis of Giani Gian Singh's Writings*, 28–30.

89 Rai Balwand and Satta the drummer, GGS, 967. For more on Balwand and Satta, see Chapter 3, note 18.

90 *Udasi* (indifferent, detached) refers to someone who withdraws from worldly affairs in the pursuit of higher spiritual goals, like an ascetic. In contrast to Guru Nanak's teachings about living in the world, the Udasi sect founded by Sri Chand preached world renunciation and celibacy. During the eighteenth and nineteenth centuries the Udasi *mahants* both gained control over major Sikh institutions, like the Harmandar Sahib in Amritsar, and set up centres in rural Punjab to spread and preach their sectarian version of the Sikh religion, in the course of which Hindu practices entered into the evolving tradition. With the advent of the Singh Sabha movement in the late 1800s and the Akali Gurdwara reform of the 1920s, the Udasis declined in importance. While they are excluded from mainstream Sikhism, they are highly revered in the Hindu tradition. Oberoi, *Construction of Religious Boundaries*, 78–80.

91 For example, *Sukhmani* 13.1 and 13.3.

92 Bhai Gurdas, *Varan* 26.33.

93 According to tradition, when Guru Gobind Singh initiated the Khalsa, he forbade members of the Sikh Panth to interact with the Minas, as also with the followers of the Dhirmalia sect founded by Dhir Mal (grandson of Guru Hargobind) and the

masands. This code (*rahit*) was incorporated in both the eighteenth-century *rahit-namas* (e.g. Chaupa Singh Chhibbar's *Rahit-nama*) and the twentieth-century *Sikh Reht Maryada* (Article 24.q).

94 Pashaura Singh, *The Guru Granth Sahib*, 93.

95 Damdami Taksal is a seminary order that regards Baba Deep Singh (1682–1757) as its first leader. Baba Deep Singh – a martyr – was the first leader of the Khalsa misl called Shaheed Taran Dal and the caretaker of the Damdama Sahib at Talwandi Sabo. The place became known as Damdama (resting or breathing place) because Guru Gobind Singh is said to have rested there following the Battle of Mukhtsar in 1705. While the Damdami Taksal was established in Talwandi Sabo, it is now based at Chowk Mehta, 25 miles north of Amritsar.

96 For Gurbachan Singh Bhindranwale's sermon on Giani Gian Singh's narrative '*Sri Chand da milaap*', see http://www.gurmatveechar.com/audios/Katha/01_Puratan_Katha/Sant_Gurbachan_Singh_%28Bhindran_wale%29/Guru_Granth_Sahib_Larivaar_Katha/Volume_04_Ang_0250-0346/31–Sant.Gurbachan.Singh.%28Bhindran.wale%29–Raag.Gourhi–Ang.285.%28Sukhmani.Sahib%29.mp3

97 Judge, 'Taksals, Akharas, and Nihang Deras', 374.

98 M.5, *GGS*, 628.

99 Unlike other sects (like the Minas and Dhirmalias), the Udasis flourished a lot in terms of their popularity and patronage. However, subsequent to the Singh Sabha movement and Akali Gurdwara reform, there emerged biographical literature about Sri Chand that was polemical, reflecting the strained relations between the Udasis and the Akali Sikhs. Sulakhan Singh, *Heterodoxy in the Sikh Tradition* (Jalandhar: ABS Publishing, 1999), 11–12, 111.

100 Ralph Singh (ed.), *The Miraculous Life of Baba Siri Chand Ji: Loving Son, and True Follower of Guru Nanak Dev Ji*, Gobind Sadan Society for Interfaith Understanding (New Delhi: Sterling Publishers, 2006), 9.

101 Gobind Sadan Society was founded in 1967 by Baba Virsa Singh (1934–2007). Although Virsa Singh did not follow the Udasi sect, he claimed that he had two visions of Sri Chand. In the second vision, Sri Chand was accompanied by his father, Guru Nanak, who asked Virsa Singh to give the mantra '*Ek Oankar satnam sri waheguru*' to the people. See http://www.gobindsadan.org/about-gobind-sadan/

102 Sri Chand's main centre was at Barath, now a town 8 kilometres southwest of Pathankot in Gurdaspur district (Pandit Tara Singh Narotam, *Sri Guru Tirath Sangreh*, 209–13). There are three types of Udasi centres: (1) those which are set up by Udasi ascetics, (2) those which are associated with the Sikh Gurus and (3) those which are associated with Sri Chand (Sulakhan Singh, *Heterodoxy in the Sikh Tradition*, 43–4). Gurdwara Barath Sahib was maintained by Udasi *mahants* until 1920, when it was taken over by the Shiromani Gurdwara Prabandhak Committee during the Gurdwara reform movement.

103 While *Gur Pratap Suraj* 4.28 states that Sri Chand sent Kamalia to Amritsar, it does not mention that Kamalia invited Guru Arjan to Barath.
104 http://gurudwarabarthsahib.weebly.com/. This narrative is also provided on the website for Gurdwara Baba Shri Chand Ji (Tahli Sahib) at Amritsar. See http://tahlisahib.com/history_english.html
105 *Sthala-puranas* (ancient story of a [sacred] place) or local temple stories are adaptations of established *sakhis* to a particular town, temple or shrine, reflecting local traditions that have evolved around a shrine and its locale in order to account for its sanctity. Kamala Elizabeth Nayar, *Hayagriva in South India: Complexity and Selectivity of a Pan-Indian Hindu Deity* (Leiden: Brill, 2004), 173–4.
106 Joseph Davey Cunningham, *A History of the Sikhs* (1849; Delhi: S. Chand, 1955), 44; John Malcolm, *Sketch of the Sikhs* (1810; London: Forgotten Books, 2012), 26–7. Sulakhan Singh, *Heterodoxy in the Sikh Tradition*, 16–17.
107 According to the Udasis, Sri Chand appointed Gurditta as his successor. However, Gurditta died in his mid-twenties, before the passing of his father (Guru Hargobind). Subsequently, Guru Hargobind appointed Gurditta's son, Har Rai, as successor in the Sikh Panth.
108 Giani Ishar Singh Nara, *Itihas Baba Sri Chand Ji Sahib Ate Udasin Sampradaie* (Delhi: Delhi Gate, 1959), 384–6.
109 For instance, Guru Arjan is described as having used his beard to wipe Sri Chand's feet. Nara, *Itihas Baba Sri Chand Ji Sahib Ate Udasin Sampradaie*, 381.
110 See note 93.
111 For a comprehensive look at the literature of the Mina sect, see Syan, 'Sectarian Works', 170–80; Jeevan Singh Deol, 'The Minas and Their Literature', *Journal of the American Oriental Society* 118, no. 2 (1998): 172–84; Gurmohan Singh Ahluwalia, 'Miharvan Sampradae di Panjabi Vartak nu Dehn', in *Khoj Patrika*, ed. Jaggi Rattan Singh (Patiala: Publication Bureau, Punjabi University, 1988), 345–59.
112 Some have suggested that Harji composed the *Sukhmani Sahasranam*. Syan, 'Sectarian Works', 177.
113 Syan, 'Sectarian Works', 177; Deol, 'The Minas and Their Literature', 180.
114 The *Sukhmani* consists of twenty-four *astapadis* with three *astapadis* for each of the eight *pehars* of the day-night cycle. For the spiritual significance of this structure, see Chapter 4.
115 While *Sahasranamavali of Lord Vishnu* is called 'The Thousand Names of Vishnu', it actually contains 1008, an auspicious number in the Hindu tradition.
116 Syan, 'Sectarian Works', 174–5.
117 For an in-depth analysis of how Indic religious literary genres (such the Upanishad, Purana and Sahasranama) are used as means to legitimize sectarian developments, see Nayar, *Hayagriva in South India*, chapters 8 and 9.
118 Syan, 'Sectarian Works', 177; Deol, 'The Minas and Their Literature', 180–1; Ahluwalia, 'Miharvan Sampradae di Panjabi Vartak nu Dehn', 172–84.

119 Syan, 'Sectarian Works', 176; Syan, 'Early Sikh Historiography', 150–2.
120 For a study on Harji's work, see Krishna Kumari Bansal, 'Sukhmani Sahasranam Parmarth', in *Khoj Patrika*, ed. Jaggi Rattan Singh (Patiala: Publication Bureau, Punjabi University, 1988), 402–10. For an edition of the text, see Krishna Kumari Bansal, 'Hariji rachit Sukhamani sahasranama da vistrit adhyain ate alochanatmak sampadan' (PhD diss.; Patiala: Punjabi University, 1977).
121 Pashaura Singh, *The Guru Granth Sahib*, 120.
122 Grewal, *The Sikhs of the Punjab*, 59; Pashaura Singh, *Life and Work of Guru Arjan*, 18.
123 For instance, Sheikh Ahmed, head of Naqshbandi Sufis of Sirhind. Cyril Glasse, *The New Encyclopedia of Islam* (New York: AltaMira Press, 2001), 432; Wilfred Cantwell Smith, *On Understanding Islam: Selected Studies* (Berlin: Walter De Gruyter, 2000), 185.
124 *Tuzuk-I Jahangiri*, 34. Wheeler M. Thackston (trans.), *The Jahangirnama: Memoirs of Jahangir, Emperor of India* (New York: Oxford University Press, 1999), 59. See also Shireen Moosvi (trans.), 'Guru Arjan's Martyrdom', in *Sikh History from Persian Sources*, ed. Grewal and Habib (New Delhi: Tulika, 2001), 57.
125 In April 1606, Emperor Jahangir's son, Prince Khusrau, accompanied by an army of 350 men, left Agra for Lahore in order to oust Emperor Jahangir from the throne and take his place. On his way, Prince Khusrau received shelter and food from Guru Arjan. Prince Khusrau was defeated in the battle of Bhairowal, and was subsequently captured by his father's army. Emperor Jahangir publicly punished Prince Khusrau in Chandni Chowk (Delhi) and also partially blinded him. Eventually, Prince Khusrau was killed in 1622 by his younger brother Prince Khurram, later known as Shah Jahan, when he succeeded Jahangir in 1627. Thackston (trans.), *The Jahangirnama*, 53–5, 56–61, 313, 376.
126 Pedro de Moura Carvalho. *Mirāt al-quds (Mirror of Holiness): A Life of Christ for Emperor Akbar: A Commentary on Father Jerome Xavier's Text and the Miniatures of Cleveland Museum of Art, Acc. No. 2005.145*, ix–x. (Leiden: E. J. Brill, 2012), 1–8. Charles Heibert Payne (trans.), *Jahangir and the Jesuits, with an Account of the Travels of Benedict Goes and the Mission to Pegu* (New York: R.M. McBride & Co., 1930), 11–12.
127 Moosvi (trans.), 'Guru Arjan's Martyrdom', 57. See also Thackston (trans.), *The Jahangirnama*, 59.
128 Thackston (trans.), *The Jahangirnama*, 59; Grewal, *The Sikhs of the Punjab*, 63.
129 Irfan Habib (trans.), 'Sikhism and the Sikhs', 67; Pashaura Singh, *Life and Works of Guru Arjan*, 216.
130 While some scholars have argued that Guru Arjan more likely made a reverent blessing gesture on Prince Khusrau's forehead because of his Mughal status (instead of explicitly supporting Khusrau's rebellion), other scholars explicitly state that the allegation of treason was entirely created as a pretext used to justify Jahangir's actions. Ganda Singh, *Guru Arjan's Martyrdom: Re-Interpreted* (Patiala: Guru Nanak Mission, 1969), 23–36; Banerjee, *Evolution of the Khalsa*, vol. 2, 1–7; Pashaura Singh, *Life and Work of Guru Arjan*, 210–15.

131 For a thorough analysis of the early references to Guru Arjan's martyrdom, see Pashaura Singh, 'Understanding the Martyrdom of Guru Arjan', *Journal of Punjab Studies* 12, no. 1 (2005): 29–62; Louis E. Fenech, 'Martyrdom and the Execution of Guru Arjan, in Early Sikh Sources', *Journal of the American Oriental Society* 121, no. 1 (2001): 20–31.

132 Macauliffe, *The Sikh Religion*, vol. 3, 87–98.

133 Kirpal Singh, *Perspectives on Sikh Gurus* (New Delhi: National Book Shop, 2000), 126; Macauliffe, *The Sikh Religion*, vol. 3, 90–100; Sukhdial Singh, *Historical Analysis of Giani Gian Singh's Writings*, 31.

134 Pashaura Singh, 'Understanding the Martyrdom of Guru Arjan', 38. From the Sikh perspective, Guru Arjan found out how Chandu spoke derogatively towards him for not having the wealth or political status that Chandu had as a minister under the Mughal regime. Subsequently, the Sikhs in Delhi also disapproved of Chandu and the marriage proposal. See Macauliffe, *The Sikh Religion*, vol. 3, 73–5.

135 Uberoi, *Religion, Civil Society and the State*, 91–2. See also Banerjee, *Evolution of the Khalsa*, vol. 2, 3–4.

136 Fenech, 'Martyrdom and the Execution of Guru Arjan', 23–4.

137 Bhai Gurdas, *Varan* 24.23.

138 M.5, *GGS*, 394. Louis E. Fenech, *Martyrdom in the Sikh Tradition: Playing the 'Game of Love'* (New Delhi: Oxford University Press, 2000), 78–9; Fenech, 'Martyrdom and the Execution of Guru Arjan', 20–31.

139 According to Fenech, Guru Arjan's execution is not mentioned in early Sikh literature because martyrdom at that time was based on a heroic death on the battlefield (*dharam yudh*). Moreover, Guru Arjan's execution was not public as was Guru Tegh Bahadur's beheading in Chandni Chowk, Delhi. Fenech, *Martyrdom in the Sikh Tradition*, 117–21; Fenech, 'Martyrdom and the Execution of Guru Arjan', 20–31.

140 Bhai Gurdas, *Varan* 24.20 suggests that Bhai Gurdas recognized his huge burden for the continuation of the Panth. See also Pashaura Singh, 'Understanding the Martyrdom of Guru Arjan', 53; Louis E. Fenech, 'Martyrdom and the Execution of Guru Arjan', 20–31. Guru Arjan's son and successor, Guru Hargobind, militarized the Panth in resistance to Mughal oppression and persecution. However, following his release from prison, Guru Hargobind's attitude towards the Mughal state changed, as a result of which he kept dogs and horses for hunting and had a relative cordial relationship with Emperor Jahangir, whose attitude towards the Gurus also changed. See Habib (trans), 'Sikhism and the Sikhs', 68–9.

141 Pashaura Singh, *Life and Work of Guru Arjan*, 233; Pashaura Singh, 'Understanding the Martyrdom of Guru Arjan', 53. See also Banerjee, *Evolution of the Khalsa*, vol. 2, 2–4. Banerjee also explains how the pretext (i.e. Chandu's role) for Guru Arjan's execution was for the purpose of hiding Mughal religious bigotry. Macauliffe, *The Sikh Religion*, vol. 3, 100.

142 For instance, Giani Gian Singh, *Tawarikh Guru Khalsa*, vol. 1, 211–14.

143 For instance, Banerjee, *Evolution of the Khalsa*, vol. 2, 1–7; Sukhdial Singh, *Historical Analysis of Giani Gian Singh's Writings*, 31–2; Ganda Singh, *Guru Arjan's Martyrdom*, 23–6; Pashaura Singh, 'Understanding the Martyrdom of Guru Arjan', 53.

Chapter 3

1. Pashaura Singh, *Life and Work of Guru Arjan: History, Memory, and Biography in the Sikh Tradition* (New Delhi: Oxford University Press, 2006), 134.
2. Khushwant Singh, *A History of the Sikhs, 1469–1838*, vol. 1 (Princeton, NJ: Princeton University Press, 1963), 95.
3. W.H. McLeod, *Guru Nanak and the Sikh Religion* (New Delhi: Oxford University Press, 1977), 2; W.H. McLeod, *Who Is a Sikh?: The Problem of Sikh Identity* (Oxford: Clarendon Press, 1989), 52–5; J.S. Grewal, *The Sikhs of the Punjab* (Cambridge: Cambridge University Press, 1998), 80.
4. Pashaura Singh, *The Guru Granth Sahib: Canon, Meaning and Authority* (New Delhi: Oxford University Press, 2003), 266–7.
5. Jaswinder Singh Sandhu, 'The Sikh Model of the Person, Suffering, and Healing: Implications for Counsellors', *International Journal for the Advancement of Counselling* 26, no.1 (2004): 35.
6. Bhai Gurdas, *Varan* 24.11.
7. Interestingly, *Sukhmani* 7.1–8 specifically expounds on the significant role of the *sadh sangat* (*GGS*, 271–2). For an elaboration of the Sikh belief in, and role of, the *sadh sangat*, see Chapter 4.
8. *Dasam Granth* (Tenth Sacred Book) is a collection of various writings attributed to Guru Gobind Singh, the tenth Sikh Guru. While the *Dasam Granth* is regarded as having the role of protecting *shabad-Guru* (Guru's words), it is a controversial text in terms of authenticity and authorship.
9. Bhai Gurdas's *Varan* is a collection of interpretive commentary on the *Guru Granth Sahib*. Bhai Gurdas (1551–1636) was a scribe and had a significant role in the writing of the *Adi Granth* under the supervision of Guru Arjan. He also composed the renowned *Varan*, which Guru Arjan designated as the 'key' to understanding *shabad-Guru*. See J.S. Grewal, *History, Literature, and Identity: Four Centuries of Sikh Tradition* (New Delhi: Oxford University Press, 2011), 119–35.
10. Bhai Nand Lal's *Diwan* is mystical contemplative poetry revealing the experience of *shabad-Guru* (Guru's words). Bhai Nand Lal Goya (*c.* 1633–1713) was a Persian poet in Guru Gobind Singh's court. He is renowned for having written the *Rahit-nama* (Code of Conduct) prior to the creation of the Khalsa and *Tankah Nama* (Code of Discipline) after the establishment of the Khalsa.

11 For a more detailed and critical discussion on the different recensions of the *Guru Granth Sahib*, see Pashaura Singh, *The Guru Granth Sahib*, 28–82, 201–35. See also, Gurinder Singh Mann, *The Making of Sikh Scripture* (New York: Oxford University Press, 2001), 82–101, 121–5.
12 Pashaura Singh, 'The Guru Granth Sahib', in *Oxford Handbook of Sikh Studies*, ed. Pashaura Singh and Louis Fenech (Oxford: Oxford University Press, 2014), 129–30; Pashaura Singh, *The Guru Granth Sahib*, 222–30.
13 Pashaura Singh, 'The Guru Granth Sahib', 129–30; Pashaura Singh, *The Guru Granth Sahib*, 225–9.
14 Pashaura Singh, 'The Guru Granth Sahib', 129–30; Pashaura Singh, *The Guru Granth Sahib*, 224.
15 Ordered by the then Prime Minister Indira Gandhi, Operation Bluestar (3–8 June 1984) was the Indian military operation to flush out militants, including Jarnail Singh Bhindranwale, who had fortified the Akal Takht of the Golden Temple complex.
16 The fifteen *bhagats* (devotional poets), whose verses have been incorporated in the *Guru Granth Sahib*, are Kabir, Ravidas, Sheikh Farid, Ramanand, Beni, Namdev, Sadhana, Sheikh Bhikhan, Parmanand, Sain Nayee, Dhanna, Pipa, Surdas, Jaidev and Trilochan. The *bhagats* belonged to the Hindu (Vaishnava) Bhakti, *nirgun* Bhakti or Sufi traditions, and either predated or lived during the Guru Nanak period.
17 The eleven *bhatts* (Hindu court bards), whose verses have been incorporated in the *Guru Granth Sahib*, are Kalashar, Balh, Bhalh, Bhika, Gayand, Harbans, Jalap, Kirat, Mathura, Nalh and Salh. Bhai Baldeep Singh, 'What Is *Kirtan*?: Observations, Interventions and Personal Reflections', *Sikh Formations* 7, no. 3 (2011), 282 n. 13. While the Brahmin ballad singers were connected with the divine courts (*darbar sahib*) of the later Sikh Gurus, their verses praise the first five Sikh Gurus. The *bhatt* verses are collectively referred to as Bhatt Bani, which is included in the concluding section of the *Guru Granth Sahib* (pp. 1389–1406).
18 Bhai Mardana (*GGS*, 553) was a Muslim *rebab* (bowed string instrument) musician, who accompanied Guru Nanak on his travels. Bhai Rai Balwand was a Muslim *rebab* musician and Satta was a Muslim drummer during the time of Guru Angad up to the time of Guru Arjan; they both sang *gurbani-kirtan* and composed a Ramkali *var* that was included in the *Guru Granth Sahib* (pp. 966–8). Baba Sundar was the great grandson of Guru Amar Das and grandson of Mohri, who wrote *Sadu* (Call of Death) (*GGS*, 923–4).
19 The *Mul Mantar* describes *Ek Oankar* and is regarded as the foundation of Sikh spirituality.
20 For details on the development of the *rag* section of the *Guru Granth Sahib*, see Pashaura Singh, *The Guru Granth Sahib*, 125–50.
21 Pashaura Singh, *Life and Work of Guru Arjan*, 144.

22 Pashaura Singh, *Life and Work of Guru Arjan*, 158–60.
23 M.5, *GGS*, 1429.
24 Ek Ong Kaar Kaur Khalsa (poetically interpreted), *Sukhmani Sahib – Jewel of Peace* (USA, 2015).
25 W.H. McLeod, *Textual Sources for the Study of Sikhism* (Manchester: Manchester University Press, 1984), 110; Nikky-Guninder Kaur Singh, *The Name of My Beloved: Verses of the Sikh Gurus* (New York: AltaMira Press, 1995), 173, 175.
26 Grewal, *History, Literature, and Identity*, 85; https://searchgurbani.com/guru_granth_sahib/chapter_index
27 Khalsa Diwan Society, *Who Are the Sikhs* (New Westminster, BC: Gurdwara Sahib Sukh Sagar, 2011), 5.
28 Khushwant Singh, *A History of the Sikhs*, vol. 1, 61; Gurbachan Singh Talib, 'Sukhmani', in *The Encyclopedia of Sikhism*, vol. 4, ed. Harbans Singh (Patiala: Punjab University, 1998), 263; S.S. Johar, *Handbook on Sikhism* (New Delhi: Vivek Publishing Company, 1977); Teja Singh, *The Psalm of Peace* (Amritsar: Khalsa Brothers, 1978).
29 Max Arthur Macauliffe, *The Sikh Religion: Its Gurus, Sacred Writings and Authors*, vol. 3 (1909; Delhi: DK Publishers, 1998), 197.
30 McLeod, *Textual Sources for the Study of Sikhism*, 110; Singh, *The Name of My Beloved*, 173.
31 While *mani* is often translated as mind or heart, *man* is the Punjabi word commonly used for the mind or heart. *Dictionary of Guru Granth Sahib* (3rd edition; Amritsar: Singh Brothers, 2005), 222.
32 According to Indian yogic traditions, there are 72,000 pathways (*nadis*), which are the arteries of the body. There are three crucial pathways: The first is the central or medial pathway called *sushumana-nadi*, which runs along the axis of the body from the base of the spine to the top of the head. Along this central pathway, the six major *cakras* are located. Twisting around the central pathway and crossing over at each *cakra* is the *ida-nadi* and *pingala-nadi*, which also originate at the base of the spine (*Hatha-yoga Pradipika* 1.41, 2.7–23, 4.18; *Goraksa Sataka* 47–50). On the one hand, when the subtle energy flows through the *ida* pathway, the result is an overall cooling or calming effect. On the other hand, the subtle energy flowing through the *pingala* pathway results in arousal activity. The *Hatha-yoga Pradipika* is the oldest text on *hatha-yoga* that was compiled around fourteenth or fifteenth century by Svatmarama. The *Goraksa Sataka* (The Hundred [Verses] of Gorakhnatha) is a Sanskrit hymn that consists of 101 verses, which focuses on the mental and physical practices of *hatha-yoga* that reverse the physiological processes of ageing and death.
33 For instance, *Siddh Goshth* 60, *GGS*, 944.
34 See note 32.
35 Nayar and Sandhu, *The Socially Involved Renunciate*, 101–2.

36 Taran Singh, *Gurbani dian Viakhia Pranalian*, 24, cited in Pashaura Singh, *The Guru Granth Sahib*, 243.
37 String can refer to either the string of an instrument or the cosmic sound.
38 M.1, *Japji* 17–18, *GGS*, 3–4.
39 The Sikh scripture is rather flexible with its use of short and long syllabled words to fit the rhyme of the particular hymn. Christopher Shackle, *An Introduction to the Sacred Language of the Sikhs* (London: SOAS, 1988), 160.
40 Pashaura Singh, *The Guru Granth Sahib*, 93.
41 Similarly, the number 13 can be read as *tera* meaning Yours. While the focus of *astapadi* 13 is on the *sants*, the last verse significantly emphasizes how everything belongs to *Prabh*: 'Everybody belongs to You, the creator, forever, forever, they bow to You'.
42 Vijay Bazaz Razdan, *Hindustani Ragas: The Concept of Time and Season* (Delhi: B.R. Rhythms, 2009), 7–19.
43 Mann, *The Making of Sikh Scripture*, 88.
44 When Guru Arjan compiled the *Adi Granth*, the canonical text contained 2,218 hymns in thirty *rags*. However, Guru Tegh Bahadur (1622–75), the ninth Guru, who wrote 116 hymns in fifteen *rags*, composed four hymns in a new additional *rag* called *Jaijaiwanti*. Since Guru Tegh Bahadur's hymns were included in the final canonical text called the *Guru Granth Sahib* (1706), *Jaijaiwanti rag* was added as the last *rag* in the *rag* section of the scripture. Gobind Singh Mansukhani, *Indian Classical Music and Sikh Kirtan* (New Delhi: Oxford & IBH Publishing, 1982), 61.
45 For more on Guru Ram Das's musical contribution to the Sikh tradition, see Surjit Hans, *A Reconstruction of Sikh History from Sikh Literature* (Jalandhar: ABS Publications, 1988), 91–4.
46 M.4, *GGS*, 368.
47 Mansukhani, *Indian Classical Music and Sikh Kirtan*, 48, 52; Grewal, *History, Literature, and Identity*, 76.
48 Mansukhani, *Indian Classical Music and Sikh Kirtan*, 52.
49 For an analysis of the evolution of the distinct genre of Sikh *gurbani-kirtan*, see Francesca Cassio, '*Gurbani Sangit*: Authenticity and Influences, A Study of Sikh Musical Tradition in Relation to Medieval and Early Modern Indian Music', *Sikh Formations* 11, nos. 1–2 (2015): 23–60.
50 Baldeep Singh, 'What Is *Kirtan*?' 248–51; K.S. Saxena's comments, cited in Cassio, '*Gurbani Sangit*', 34. On the other hand, Kalra describes *gurbani-kirtan* as a 'strand of revivalism' that differentiates itself from the 'modernity' framework of the Singh Sabha movement. Virinder S. Kalra, *Sacred and Secular Musics: A Postcolonial Approach* (London: Bloomsbury, 2015), 79.
51 Baldeep Singh, 'What Is *Kirtan*?' 247.
52 M.5, *GGS*, 404.

53 In *gurbani-kirtan*, the term 'light music' refers to folk music. Cassio, *Gurbani Sangit*, 41. However, it can also refer to popular Indian film music.
54 Baldeep Singh, 'What Is *Kirtan*?' 263.
55 There are eight watches (*aath pehar*) of the day and night cycle and six seasons. For more information on the times for the *rags*, see Razdan, *Hindustani Ragas*, 21–62.
56 M3, GGS, 311.
57 *Bavan Akhri* (GGS, 250–62) consists of fifty-five stanzas (*pauris*) of eight lines each. Each stanza is preceded by a couplet (*salok*), except for the last stanza which consists of four lines. The central theme of this sacred text revolves around seeking the True *Guru*'s grace with humility. See Jaswinder Singh, *Discovering Divine Love in the Play of Life: The Teachings from Guru Arjun's Bhawan Akhri* (Surrey, BC: Journal of Contemporary Sikh Studies, 2000).
58 The Gauri *rag* variants include Gauri Bairagan, Gauri Cheti, Gauri Dipaki, Gauri Purbi Dipaki, Gauri Purbi, Gauri Guareri, Gauri-Manjh, Gauri Malava, Gauri Mala, Gauri Sorath, Gauri Sulakhni and Gauri Dakhani. Mansukhani, *Indian Classical Music and Sikh Kirtan*, 69.
59 Variants may be assigned for other times of the day; such as, Gauri Mala is to be sung in the early night. Mansukhani, *Indian Classical Music and Sikh Kirtan*, 82.
60 Mansukhani, *Indian Classical Music and Sikh Kirtan*, 65. In fact, all serious questions about cosmology are raised in the Gauri *rag* in the *Guru Granth Sahib*. This *rag* is used to bring seriousness and depth to one's understanding even as it evokes a spirit of balance. For instance, Guru Nanak employs the mixed form of Gauri-Deepaki *rag* (e.g. Sohila, GGS, 12), where the Gauri equalizes the melancholic mood of Deepak *rag*, a *rag* which is never used independently in the scripture.
61 Sikh scholars in support of the *Ragmala* as an authentic part of the *Guru Granth Sahib* include Bhai Sahib Vir Singh and Dr Jodh Singh. For a discussion on the historical significance of the *Ragmala* in the Punjab, see Pashaura Singh, *The Guru Granth Sahib*, 145–50.
62 Questions about the authenticity of the *Ragmala* have been longstanding. Bhai Santokh Singh (1783–1843), author of *Gur Pratap Suraj Granth*, was the first Sikh scholar to challenge the authenticity of the *Ragmala*. He argued that the text is inauthentic because it is not *gurbani*. Subsequently, Pandit Tara Singh Narotam (1822–91), a Nirmala scholar, who received the patronage of Maharaja Narinder Singh (1824–62) of Patiala (where he established a permanent seat), asserted that the *Mundavani* is the seal of the *Guru Granth Sahib*. Therefore, the *Ragmala*, which follows the seal, is a later addition and therefore inauthentic (*Guru Giraarathh Kosh*). During the Singh Sabha movement, both the Tat Khalsa and the Chief Khalsa Diwan as well as scholars (such as Dr Charan Singh and Bhai Kahn Singh Nabha) also asserted that the *Ragmala* is not *gurbani*. Subsequently, the Chief Khalsa Diwan in Amritsar published the scripture without the *Ragmala*.

63 *Sree Guru Granth Sahib*, Gopal Singh (trans.), xix. Bhai Santokh Singh (1783–1843) also claimed that the *Ragmala* was composed by the poet Alam.
64 *Dharamsal* (religious sanctuary or resting place) was the initial term used for a Sikh place of worship.
65 McLeod, *Guru Nanak and the Sikh Religion*, 230; Macauliffe, *The Sikh Religion*, vol. 1, 180–1; Pashaura Singh, *Life and Work of Guru Arjan*, 105–6; Mansukhani, *Indian Classical Music and Sikh Kirtan*, 57.
66 M.4, *GGS*, 305.
67 *Gianis*, as part of Sikh oral tradition, widely use the metaphor of the water droplet amid the river to illustrate the role of the *sadh sangat*.
68 Article IV 'Meditating on Naam (Divine Substance) and Scripture', *The Sikh Reht Maryada* (Amritsar: Shiromani Gurdwara Parbhandak Committee, 1982), 2.
69 It is a common practice for baptized Sikhs to recite two additional hymns (*Chaupi* and *Anand*) in the morning. Baptized Sikhs maintain that these five hymns were recited by the five beloved ones (*panj piare*) when the Khalsa was created in 1699.
70 *Sodar Rehras* consists of the following compositions: (1) Nine hymns of the *Guru Granth Sahib*, occurring in the holy book after the *Japji Sahib*, the first of which begins with *Sodar* and the last of which ends with '*saran pare ki rakh sarma*'; (2) *Benti Chaupai* of the tenth Guru (beginning '*hamri karo hath dai rachha*' and ending with '*dusht dokh te leho bachai*'); (3) *Sawayya* beginning with the words '*pae geho jab te tumre*'; (4) *Dohra* beginning with the words '*sagal duar kau chhad kai*'; (5) The first five *pauris* (stanzas) and the last *pauri* of *Anand*; (6) *Mundawani* and the *Slok* Mahala 5 beginning '*tere kita jato nahi*'. *Sikh Reht Maryada* III, Article IVb.
71 Isabel Dyck and Parin Dossa, 'Place, Health and Home: Gender and Migration in the Constitution of Healthy Place', *Health & Place* 13 (2017): 698–9.
72 McLeod, *Textual Sources for the Study of Sikhism*, 110; Beryl Dhanjal, 'Sikhism', in *Worship*, ed. Jean Holm with John Bowker (London: Pinter Publishers, 1994), 149. See also G.S. Sharma, *Sukhmani Sahib – Reflections* (Acharya Sri Agyaatdarshan, n.d.). Moreover, in analysing the relations between Hindus and Sikhs in Southall, London, Baumann notes that the *Sukhmani* was 'a Hindu prayer as much as a Sikh one'. Gerd Baumann, *Contesting Culture: Discourses of Identity in Multi-ethnic London* (Cambridge: Cambridge University Press, 1996), 118.
73 For instance, see http://www.gurmatsagar.com/Nitnem-Baanis-Japji-sahib
74 While there may be different versions of the *Panj Granthi* in circulation, it is important to note that the original *Panj Granthi* only contained selections of hymns taken from the *Guru Granth Sahib*. The *Panj Granthi* literally means the 'booklet of five'. There are, however, two common ways that oral tradition interprets 'five'. Some Sikh followers and traditional Sikh scholars regard the word 'five' as referring to the fact that the small book (*pothi*) of sacred texts was compiled by the fifth guru, Guru Arjan, whereas other Sikh scholars contend that the 'five' refers to the actual number of sacred texts that existed in the original version, which then later grew

larger over time, with the title of the original prayer book retained for its symbolic significance. Giani Sant Singh Maskeen, interview, 22 January 2003.
75 *Sri Guru Granth Sahib-ji Vichon: Panj Granthi* (Amritsar: Khalsa Brothers, n.d.).
76 Dhanjal, 'Sikhism', 149; Nikky-Guninder Kaur Singh, *The Name of My Beloved*, 173.
77 *Hukam-nama* (letter of command) refers to an order given to Sikhs. Originally, it was given by the Sikh Gurus. However, the daily *hukam-nama* now refers to the daily practice of random selection of a hymn from the *Guru Granth Sahib*, which is regarded as an order to Sikhs for that particular day.
78 Talib, '*Sukhmani*', 263; Nikky-Guninder Kaur Singh, *The Name of My Beloved*, 173; Pashaura Singh, 'Sikh Perspectives on Health and Suffering: A Focus on Sikh Theodicy', in *Religion, Health, and Suffering*, ed. John R. Hinnells and Roy Porter (London: Kegan Paul, 1999), 126–7.
79 Out of the total sample of 748 participants, there were 336 participants who regularly recited the *Sukhmani* and 412 participants who did not recite the text. The study found that the blood pressure (especially the diastolic) was significantly lower in those who recited the *Sukhmani*, and therefore required fewer drugs to control their blood pressure. The study established that the regular recitation of the *Sukhmani* is an effective, economical and non-pharmaceutical means to reduce high blood pressure, either as part of an anti-hypertensive therapy or as an alternative to anti-hypertensive medications. Harcharan Singh and Ajinder Singh, 'The *Sukhmani* and Blood Pressure', *Journal of Sikh Studies* 6 (1980): 45–62.
80 For example, see Dharma Singh Khalsa, Daniel Amen, Chris Hanks, Nisha Money and Andrew Newberg, 'Cerebral Blood Flow Changes during Chanting Meditation', *Nuclear Medicine Communications* 30, no. 12 (2009): 956–61; Ajay Anil Gurjar and Siddharth A. Ladhake, 'Analysis and Dissection of Sanskrit Divine Sound "Om" Using Digital Signal Processing to Study the Science behind "Om" Chanting', 7th Annual Conference on Intelligent Systems, Modelling and Simulation. doi: 10.1109/ISMS.2016.79: 169–73; Ajay Anil Gurjar and Siddharth A. Ladhake, 'Time-Frequency Analysis of Chanting Sanskrit Divine Sound "OM" Mantra', *International Journal of Computer Science and Network Security* 8, no. 8 (August 2008): 170–5.
81 For example, see Wolf, David B. and Neil Abell. 'Examining the Effects of Meditation Techniques on Psychosocial Functioning', *Research on Social Work Practice* 13, no. 1 (2003): 27–42.
82 For instance, Mohinder Singh was recorded as having been cured of tuberculosis. See Bhai Guriqbal Singh, *Nine Special Characteristics of Sukhmani Sahib Ji* (Amritsar: Chattar Singh Jeevan, 2008), 42–3.
83 Wazir Khan or Ilam-ud-din Ansari (d. 1634) was governor during the rule of Mughal emperor Shah Jahan.
84 Macauliffe, *The Sikh Religion*, vol. 3, 17–18.

85 People who have received minimal or no education possess the communication patterns associated with orality, which includes concrete thought and speech forms that express a collectivity-orientation. People, who have received some formal education so that they can read and write, tend towards a literacy mode of thinking. This mode enables a literal interpretation that is expressed in a concrete thought form based on what has been experienced or exposed through print, along with some prioritizing and distancing from the subject matter. Lastly, people who have received higher education tend towards an analytics mode of thinking, wherein there is greater conceptual and abstract thought that can be articulated in a self-reflective manner. For an elaboration of the three communication types, see Kamala Elizabeth Nayar and Jaswinder Singh Sandhu, 'Intergenerational Communication in Immigrant Punjabi Families: Implications for Helping Professionals', *International Journal for the Advancement of Counselling* 28, no. 2 (2006): 147–8; Kamala Elizabeth Nayar, *The Sikh Diaspora: Tradition, Modernity, and Multiculturalism* (Toronto: University of Toronto Press, 2004), chapter 2.

86 Ek Ong Kaar Kaur Khalsa, 'The Essence of Prosperity in Sukhmani', *Sikh Dharma Ministry Newsletter* (November 2012), retrieved from http://www.sikhnet.com/news/essence-prosperity-sukhmani (5 January 2016).

87 Hans, *A Reconstruction of Sikh History from Sikh Literature*, 271.

88 Giani Ishar Singh Nara, *Itihas Baba Sri Chand Ji Sahib Ate Udasin Sampradaie* (Delhi: Delhi Gate, 1959), 385. See also Giani Gian Singh, *Tawarikh Guru Khalsa*, vol. 1 (Amritsar: Giani Gian Singh Ji, 1897), 42.

89 In Hindu mythology, *nau nidhi* refers to a treasure of nine belonging to the god of wealth (Kuvera or Kubera). Although Kuvera was the chief of evil spirits in the Vedic texts, he acquired the status of god in the *smriti* literature (Epics and Puranas). According to *Amarakosha*, the nine treasures are: (1) great lotus flower (*mahapadma*), (2) lotus flower (*padma*), (3) conch shell (*shankha*), (4) crocodile (i.e. skin) (*makara*), (5) tortoise (i.e. shell) (*kachchhapa*), (6) a precious stone (*kumud*), (7) jasmine (*kunda*), (8) sapphire (*nila*) and (9) vessel baked in fire (*kharva*).

90 Bhai Guriqbal Singh belongs to the Nanaksar sect of Sikhism, which was founded by Nand Singh (1869–1943), a celibate who engaged in austerities and meditation. The movement was established near Kaleran village (close to Jagraon), Punjab. He was succeeded by Ishar Singh, also a celibate. In 1950 Ishar Singh began to construct the *gurdwara* at the location where the *Sukhmani* had been constantly recited. Since Ishar Singh did not appoint a successor, there have been several splinter groups after his passing. See http://www.nanaksarkaleran.net

91 Bhai Guriqbal Singh, *Nine Special Characteristics of Sukhmani Sahib Ji*, 7–8.

92 Bhai Guriqbal Singh, *Nine Special Characteristics of Sukhmani Sahib Ji*, 135–58. See also https://khojee.wordpress.com/2010/05/18/shri-sukhmani-sahib-grants-protection-from-black-magic/

93 McLeod, *Guru Nanak and the Sikh Religion*, 208–13. See Guru Nanak's texts like *Japji* and *Asa di Var*.
94 For a Sikhnet blog discussion on the benefits of the *Sukhmani*, see http://www.sikhnet.com/discussion/viewtopic.php?f=2&t=815&start=20
95 Giani Sant Singh Maskeen, interview, 22 January 2003.
96 Seema Mehta, 'California Lawyer Delivers Sikh Prayer at GOP Convention', *Los Angeles Times* (19 July 2016), retrieved on http://www.latimes.com/politics/la-na-pol-republicans-harmeet-dhillon-20160719-snap-story.html
97 The standard *Ardas* comprises three distinct sections: (1) a plea to contemplate on *Ek Oankar* along with Guru Nanak and the nine successors, (2) describes the sacrifices various Sikhs have made throughout Sikh history and (3) asking for forgiveness and guidance. To view Harmeet Dhillon recite the prayer at the Republican Nomination Convention, see https://www.youtube.com/watch?v=0U4SFRJI1lc
98 Baldeep Singh, 'What Is *Kirtan*?' 251–2.
99 Vishnu Narayan Bhatkhande, *A Short Historical Survey of the Music of Upper India, a Reproduction of a Speech Delivered by Pandit V. N. Bhatkhande at the First All-India Music Conference, Baroda, in 1916* (1916; Baroda: Indian Musicological Society, 1974). See also Vishnu Narayana Bhatkhande, *Hindusthani Sangeet Paddhati Kramik Pustak Malika*, 6 vols. (Allahabad: Sangit Sadan Prakashan, 1999).
100 Cassio, 'Gurbani Sangit', 24; Baldeep Singh, 'What Is *Kirtan*?' 269. For an in-depth look at the introduction and popularization of the harmonium in Sikh music from the mid-nineteenth to early twentieth century, see Harjinder Singh Lallie, 'The Harmonium in Sikh Music', *Sikh Formations* 12, no. 1 (2016): 53–66.
101 Lallie, 'The Harmonium in Sikh Music', 53–7; Cassio, 'Gurbani Sangit', 24; Baldeep Singh, 'What Is *Kirtan*?' 272.
102 For an analysis of the role of the Singh Sabha movement and the Sikh reformers in *kirtan* as a part of a larger process of modern Sikh identity formation, see Bob van der Linden, 'Sikh Music and Empire: The Moral Representation of Self in Music', *Sikh Formations* 4, no. 1 (2008): 1–15. See also Kalra, *Sacred and Secular Musics*, 67–95.
103 During the Swadeshi movement (against the purchase of British products), an anti-harmonium debate emerged. Lallie, 'The Harmonium in Sikh Music', 60. Moreover, following the partition of the Punjab, the Sikhs distanced themselves from the Sikh tradition of *rababis* or Muslim musicians who played the string instrument, called the *rebab*. N.K. Purewal, 'Sikh Muslim Bhai-Bhai: Towards a Social History of the Rababi Tradition of Shabad Kirtan', *Sikh Formations* 7, no. 3 (2011): 377.
104 Baldeep Singh, 'What Is *Kirtan*?' 272.

105 Baldeep Singh, 'What Is *Kirtan*?' 272.
106 The harmonium took the place of the more traditional string instruments like the *rabab*. Similarly, the *tabla* replaced the *pathavaj* and *jori*. For more on the instruments used at the time of the Sikh Gurus, see Baldeep Singh, 'What Is *Kirtan*?' 254–9; Mansukhani, *Indian Classical Music and Sikh Kirtan*, 73.
107 For example, see https://www.youtube.com/watch?v=igK8xLbBH1c where one can view Bhai Niranjan, Jawaddi Kalan (Ludhiana), chant the *mangala-charan* of the *Sukhmani* at the Ram Das Darbar (Calgary, Canada) in 2012.

Chapter 4

1 For instance, the transformative Sri Vaishnava worldview is contained in the devotional poetry of Kuresha and Bhattar (disciples of the eminent philosopher Ramanuja). See Nancy Ann Nayar, *Poetry as Theology: The Srivaisnava Stotra in the Age of Ramanuja* (Wiesbaden: Otto Harrassowitz, 1992).
2 The mantra *Oan* (Punjabi for the Sanskrit mantra *Aum*) was recited as early as the Vedic period *c.* 1500 BCE. *Oan* is found in both the Vedic and Buddhist traditions and is also a sacred mantra in the Jain religion.
3 Kamala Elizabeth Nayar and Jaswinder Singh Sandhu, *Socially Involved Renunciate: Guru Nanak's Discourse to the Nath Yogis* (Albany: State University of New York Press, 2007), 72–5.
4 Gobind Singh Mansukhani, *Indian Classical Music and Sikh Kirtan* (New Delhi: Oxford & IBH Publishing, 1982), 17–18. 'Pahar', https://en.wikipedia.org/wiki/Pahar, (accessed 19 January 2017).
5 While in the first half of the *Sukhmani* the term *aath pehar* is employed four times with respect to the act of remembering *Nam* 'all day and all night' (2.7, 6.1, 6.2 and 6.5), in the second half of the text the term is used four times in reference to the process of spiritual attainment (17.7, 18.3, 18.6 and 22.5).
6 Similarly, as underscored by Pashaura Singh, Guru Arjan offers a balanced approach to birth and death in his arrangement of the *Adi Granth* by having placed the hymn celebrating bliss (*Anand*) immediately before the hymn about death (*Sad*). Pashaura Singh, *The Guru Granth Sahib* (New Delhi: Oxford University Press, 2003), 161–5.
7 Interestingly, the *Bhagavad Gita* (*c.* 200 BCE–200 CE), a popular Hindu text, uses day and night metaphorically to differentiate the state of consciousness of a mundane being and of an enlightened being. That is, while a mundane being is awake during the day yet paradoxically wandering through the darkness of the illusory world as if asleep or in a dream, an enlightened being is 'awake' at night when mundane beings are asleep. See *Bhagavad Gita* 2.64.

8. M.1, *GGS*, 1256.
9. M.1, *GGS*, 469; M.1, *Siddh Goshth* 25, *GGS*, 940–1; M.1, *GGS*, 149.
10. W.H. McLeod, *Guru Nanak and the Sikh Religion* (New Delhi: Oxford University Press, 1988), 8.
11. M.5, *GGS*, 960.
12. For more on family conflict over the *gur-gaddi* title, see the section on 'The Panth inherited by Guru Arjan' in Chapter 2.
13. Diane L. Eck, *Darsan: Seeing the Divine Image in India* (New York: Columbia University Press, 1996).
14. According to some scholars, the *Bhagavata Purana* (ca. 900 CE) is the medium through which Vaishnava Bhakti travelled to North India. *Bhagavata Purana* 7.5.23–4 describes nine modes of devotion (*navadha-bhakti*): (1) *sunan*, hearing the *shabad*; (2) *kirtan*, singing the praises of God; (3) *simran*, remembrance of God; (4) *puja*, love-worship of a deity; (5) *pad-sevan*, surrender at the Lord's feet; (6) *vandhana*, supplication to the Lord; (7) *dasa-bhava*, considering oneself as God's servant; (8) *maitri bhava*, friendship with God; and (9) *atma*-nivedan, self-surrender to God.
15. For a comparative study of Bhakti and Sikh philosophy, see Nirbhai Singh, 'Gurbani and Bhakti Bani: A Philosophical Analysis', in *The Sikh Tradition: A Continuing Reality*, ed. Sardar Singh Bhatia and Anand Spencer (Patiala: Punjabi University, 1999), 114–32.
16. M.1, *Siddh Goshth* 50, *GGS*, 943. Gobind Singh Mansukhani, *Indian Classical Music and Sikh Kirtan*, 47.
17. M.5, *GGS*, 202.
18. M.1, *Japji* 5, *GGS*, 2.
19. These four vices, along with the ego (*ahankar*), are regarded as the five evils (also spoken of as the five rivals, thieves or demons) that rob consciousness (*chit*) from gaining an awareness of the soul (*atma*). The four vices include attachment (*moh*), greed (*lobh*), anger (*karodh*) and lust (*kam*).
20. M.1, *GGS*, 687. In Theravada Buddhism, right or correct mindfulness (*samma-sati*) is the seventh practice of the Eightfold Path to liberation. This concept of *sati* is also critical in Tibetan and Zen Buddhism. In the 1970s, mindfulness became popular in the West as a popular therapeutic technique (like vipassana meditation) of bringing one's attention to experiences occurring in the present moment.
21. In fact, the *Guru Granth Sahib* (M.4, 982; M.9, 1429) makes reference to a popular Bhakti myth called 'Gajendra Moksha'. It is about how Lord Vishnu liberates Gajendra (Lord of elephants) when Gajendra – while being killed by a crocodile – selflessly offers a flower to Vishnu (*Bhagavata Purana* 8.2–3). For the Sikh view on the relation between grace and effort, see Chapter 5.

22 For instance, 'Through *Guru's* grace one becomes self-aware' (14.4); 'Nanak: With *Guru's* grace they realize the One' (19.8); and 'Nanak: With *Guru's* grace one attains happiness' (23.2).
23 In fact, Gautama Buddha founded the *sangha* (Skt.) – the monastic order of monks and nuns – and designated it as one of the three jewels (*triratna*) or refuges in Buddhism (*Dhammapada* 190-4, 296-301). According to the Buddha's teachings and Theravada Buddhism, becoming a member of the monastic community is a prerequisite for attaining liberation.
24 See Guru Nanak's well-known texts like the *Japji*, *Asa di Var*, *Siddh Goshth* and *Dakhini Oankar*.
25 While the *sangat* did eventually evolve into a dynamic communal institution, I do not think this development occurred during Guru Nanak's mission.
26 There are numerous accounts of Guru Nanak's *udasis* in both Bhai Gurdas's *Varan* and the *janam-sakhis*. Guru Nanak travelled to a great number of places where he engaged in religious dialogue with many persons belonging to a variety of traditions, including Brahmin priests, Muslim sheikhs, Sufi mystics, Jain and Buddhist monks, Hindu yogis etc.
27 M.1, *GGS*, 1256.
28 M.1, *GGS*, 20.
29 Nayar and Sandhu, *Socially Involved Renunciate*, 86-7.
30 M.1, *GGS*, 72. See also McLeod, *Guru Nanak and the Sikh Religion*, 217-18.
31 Indubhusan Banerjee, *Evolution of the Khalsa*, vol. 1 (1936; Calcutta: University of Calcutta, 1972), 257-8.
32 M.3, *GGS*, 29. Surjit Singh Hans, *A Reconstruction of Sikh History from Sikh Literature* (Jalandhar: ABS, 1988), 57-8.
33 M.3, *GGS*, 26, 30, 31, 37-8, 67-8.
34 M.3, *GGS*, 129. See also M.3, *GGS*, 114, 115 and 120.
35 M.3, *GGS*, 1417.
36 M.4, *GGS*, 94, 1314.
37 M.4, *GGS*, 94, 1316.
38 M.4, *GGS*, 95, 96.
39 M.5, *GGS*, 1098.
40 'Three qualities' refers to the qualities of the material world: goodness (*sat*), passion (*raj*) and darkness (*tam*).
41 Guru Nanak's view about ego-renunciation and social involvement is most prominently explained in the text called *Siddh Goshth*.
42 The snake-rope story is told for the purpose of teaching the concept of *maya*. The story is about a blind man who is taught to identify a snake based on its qualities. However, the man misidentifies a rope for a snake. The story demonstrates how qualities are deceptive in discerning the true nature of reality (i.e. Brahman).

43 See also *Sukhmani* 17.3, 19.3, 22.3 and 23.3.
44 See also *Sukhmani* 19.1.
45 Nayar and Sandhu, *Socially Involved Renunciate*, 72–5. See also Parma Nand, 'Ek Onkar', in *Sikh Concept of the Divine*, ed. Pritam Singh (Amritsar: Guru Nanak Dev University Press, 1985), 45; Maskeen, lecture, 1994.
46 *Satgur* (Skt. *satguru*) means True *Guru*. While in Hinduism the term *guru* refers to spiritual master or teacher, Bhagat Kabir began to use the word to connote an enlightened *sant* who has attained self-realization and realization of *nirgun* (formless God) or the Truth – that is, the embodiment of *Guru* in human form. Kabir explicitly describes *Satgur* as one who teaches and guides one on the spiritual path: 'When I met the *Satgur*, He showed me the path' (Bhagat Kabir, Asa, *GGS*, 476; Kabir, *Bijak*, *Sabda* 69). There is, however, ambiguity as to whether Kabir is specifically referring to a human Guru or the 'inner *guru*' as in *antarajami* (Skt. *antaryamin*). Regardless, the Kabir Panth reveres its leader as *guru*.
47 Bhai Gurdas, *Varan* 20.9.
48 M.4, *GGS*, 366.
49 M.5, *GGS*, 614. For more information about the cycle of vices, see note 18.
50 For a Sikh perspective on alcohol misuse, see Jaswinder Singh Sandhu, 'A Sikh Perspective on Alcohol and Drugs: Implications for the Treatment of Punjabi-Sikh Patients', *Sikh Formations* 5, no. 1 (2009): 23–37.
51 M.5, *GGS*, 406.
52 There are three forms of *seva*: *tan* (physical), *man* (mental) and *dhan* (philanthropy). For an elaboration on the three types of *seva*, see Nayar and Sandhu, *Socially Involved Renunciate*, 87–8.
53 Bhai Gurdas, *Varan* 20.10.
54 Bhai Gurdas, *Varan* 29.15.
55 Bhai Gurdas, *Varan* 24.19.1–7.
56 Banerjee, *Evolution of the Khalsa*, vol. 1, 259–60.

Chapter 5

1 Christopher Peterson, *A Primer in Positive Psychology* (New York: Oxford University Press, 2006), 6. See also Richard Schoch, *The Secrets of Happiness: Three Thousand Years of Searching for the Good Life* (New York: Scribner, 2008).
2 Kiran Kumar Salagame, 'Meaning and Well-Being: Indian Perspectives', *Journal of Constructivist Psychology* 30, no. 1 (2017): 64–5. It is important to note here that while meaningful living can be a dimension found in Indic religions, Western concerns over the meaning of life are not inherent to religions born out of the Indian subcontinent.

3   While the term 'Sikhism' is more popularly used, that term was coined by the British in the nineteenth century and it inaccurately objectifies the religion and its teachings. Arvind-Pal Mandair, *Sikhism: A Guide for the Perplexed* (New York: Bloomsbury Academic, 2013), 3–14.
4   In part, the explanation for the difference in orientation internally lies in their respective worldviews; that is, West Asian religions tend towards a linear view of existence with the primary goal of salvation or a good afterlife in heaven, whereas religions born out of the Indian subcontinent hold a cyclical view of birth, death and rebirth (*sansar*; Skt. *samsara*) with the primary goal of liberation (*mukat*; Skt. *moksha*; Pali *nibbana*) from the continual cycle of suffering, also described as self-realization and/or God-realization.
5   Salagame, 'Meaning and Well-Being', 67.
6   However, Abraham Maslow, founder of humanist psychology, later added 'self-transcendence' to his hierarchy of human needs, setting the stage for transpersonal psychology, which is regarded as a sub-field in psychology. See Abraham H. Maslow, *The Farther Reaches of Human Nature* (New York: The Viking Press, 1971).
7   For instance, see Susan A. David, Ilona Boniwell and Amanda Conley Ayers, *The Oxford Handbook of Happiness* (Oxford: Oxford University Press, 2013).
8   Theo Theobald and Cary Cooper, 'The Relationship between Happiness and Well-Being', in *Doing the Right Thing: The Importance of Well-Being in the Workplace* (London: Palgrave Macmillan, 2012), 13–18.
9   Naci Huseyin and John P.A. Ioannidis, 'Wellness-Evaluation of Wellness Determinants and Interventions by Citizen Scientist', *The Journal of the American Medical Association* 314, no. 2 (2015): 121–2.
10 Huseyin and Ioannidis, 'Wellness-Evaluation of Wellness Determinants and Interventions by Citizen Scientist', 121–2.
11 Jaswinder Singh Sandhu, 'The Sikh Model of the Person, Suffering, and Healing: Implications for Counselors', *International Journal for the Advancement of Counselling* 26, no. 1 (2004): 34.
12 Bhagat Pipa, *GGS*, 695.
13 Sandhu, 'The Sikh Model of the Person, Suffering, and Healing', 36–7.
14 The four states of consciousness originated from the *Mandukya Upanishad* I.2-7.
15 Sandhu, 'The Sikh Model of the Person, Suffering, and Healing', 37.
16 For example, see Tamas Chamorro-Premuzic, *Personality and Individual Differences* (3rd edn.; West Sussex: The British Psychological Society and John Wiley & Sons, 2015), 12.
17 Sandhu, 'The Sikh Model of the Person, Suffering, and Healing', 37.
18 Bhai Gurdas, *Kabitt Savaiyye*, 111.
19 The concept of *antahkaran* (Skt. *antahkarana*), consisting of four parts, originated from Advaita Vedanta philosophy based on the Upanishadic concept of the mind

(*Chandogya Upanishad* VI.5.4; VI.6.5; and VI.7.6). While Indian philosophical terms are used by the Sikh Gurus, they are adapted to fit the Sikh worldview.

20 Sandhu, 'The Sikh Model of the Person, Suffering, and Healing', 38. According to Guru Nanak, the five elements are the basic constituents of both the whole creation (M.1, *GGS*, 1038) and the human body (M.1, *GGS*, 1039).

21 For example, in *Anand* (*GGS*, 917–22), Guru Amar Das addresses the mind (*man*), and describes it as both beloved and clever.

22 *Sahaskriti saloks* are verses in a language form that combines Sanskrit, Pali and Prakrti. Both Guru Nanak and Guru Arjan wrote *Sahaskriti saloks* which are included in the *Guru Granth Sahib* (M.1, *GGS*, 1353; M.5, *GGS*, 1358)

23 M.5, *GGS*, 1358.

24 Guru Amar Das also makes reference to the cycle of the five thieves: 'within this body are hid five thieves – lust, anger, greed, attachment and ego' (M.3, *GGS*, 600).

25 For instance, Giani Sant Singh Maskeen, *North American Lecture Series* (audiotape) (Vancouver, BC: Ross Street Gurdwara, 1982); Giani Sant Singh Maskeen, *Guru Chintan* (Amritsar: Singh Brothers, 1993). Jaswinder Singh Sandhu, 'A Sikh Perspective on Life-Stress Implications for Counseling', *Canadian Journal of Counseling*, 39, no. 1 (2005): 43.

26 Elie G. Karam et al., 'The Role of Anxious and Hyperthymic Temperaments in Mental Disorders: A National Epidemiologic Study', *World Psychiatry* 9, no. 2 (2010): 103–10.

27 Taiki Takahashi et al., 'Anxiety, Reactivity, and Social Stress-Induced Cortisol Elevation in Humans', *Neuroendocrinology Letters* 26, no. 4 (2005): 351–4.

28 Gregory E. Miller, E. Chen and E.S. Zhou, 'If It Goes Up, Must It Come Down? Chronic Stress and the Hypothalamic-Pituitary-Adrenocortical Axis in Humans', *American Psychological Association* 133, no. 1 (2007): 25–45.

29 For a discussion on how the *Guru Granth Sahib* describes the modern understanding of depression, see Gurvinder Kalra, Kamaldeep Bhui and Dinesh Bhugra, 'Does *Guru Granth Sahib* Describe Depression?' *Indian Journal of Psychiatry* 55, no. 2 (2013): S195–S200.

30 M. 3, *Anand*, *GGS*, 922.

31 Sandeep Kumar Kar, Chaitali Sen and Anupam Goswami. 'Effect of Indian Classical Music (Raga Therapy) on Fentanyl, Vecuronium, Propofol Requirement and Cortisol Levels in Cardiopulmonary Bypass', *British Journal of Anaesthesia* 108, no. S2 (2012): ii216, doi: 10.1093/bja/aer485.

32 Based on the Goldberg Depression questionnaire findings before and after music therapy of 45 to 60 minutes per day for 15 days, participants aged from fifteen to forty-five years demonstrated a substantial decrease in depressive symptoms. Mounika Akkera, Srilatha Bashetti, Neetha Kundoor, Krishnaveni V. Desai, Radha Kishan N and Aparna V. Bhongir, 'Indian Music Therapy: Could It Be Helpful in the Management of Mental Depression?' *International Journal of Medical Research & Health Sciences* 3, no. 2 (2014): 354–7.

33 Avantika Mathur et al., 'Emotional Responses to Hindustani Raga Music: The Role of Musical Structure', *Frontiers in Psychology* 6, no. 513 (2015), doi: 10.3389/fpsyg.2015.00513.
34 Joseph E. LeDoux, 'Emotion Circuits in the Brain', *Annual Review of Neuroscience* 23 (2000): 155–84.
35 While God is praised by way of various epithets, the favourite one among the Sikhs is *Waheguru* (infinite light that dispels darkness).
36 There are three forms of *seva*: (1) *tan* (physical), (2) *man* (mental) and (3) *dhan* (philanthropy). First, *tan-seva* involves the adherent serving humanity through physical efforts, such as feeding the poor, constructing shelters for the homeless or cleaning the Sikh place of worship. Second, *man-seva* involves serving humanity through mental efforts, such as tutoring disadvantaged children, giving managerial support or teaching others in the *gurdwara*. Last, *dhan-seva* pertains to serving humanity through philanthropic efforts, such as donating money or material goods. The purpose of *dhan-seva* is to break worldly attachments instead of accumulating honours. Kamala Elizabeth Nayar and Jaswinder Singh Sandhu, *The Socially Involved Renunciate: Guru Nanak's Discourse to the Nath Yogis* (Albany: State University of New York Press, 2007), 87–8.
37 *Laws of Manu* 4.6 and 4.160.
38 Nayar and Sandhu, *The Socially Involved Renunciate*, 87–8.
39 As aforementioned in Chapter 1, suffering is a result of both inner forces (ego-centeredness) and external forces (social and political oppression). For the inner forces, one should follow the path of inner awareness, whereas for the external forces, one should perform *seva* (selfless service) for the betterment of humanity, including helping those in need or fighting against social injustice and political oppression. That is, the external forces need to be acknowledged and addressed. Sandhu, 'The Sikh Model of the Person, Suffering, and Healing', 39–40.
40 Peterson, *A Primer in Positive Psychology*, 142.
41 Britta K. Holzel, James Carmody, Mark Vangel, Christina Congleton, Sita M. Yerramsetti, Tim Gard and Sara W. Lazar, 'Mindfulness Practice Leads to Increases in Regional Brain Grey Matter Density', *Psychology Research* 191, no. 1 (2011): 36–43.
42 Robert Lane, 'The Loss of Happiness', in *The World Book of Happiness*, ed. Leo Bormns (Buffalo, NY: Firefly Books, 2011), 180.
43 The Sikh concept of *sunn* should not be confused with the Theravada concept of non-self (Pali *anatta*) or the Mahayana Buddhist concept of void (Skt. *shunyata*), both of which are understood as an experience or meditative state of being devoid of an intrinsic nature.
44 Peterson, *A Primer in Positive Psychology*, 140.
45 Robert Lane, 'Diminishing Returns to Income, Companionship, and Happiness', *Journal of Happiness Studies* 1, no. 1 (2000): 103–19.

46 Shigehiro Oishi and Selin Kesebir, 'Income Inequality Explains Why Economic Growth Does Not Always Translate to an Increase in Happiness', *Psychological Science* 26, no. 10 (2015): 1630–8.

47 Richard A. Easterlin, 'Happiness and Economic Growth: The Evidence', in *Global Handbook of Quality of Life*, ed. Wolfgang Glatzer (Dordrecht: Springer, 2015), 283–99.

48 For instance, see Lane, 'Diminishing Returns to Income, Companionship, and Happiness', 103–19.

49 Leaf van Boven, 'Experientialism, Materialism, and the Pursuit of Happiness', *Review of General Psychology* 9, no. 2 (2005): 139.

50 Helena Hnilicova, 'The Revolutionary Experience', in *The World Book of Happiness*, ed. Leo Bormns (Buffalo, NY: Firefly Books, 2011), 107; James Burroughs and Aric Rindfleisch, 'Materialism and Well-Being: A Conflicting Values Perspective', *Journal of Consumer Research* 29, no. 3 (2002): 348–70.

51 Hnilicova, 'The Revolutionary Experience', 107.

52 For instance, see Stefano Bartolini, 'Did the Decline in Social Connections Depress Americans?' *Social Indicators Research* 110, no. 3 (2013): 1033–59.

53 Daniel Kahneman, Edward Diener and Norbert Schwarz, *Well-being: Foundations of Hedonic Psychology* (New York: Russell Sage Foundation, 1999), 365–6.

54 E. Martz, 'Principles of Eastern Philosophies Viewed from the Framework of Yalom's Four Existential Concerns', *International Journal for the Advancement of Counseling* 24 (2002): 31–42.

55 M.1, *GGS*, 954.

56 M.1, *GGS*, 469.

57 Aaron Antonovsky, *Unraveling the Mystery of Health – How People Manage Stress and Stay Well* (San Francisco: Jossey-Bass Publishers, 1987).

58 M.B. Mittelmark, T. Bull and L. Bouwman, 'Emerging Ideas Relevant to the Salutogenic Model of Health', in *The Handbook of Salutogenesis*, ed. M. Mittelmark et al. (Cham, Switzerland: Springer, 2017), 45–56.

59 Crystal L. Park, 'Religion as a Meaning-Making Framework in Coping with Life Stress', *Journal of Social Issues* 61, no. 4 (2005): 707–29. See also Sukhmani Pal and Rupali Bhardwaj, 'Personality, Stress and Coping Resources among Working Women', *Indian Journal of Health and Wellbeing* 7, no. 9 (2016): 877–83.

60 D.N. McIntosh, 'Religion as a Schema, with Implications for the Relation between Religion and Coping', *The International Journal for the Psychology of Religion* 5 (1995): 1–16.

61 Rebecca L. Carter, 'Understanding Resilience through Ritual and Religious Practice: An Expanded Theoretical and Ethnographical Framework', http://www.ehs.unu.edu/file/get/3736 (accessed 21 August 2010), 1.

62 Interestingly, Kirpal Singh found – in his psychiatric practice – that those who attend the *gurdwara* and pray regularly recover more quickly that those who depend solely on medicine. Kirpal Singh, 'In Pursuit of Happiness', *Indian Journal of Psychiatry* 25, no. 1 (1983): 10–11.

Chapter 6

1. M.1, *Siddh Goshth* 4–8, *GGS*, 938–9.
2. *Dhammapada* 296–305.
3. M.5, *Sukhmani* 7.1–8; 22.4. See also Bhai Gurdas, *Varan* 29.15; 24.19.1–7.
4. M.1, *GGS*, 1256.
5. Kamala Elizabeth Nayar and Jaswinder Singh Sandhu, *Socially Involved Renunciate: Guru Nanak's Discourse to the Nath Yogis* (Albany: State University of New York Press, 2007), 72–5.

The *Sukhmani*: *The Pearl of Happiness*

1. 'Vedas, Simritis and Puranas' refer to the religious literature from the Vedic Period (*c.* 1500–500 BCE), Classical Hindu Period (*c.* 500 BCE–500 CE) and Medieval Hindu Period (*c.* 600–1500 CE), respectively.
2. Nine treasures (*nau nidhi*) may be an allusion to the nine treasures (*nau nidhi*) found in Hindu mythology and, therefore, be a motif to express 'everything' or 'abundance' that one will receive from *Ek Oankar*. For more information, see Chapter 3.
3. 'Posture is unmovable' means 'yogic positions are held steadfast' and is used figuratively to refer to mental and physical stability.
4. 'Swim across' refers to swimming across the ocean of *sansar*. It is a metaphor for liberation.
5. While *maya* (illusions of the material world) is frequently written as *maia* in the *Guru Granth Sahib*, we write *maya* for consistency and readability.
6. 'Eight watches' refers to the eight watches (*pehar*) of the day-night cycle.
7. 'Cutting the body into pieces and offering them' refers to a Jain practice of self-mortification and self-torture.
8. The 'four blessings' refer to the four classical Hindu human goals (Skt. *purusartha*): (1) righteousness (Skt. *dharma*), (2) wealth (Skt. *artha*), (3) sensual-pleasures (Skt. *kama*) and (4) liberation (Skt. *moksha*). For more information, see Chapter 1.
9. 'Womb's fire' refers to rebirth; that is, one will be saved or liberated from the cycle of birth, death and rebirth.
10. Fire is a necessity for keeping warm and cooking.
11. Sandalwood paste is traditionally used to protect the skin.
12. The 'ten possessions' is a figure of speech for worldly possessions.
13. According to *Sikhi*, lust (*kam*), anger (*krodh*), greed (*lobh*), attachment (*moh*) and ego (*ahankar*) are the five vices or thieves (*panj chor*) that rob humans from realizing their true nature (*atma*) and connection with *Ek Oankar*. For more information, see Chapter 5.
14. 'Thirty-six' refers to the many types of delicacies eaten on auspicious occasions.

15 'The god of justice engages in service' can be interpreted literally. However, the line can also be metaphorically understood as the fear of death dissipates because even the god of justice performs *seva*.
16 'Three qualities' (*gun*; Skt. *guna*) refers to the attributes of material world: purity (*sat*; Skt. *sattva*), passion (*raj*; Skt. *rajas*) and darkness (*tam*; Skt. *tamas*).
17 Here, 'dug' refers to slander, and 'anointed with sandalwood paste' refers to flattery.
18 *Brahamgiani* refers to an enlightened one. At times in the *Sukhmani*, *brahamgiani* is described as *Guru*, since there is no difference between an enlightened one and *Prabh*.
19 'Four classes' refers to the four *varnas* (colour) described in the Vedas. According to *RgVeda* 10.90, the four *varnas* are: (1) *brahmin* 'priestly' class, (2) *kshatriya* 'warrior' class, (3) *vaishya* 'agriculturalist' class and (4) *shudra* 'serving' class.
20 The four sources of creation are the (1) egg, (2) womb, (3) earth and (4) moisture.
21 'Ten directions' is used figuratively, signifying 'all around'.
22 'Four quarters' refers to either the four cardinal points (i.e. north, south, east and west) or the four stages in life: (1) infancy, (2) childhood and youth, (3) adulthood and (4) old age. Kamala Elizabeth Nayar and Jaswinder S. Sandhu, *The Socially Involved Renunciate: Guru Nanak's Discourse to the Nath Yogis* (Albany: State University of New York Press, 2007), 76–80.
23 For an explanation of the three qualities (*gun*), see note 16.
24 The four states are: (1) wakefulness, (2) dream sleep, (3) deep sleep and (4) pure consciousness. See 'The Multi-Layered Person' in Chapter 5.
25 For an analysis on the significance of this *salok*, see 'Narrative about the *Sukhmani*' in Chapter 2.
26 'Devotee' refers to the perfected or enlightened one (*brahamgiani*), who is completely absorbed in *Prabh*. Since the perfected one is void of ego, there is no difference between the devotee and *Prabh*. See Chapters 4 and 5.
27 The 'hidden record' (*chitr gupt*) is regarded as the unconscious sphere of the human person. It stores cognitive, emotional and behavioural impressions (*sanskar*) that have accumulated both in the past and in current life.
28 *Kitab* is the Urdu word for book, and in this verse it refers to Muslim scripture, the Qur'an.
29 'Collyrium' means eye wash or the black substance (*kajal*) placed in the eyelids to either ward off the evil eye or highlight the beauty of the eyes. It is used here figuratively to refer to highlighting the beauty of the eyes, which can also be symbolic for pure vision or awareness.
30 'Ocean of fire' refers to the ocean of desire that binds one to the cycle of rebirth (*sansar*).
31 'Merchandise' is used figuratively to refer to the accumulation of virtuous actions.
32 This line can also be translated as 'The *Sukhmani* (as in the text) embodies *Gobind's* virtues and *Nam*'.
33 For an explanation of 'four blessings', see note 8.

References

Primary Sources

Abhidhamma, Bhikkhu Bodhi, trans. *A Comprehensive Manual of Abhidhamma* (Series: Vipassana Meditation and the Buddha's Teachings). Onalaska, WA: Pariyatti Publishing, Buddhist Publication Society, 2003.

Adi Sri Guru Granth Sahib (Sri Damdami Bir). Amritsar: Sri Gurmat Press, standard pagination.

Bhagavad Gita, W.J. Johnson, trans. Oxford: Oxford University Press, 1994.

Dhammapada: The Sayings of the Buddha, John Ross Carter and Mahinda Palihawadana, trans. Oxford: Oxford University Press, 2000.

Hatha-yoga Pradipika, Pancham Singh, trans. Reprint [1915]; New York: AMS, 1974.

The Jahangirnama: Memoirs of Jahangir, Emperor of India, Wheeler M. Thackston, trans. New York: Oxford University Press, 1999.

The Law Code of Manu, Patrick Olivelle, trans. New York: Oxford University Press, 2009.

Majjhima Nikaya, Bhikkhu Bodhi, trans. *Teachings of the Buddha: Middle Length Discourses of the Buddha: A Translation of the Majjhima Nikaya*. Boston: Wisdom Publishers, 1995.

Patanjali's Yoga Sutras with Commentary of Vyasaand the Gloss of Vacapati Misra, Rama Prasada, trans. Reprint [1912]; New York, AMS Press, 1974.

Samyutta Nikaya, Bhikkhu Bodhi, trans. *The Connected Discourses of the Buddha: A Translation of the Samyutta Nikaya*. Boston: Wisdom Publications, 2000.

Sikh Reht Maryada. Amritsar: Shiromani Gurdwara Parbhandak Committee, 1982.

Tankhah Nama, (Bhai) Nand Lal Goya, n.p, n.d.

Upanisad Samgrahah, edited by J.L. Shastri. Delhi: Motilal Banarsidass, 1984.

Visuddhimagga: The Path of Purification by Bhadantacariya Buddhaghosa, Bhikkhu Nanamoli, trans. Reprint [1975, 1991]; Onalaska, WA: Pariyatti Publishing, Buddhist Publication Society 1999.

Punjabi Sources

Bansal, Krishna Kumari. 'Hariji rachit Sukhamani sahasranama da vistrit adhyain ate alochanatmak sampadan'. PhD diss.; Patiala: Punjabi University, 1977.

Bansal, Krishna Kumari. 'Sukhmani Sahasranam Parmarth'. In *Khoj Patrika*, edited by Jaggi Rattan Singh, 402–10. Patiala: Publication Bureau, Punjabi University, 1988.

Bhalla, Sarup Das. *Mahima Prakash* part II, edited by Gobind Singh Lamba et al. Patiala: Bhasha Bibhag, 1971.

Chhibbar, Kesar Singh. *Bansavalinama Dasan Patishahian Ka*, edited by R.S. Jaggi, published in Parakh: Research Bulletin of Punjabi Language and Literature. Chandigarh: Punjab University, 1972.

Gurdas, Bhai. *Kabitt Savaiyye Bhai Gurdas Ji Ke*. Lahore: Munsi Gulab Singh and Sons, n.d.

Gurdas, Bhai. *Varan Bhai Gurdas: Text, Transliteration and Translation*, 2 vols. Jodh Singh, trans. New Delhi: Vision and Venture, 1998.

Maskeen, (Giani) Sant Singh. *Prabhu Simran*. Amritsar: Singh Brothers, 1992.

Maskeen, (Giani) Sant Singh. *Guru Chintan*. Amritsar: Singh Brothers, 1993.

Maskeen, (Giani) Sant Singh. *Teeja Netr*. Amritsar: Singh Brothers, 1995.

Nabha, Kahn Singh. *Gurshabad Ratnakar Mahankosh*. Patiala: Punjab State University, [1930] 1974.

Nara, Giani Ishar Singh. *Itihas Baba Sri Chand Ji Sahib Ate Udasin Sampradaie*. Delhi: Delhi Gate, 1959.

Narotam, (Pandit) Tara Singh. *Sri Guru Tirath Sangreh*. Reprint Ambala, 1884; Kankhal: Sri Nirmal Akhara, 1975.

Singh, (Giani) Gian. *Tawarikh Guru Khalsa*. Amritsar: Bhai Budh Singh, 1897.

Singh, Raijasbir. 'Nirmala bekh da arambh'. In *Nirmala Sampraday*, edited by Pritam Singh. Amritsar: Guru Nanak Dev University, 1981.

Singh, Sahib. *Sri Guru Granth Sahib Darpan*, 10 vols. Jalandhar: Raj Publishers, 1962–1964.

Singh, (Bhai) Santokh. *Sri Gurpratap Suraj Granth*. Patiala: Punjab University, n.d.

Singh, (Bhai) Vir. *Sri Gurpratap Suraj Granth*, 14 vols. [1927–1935]. Amritsar: Khalsa Samachar, 1963.

English Secondary Sources

Ahluwalia, Gurmohan Singh. 'Miharvan Sampradae di Panjabi Vartak nu Dehn'. In *Khoj Patrika*, edited by Jaggi Rattan Singh, 345–59. Patiala: Publication Bureau, Punjabi University, 1988.

Ahluwalia, Muninder K., Anne Flores Locke, and Steven Hylton. 'Sikhism and Positive Psychology'. In *Religion and Spirituality across Cultures*, edited by Chu Kim-Prieto, 125–36. New York: Springer, 2014.

Akkera, Mounika, Srilatha Bashetti, Neetha Kundoor, Krishnaveni V. Desai, Radha Kishan N., and Aparna V. Bhongir, 'Indian Music Therapy: Could It Be Helpful in the Management of Mental Depression?' *International Journal of Medical Research & Health Sciences* 3, no. 2 (2014): 354–7.

Antonovsky, Aaron. *Unraveling The Mystery of Health – How People Manage Stress and Stay Well*. San Francisco: Jossey-Bass Publishers, 1987.

Avari, Burjor. *India: The Ancient Past, A History of the Indian Subcontinent from 7000 BC to AD 1200*. New York: Routledge, 2007.

Banerjee, Indubhusan. *Evolution of the Khalsa*, vol. 2. Calcutta: Mukherjee & Co., 1947.

Banerjee, Indubhusan. *Evolution of the Khalsa*, vol. 1. Reprint [1936]; Calcutta: University of Calcutta, 1963.

Bartolini, Stefano. 'Did the Decline in Social Connections Depress Americans?' *Social Indicators Research* 110, no. 3 (2013): 1033–59.

Baumann, Gerd. *Contesting Culture: Discourses of Identity in Multi-Ethnic London*. Cambridge: Cambridge University Press, 1996.

Bhatkhande, Vishnu Narayan. *A Short Historical Survey of the Music of Upper India, A Reproduction of a Speech Delivered by Pandit V. N. Bhatkhande at the First All-India Music Conference, Baroda, in 1916*. Reprint [1916]; Baroda, Gujarat: Indian Musicological Society, 1974.

Bhatkhande, Vishnu Narayan. *Hindusthani Sangeet Paddhati Kramik Pustak Malika*, 6 vols. Allahabad: Sangit Sadan Prakashan [first published in Marathi in 6 vols. 1910–1932], 1999.

Bhogal, Balbinder Singh. 'Postcolonial and Postmodern Perspectives on Sikhism'. In *The Oxford Handbook of Sikh Studies*, edited by Pashaura Singh and Louis Fenech, 282–97. Oxford, UK: Oxford University Press, 2014.

Bir, Raghbir Singh. *Bangdi Nama: Communion with the Divine*. Calcutta: Atam Science Trust, 1981.

Bodhi, Bhikkhu. *In the Buddha's Words*. Boston: Wisdom Publications, 2005.

Briggs, George Weston. *Gorakhnath and the Kanphata Yogis*. Reprint [1938]; Delhi: Motilal Banarsidass, 2001.

Bronkhorst, Johannes. *Buddhism in the Shadow of Brahmanism Handbook of Oriental Studies*. Leiden: Brill, 2011.

Burroughs, James and Aric Rindfleisch. 'Materialism and Well-Being: A Conflicting Values Perspective'. *Journal of Consumer Research* 29, no. 3 (2002): 348–70.

Carter, Rebecca L. 'Understanding Resilience through Ritual and Religious Practice: An Expanded Theoretical and Ethnographical Framework', http://www.ehs.unu.edu/file/get/3736 (accessed 21 August 2010), 1.

Carvalho, Pedro de Moura. *Mirāt al-quds (Mirror of Holiness): A Life of Christ for Emperor Akbar: A Commentary on Father Jerome Xavier's Text and the Miniatures of Cleveland Museum of Art, Acc. No. 2005.145*, ix–x. Leiden: Brill, 2012.

Cassio, Francesca. '*Gurbani Sangit*: Authenticity and Influences, A Study of Sikh Musical Tradition in Relation to Medieval and Early Modern Indian Music'. *Sikh Formations* 11, nos. 1–2 (2015): 23–60.

Chamorro-Premuzic, Tamas. *Personality and Individual Differences*. 3rd edn. West Sussex, UK: The British Psychological Society and John Wiley & Sons, 2015.

Cole, W. Owen and Piara Singh Sambhi. *A Popular Dictionary of Sikhism: Sikh Religion and Philosophy*. London: Routledge, 1997.

Cunningham, Joseph Davey. *A History of the Sikhs*. Reprint [1849]; Delhi: S. Chand, 1955.

David, Susan A., Ilona Boniwell, and Amanda Conley Ayers. *The Oxford Handbook of Happiness*. Oxford: Oxford University Press, 2013.

Davids, Carline Augusta Rhys. *The Vibhanga: Being the Second Book of the Abhidhamma Pitaka*. Reprint [1904]; Whitefish, MT: Kessinger Publishing LLT, 2010.

Deol, Jeevan Singh. 'The Minas and Their Literature'. *Journal of the American Oriental Society* 118, no. 2 (1998): 172–84.

Dhanjal, Beryl. 'Sikhism'. In *Worship*, edited by Jean Holm with John Bowker, 141–58. London: Pinter Publishers, 1994.

Dictionary of Guru Granth Sahib. 3rd edn. Amritsar: Singh Brothers, 2005.

Doniger, Wendy. *The Hindus: An Alternative History*. New York: Penguin, 2010.

Duggal, K.S. *Sikh Gurus: Their Lives and Teachings*. New Delhi: UBS Publishers, 1993.

Dyck, Isabel and Parin Dossa. 'Place, Health and Home: Gender and Migration in the Constitution of Healthy Place'. *Health & Place* 13 (2017): 691–701.

Easterlin, Richard A. 'Happiness and Economic Growth: The Evidence'. In *Global Handbook of Quality of Life*, edited by Wolfgang Glatzer, 283–99. Dordrecht, Springer, 2015.

Eck, Diane L. *Darsan: Seeing the Divine Image in India*. New York: Columbia University Press, 1996.

Eliade, Mircea. *Yoga: Immortality and Freedom*. Princeton: Princeton University Press, 1969.

Fenech, Louis E. *Martyrdom in the Sikh Tradition: Playing the 'Game of Love'*. New Delhi: Oxford University Press, 2000.

Fenech, Louis E. 'Martyrdom and the Execution of Guru Arjan in Early Sikh Sources'. *Journal of the American Oriental Society* 121, no. 1 (2001): 20–31.

Fenech, Louis E. *The Darbar of the Sikh Gurus: The Court of God in the World of Men*. New Delhi: Oxford University Press, 2008.

Feuerstein, Georg. *The Philosophy of Classical Yoga*. Manchester: University of Manchester Press, 1982.

Glasse, Cyril. *The New Encyclopedia of Islam*. New York: AltaMira Press, 2001.

Grewal, J.S. *Sikh Ideology, Polity, and Social Order*. New Delhi: Manohar Publications, 1996.

Grewal, J.S. *Contesting Interpretations of the Sikh Tradition*. Delhi: Manohar Publishers, 1998.

Grewal, J.S. *The Sikhs of the Punjab*. Cambridge: Cambridge University Press, 1998.

Grewal, J.S. *Four Centuries of Sikh Tradition: History, Literature, and Identity*. New Delhi: Oxford University Press, 2011.

Grewal, J.S. and Irfan Habib, eds. *Sikh History from Persian Sources*. New Delhi: Tulika, 2001.

Gurjar, Ajay Anil and Siddharth A. Ladhake. 'Analysis and Dissection of Sanskrit Divine Sound "Om" Using Digital Signal Processing to Study the Science behind "Om"

Chanting'. *7th Annual Conference on Intelligent Systems, Modelling and Simulation.* doi: 10.1109/ISMS.2016.79: 169–73.

Gurjar, Ajay Anil and Siddharth A. Ladhake. 'Time-Frequency Analysis of Chanting Sanskrit Divine Sound "OM" Mantra'. *International Journal of Computer Science and Network Security* 8, no. 8 (2008): 170–5.

Habib, Irfan. *The Agrarian System of Mughal India, 1556–1707*. New Delhi: Oxford University Press, 1999.

Hans, Surjit. *A Reconstruction of Sikh History from Sikh Literature*. Jalandhar: ABS Publications, 1988.

Hess, Linda and Shukhdev Singh, trans. *Bijak of Kabir*. Delhi: Motilal Banarsidass, 1983.

Hnilicova, Helena. 'The Revolutionary Experience'. In *The World Book of Happiness*, edited by Leo Bormns, 106–9. Buffalo, NY, Firefly Books, 2011.

Holzel, Britta K., Mark Vangel, James Carmody, Sita M., Yerramsetti, Christina Congleton, Tim Gard, and Sara W. Lazar. 'Mindfulness Practice Leads to Increases in Regional Brain Grey Matter Density'. *Psychology Research* 191, no. 1 (2011): 36–43.

Huseyin, Naci and John P.A. Ioannidis. 'Wellness-Evaluation of Wellness Determinants and Interventions by Citizen Scientist'. *The Journal of the American Medical Association* 314, no. 2 (2015): 121–2.

Jaspers, Karl. *The Origins and Goal of History*. London: Routledge Revivals, 2011.

Johar, S.S. *Handbook on Sikhism*. New Delhi: Vivek Publishing Co., 1977.

Judge, Paramjit Singh. 'Taksals, Akharas, and Nihang Deras'. In *The Oxford Handbook of Sikh Studies*, edited by Pashaura Singh and Louis Fenech, 372–81. Oxford, UK: Oxford University Press, 2014.

Kahneman, Daniel, Edward Diener, and Norbert Schwarz, *Well-Being: Foundations of Hedonic Psychology*. New York: Russell Sage Foundation, 1999.

Kalra, Gurvinder, Kamaldeep Bhui, and Dinesh Bhugra. 'Does Guru Granth Sahib Describe Depression?'. *Indian Journal of Psychiatry* 55, no. 2 (2013): S195–S200.

Kalra, Virinder S. *Sacred and Secular Musics: A Postcolonial Approach*. London: Bloomsbury Academic, 2015.

Kar, Sandeep Kumar, Chaitali Sen, and Anupam Goswami. 'Effect of Indian Classical Music (Raga Therapy) on Fentanyl, Vecuronium, Propofol Requirement and Cortisol Levels in Cardiopulmonary Bypass'. *British Journal of Anaesthesia*, 108 (S2) (2012): ii216. doi: 10.1093/bja/aer485.

Karam Elie G., Mariana M. Saloman, Joumana S. Yeretzian, Zeina N. Mneimneh, Aimee N. Karam, John Fayyad, Elie Hantouche, Kareen Akiskal, and Hagop S. Akiskal. 'The Role of Anxious and Hyperthymic Temperaments in Mental Disorders: A National Epidemiologic Study'. *World Psychiatry* 9, no. 2 (2010): 103–10.

Kaur, Madanjit and Piar Singh, eds. *Selected Works of Sardar Kapur Singh: Guru Arjan and His Sukhmani*. Amritsar: Guru Nanak Dev University, 1992.

Khalsa, Dharma Singh, Daniel Amen, Chris Hanks, Nisha Money, and Andrew Newberg. 'Cerebral Blood Flow Changes during Chanting Meditation'. *Nuclear Medicine Communications* 30, no. 12 (December 2009): 956–61.

Khalsa Diwan Society. '*Who Are the Sikhs*'. New Westminster, BC: Gurdwara Sahib Sukh Sagar, 2011.
Khalsa, Ek Ong Kaar Kaur. 'The Essence of Prosperity in *Sukhmani*'. *Sikh Dharma Ministry Newsletter* (November 2012). 5 January 2016. http://www.sikhnet.com/news/essence-prosperity-sukhmani
Khalsa, Ek Ong Kaar Kaur. *Sukhmani Sahib – Jewel of Peace* (poetically interpreted). USA, 2015.
Klostermaier, Klaus. *A Survey of Hinduism*. Albany: State University of New York Press, 1989.
Kohli, Surinder Singh. *Yoga of the Sikhs*. Amritsar: Singh Brothers, 1991.
Lallie, Harjinder Singh. 'The Harmonium in Sikh Music'. *Sikh Formations* 12, no. 1 (2016): 53–66.
Lane, Robert. 'Diminishing Returns to Income, Companionship, and Happiness'. *Journal of Happiness Studies* 1, no. 1 (2000): 103–19.
Lane, Robert. 'The Loss of Happiness'. In *The World Book of Happiness*, edited by Leo Bormns, 180–1. Buffalo, NY: Firefly Books, 2011.
LeDoux, Joseph E. 'Emotion Circuits in the Brain'. *Annual Review of Neuroscience* 23 (2000): 155–84.
Levine, Marvin. *The Positive Psychology of Buddhism and Yoga: Paths to a Mature Happiness*. New York: Routledge, 2009.
Macauliffe, Max Authur. *The Sikh Religion: Its Gurus, Sacred Writings and Authors*, 6 vols. in 3 books. Reprint [1909]; Delhi: DK Publishers, 1998.
Malcolm, John. *Sketch of the Sikhs*. Reprint [1810]; London: Forgotten Books, 2012.
Mandair, Arvind-Pal Singh. *Religion and the Specter of the West: Sikhism, India, Postcoloniality, and the Politics of Translation*. New York: Columbia University Press, 2009.
Mandair, Arvind-Pal Singh. *Sikhism: A Guide for the Perplexed*. London: Bloomsbury Academic, 2013.
Mann, Gurinder Singh. *The Goindval Pothis: The Earliest Extant Source of the Sikh Canon*. Cambridge, MA: Harvard University Press, 1996.
Mann, Gurinder Singh. *The Making of Sikh Scripture*. New York: Oxford University Press, 2001.
Mann, Gurinder Singh. 'Guru Nanak's Life and Legacy: An Appraisal'. *Journal of Punjab Studies* 17, nos. 1–2 (2010): 3–44.
Mansukhani, Gobind Singh. *Indian Classical Music and Sikh Kirtan*. New Delhi: Oxford & IBH Publishing, 1982.
Martz, E. 'Principles of Eastern Philosophies Viewed from the Framework of Yalom's Four Existential Concerns'. *International Journal for the Advancement of Counseling* 24 (2002): 31–42.
Maslow, Abraham H. *The Farther Reaches of Human Nature*. New York: The Viking Press, 1971.

Mathur, Avantika, Suhas H. Vijayakumar, Bhismadev Chakrabarti, and Nandini C. Singh. 'Emotional Responses to Hindustani Raga Music: The Role of Musical Structure'. *Frontiers in Psychology* 6, no. 513 (2015). doi: 10.3389/fpsyg.2015.00513.

McIntosh, D.N. 'Religion as a Schema, with Implications for the Relation between Religion and Coping'. *The International Journal for the Psychology of Religion* 5 (1995): 1–16.

McLeod, W. H. *Evolution of the Sikh Community*. Oxford: Clarendon Press, 1975.

McLeod, W. H. *Early Sikh Tradition*. Oxford: Clarendon Press, 1980.

McLeod, W. H. *Textual Sources for the Study of Sikhism*. Manchester, UK: Manchester University Press, 1984.

McLeod, W. H. *Guru Nanak and the Sikh Religion*. New Delhi: Oxford University Press, 1988.

McLeod, W. H. *Exploring Sikhism: Aspects of Sikh Identity, Culture and Thought*. New Delhi: Oxford University Press, 2000.

McLeod, W. H. *Sikhs of the Khalsa: A History of the Rahit*. New Delhi: Oxford University Press, 2003.

Mehta, Seema. 'California Lawyer Delivers Sikh Prayer at GOP Convention'. *Los Angeles Times*. 19 July 2016. http://www.latimes.com/politics/la-na-pol-republicans-harmeet-dhillon-20160719-snap-story.html

Miller, Gregory E., E. Chen, and E.S. Zhou. 'If It Goes Up, Must It Come Down? Chronic Stress and the Hypothalamic-Pituitary-Adrenocortical Axis in Humans'. *American Psychological Association* 133, no. 1 (2007): 25–45.

Mittelmark, M.B. T. Bull, and L. Bouwman, 'Emerging Ideas Relevant to the Salutogenic Model of Health'. In *The Handbook of Salutogenesis*, edited by M. Mittelmark, S. Sagy, M. Eriksson et. al., 45–56. Cham, Switzerland: Springer, 2017.

Nand, Parma. 'Ek Onkar'. In *Sikh Concept of the Divine*, edited by Pritam Singh, 36–63. Amritsar: Guru Nanak Dev University Press, 1985.

Nayar, Kamala Elizabeth. *Hayagriva in South India: Complexity and Selectivity of a Pan-Indian Hindu Deity*. Leiden: Brill, 2004.

Nayar, Kamala Elizabeth. *The Sikh Diaspora: Tradition, Modernity, and Multiculturalism*. Toronto: University of Toronto Press, 2004.

Nayar, Kamala Elizabeth and Jaswinder Singh Sandhu. 'Intergenerational Communication in Immigrant Punjabi Families: Implications for Helping Professionals'. *International Journal for the Advancement of Counselling* 28, no. 2 (2006): 139–52.

Nayar, Kamala Elizabeth and Jaswinder Singh Sandhu. *The Socially Involved Renunciate: Guru Nanak's Discourse to the Nath Yogis*. Albany: State of New York Press, 2007.

Nayar, Nancy Ann. *Poetry as Theology: The Srivaisnava Stotra in the Age of Ramanuja*. Wiesbaden: Otto Harrassowitz, 1992.

Novetzke, Christian Lee. 'The Theographic and the Historiographic in an Indian Sacred Life Story'. *Sikh Formations: Religion, Culture, Theory* 3, no. 2 (2007): 169–84.

Oberoi, Harjot Singh. *Construction of Religious Boundaries: Culture, Identity, and Diversity in the Sikh Tradition*. Delhi: Oxford University Press, 1994.

Oishi, Shigehiro and Selin Kesebir. 'Income Inequality Explains Why Economic Growth Does Not Always Translate to an Increase in Happiness'. *Psychological Science* 26, no. 10 (2015): 1630–8.

Olivelle, Patrick. *Between the Empires: Society in India 300 B.C.E.–400 C.E.* New York: Oxford University Press, 2006.

Olivelle, Patrick. *Upanisads*. New York: Oxford University Press, 2008.

'Pahar'. 19 January 2017. https://en.wikipedia.org/wiki/Pahar

Pal, Sukhmani and Rupali Bhardwaj. 'Personality, Stress and Coping Resources among Working Women'. *Indian Journal of Health and Wellbeing* 7, no. 9 (2016): 877–83.

Park, Crystal L. 'Religion as a Meaning-Making Framework in Coping with Life Stress'. *Journal of Social Issues* 61, no. 4 (2005): 707–29.

Payne, Charles Heibert, trans. *Jahangir and the Jesuits, with an Account of the Travels of Benedict Goes and the Mission to Pegu*, from the Relations of Father Fernao Guerreiro. New York: R.M. McBride & Co., 1930.

Peterson, Christopher. *A Primer in Positive Psychology*. New York: Oxford University Press, 2006.

Purewal, N.K. 'Sikh Muslim Bhai-Bhai: Towards a Social History of the *Rababi* Tradition of *Shabad Kirtan*'. *Sikh Formations* 7, no. 3 (2011): 365–82.

Razdan, Vijay Bazaz. *Hindustani Ragas: The Concept of Time and Season*. Delhi: B.R. Rhythms, 2009.

Salagame, Kiran Kumar. 'Meaning and Well-Being: Indian Perspectives'. *Journal of Constructivist Psychology* 30, no. 1 (2017): 63–8.

Sandhu, Jaswinder Singh. 'The Sikh Model of the Person, Suffering, and Healing: The Implications for Counselors'. *International Journal for the Advancement of Counseling* 26, no. 1 (2004): 33–46.

Sandhu, Jaswinder Singh. 'A Sikh Perspective on Life-Stress: Implications for Counseling'. *Canadian Journal of Counseling*, 39, no. 1 (2005): 40–51.

Sandhu, Jaswinder Singh. 'A Sikh Perspective on Alcohol and Drugs: Implications for the Treatment of Punjabi-Sikh Patients'. *Sikh Formations* 5, no. 1 (2009): 23–37.

Schoch, Richard. *The Secrets of Happiness: Three Thousand Years of Searching for the Good Life*. New York: Scribner, 2008.

Shackle, Christopher. *An Introduction to the Sacred Language of the Sikhs*. London: SOAS, 1988.

Shackle, Christopher. 'Survey of Literature in the Sikh Tradition'. In *The Oxford Handbook of Sikh Studies*, edited by Pashaura Singh and Louis Fenech, 109–24. Oxford, UK: Oxford University Press, 2014.

Sharma, G.S. *Sukhmani Sahib – Reflections*. New Delhi: Acharya Sri Agyaatdarshan, n.d.. https://agyaatdarshan.wordpress.com/2011/10/13/a-book-written-by-shri-gs-sharma-on-sukhmani-sahib/

Singh, Bhai Baldeep. 'What Is Kirtan?: Observations, Interventions and Personal Reflections'. *Sikh Formations* 7, no. 3 (2011): 245–95.

Singh, Bhai Guriqbal. *Nine Special Characteristics of Sukhmani Sahib Ji*. Amritsar: Chattar Singh Jeevan, 2008.

Singh, Daljeet. *The Sikh Ideology*. Amritsar: Singh Brothers, 1991.

Singh, Fauja. *Guru Amardas: Life and Teachings*. New Delhi: Sterling, 1978.

Singh, Ganda. *Guru Arjan's Martyrdom: Re-Interpreted*. Patiala: Guru Nanak Mission, 1969.

Singh, Harbans. *The Heritage of the Sikhs*. New York: Asia Publishing, 1964.

Singh, Harbans, chief ed. *The Encyclopedia of Sikhism*, vols. 1–4. Patiala: Punjabi University, 1998.

Singh, Harcharan and Ajinder Singh. 'The *Sukhmani* and Blood Pressure'. *Journal of Sikh Studies* 6 (1980): 45–62.

Singh, Jaswinder. *Discovering Divine Love in the Play of Life: The Teachings from Guru Arjun's Bhawan Akhri*. Surrey, BC: Journal of Contemporary Sikh Studies, 2000.

Singh, Khushwant. *A History of the Sikhs, 1469–1838*, vol. 1. Princeton: Princeton University Press, 1963.

Singh, Kirpal. 'In Pursuit of Happiness'. *Indian Journal of Psychiatry* 25, no. 1 (1983): 7–13.

Singh, Kirpal. *Perspectives on Sikh Gurus*. Delhi: National Book Shop, 2000.

Singh, Nikky-Guninder Kaur. 'The Myth of the Founder: The Janamsakhis and Sikh Tradition'. *History of Religions* 31, no. 4 (1992): 329–43.

Singh, Nikky-Guninder Kaur. *The Name of My Beloved: Verses of the Sikh Gurus*. New York: AltaMira Press, 1995.

Singh, Nirbhai. *Philosophy of Sikhism: Reality and Its Manifestations*. New Delhi: Atlantic Publishers, 1990.

Singh, Nirbhai. 'Gurbani and Bhakti Bani: A Philosophical Analysis'. In *The Sikh Tradition: A Continuing Reality*, edited by Sardar Singh Bhatia and Anand Spencer, 114–32. Patiala: Punjabi University, 1999.

Singh, Pashaura. 'Sikh Perspectives on Health and Suffering: A Focus on Sikh Theodicy'. In *Religion, Health, and Suffering*, edited by John R. Hinnells and Roy Porter, 111–38. London: Kegan Paul, 1999.

Singh, Pashaura. *The Guru Granth Sahib: Canon, Meaning and Authority*. New Delhi: Oxford University Press, 2003.

Singh, Pashaura. 'Understanding the Martyrdom of Guru Arjan'. *Journal of Punjab Studies* 12, no. 1 (2005): 29–62.

Singh, Pashaura. *Life and Work of Guru Arjan: History, Memory, and Biography in the Sikh Tradition*. New Delhi: Oxford University Press, 2006.

Singh, Pashaura. 'Revisiting the "Evolution of the Sikh Community"'. *Journal of Punjab Studies* 17, nos. 1–2 (2010): 45–74.

Singh, Pashaura and Louis Fenech, eds. *The Oxford Handbook of Sikh Studies*. Oxford, UK: Oxford University Press, 2014.

Singh, Pritam, ed. *Sikh Concept of the Divine*. Amritsar: Guru Nanak Dev University Press, 1985.

Singh, Ralph, ed. *The Miraculous Life of Baba Siri Chand Ji: Loving Son, and True Follower of Guru Nanak Dev Ji*. Gobind Sadan Society for Interfaith Understanding. New Delhi: Sterling Publishers, 2006.

Singh, Sukhdial. *Historical Analysis of Giani Gian Singh's Writings*. Jalandhar: UICS, 1996.

Singh, Sulakhan. *Heterodoxy in the Sikh Tradition*. Jalandhar: ABS Publishing, 1999.

Singh, Teja. *Sikh Dharam*. Reprint [1952]; Amritsar: Singh Brothers, 1977.

Singh, Teja. *The Psalm of Peace*. Amritsar: Khalsa Brothers, 1978.

Singh, Teja. *Sikhism: Its Ideals and Institutions*. Reprint [1951, 1962]; Bombay: Orient Longman, 2009.

Singh, Trilochan. *Ernest Trumpp and W. H. McLeod as Scholars of Sikh History, Religion and Culture*. Chandigarh: International Centre of Sikh Studies, 1994.

Smith, Wilfred Cantwell. *On Understanding Islam: Selected Studies*. Berlin: Walter De Gruyter, 2000.

Stoler Miller, Barbara. *Yoga: Discipline of Freedom: The Yoga Sutra Attributed to Patanjali*. New York: Bantam Books, 1998.

Syan, Hardip Singh. 'Early Sikh Historiography'. *Sikh Formations: Religion, Culture, Theory* 7, no. 2 (2011): 145–60.

Syan, Hardip Singh. 'Sectarian Works'. In *The Oxford Handbook of Sikh Studies*, edited by Pashaura Singh and Louis Fenech, 170–80. Oxford, UK: Oxford University Press, 2014.

Takahashi, Taiki, K. Ikeda, M. Ishikawa, N. Kitamura, T. Tsukasaki, D. Nakama, and T. Kameda. 'Anxiety, Reactivity, and Social Stress-Induced Cortisol Elevation in Humans'. *Neuroendocrinology Letters* 26, no. 4 (2005): 351–4.

Talib, Gurbachan Singh. '*Sukhmani*'. In *The Encyclopedia of Sikhism*, vol. 4, edited by Harbans Singh, 263–5. Patiala: Punjabi University, 1998.

Theobald, Theo and Cary Cooper. 'The Relationship between Happiness and Wellbeing'. In *Doing the Right Thing: The Importance of Wellbeing in the Workplace*, edited by Theo Theobald and Cary Cooper, 13–18. London: Palgrave Macmillan, 2012.

Trumpp, Ernest. *The Adi Granth: The Holy Scripture of the Sikhs*. Reprint [1877]; New Delhi: Munisharam Manoharlal, 1989.

Uberoi, J.P.S. *Religion, Civil Society and the State: A Study of Sikhism*. Delhi: Oxford University Press, 1996.

Valliere, Paul. 'Tradition'. In *The Encyclopedia of Religion*, vol. 13, edited by Mircea Eliade, 9267–9281. 1st edn. New York: Macmillan, 2005.

van Boven, Leaf. 'Experientialism, Materialism, and the Pursuit of Happiness'. *Review of General Psychology* 9, no. 2 (2005): 132–42.

van der Linden, Bob. 'Sikh Music and Empire: The Moral Representation of Self in Music'. *Sikh Formations* 4, no. 1 (2008): 1–15.

van der Linden, Bob. 'Sikh Sacred Music, Empire and World Music'. *Sikh Formations* 7, no. 3 (December 2011): 383–97.

Wolf, David B. and Neil Abell. 'Examining the Effects of Meditation Techniques on Psychosocial Functioning'. *Research on Social Work Practice* 13, no. 1 (2003): 27–42.

Yalom, Irvin D. *Existential Psychotherapy*. New York: Basic Books, 1980.

Other Sources

Bhai Baldeep Singh. Email Communication. 27 to 29 June 2016, Anad Foundation, New Delhi, India.

Giani Gurbachan Singh Bhindranwale. Sermons on mp3 at http://www.gurmatveechar.com

Giani Sant Singh Maskeen. *North American Lecture Series* (audiotape). Vancouver, BC: Ross Street Gurdwara, 1982.

Giani Sant Singh Maskeen. Lecture on audiotape. Vancouver, BC: Khalsa Diwan Society, 1994.

Giani Sant Singh Maskeen. Interview with authors. Surrey, BC, 22 January 2003.

Giani Thakur Singh. Sermons. https://www.youtube.com/watch?v=SJCuFHz2SJM

Index

aath pehar. *See* watches of the day/night
abuse 14, 93
acceptance
    form of happiness 13, 92–4, 128
    gurmat value 44, 84, 114–15, 120, 131
Adi Granth 21, 24, 29, 34–5, 41, 47, 89, 98,
    211 n.72, 212 n.77, 221 n.44
    compilation of 30–1, 207 n.10, 212
        n.75, 218 n.9
    organization of 49–50, 227 n.6
    recensions 30, 41, 48–9
    see also Guru Granth Sahib
addiction 10, 12–13, 92, 109
    see also five thieves
Advaita Vedanta. *See* Vedanta
affliction (*kalesh/klesha*) 1, 9
    in Buddhism 6–8
    in *Sikhi* 1, 92
    in *Yoga Sutras* 4–6
    see also suffering
ahankar. *See* ego
Akal Purakh. *See* Sat Purakh
Akbar. *See* Mughal – Akbar
Akhand Kirtani Jatha 58
alcohol. *See* addiction
Amritsar/Ramdaspur 21, 24–7, 31, 48,
    73
Anand 25, 50, 60, 232 n.21
anger 112, 115, 117, 130
    see also distress cycle, five thieves
anhat nad. *See* unstruck sound
antahkaran. *See* inner controller
anxiety 5, 11–12, 36, 70, 92–3, 109, 116,
    124, 131
    see also psychological distress
Ardas 47, 59–60, 64, 226 n.97
asceticism 1, 3, 6, 9, 199 n.3
    see also renunciation
atma 3–6, 103–6
attachment
    in Buddhism 6
    in Hinduism 3–6
    in *Sikhi* 74, 78, 90–1, 93, 109, 130 *see
        also* five thieves, distress cycle
Aurangzeb. *See* Mughal – Aurangzeb
avatar(a). *See* incarnation
axial age 2–3, 9, 200 n.11

Babur. *See* Mughal – Babur
balanced approach to living 15, 30, 85–8,
    110, 124
    see also meaningful engagement/living
(Bhai) Balwand, Rai 33–4, 49, 219 n.18
Banda Singh Bahadur 22
bani 26–7, 29–30, 36, 39–41, 55–6, 59, 90,
    125
    about Babur 11–12, 203–4 n.61
    nitnem (daily), 59–60, 223 nn.69–70
    unripe (*kachi*), 25, 29–30
    see also kirtan
Banno Bir 41, 49
Bansavalinama Dasan Patishahian Ka 207
    n.11, 209–10 n.49, 210 n.55
Barath 32–3, 37–9
    Gurdwara Sahib 38–9, 214 n.102
Bavan Akhri 57, 60, 222 n.57
bhagat 16, 31, 49, 219 n.16
    -*bani* 31, 49
Bhagavad Gita 10, 101, 131, 203 nn.56–7,
    227 n.7
Bhai Gurdas. *See* (Bhai) Gurdas
Bhakti. *See* Hinduism – Bhakti, Nirgun
    Bhakti
Bhatkhande, Vishnu Narayan 65
bhatts 49–50, 219 n.17
    see also (Bhatt) Mathura
body (*sarir*) 103, 106
Braham (*Brahman*). *See* Ek Oankar
brahamgiani 102, 110, 119, 121–2, 132
    see also gurmat values
Brahmin. *See* varna
Brahminical hegemony 3, 15, 201 n.33
breathing technique. *See* meditation –
    breathing (*pranayam*)

(Bhai) Buddha 27, 29, 62
Buddha, Gautama 6, 123, 229 n.23
    see also Dhammapada, Four Noble Truths
Buddhaghosa 8
Buddhism 1, 2, 19, 201 n.33
    Mahayana 199 n.4, 233 n.43
    Theravada 3, 6–8, 30, 123, 132, 199 n.3, 202 n.35, 202 n.41, 228 n.20, 229 n.23, 233 n.43

caste. See varna
Chandu Shah 43–5, 217 n.134
Chibber, Chaupa Singh. See rahit-nama
Chibber, Kesar Singh. See Bansavalinama Dasan Patishahian Ka
chinta. See anxiety
Christianity 65, 101
cit (consciousness) 103–4, 106, 231 n.14
cit (memory) 105
colonialism 18, 65, 123, 199 n.2
compassion 15, 77, 90–1, 94–7, 115, 118
    see also grace, seva
Confucius 101
coping 92
    see also resilience
core needs 108–9, 116, 119
    see also humanitarian goals, material goals/needs
cosmology 47, 82–5, 103, 232 n.20
    see also Ek Oankar
courage 88, 118, 132
critical historians 18, 22, 30, 205 n.93
Cunningham, Joseph D. 18

Dabistan-i-Mazahab 42–3, 210 n.52
Dakhni Oankar 60
Damdami Bir 49
Damdami Taksal 36, 214 n.95
    see also Gurbachan Singh (Bhindranwale)
dan. See Nam–dan–ishnan, seva
Dasam Granth 44, 98, 218 n.8
Dasu 24, 35, 73
Datu 24, 35, 73, 208 n.27
death/dying 11–12, 70, 120–1
Delhi 216 n.125, 217 n.134, 217 n.139
desire 9, 19, 92, 101
    in Buddhism 3–6, 8
    in Classical Hinduism 9–10, 71, 81
    in *Sikhi*. see kam (lust)
    in Yoga 4–6
detached engagement 2, 68, 95, 98, 100
Dhammapada 6–7, 101, 131
dharam (dharma)
    in Hinduism 9–10, 15, 71, 200 n.7, 202–3 n.50, 203 nn.51–2
    in *Sikhi* 10, 15, 81
dharamsal 17, 59, 79
    see also gurdwara
disease 11, 70, 92, 121
distress cycle (figure 5.2) 106–10
Diwan of Bhai Nand Lal. See (Bhai) Nand Lal
duality 13–14, 69, 95–6, 115, 131–2
dukh. See suffering
dvija 9, 127, 203 n.52
    see also varna

Easterlin paradox 119
ego
    in Indic religions 3–4
    in modern/Western psychology 105, 199 n.5
    in *Sikhi* 2, 12, 14, 74, 76–8, 80, 82–5, 90, 97, 103, 105–6, 116, 199 n.5. see also manmukh
    renunciation 1–2, 10
Ek Oankar 14–15, 25, 40, 48, 57, 64, 67–8, 76–7, 88–90, 103–4, 110–12, 115, 126, 128–30
    see also Guru
emotional distress. See psychological distress
emotions 55–6, 66, 101–2, 109–12, 115, 120
    see also happiness, suffering
emptiness (sunn)
    in Buddhism 233 n.43
    in *Sikhi* 118
existential
    psychotherapy 120–1
    suffering/concerns 1–2, 14, 17, 19, 70, 74–5, 92–3, 96, 102, 109, 120–1

faith 87, 95
(Baba/Sheikh) Farid 31, 50
fear 6, 11, 61, 70, 73, 92–3, 95, 99, 107, 120, 124
Fenech, Louis E. 44, 217 n.139

five thieves 13, 76, 82–3, 92, 117, 130, 232 n.24
  see also distress cycle
Four Noble Truths 6–7
Freudian perspective 105, 199 n.5
frontal cortex 117

Gauri *rag*. *See rag* – Gauri
gian. *See* knowledge (*gian*)
giani (preacher-scholar) 19, 108, 223 n.67
(Giani) Gian Singh 32, 212 n.80
  see also Tawarikh Guru Khalsa
Gobind Sadan Society 38–9, 214 n.101
Goindval 25, 27, 30, 79, 209 n.35
  Pothis 25, 30, 211–12 nn.73–4, 211–2 n.74
Golden Temple. *See* Harmandar Sahib
grace
  in Bhakti 124, 228 n.21
  in *Sikhi* 52, 66, 77, 97–8, 229 n.22
greed. *See* distress cycle, five thieves
gun. *See* qualities (*gun*)
Gurbachan Singh (Bhindranwale) 36–7
gurbani. *See* bani
gurbilas 44, 207 n.11
(Bhai) Gurdas 26–9, 35, 44, 96, 98, 207 n.10, 209 n.35, 217 n.140, 218 n.9
  see also Varan
Gurdaspur 32
Gurditta 39, 215 n.107
gurdwara 27, 45, 47, 58–60, 76, 91, 108, 112–13, 121
Gurdwara reform 65, 213 n.90, 214 n.99
Gurdwara Tap Asthan Baba Sri Chand Ji. *See* Barath – Gurdwara Sahib
gur-gaddi 16, 24, 27, 45
  rivalry over 24–7, 33–5, 73, 124–5, 209 n.35
  see also Guru Arjan – Prithi Chand's conflict with
(Bhai) Guriqbal Singh 63–4, 225 n.90
gurmat values 67, 114–19, 130–1
gurmukh 14–15, 78–9, 84–6, 94–5
  see also brahamgiani
Gurmukhi script 24–5
Guru 68, 79, 199 n.1
  Guru Arjan's conception of 68, 88–91, 129–30
  see also Ek Oankar

(Sikh) Gurus 23–4, 35, 47, 64–5, 71–2, 89–90, 199 n.1
Guru Nanak (First) 1–2, 10–17, 21, 24, 25, 30, 49, 50, 55, 57, 78–9, 97, 203–4 n.61, 208 n.15, 208 n.21, 229 n.26
  see also Japji, *Siddh Goshth*
Guru Angad (Second) 24–5, 34, 49, 79
Guru Amar Das (Third) 24–5, 27, 49, 50, 57, 72, 79
  see also Anand, *Goindval* – *Pothis*
Guru Ramdas (Fourth) 25–8, 34, 49, 55, 57, 79, 90, 209 nn.34–5
Guru Arjan (Fifth) 1–2, 17–19, 21–3, 49, 50, 66, 124–5, 132, 210 n.62
  execution/martyrdom 21, 30, 41–5, 60, 125, 132, 216 n.130, 217 n.131, 217 n.134, 217 n.139, 217 n.141
  life 26–9, 124–5, 209–10 n.49
  Panthic contributions of 21, 27–30, 45, 47, 68, 72–3, 125
  Prithi Chand's conflict with 21, 26–9, 31, 45, 124
  see also Adi Granth, *Bavan Akhri*, *Sukhmani*
Guru Hargobind (Sixth) 27–8, 30, 39, 49, 209–10 n.49, 215 n.107, 217 n.140
Guru Tegh Bahadur (Ninth) 49–50, 57, 217 n.139, 221 n.44
Guru Gobind Singh (Tenth) 47–9, 207 n.13, 213–14 n.93
  see also Dasam Granth
Guru Granth Sahib 16, 22, 32–3, 47–50, 126–7, 199 n.1, 221 n.44, 227 n.6
  closing of 48–9
  function of 47–8, 67
  see also Adi Granth

hagiographies 7, 18–19, 22, 29, 36, 38, 207 n.6, 213 n.88
  about the *Sukhmani*. *See Sukhmani* – narratives
happiness 1–2, 12–14
  extrinsic/intrinsic 19, 92, 101
  ingredients for, (figure 4.2) 96–8, 128
  pursuit of 2, 6–7, 17, 69–70, 101–2, 127, 130–2, 128
  six forms of, (figure 4.1) 92–6, 128

Western notions of 19, 101, 119-20
see also liberation, wellbeing/wellness, suffering – and happiness
Harji 41, 215 n.112, 216 n.120 *see also Sukhmani Sahasranama*
Harmandar Sahib 21, 27, 31, 48, 98, 206 n.1
healing 6, 19, 58, 61-2, 102, 122, 131-2
   practices 110-13
   and music. See *rag* – and healing
Heran 73
hidden record 103-6, 110-12
Hinduism 1, 19, 22, 31, 63, 73
   Bhakti 15-16, 41, 75, 124, 126, 199 n.4, 228 n.14, 228 n.21
   Classical 9-10, 15, 202-3 nn.50-2, 203 nn.56-7
   Puranic 40-1, 215 n.105, 215 n.117, 225 n.89, 228 n.14
   Upanishadic 2-4, 6, 41, 199 n.3, 200 n.14, 201 n.19, 215 n.117. *see also* Vedanta
   Vedic 3, 4, 16, 30, 72, 127, 200 n.13, 227 n.2
   see also Sikhi – critique of Hinduism
historiography 18-19, 22
   see also hagiographies
hope 6, 9, 61, 66-7, 70-1, 87-8, 99, 127, 129
householder
   traditional conception of 9-10, 200 n.7, 200 n.10
   Sikh understanding of 1, 10, 82, 124
hukam 14, 83-4, 92-3
hukanama 60, 66, 224 n.77
humanistic goals/needs 108, 130
humanitarian action 16-17, 82, 113
   see also seva
humility 84-5, 113

icon. *See* incarnation
illness. *See* disease
illusion. *See maya*
impermanence
   in Buddhism 6-7, 115
   in *Sikhi* 13. see also *maya*
   a *gurmat* value 115-16
incarnation 40-1, 47, 75
independence/nationalist movement 65, 226 n.103

inner controller 103, 105-6, 231-2 n.19
   see also ego
interdependence 114
interpretation xi-xii 18-19, 62-3, 123, 225 n.85
Islam 25, 31, 42, 44, 58, 101, 216 n.123
Itihas Baba Sri Chand Ji Sahib Ate Udasin Sampradaie 37, 39-40

Jahangir. *See* Mughal – Jahangir
Jahangirnama 42-3, 45
   see also Mughal – Jahangir
Jainism 1-4, 199 n.3
Japji 31-3, 35-9, 49, 52-4, 59, 60

(Bhagat) Kabir 16, 25, 31, 50, 57, 230 n.46
kachi bani. See bani – unripe *(kachi)*
kalesh. See affliction *(kalesh/klesha)*
kam (lust) 10, 12-13, 71, 81, 92, 101, 106-9, 117, 203 n.51, 203 n.54
   see also desire, five thieves
karam (karma) 3, 6-7, 10, 14, 110-12, 130
karodh. See anger, five thieves
Kartarpur (West Punjab) 16, 48-9
Kartarpur Bir 41, 48
katha 22, 48, 66-7, 75
Khadur 24
Khatri 24, 26
   see also varna
(Prince) Khusrau. *See* Mughal – Khusrau
Kiratpur 41, 49
kirtan 48, 55-9, 64-6, 75, 111-13, 117, 121, 219 n.18, 221 n.50, 222 n.53, 226 nn.102-3, 227 n.106
   see also rag
knowledge *(gian)* 3-5, 104-5
Krishna 10, 40, 126, 203 n.56
kundalini-yoga. See yoga – *kundalini*

Lahore 28, 42-3, 73
Lahori Bir 49
Lakhmi Das 24, 33, 35
langar 17, 24-6, 60, 79, 113
(Bhai) Lehna. *See* (Sikh) Guru – Angad
liberation 1-3, 6, 8-10, 16, 57, 63, 67, 75, 77, 79, 82, 126, 231 n.4
lila 82, 84
lobh (greed). *See* distress cycle, five thieves

Macauliffe, A. Max 18, 32–3, 213 n.83
Mahima Prakash Vartak of Sarup das Bhalla 43, 207 n.11
man (mind) 103–6
   -*tan* (body). *see* mind and body
   see also ego, *seva*
Mandair, Arvind-Pal Singh 199 n.2
manji system 25, 79, 209 n.30
manmukh 12, 83–6, 130–1
Mann, Gurinder Singh 16, 211–12 n.74, 212 n.75
Mansukhani, Gobind Singh 56
(Bhai) Mardana 49, 219 n.18
martyrdom. *See* Guru Arjan – execution/martyrdom
masand 26, 28, 45, 72, 79, 98–9, 213–14 n.93
(Giani) Maskeen, Sant Singh 64
Maslow, Abraham H. 206 n.97, 231 n.6
material goals/needs 9, 108, 119–20, 130
(Bhatt) Mathura 50
maya 3–4, 6, 82–4, 100, 131
   in Advaita Vedanta 82, 229 n.42
   in Sikhi 82–4
McLeod, W.H 16, 18, 31, 72
meaningful engagement/living 19, 54, 92–5, 100–2, 110, 113, 119–21, 128, 131–2, 230 n.2
medicine
   in Buddhism 77, 128
   in Sikhi 11, 77, 128. *see also* Nam – as panacea
meditation
   breathing (*pranayam*) 111
   in Buddhism 6, 8, 111
   in Hinduism 3, 6, 37–8, 51, 61
   in Sikhi 16, 61, 106, 110–11. *see also* Nam simran
mental distress. *See* psychological distress, suffering – sources of
Miharvan 28–30, 40–1, 125–6, 210 n.59
   see also Mina sect (Miharvan *sampraday*), *Sukhmani Sahasranama*
Mina sect (Miharvan *sampraday*) 210 n.55
   and the Sikh Panth 28–30, 35, 40–1, 49, 125–6, 213–14 n.93
   see also Harji, Miharvan, Prithi Chand

mind and body 12, 15, 61, 97, 102, 110–11, 116, 131
   see also person(hood)
mindfulness
   in Buddhism 7, 77, 128, 228 n.20
   in Sikhi 70, 75, 77, 106, 128
moh. *See* attachment
Mohan 25, 30, 35, 38, 73, 209 n.35, 211–12 n.74
Mohari 25–6, 35, 209 n.35
Mohsin Fani 42–3
Mughal
   Aurangzeb, Emperor 211 n.65
   Akbar, Emperor 21, 25–6, 29–31, 41–3, 125, 207 n.2, 211 n.65, 212 n.77
   authorities/empire 29, 31, 45, 73, 211 n.67, 217 n.140. *see also* Wazir Khan
   Babur, Emperor 11–12, 203–4 n.61
   Jahangir, Emperor 21, 42–3, 45, 125, 216 n.125, 217 n.140
   Khusrau, Prince 42–3, 216 n.125, 216 n.130
   Shah Jahan, Emperor 216 n.125
mukat. *See* liberation
Mul-mantar 49, 88–9, 219 n.19
Mundavani 50, 222 n.62
Muslim. *See* Islam

Nam 1, 14, 16, 51, 69, 92, 111, 114, 116, 131–2
   and *Ek Oankar* 75–7, 104
   as the panacea 2, 57, 61–2, 70–4, 77, 110
   dan-ishnan 11–12, 204 n.78
   separation from 11–13, 70, 75
Nam simran 15–16, 71–2, 74–5, 78–9, 81, 86, 96–8, 111–13, 127–8, 130–1
   three stages of 76–7
(Bhagat) Namdev 16, 25, 57
Nanaksar sect 225 n.90
   see also (Bhai) Guriqbal SIngh
(Bhai) Nand Lal 48, 218 n.10
(Giani) Nara, Ishar Singh. *See Itihas Baba Sri Chand Ji Sahib Ate Udasin Sampradaie*
(Pandit) Narotam, Tara Singh 212 n.80, 213 n.85
   see also Sri Guru Tirath Sangreh
Nath tradition 16, 51
   see also yoga – *hatha*

Nirgun Bhakti 16, 199 n.4, 219 n.16
    see also Farid, Kabir, Namdev, Ravidas
Nirmala sect 22, 32–3, 35–6, 125, 207–8 n.13, 208 n.14
    see also Sukhmani - narratives
nitnem bani (daily prayers). *See bani* - *nitnem*

Oberoi, Harjot Singh 18
Operation Bluestar 49, 219 n.15
oral tradition 62, 67, 127, 225 n.85

Pali Canon 7–8, 30
Panj Granthi 59–60, 66, 223–4 n.74
panj chor. See five thieves
Panth. *See* Sikh Panth
Patanjali. *See Yoga Sutras*
pehar. See watches of day-night
person(hood)
    and *Ek Oankar* 103–4, 106
    in *Sikhi* (figure 5.1) 103–6
pilgrimage 16, 25, 29, 32, 73, 79
post-colonialism/post-modernism 18, 123
pranayama(a). See meditation
Prithi Chand 26, 28, 30–1, 35, 40–1, 49, 73, 124, 210 n.55, 210 n.62
    see also Mina sect (Miharvan sampraday); Guru Arjan, conflict with Prithi Chand
psychiatry 102, 234 n.62
psychological distress 14, 17, 63, 86, 92, 102, 121, 127, 131
    see also anxiety, distress cycle, suffering
psychology (modern) 19, 101–2, 120–1
psychotherapy 102, 120–1
Punjab society 21, 25, 65
Puranas. *See* Hinduism - Puranic

qualities (*gun*) 4, 82, 89
Qur'an 16, 30

rag 25, 27, 49–50, 54–5, 221 n.44
    and healing 111–12
    Asa 57
    Gauri 40, 57–8, 60, 66, 118, 126–7, 222 nn.58–60
    in medical studies 112, 232 n.32
    role in *Sikhi* 55–7
Rag-mala 50, 58, 222 nn.61–2
rahit-nama 204 n.80, 213–14 n.93
    see also Sikh Reht Maryada

Ramdaspur. *See* Amritsar
Ramsar 27, 31, 36–7
(Bhai) Randir Singh. *See* Akhand Kirtani Jatha
(Bhagat) Ravidas 16, 25, 31, 57
Rehras 49, 59–60
renunciation 9
    in Buddhism 6, 123
    in Hinduism 3–4, 123, 200 n.10
    Guru Nanak's critique of 1–2, 10–11, 200 n.7
Republican party (USA) 64
resilience 110, 121–2
ritual(ism)
    Brahminical/Vedic 3, 72
    in *Sikhi* 25–6, 58–60, 65–6, 126–7
    Sikhi critique of 16–17, 63, 72–5, 117–18

sacred word (*sabad*). *See Nam, shabad-Guru*
sadh sangat. See sangat - sadh
Sahaskriti salok 106–7, 232 n.22
Salutogenesis model 121
Samkhya School 4, 6
Sanatan Sikhism. *See* Nirmala sect
sangat
    in Buddhism 123–4, 229 n.23
    in the Sikh Panth 17, 24, 78–9, 229 n.25
    sadh- 48, 58–60, 66, 78–81, 90–1, 96–100, 117–18, 128, 218 n.7, 223 n.67
sangha. See sangat
sansar 1, 3, 11–13, 70–1, 82–3, 91, 99, 114, 124, 126, 129, 200 n.14, 231 n.4
(Bhai) Santokh Singh. *See Gur Pratap Suraj*
sarbat da bhalla. See humanitarian effort
sargun 14, 82–5
    see also incarnation
sarovar 25–7
Satgur 47, 68, 80, 89–91, 129, 131
Sat Purakh 54, 68–9, 75, 80, 88–91, 93, 97–8, 128–9, 131
    see also Ek Oankar
(Bhai) Satta 33–4, 49
Sense of Coherence (SOC) 121
seva 14–17, 94–9, 112–13, 117, 121, 128, 131, 210 n.51, 233 n.36

Shiromani Gurdwara Prabandhak Committee (SGPC) 204 n.80, 205 n.81
shabad-Guru 17, 22, 28, 35–6, 39–40, 47, 56, 79, 86, 89, 91, 111, 115, 199 n.1, 212 n.77
Shiva consciousness. *See* yoga – *kundalini*
Siddh Goshth 1, 10, 50–1, 60
Sikh Reht Maryada 16, 59, 64, 204 n.80, 205 n.81, 213–14 n.93, 223 n.68
Sikh
   definition of 88, 91, 98–100, 129, 131
Sikh Panth
   consolidation of 23, 28–31, 41, 45, 47, 49, 72–3, 98–9, 124–5, 129, 132
   evolution of 16–17, 21, 24–6, 59, 210 n.52
   and Mughal tensions 21, 41–5
   -sectarian rivalry. *see* Mina sect (Miharvan *sampraday*), Udasi sect
Sikh studies 17–18, 123, 205 n.89, 206 nn.94–5
   see also critical historians, traditional historians
Sikhi 1, 16–18, 23–5, 32, 67–8, 101, 126, 199 n.2, 199 n.4
   critique of Hinduism 10–11, 25, 72–3, 75, 113, 127, 200 n.10
   redefinition of Hindu concepts 10–11, 47, 51, 75–6, 81, 212 n.77
   frames 18–19, 123–4, 206 n.95
Singh, (Bhai) Baldeep 65
Singh, Daljeet 18
Singh, Pashaura 18, 44, 53–4, 217 n.134, 227 n.6
Singh, Sahib 18
Singh, Teja 18
Singh, Trilochan 18
Singh Sabha movement 18, 65, 123, 213 n.90, 222 n.62, 226 n.102
social involvement
   according to Guru Arjan 97–8, 113, 121, 131–2
   according to Guru Nanak 1–2, 10–11, 14–17, 34
   see also seva
Sohila 49, 59–60
Sri Chand 214 n.99, 214 n.101
   discord with Sikh Gurus 24, 34–5, 63, 73

   meet with Guru Arjan 31–3, 36–40, 54, 125, 212–13 n.82, 215 n.109
   reconciliation with Sikh Panth 36, 40
   see also Udasi sect
Sri Gur Pratap Suraj 22, 27, 31–3, 207 n.11, 208 n.16
Sri Guru Tirath Sangreh 32–3, 222 n.62
stress hormone 109
(Baba) Sundar 49
suffering
   and happiness 12–14, 66, 69, 95–6, 100, 120–1
   in Hinduism 3–6
   in Buddhism 6–8
   removal of 92–3, 124, 130–1. *see also* Nam – as the panacea
   sources of, (figure 1.1) 1–14, 70–1, 86–7, 124, 233 n.39
   see also affliction (*kalesh/klesha*), distress cycle
Sufism 16, 211 n.65, 216 n.123, 219 n.16, 229 n.26
sukh. *See* happiness, liberation
Sukhmani 1–2, 17, 31, 44
   and Hindus 59, 223 n.72
   application of 101–22, 130–1
   audience 45, 54, 58, 66, 127
   benefits of 60–4, 66, 127
   meaning of 50–1
   medical studies on 61, 224 n.79
   narratives (tables 2.1 and 2.2) 21, 23, 31–41, 45, 54, 62–3, 123, 125–6
   ritual function/practice 48, 57–60, 64–7, 126–7
   structure of 40–1, 50–4, 68–9, 227 n.5
   teachings 54, 66–100, 128
Sukhmani Sahasranama 40–1, 123, 125–6
sunn. *See* emptiness (*sunn*)
superstition 60–4
Suraj Prakash. *See Sri Gur Pratap Suraj*

Talib, Gurbachan Singh 37
tan (body). *See* mind and body, *seva*
Tawarikh Guru Khalsa 32–3, 36–7, 54
temperance 117
tirath. *See* pilgrimage
traditional historians 18, 205 n.92
transcendence
   ego/duality 13–14, 95–8

gurmat value 117–19
  see also Maslow, Abraham H.
transpersonal experience 13–14, 95–8,
   101, 110
  see also brahamgiani
trauma 112
Trump, Donald. *See* Republican party (USA)
Trumpp, Ernest 18
Tuzuk-i-Jahangiri. *See* Jahangirnama

Uberoi, J.P.S.
Udasi sect 34–6, 39–40, 125, 207–8 n.13,
   213 n.90, 214 n.99, 214 n.102, 215
   n.107
  see also Sri Chand
United States of America. *See* Republican
   party (USA)
unstruck sound 76–7, 118
Upanishad. *See* Hinduism – Upanishadic

Vaishnav(a) Bhakti. *See* Hinduism – Bhakti
Varan of Bhai Gurdas 22, 33, 35, 44, 48, 125
varna 3, 9–10, 15, 17, 25, 31, 71–2, 127,
   200 n.13, 205 n.87
  see also dvija
Vedanta 82, 201 n.19, 231 n.19
Vedas. *See* Hinduism – Vedic
vipassana meditation. *See* meditation – in
   Buddhism
(Bhai) Vir Singh 60, 208 n.16

(Baba) Virsa Singh. *See* Gobind Sadan
   Society
Vishnu 40–1, 126
Vishnu Sahasranama 40, 215 n.115, 215
   n.117

Waheguru 113, 233 n.35
watches of the day/night 40, 56–7, 68–9,
   126, 128, 215 n.114, 222 n.55
Wazir Khan 62, 224 n.83
welfare of humanity. *See* humanitarian
   effort
wellbeing/wellness 13, 19, 101–2
  in *Sikhi* 2, 17, 59, 61, 71–2, 92–3, 127,
    130–2
  studies 101–2, 130–1. *see also* Easterlin
    paradox, Salutogenesis model,
    Sense of Coherence (SOC)
women 9, 25, 59

(Father) Xavier, Jerome 42

Yalom, Irvin D. 120
yoga 1, 61, 111
  classical school of 4–6, 17, 123, 201
    n.22, 201 n.32. *see also* Yoga Sutras
  hatha- 16, 51, 220 n.32
  in *Bhagavad Gita* 10
  kundalini- 51
Yoga Sutras 5–6, 123, 132

www.ingramcontent.com/pod-product-compliance
Lightning Source LLC
Chambersburg PA
CBHW070027010526
44117CB00011B/1736